The Definitive Guide to Plone

Second Edition

Maurizio Delmonte, Davide Moro, Alice Narduzzo,
Fabrizio Reale, and Andy McKay
with contributions from
Enrico Barra, Andrea Cannizzaro, Andrea D'Este,
Maurizio Lupo, Giuseppe Masili, and Matteo Sorba

The Definitive Guide to Plone, Second Edition

Copyright © 2009 by Redomino SRL and Andy McKay

ISBN-13 (pbk): 978-1-4302-1893-7

ISBN-13 (electronic): 978-1-4302-1894-4

9 8 7 6 5 4 3 2 1

Trademarked names may appear in this book. Rather than use a trademark symbol with every occurrence of a trademarked name, we use the names only in an editorial fashion and to the benefit of the trademark owner, with no intention of infringement of the trademark.

Java™ and all Java-based marks are trademarks or registered trademarks of Sun Microsystems, Inc., in the US and other countries. Apress, Inc., is not affiliated with Sun Microsystems, Inc., and this book was written without endorsement from Sun Microsystems, Inc.

Lead Editors: Clay Andres, Joohn Choe
Technical Reviewers: Carlos de la Guardia, William C. Hayes
Editorial Board: Clay Andres, Steve Anglin, Mark Beckner, Ewan Buckingham, Tony Campbell,
    Gary Cornell, Jonathan Gennick, Michelle Lowman, Matthew Moodie, Jeffrey Pepper,
    Frank Pohlmann, Ben Renow-Clarke, Dominic Shakeshaft, Matt Wade, Tom Welsh
Project Manager: Beth Christmas
Copy Editors: Damon Larson, Kim Wimpsett
Associate Production Director: Kari Brooks-Copony
Production Editor: Ellie Fountain
Compositor and Artist: Diana Van Winkle, Van Winkle Design
Proofreader: Linda Seifert
Indexer: BIM Indexing & Proofreading Services
Interior Designer: Diana Van Winkle, Van Winkle Design
Cover Designer: Kurt Krames
Manufacturing Director: Tom Debolski

Distributed to the book trade worldwide by Springer-Verlag New York, Inc., 233 Spring Street, 6th Floor, New York, NY 10013. Phone 1-800-SPRINGER, fax 201-348-4505, e-mail orders-ny@springer-sbm.com, or visit http://www.springeronline.com.

For information on translations, please contact Apress directly at 2855 Telegraph Avenue, Suite 600, Berkeley, CA 94705. Phone 510-549-5930, fax 510-549-5939, e-mail info@apress.com, or visit http://www.apress.com.

Apress and friends of ED books may be purchased in bulk for academic, corporate, or promotional use. eBook versions and licenses are also available for most titles. For more information, reference our Special Bulk Sales–eBook Licensing web page at http://www.apress.com/info/bulksales.

The information in this book is distributed on an "as is" basis, without warranty. Although every precaution has been taken in the preparation of this work, neither the author(s) nor Apress shall have any liability to any person or entity with respect to any loss or damage caused or alleged to be caused directly or indirectly by the information contained in this work.

The source code for this book is available to readers at http://www.apress.com.

A limited electronic version of this book is available at http://redomino.com/plonebook.

To all those who haven't met Plone yet,
because life is too short to use bad software.

Contents at a Glance

Foreword xv

About the Authors. xvii

About the Technical Reviewers xix

About the Foreword Writer xxi

Introduction xxiii

PART 1 ■ ■ ■ Using Plone

CHAPTER 1   Introducing Plone 3

CHAPTER 2   Installing Plone 13

CHAPTER 3   Managing Content with Plone. 35

CHAPTER 4   Administering a Plone Site. 81

PART 2 ■ ■ ■ Configuring Plone

CHAPTER 5   Behind the Scenes 133

CHAPTER 6   Customizing Plone's Look and Feel. 161

CHAPTER 7   Managing Security and Workflows 181

CHAPTER 8   Advanced User Management 205

PART 3 ■ ■ ■ Developing Plone

CHAPTER 9   Writing an Add-On Product 223

CHAPTER 10   Integrating Plone with Other Systems 277

CHAPTER 11   System Architectures and Deployment Configurations 295

CHAPTER 12   Case Studies. 315

APPENDIX   Creative Commons Legal Code. 331

INDEX 339

Contents

Foreword xv

About the Authors. xvii

About the Technical Reviewers xix

About the Foreword Writer xxi

Introduction xxiii

PART 1 ▪▪▪ Using Plone

▪CHAPTER 1   **Introducing Plone** 3

What Is a Content Management System? 4
        The History of Web Development and CMSs. 4
        What a CMS System Gives You 4
What Needs Plone?. 5
        Packaging 6
        Internationalization 6
        Usability. 6
        Easy Theming. 7
        Registration and Personalization. 7
        Workflow and Security 7
        Extensibility. 7
        Content Customization 7
        Documentation. 7
        Reliability, Growth, and the CMS Future 8
The History and Origins of Plone. 8
        Zope and the CMF 8
Python 9
The Plone World. 9
        The Community 10
        The Foundation. 10
        The Framework Team 10
        Getting Involved 10
        Plone.org and Plone.net 11
Summary. 11

■CHAPTER 2   **Installing Plone**. 13

Installing Plone on Windows 2000/XP/Vista 14
Configuring the Server on Windows. 18
    Changing the Ports 18
    Starting Plone in Debug Mode. 19
Installing Plone on Mac OS X 19
Installing Plone on Gnu/Linux 20
    Ubuntu and Other Debian-Like Distributions. 20
    Installing on Fedora and Red Hat/CentOs 21
    Installing with the Unified Installer 22
Installing Plone with zc.buildout 24
    The Buildout Directory Tree 27
    Managing Your Buildout 28
Adding a Plone Site. 31
Installing an Add-on Product 33
    Installing a Traditional Zope 2 Product. 33
    Installing a Product Packaged As an Egg with Buildout 34
Summary. 34

■CHAPTER 3   **Managing Content with Plone** 35

Logging in As a New User 35
A First Look at the Plone Interface 38
Organizing Your Site 40
    Setting Up Your Dashboard 43
    Setting Up Your Preferences 44
Adding and Editing Site Content 46
    Adding and Editing Pages. 47
    Adding and Editing Images. 52
    Adding and Editing Files 54
    Adding and Editing Events 55
    Adding and Editing Links 56
    Adding and Editing News Items. 57
    Inline Editing 59
    Automatic Item Locking and Unlocking 59
Managing and Sharing Your Content 60
    Publishing Your Documents. 60
    Restricting Content Types in a Folder. 63
    Using the Display Drop-Down Menu. 64
    Tracking the History of Content and Versioning 68
    Sharing Your Content 71

Gathering Disparate Elements into Coherent Collections 72

    Adding a New Collection. 72

    Setting the Search Criteria 74

Finding Content in Your Site 77

    Performing an Advanced Search. 78

    The LiveSearch Feature 79

Commenting Content 79

Summary. 80

CHAPTER 4   **Administering a Plone Site** 81

Main Site Setup 81

    Managing Your Site Settings 83

    Managing Language Settings 85

    Managing Security Settings 86

    Managing Theme Settings 87

    Managing Mail Settings 88

    Managing the Site Maintenance Options. 89

    Using the Error Log 89

    Navigation Settings 93

    Managing Search Settings 94

    Adding/Removing Products in Your Site. 95

    Managing the Calendar Settings. 96

    Managing the Collection Settings 97

    Markup Settings. 98

    Type Settings 99

Managing Users and Permissions. 100

    Users, Roles, and Groups 101

    Managing Users Through the Web 102

    Managing Groups Through the Web. 105

Configuring the WYSIWYG Editor. 108

    Main Configuration. 109

    Library Configuration. 109

    Kupu Resource Types 111

    Documentation. 112

    Links 112

    Toolbar Configuration 113

Managing HTML Filtering. 113

    Tags 114

    Attributes. 115

    Styles 115

Managing Portlets 116
    Managing and Adding Portlets. 117
    Using the Block/Unblock Portlets Controls 119
    Using Classic Portlets 121
Managing Automatic Rules 122
    Creating a New Rule 123
    Assigning Rules 127
Summary. 129

PART 2 ■ ■ ■ Configuring Plone

■CHAPTER 5   **Behind the Scenes** 133

Understanding Object-Oriented Web Development. 133
Doing Through-the-Web Development: The ZMI 134
Understanding Object Publishing and Acquisition 135
Managing Content Types Through the ZMI. 137
    Configuring Content Types. 137
    Changing Icons for a Content Type. 140
    Looking at Actions 142
    Exporting Your Configuration 144
    Creating a New Content Type from an Existing Type. 145
Understanding the Portal Catalog. 147
    Indexing Content 148
    Searching the Catalog. 150
    Using Search Results. 153
    Tying It All Together: Making a Search Form 154
    Taking Advantage of the ZCA: Searching by Interfaces 157
Summary. 159

■CHAPTER 6   **Customizing Plone's Look and Feel**. 161

Changing the Entire Site's Look Quickly 161
Introducing Plone Skins 163
    Using Layers Within a Skin. 163
    Your First Customization. 165

Templates and CSS: Customizing Your Plone Skin 167
    DTML and ZPT 167
    Managing Viewlets. 169
    Editing CSS 172
    Examining Example Customization Snippets 173
Working with JavaScript. 175
KSS: Ajax Made Easy 175
    What Can You Do with KSS? 177
    How to Disable KSS in Plone 179
Summary. 179

CHAPTER 7   **Managing Security and Workflows** 181

Implementing Security in Zope 181
    Adding New Roles 183
    Understanding the Way Zope Stores Users' Information. 184
Using Plone Workflows. 186
    Using the portal_workflow Tool. 186
    Managing an Existing Workflow 188
Adding Plone Policy Support 197
Creating and Customizing Plone Workflows 201
    Customizing an Existing Workflow 201
    Duplicating and Creating New Workflows 202
Summary. 204

CHAPTER 8   **Advanced User Management** 205

The Pluggable Authentication Service (PAS) 206
    The PAS in Plone 207
    The Plug-in Types 207
    Managing Users Through the acl_users Tool 209
Authentication with LDAP. 212
    Installing Plone.app.ldap. 213
    Configuring Your LDAP Connection. 213
    Configuring Your LDAP Connection Through the ZMI 215
Authentication with Relational Databases. 216
Summary. 219

PART 3 ■ ■ ■ Developing Plone

■CHAPTER 9   **Writing an Add-On Product**.................................223

Structure of a Plone Product 223
    Building a Regional News Reader: Requirements and Discussion. . 226
Building a Plone Product the Easy Way 227
Writing a Custom Content Type..233
Theming 240
Forms..246
    Getting and Using z3c.form 247
    Understanding the Plone Catalog 255
Viewlets and Portlets..256
Plone Configuration..265
Tools and Utilities 270
Summary..275

■CHAPTER 10   **Integrating Plone with Other Systems**...................277

Publishing the File System...277
Relational Databases...279
    ZODB vs. Relational Databases 279
    Adopting a Relational Database in Zope 280
    SQLAlchemy and Plone...283
Accessing Plone Without a Web Browser 288
    Accessing Plone over FTP...288
    Using Plone Through the WebDAV Protocol..........................289
Integrating Plone with Other Frameworks..............................291
    RSS Integration into Plone 291
    XML-RPC and Plone..292
    And Now for Something Completely Different: Plone on WSGI . . . 292
Summary..294

■CHAPTER 11   **System Architectures and Deployment Configurations**. . .295

Optimizing Storage Configurations....................................296
    Configuring BLOB Storage 296
    Configuring RelStorage...297
Asynchronous Indexing..299

Plone Behind a Web Server 300
Caching, Clustering, and Load Balancing 301
    Zope Clustering with ZEO 302
    Installing a Load-Balancing ZEO Cluster with buildout 304
    Caching Proxies and Your Plone Site 306
    Installing a Proxy Cache Server with buildout. 308
Multiple ZODBs 308
    Speeding Up Plone by Putting portal_catalog
        on a Different ZODB with a Stand-Alone Zope Instance 309
    Speeding Up Plone by Putting portal_catalog
        on a Different ZODB with a ZEO Cluster 310
Automatic ZODB Packing 312
Summary. 313

■CHAPTER 12   **Case Studies**. 315

Management of Enterprise Workflow. 315
E-Commerce with Plone: Your Business Online. 317
    Integrating E-Commerce Functionality into a Plone Portal 317
    Atypical E-Commerce Use Cases with Plone 318
Automatic Handling of Documents and Images. 318
    Watermarks on Images 318
    Dynamic Document Generation from Your Web Content 319
Plone and Multimedia. 319
Handling Many Large Objects with Plone 321
Integration of External Applications and Single-Sign-On 323
Custom Member Profiles 325
Community Portals and Social Networks. 326
Intranets and Document Management Systems 327
Plone: Faster Than Light. 328
Summary. 329

■APPENDIX   **Creative Commons Legal Code**. 331

Attribution-NonCommercial-ShareAlike 3.0 Unported 331
License 331
Creative Commons Notice 337

■INDEX 339

Foreword

When *The Definitive Guide to Plone* first arrived on bookshelves in 2004, Plone 2.0 had just been released and had little notable open source competition. The first edition of *The Definitive Guide* provided a truly comprehensive overview of the features of this early version of Plone and brought many new users to Plone. It was a major landmark for Plone and for open source content management systems (CMSs) in general. In the intervening years, the open source CMS universe has expanded rapidly. There are now dozens of competing open source CMSs, from humble blogging platforms to flexible enterprise-capable systems. Through all of this, Plone has managed to innovate, expand its vibrant community, and remain a vital, flexible, and popular CMS.

Since the publication of the first edition, the Plone community has produced a number of major revisions to the Plone CMS. Many new books have been published covering Plone from different perspectives (developers, administrators, and end users), but few have provided the comprehensive treatment provided by this book's first edition. Thankfully, Redomino, a successful Italian Plone consultancy, has updated *The Definitive Guide* so that this landmark book remains—true to its title—definitive. This updated volume reflects the many changes to Plone's user interface, nomenclature, and infrastructure. Redomino has asked me to provide a brief overview of Plone's recent evolution from the perspective of someone involved directly in the development and release of Plone during this period of change. The following is a brief summary of the major Plone releases since the original publication of *The Definitive Guide to Plone*, reflecting the new features covered in this edition.

Plone 2.1

The primary goal of this release was to convert all of the built-in Plone content types to use the Archetypes framework. This was a dramatic change to Plone's infrastructure, but one that made it much easier for developers to customize and extend the built-in types. By this point, Archetypes was in wide use among third-party developers; making the core types utilize the framework most used by the Plone developer community brought major advantages. Additionally, the user interface was significantly improved; this included moving many configuration tasks out of the ZMI and into Plone's control panels. Plone 2.1 also included a number of new features, such as selectable default pages, an improved Collection type (originally called Topics, and later Smart Folders), and Ajax LiveSearch.

Plone 2.5

This release focused almost entirely on infrastructure improvements. Though the outward appearance of Plone changed little for this release, there were a number of major internal changes that laid the groundwork for future improvements. Perhaps the most significant of these was support for using the Zope 3 framework when developing add-on products. The existing authentication and user management system was replaced with a more flexible version called the Pluggable Authentication System. This release also included support for locally customizable workflow policies.

Plone 3.0

Plone 3.0 arrived with a huge array of new features. A new portlet engine was added, providing tremendous flexibility in portlet definition and assignment. The user interface was redesigned, making heavy use of customizable Zope 3 "viewlet" components. Many improvements to the user interface were made, particularly to the administration control panels. The KSS Ajax framework was added, providing inline editing support and other dynamic user interface features. Additionally, this release included support for keeping a full revision history and for locking content during editing. It also added a content rules engine—allowing users to assign custom behaviors triggered by system events; these features greatly improved collaborative editing in Plone.

Post-3.0

There have been two subsequent releases, 3.1 and 3.2, since the tremendous milestone of Plone 3.0. These releases have had a somewhat limited scope; nonetheless, many interesting changes have happened during this time. Most significantly, the Plone community has standardized on zc.buildout for installing and deploying Plone, and WSGI has been gaining popularity as a means of integrating Plone with other Python applications and technologies.

This new edition of *The Definitive Guide to Plone* provides a much-needed update to the comprehensive view of the original. It covers everything from basic installation and setup tasks to advanced Python customizations, and has been updated to reflect Plone in its current—greatly improved—state. Hopefully, it will guide you to success in all your content management endeavors.

Alec Mitchell
Plone Core Developer

About the Authors

 REDOMINO is an Italian company founded by a group of software consultants who truly believe in the open source culture and have worked with Plone since this software was born, participating in the community as developers and supporters. Translating their passion into a business, they've had the opportunity to bring Plone to many major Italian companies.

Redomino is a content management solutions provider; its team specializes in the production of competitive, innovative, and practical e-business solutions, professional web sites, intranets, e-commerce solutions, and other web applications in consulting, design, and hosting services. It has years of training skills and experience in Plone, Zope, Python, and Linux.

| Maurizio Delmonte | Davide Moro | Alice Narduzzo | Fabrizio Reale | Enrico Barra | Andrea Cannizzaro | Andrea D'Este | Maurizio Lupo | Guiseppe Masili | Matteo Sorba |

 **ANDY MCKAY** has been building web sites for more than nine years and developing in Python for ages. Andy has a degree in economics from Bath University and has taken postgraduate courses at the British Columbia Institute of Technology.

He started his career at ActiveState, where he got lured into the world of Zope and Python. This was followed by cofounding Enfold Systems. These days he runs his own consulting company, Clearwind.

Most of his time is now spent using Django and jQuery rather than developing Plone. But he still uses Plone, enjoys hanging out with Plone developers, and thinks that Plone is just spiffy. When not kayaking rivers, he can be found walking his dog or having a good cup of tea.

About the Technical Reviewers

 **BILLY HAYES**'s experience with Plone includes planning, management, coding, and delivery of many major sites, including www.siggraph.org and www.tigerturf.com.au. His work for Labnow used Plone, Linux, and OpenOffice to create a documentation control system for the medical device company's work in developing HIV-monitoring tools for use in resource-poor communities. That system has been used for regulatory, quality, HR, and MSDS materials, as well as internal software maintenance, documentation, and training materials.

Billy is currently a web administrator for the Texas Parks & Wildlife Department, and is conducting the migration of the agency's content-rich sites from LAMP to Plone.

 **CARLOS DE LA GUARDIA** has been doing web consulting and development since 1994, when selling any kind of project required two meetings just to explain what the Internet was in the first place. He was cofounder of Aldea Systems, a web consulting company where he spent ten years working on all kinds of web projects using a diverse range of languages and tools. In 2005, he became an independent developer and consultant, specializing in Zope and Plone projects. He frequently blogs about Plone and other Zope-related subjects.

About the Foreword Writer

ALEC MITCHELL is a Plone core developer and has been an active member of the Plone community since 2004. He was the release manager for Plone 2.5 and a member of the inaugural framework team.

Alec is an independent consultant; he is working on various projects and at present maintains the Plone core content types (ATContentTypes) and a few popular add-on products for Plone.

Introduction

Plone is a great success. I know very few open source projects with a longer life and a more widespread trend—above all in the web field, where the turnover is high. I have seen so many content management systems (CMSs) rise and fall since Plone was born. And Plone is still here and it seems to me that it will be with us for a very long time.

Besides, Plone is not a toy like many other small CMSs, but competes with the most famous enterprise solutions and overreaches them on many features.

So you might wonder why Plone isn't as widely used as many other well-known technologies. The best answer I can find is that Plone is different. Its approach to development is a far cry from how other frameworks work. This is the force of Plone, since it is what lets us develop in an easy, reliable, and modular way. But the other side of the coin is that it seems difficult for people who know other technologies. They feel less productive and often try to bend Plone to a way of working that is not the best one for it.

So some urban legends are born. The most famous and, in my opinion the most damaging, is that the Plone learning curve is steep. This is not true if you start off with Plone on the right path. On the contrary, learning Plone can be easy and pleasant, because you can get results very fast. Just using the front-end user interface, it is possible to manage content and workflow, create reserved areas to share information, organize the way your content is shown to visitors regardless of where they are created, and so on. Usually this requires no more than a one-day training class for people who have never seen Plone. The next step is to begin to use the back end, where you can change the look and behavior of Plone. And you can do this without programming—you just need to know a minimal amount of HTML and CSS. The last step is to start programming Plone by writing your own modules, which will of course require some knowledge of the Python language.

The important thing to understand is that, to learn Plone, you need to proceed stepwise. Sometimes web developers hear about the great potential of Plone, but do not consider it until they have a big project, so they do not follow the best training path, and deduce that it is hard to learn Plone. In these cases, it is better to rely on an expert who can lead you through the best choices and help you think in the Plone way. Thus, if you want to work with Plone, you must think like a Plonista—then the learning curve will be flat.

The goal of this book is just to help you approach Plone in the right way. We will guide you from the usage of the interface to the programming of new extensions, following the best training path.

After years of experience of training courses, we have identified three steps that lead to mastering Plone, and we have divided this book along these lines. They are the same as I described before: learn how to use Plone as a user, learn how to configure it, and then learn how to develop with it.

Please do not go on until you are familiar with the concepts of the previous parts. This is really important, above all when you are a skilled web developer, because otherwise you'll be tempted to follow poor coding practices. If you have a doubt about the correct way to develop a feature of your application, we recommend that you discuss it in the community, where you will get good advice.

There is only one chapter you might look at before the others: Chapter 12. It is a collection of use cases that can be solved with Plone. It can give you an idea about what you can achieve, and it can motivate you to use Plone as a solution for your own needs. Obviously, it is also important to read it when you have become an expert in Plone development.

The structure of this book can also be useful if you need only the knowledge covered by Parts 1 or 2 of this book. For example, there may not be a need for your customers to become expert Plone developers—they may just need to know how to use your Plone applications (covered in Part 1); or your colleagues may just need to do some simple configurations (covered in Part 2).

▮**Note** To ensure that your *Definitive Guide to Plone* is up to date, please visit `http://redomino.com/plonebook`. Here, you can find periodic updates, download additional code and practical examples, view errata, ask for support, and provide feedback to the authors. Keep your book vital!

I am very pleased to welcome you to the wonderful world of Plone. I am sure you will enjoy this book, and I await your feedback to improve it for the next editions.

Fabrizio Reale
Cofounder of Redomino

PART 1

■■■

Using Plone

You are at the start of your journey, a path that will allow you to get acquainted with a powerful tool to build flexible web sites and content management solutions. We are glad you chose to travel with us!

We'll remind you that it is very important to proceed stepwise. So, even if you already know other content management systems or similar applications, or you're a webmaster or web developer but you don't know Plone yet, it is important you start here and get familiar with the front-end user interface, its structure, and its logic.

In Part 1 of the book, you will learn how to use Plone as a basic user and an administrator. We will go over the general concept of a content management system and then introduce Plone, the technologies that lie behind it, the project that gave life to it, its history, and its wide community. You will see how to install Plone on different operating systems, and you will finally start getting your hands on the Plone user interface: you will learn how to add and manage content and use all the available features.

You will see how to do simple configurations: how to add and manage users and groups so that different people can work on your platform while you maintain control over content and publication; and how to manage the user interface elements and the way the content is viewed, published, and managed through custom rules. In other words, you will be able to perform the administration tasks that a site manager performs.

If you need further documentation about the basic use of Plone, the best source of help is the official Plone site, at http://plone.org. In particular, to get started, you can consult the Plone 3 User Manual at http://plone.org/documentation/manual/plone-3-user-manual; you can read more about installing Plone 3 with the Unified Installer at http://plone.org/documentation/tutorial/installing-plone-3-with-the-unified-installer; and you can browse the frequently asked questions (FAQs) at http://plone.org/documentation/faq.

CHAPTER 1

■■■

Introducing Plone

Plone is a content management system (CMS)—a platform that lets you build content-rich sites very quickly; it is built on top of Zope, a powerful web application server written in Python (see Figure 1-1). Plone is open source software licensed under the General Public License (GPL), which ensures freedom to users as well as developers. Most importantly, Plone is a user-friendly, powerful solution that lets you add and edit any kind of content through the Web, produces navigation and searches for that content, and applies security and workflow to that content.

Plone enables you to put together almost any web site and easily update it. It is easily customizable and extensible; there are many add-on products you can integrate into your site to add more features and meet almost any kind of need. In other words, using Plone lets you gain a competitive advantage; plus, it is free and open source, so that you can download and install it on your computer and start building and customizing your application for free. You can examine any aspect of Plone's code and alter it to fit your application. There are no licensing fees to pay, there is no license that will expire, and all the code is visible.

By using Plone, you will understand how its architecture works, and then you will also discover the power of this system. So, let's start our journey, beginning with an overview of the way we can build web sites, the features that Plone provides, some history, and a glance into the big world of Plone and its community.

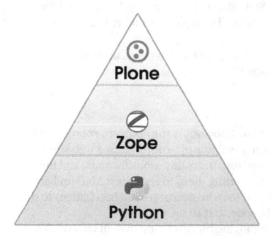

Figure 1-1. *The relationship among Plone, Zope, and Python: Plone is built on top of Zope, which is written in Python.*

What Is a Content Management System?

With the term *content management system*, we usually refer to a software application used to create, edit, manage, and publish content in a consistently organized way. But let's break the term down into smaller parts for a deeper explanation.

What do we mean by *content*? Content is a unit of data with some extra information attached to it. That piece of data could be a web page, information about an upcoming event, a Microsoft Word or PDF file, an image, a movie clip, or any piece of data that has meaning to the organization deploying the system.

All these items are called content and they all share similar attributes, such as the need to be added or edited by certain users and to be published in various ways. The system controls these attributes, following the type of workflow you chose, in accordance with the logic defined by the organization's business rules for managing content.

With the ubiquity of the Web, many CMSs are now classified as *web CMSs*, either because they have a web-based interface or because they focus on a web-based delivery system over the Internet or an intranet. Plone provides a web management interface and web-based delivery system.

The History of Web Development and CMSs

The Internet was first proposed in 1962; the idea was to create a global network of computers for sharing information and data. The feature that characterized the Web among other means of communication was the ability to link pages together using hyperlinks. We needed a way to collect, share, and show information, so web sites came to life.

At first, creating a web site meant using a simple markup language, called HTML, that included some formatting options and the ability to link pages together using hyperlinks. So, at this time, we had to write the HTML code from scratch for every page of our web sites, manually creating links among pages for managing content and allowing visitors to surf through it.

With the passing of time, HTML became more complex and flexible. But still, building a web site was almost impossible for nontechnicians—you had to know the language and its behavior very well. With the advent of Cascading Style Sheets (CSS), we finally achieved the ability to separate the content of pages from their looks—but again, we had to know how to write CSS.

One of the advantages a CMS gives you is the ability to build web pages through a user-friendly interface, without having to write any HTML or manage the layout.

What a CMS System Gives You

Although it's not the only advantage of a CMS, the most obvious is the ability to coordinate a web site easily. Take a situation where one person, a webmaster, coordinates a web site—either an intranet or an external site. Contents come from users in various formats, and the webmaster turns them into usable web pages by converting them to Hypertext Markup Language (HTML). If a user wants to change those pages, then he needs to send his changes to the webmaster, who takes care of changing the HTML code, and so on.

This presents many problems for an organization, the biggest being that all content flows through one person, creating an obvious bottleneck. That one person can do only so much work, and if he is sick or leaves the company, a great deal of productivity is lost in finding a replacement. The publishing process can be quite frustrating as e-mails fly between the webmaster and the user trying to get content published.

What is needed is a system that does the following:

- *Separates the content of a page from its presentation*: If the actual content is separated from the presentation method, then the content author doesn't need to know any HTML or how the page is delivered. In fact, one piece of content could have many different templates applied to it, including formats other than HTML, such as Portable Document Format (PDF) or Scalable Vector Graphics (SVG). Thus, if you want to change the look and feel of the site, you only have to change the template file, rather than all the content.

- *Allows certain users to add and edit content*: If specified users can add and edit content easily, then there is no need to send content to the webmaster or web team. Instead, the user who wants to create a page can do so and edit it as much as necessary.

- *Applies rules regarding who can publish what and when*: Your organization might not want just anybody publishing content on your web site. For example, people in marketing should be able to publish in the press release area of the site, but not the engineering section.

- *Can apply business rules to content*: If a person from marketing creates a press release, somebody in legal might need to review that document. In this case, the document will be passed through a review process that ensures it won't go live until reviews are done.

- *Can search and index information intelligently*: Since the CMS can keep track of structured metadata about the content (such as author's name, publication date, modification dates, categories, and so on), it can produce listings of content by author, recent content, and so on. It can also provide searching capabilities that are much smarter and more useful than just a simple text search.

These are all aspects and advantages that a CMS provides. Although this example lists advantages that are more significant for large organizations, groups of all levels benefit from this approach.

The key factor of any CMS is that it provides a clear separation of the various elements in it: security, workflow, templates, and so on. For example, as we have already mentioned, the templates presenting an item are separated from the content. This allows you to easily modify the presentation.

So, Plone is a CMS, but it isn't just a simple CMS, it is a great deal more! Let's discuss why.

Who Needs Plone?

In the 21st century, a company without a web site is unthinkable, and many companies and organizations have more than one. As we have already mentioned, whether it is an external site for communicating with clients, an intranet for employees to use, or an e-commerce or e-learning site, all web sites have a common problem: how to manage content. This is a challenge that can often cost organizations large amounts of time and effort. Producing a powerful yet flexible system for these sites that meets ever-changing requirements while growing to meet your company's emerging needs isn't easy. This is what Plone does.

No matter what the requirements for your web site or the amount of content or users, Plone is a powerful and flexible solution for managing and updating a site. Being open source software, Plone already has a large user base and legions of developers, usability experts, translators, technical writers, and graphic designers who are able to work on it. By choosing Plone, you are not locked into one company; rather, many companies offer different Plone services all around the world.

Is there a better warranty than a successful case study? Many important and famous companies have chosen Plone to build and manage their web sites; some of them are easily recognizable because of their look, and some of them aren't. The following is just a small sample of the diverse range of sites:

- The official Plone site: `http://plone.org`
- Central Intelligence Agency (CIA): `https://www.cia.gov`
- International Planetary Data Alliance: `http://planetarydata.org`
- Chicago History Museum: `www.chicagohistory.org`
- Novell: `www.novell.com/home/index.html`
- International Training Center of the International Labour Organization (ITC ILO): `www.itcilo.org`

Let's summarize the particulars of Plone, which will help you to understand why you would want to choose Plone for your projects.

Packaging

Plone maintains installers for Windows, Linux, and Mac (we will talk about installation in Chapter 2). Other third-party products and add-ons also come with the installers. Maintaining quality releases of these products makes installation and management easy. Also, each new release maintains migration paths and updates so that your Plone site will keep working and stay up to date.

Internationalization

The whole Plone user interface is translated into more than 35 languages, including Chinese, Japanese, Korean, and even right-to-left languages such as Arabic and Hebrew, with ease. Inserting your own translation is easy (see the "Managing Language Settings" section of Chapter 4).

Usability

Plone offers an excellent user experience that provides high levels of usability and accessibility. This isn't just a matter of presenting pretty HTML, but instead goes to the core of Plone. Plone provides an interface that is compatible with industry and government standards, and it meets or exceeds the US government Section 508 and the W3C's WAI-AA standards. This allows sites built with Plone to be used by people with visual disabilities. In addition, this provides the unexpected but related benefit that your page may index better in search engines such as Google—and you know, search engine optimization (SEO) is important for almost any kind of web site.

Easy Theming

Plone separates the content from the actual templates, or skins, used to present it. The skins are written in an excellent HTML templating system, Zope Page Templates, and a large amount of CSS is provided. With little knowledge of Plone, you can apply multiple skins, achieve a variety of looks, and totally customize your web site's appearance.

Registration and Personalization

Plone features a complete user registration system. On a Plone site, users register using their own username and password. The site administrator can add and manage users through the Plone user interface, and each user can create and modify a personal profile and dashboard, and manage personal preferences. In addition, with add-ons, you can use information you already have about users, coming from many places, such as relational databases, Lightweight Directory Access Protocol (LDAP), Active Directory, and more.

Workflow and Security

Workflow controls the logic of processing content through the site. You can configure this logic through the Web using graphical tools. Site administrators can make sites as complex or as simple as they would like; for example, it is possible to add notification capabilities, such as sending e-mails or instant messages to users. Chapter 7 covers workflow in great detail. For every item of content in a Plone site, you can set up access control lists to decide who has access to that item and how users will be able to interact with it. Will they be able to edit it, view it, or comment on it? All this is configurable through the Web.

Extensibility

Since Plone is open source software, it can be easily altered. You can change and configure almost any aspect of Plone to suit your needs. Countless packages and tools for Plone provide a wide array of options for smaller sites and for large-scale enterprises. Repositories of free add-ons for Plone are available at `http://plone.org`. With development tools such as Archetypes, you can generate and alter Plone code easily through the Web or using Unified Modeling Language (UML) tools.

Content Customization

Users of a Plone site can add every kind of content: there are no limits or constrains on data. Plone developers can create their own content types so that almost any type of content can be managed; the only limit is your own imagination.

Documentation

The Plone project maintains documentation, including this book, which is published under the Creative Commons license. The best starting place for the community documentation is `http://plone.org/documentation`. Many teams of users and developers all over the world have provided documentation in languages other than English as well.

Reliability, Growth, and the CMS Future

Hundreds of developers are involved to some degree in the Plone project around the world; they work every day to improve the features of the software and to quickly solve any bugs that arise.

Many CMSs have been born in the past several years, but many of them have already disappeared. Plone, on the other hand, has been around for over seven years. It has grown, and so has its community and the number of users around the world. If you are working with Plone, you can always find a Plone developer online who is willing and able to help you. And this should be increasingly true in the future as Plone continues to grow and mature.

The History and Origins of Plone

Plone was created by Alan Runyan, Alexander Limi, and Vidar Andersen, and the first version was released in 2001. The history of Plone is tied with the application server Zope and the development of the content management framework (CMF) on which the CMS is built. Since the first distribution, Plone grew quickly, its community started to take form, and the project received many new add-on products from its users.

As the community began to grow, some important events were organized, like the first annual Plone Conference (2003), which is still running today. Sprints and other events were (and are still) held in different parts of the world to gather Plone developers to work together to improve the software and discuss the future of the community.

In 2004, the Plone Foundation was created, an organization that has ownership rights over the Plone code base, trademarks, and domain names; and that manages the development, marketing, and protection of Plone.

Zope and the CMF

To understand Plone, you have to understand Zope and its CMF as the underlying architecture. For this reason, we will explain these two items and how they integrate with Plone in this section.

Zope is a powerful and flexible open source web application server developed by Zope Corporation (www.zope.org). Originally, Zope was developed as a stand-alone CMS, but over time it didn't satisfy the needs of its users. Then Zope Corporation developed the CMF as an open source project. The CMF provides developers with the tools necessary to create complex CMSs; it enables workflow, provides site skinning, and offers other functions.

The CMF is a framework for a system; in other words, it provides developers with the tools for building a product, rather than just providing an out-of-the-box system that users can use immediately. Plone takes this and many other features and improves upon them in order to provide users with a high-quality product. Plone is a layer on top of the CMF, which is an application running on top of Zope. Understanding the CMF is the key to understanding Plone. Most administration functions require the use of Zope's administration interface, and developing Plone requires an understanding of Zope and its objects.

This book doesn't go into depth about pure Zope applications; rather, it gives you enough information to complete tasks in Plone and directions on where to widen your knowledge of the CMF. Just reading this book will give you enough information to customize and modify almost anything you want in Plone.

Both Zope and the CMF are key technologies that Plone needs; without them, Plone wouldn't exist. The Plone team owes a great deal of thanks to everyone at Zope Corporation for having the vision to create and then offer both Zope and the CMF as open source.

Python

Zope is written in Python, a powerful object-oriented open source programming language comparable to Perl or Tcl. Knowledge of Python isn't required to use Plone or even to do basic administration; however, customizing products and scripting Plone does require some Python.

If you plan to do anything sophisticated with Plone, take a day or two to learn the basics of Python. This will not only allow you to customize Plone substantially, but to familiarize yourself with objects and how they interact in the Plone environment. Teaching you Python is outside the scope of this book; instead, for the most advanced parts, we assume you have a basic knowledge of Python. That fundamental knowledge will be enough to get you through this book and allow you to easily customize the Plone installation.

Fortunately, Python is an easy-to-learn programming language; on average, it takes an experienced programmer a day to become productive in it. New programmers might take a little longer.

If you are installing Plone using the Windows or Mac installers, then the correct version of Python will be included. To download Python as a separate product, for almost any operating system, go to `www.python.org`.

The Python web site has excellent documentation, especially the tutorial. Also, the following books provide a good overview of Python:

- *Expert Python Programming*, by Tarek Ziadé (Packt, 2008) (see `http://plone.org/documentation/books/expert-python-programming`).

- *Dive Into Python*, by Mark Pilgrim (Apress, 2004) (see `http://plone.org/documentation/books/dive-into-python`).

- *Python Programming: An Introduction to Computer Science*, by John Zelle (Franklin Beedle & Associates, 2003) (see `http://plone.org/documentation/books/python-programming-an-introduction-to-computer-science`).

The Plone World

One of the best things about Plone is the community of developers, users, and companies that support and develop it. The Plone community is spread worldwide; it is one of the largest open source teams in the world. Speaking about Plone without mentioning its community doesn't make any sense, because Plone is first and foremost a community.

As soon as you get in touch with Plone, you will realize how big and involved the Plone world is. So, let's give it a glance, to understand why we belong in the community if we use Plone, how to exploit all the advantages of being part of it, and how to contribute to its growth.

The Community

The Plone community, of course, is not only the Plone core developers. It involves users, designers, contributors, sponsors, and companies. Many core contributors are friends in real life, and the community members have the chance to personally meet during the various events that are held over the year.

In brief, what does the community do for us? Besides working on the core of the software, many contributors provide end users with third-party add-on products; many developers and end users work every day to answer questions on mailing lists, produce quality documentation and translations for non-English speakers, report bugs, and discuss the future of Plone.

The Foundation

As we have mentioned before, the Plone Foundation was formed in May 2004 to serve as a supporting organization for Plone. The goals and objectives of this organization, as given on the Plone official site (http://plone.org/foundation), are listed here:

- *Provide clear, neutral, and sustainable ownership of code, trademarks, and domains.*

- *Provide a decision-making structure for essential community activities.*

- *Ensure that, as Plone grows, it remains a level playing field.*

- *Act as the voice of Plone for official announcements, press releases, and other communications.*

- *Help create promotional material, interviews, speeches, and other activities to market Plone.*

The Plone Foundation is governed by an elected board of directors (http://plone.org/foundation/about/team/FoundationBoard). You can see a list of all the members of the foundation at http://plone.org/foundation/members, where you can also fill out a new membership application if you have significantly contributed to the Plone community.

The Framework Team

The Framework Team mainly works for the future of Plone; it reviews and suggests features for inclusion in new releases; it is responsible for feature evaluation and general guidance on architectural decisions. The existence of such a group is a further demonstration of the constant effort to improve and grow the Plone project.

Getting Involved

Although Plone has an impressive list of features, its list of "wants" is even more impressive. For this reason, the project is always on the lookout for new people willing to contribute to it.

Fortunately, since Plone is focused on the end user, there is a need for a very broad spectrum of disciplines. Volunteers in a range of areas—not just coders or web developers—are welcomed. Plone needs user interface developers, usability experts, graphic designers, translators, writers, and testers. You can find the current development status on the Plone web site at http://plone.org/development, and the best way to get involved is to join the mailing lists or the developers on an Internet Relay Chat (IRC) channel.

Plone.org and Plone.net

As you may have already noticed, the official Plone site (http://plone.org) is a good starting point for anything you are looking for. First, you can download Plone (http://plone.org/products/plone)! You can navigate through almost 1,000 add-on products that you can download and install to extend the features of your site, and you can refer to hundreds of tutorials, how-tos, and FAQs to stay updated about news and events in the Plone world, inquire about the current development status, and discover ways you can contribute and sponsor.

In contrast to Plone.org, Plone.net is dedicated to Plone providers. As mentioned on the site, it "showcases Plone websites, consultants, hosting providers, case studies, and media coverage, in order to promote the use and adoption of Plone." Navigating Plone.net, you'll have the chance to see many of the Plone sites that populate the Web, together with the companies and organizations that have chosen this CMS for their projects, and you'll have the chance to get in touch with the Plone providers that work all around the world.

Summary

Plone lets you create and manage a web site with no special technical background; it is also a good groupware collaboration tool; its flexibility lets you choose a workflow system to control access to and permissions on your content. Using Plone as a development platform, developers will be able to customize every part of the software.

In this first chapter, you started your journey toward discovering and understanding this powerful open source tool. You began to see what a CMS is and why Plone is a good one, and you got an introduction to its history, its structure, and what lies behind it. You learned that since Plone is a mature open source project, you can enter a big and enthusiastic community where you will always find help and support. You were given a quick overview of the Plone world, including how you can get involved in the project.

You can now go on with your journey, starting with the installation of the software on your operating system (Chapter 2). Once Plone is correctly installed on your system, you will start working with it. In Chapter 3 you'll see how to create and manage content, and in Chapter 4 you'll see how to administer a Plone site.

CHAPTER 2

■ ■ ■

Installing Plone

This chapter explains how to install Plone and all its dependencies on a variety of platforms, and how to set the basic configuration options for Plone. Unlike the other chapters, reading this chapter from one end to the other may not make the most sense. Instead, you may want to read only the sections you need in order to install Plone on your operating system.

To get through this chapter, it is useful to know the dependences between Python, the programming language, Zope, the application server, and Plone. The Plone software is installed on top of the Zope application server, so when we talk about starting Plone, we really mean starting the Zope service. The same applies for the installation steps. It is important to know that installing Plone means installing Python (if not already installed), Zope, and then Plone. Automatic installation methods normally hide these details.

Tip All the different versions of Zope available can be a source of confusion. Plone 3 is based on Zope 2. Zope 3 is a completely new project that aims to improve the development experiences through the use of component architecture. As versions of Plone advance, Zope 3 components are becoming more and more important.

We can already take advantage of the Zope 3 component architecture using Zope 2, thanks to the Five product, which is already installed with a normal Zope installation and backports Zope 3 technologies into the Zope 2 world. This architecture permits the importation of several key Zope 3 components into Zope 2.

Plone will install on any of the platforms that Zope supports: Windows, Mac OS X, Linux, most UNIX platforms, and Solaris. For most of these operating systems, ready-to-use packages that can make the installation very easy are available. You can also always choose to install Plone from source (in other words, you can download the source code of the software and of all its dependences and compile it by hand on your server machine). This procedure gives you more control over directory layout, dependencies, and versions, but it can be kind of daunting. Another possibility for source installation is `zc.buildout`, a system that automatically builds and configures software installation based on recipes (which are like rules that allow you to automate the installation procedures; this concept will become clearer in the "Installing Plone with zc.buildout" section). This is the recommended way to install Plone in production environments. Using the same collection of recipes lets you replicate the same environment on different machines. It is more convenient than building each separate source of Zope and

Plone, and it also embeds a very useful set of commands to keep the versions of Plone and installed products under control. We will cover Windows, Mac, Linux, and source installation in this chapter.

For a Plone server, a high-performance computer will obviously make Plone perform better. Plone is a complicated system that requires processing power and memory. Plone works fine with setups as low as 500 MHz and 64 MB of memory for more modest sites. However, for a production system, it is recommended that your server be at least as fast as 2 GHz with at least 1 GB of RAM if you are serving a large web site.

For a base installation of Plone, you will need about 50 MB of hard drive space. If you already have installations of Zope or Python, then this will be a great deal less; you will need about 2 MB. However, using Plone with a preexisting installation of Zope or Python is not always recommended. You should do that only if you are familiar with the technologies and you have specific requirements; otherwise, we suggest fresh installs of everything in order to follow this book. You should also consider the Plone object database, which can grow to almost any size depending upon the amount of data you store.

To use Plone, you need a web browser that can access the server. If users want to log into your site, then they must have cookies enabled. JavaScript is not required but will provide a richer user experience. Because of the extensive use of CSS in Plone, typical browsers will see the correct Plone interface in a richer, more attractive way; however, it should be quite functional in most browsers.

Tip Before installing Plone, you should make note of any current web servers you have running. For example, some versions of Windows automatically install and start Microsoft Internet Information Services (IIS), which listens on port 80. In a Linux/UNIX environment, you can easily find that Apache listens on port 8080, which is used by Plone. You can either disable that web server or change the ports for Plone; see "Configuring the Server on Windows" later in this chapter. If you want to run Plone behind another web server or create a cluster to serve your Plone site and other web servers on the same machine at the same time, see Chapter 11 for more information. At the moment, however, it is probably easiest to just disable the service that busies the port usually used by Plone.

Installing Plone on Windows 2000/XP/Vista

By far the easiest way to install Plone is to use the Plone Windows installer, which automates the installation of Plone on Windows. The installation includes extra packages and options, a Hypertext Transfer Protocol (HTTP)–loaded database, the setup of services, and Python for Windows packages. You can download this installer from www.plone.org/download.

The installer has been tested on Windows 2000, XP, and Vista, but it should also work on other Windows versions. It is recommended you have administrator access on the computer you want to install Plone on, since the installer will try to set up as a service and install settings into the Windows registry.

Once you have downloaded the installer, double-click the installer to begin; you should get a panel similar to the one shown in Figure 2-1.

The installation setup asks you to accept the GPL license agreement (see Figure 2-2). Then it will ask you to choose the folder in which you want to install the product (see Figure 2-3).

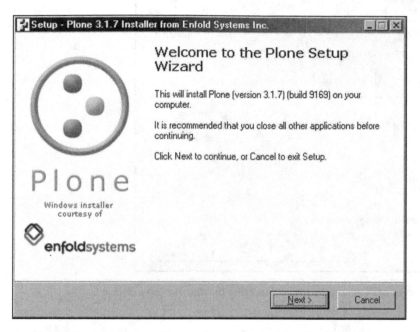

Figure 2-1. *The Plone Setup Wizard will lead you through the installation of Plone on your Windows PC.*

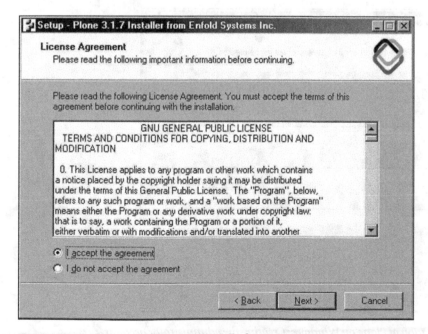

Figure 2-2. *The installation of Plone on Windows: Accepting the license agreement*

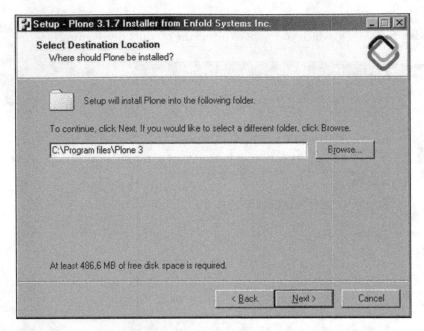

Figure 2-3. *The installation of Plone on Windows: Selecting the destination location*

Then, before beginning to copy the files, it asks you to choose a username and a password (Figure 2-4). This user account will be the administrator of your Zope instance.

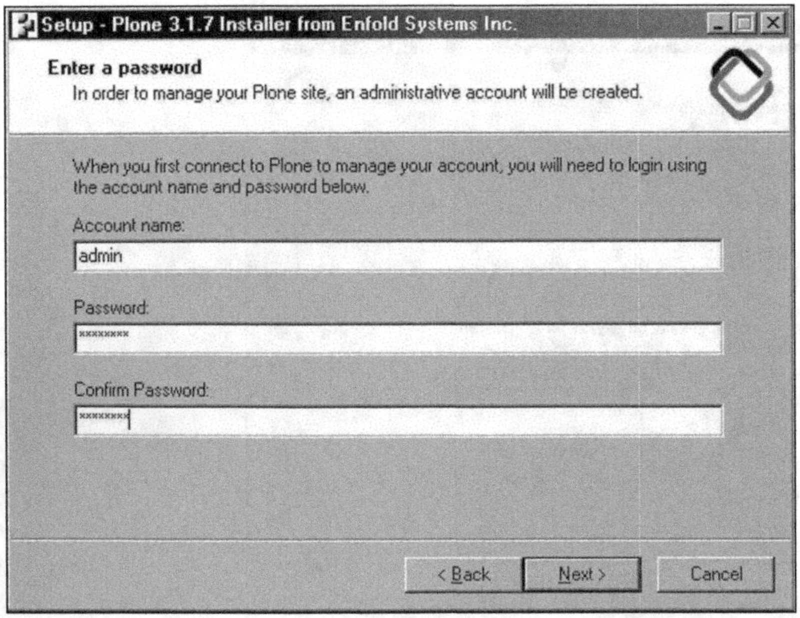

Figure 2-4. *The installation of Plone on Windows: Creating the administrator account*

Often people create one user called *admin* or something similar for this role. You will need this username and this password later, so remember them. However, if you lose your password, you can enter a new one later.

The installation takes about 5 minutes, depending upon the speed of your computer. The installation performs a few tasks at the end of the installation, such as compiling all the Python files and setting up the database. When the installation has finished, a message displays to let you know that it is done.

To start Plone, access the Plone Controller by going to Start ➤ Programs ➤ Plone ➤ Plone (see Figure 2-5). The Plone Controller is an application that provides a nice user interface for starting and stopping Plone. It begins with the Status page, which lets you easily start or stop your Plone installation.

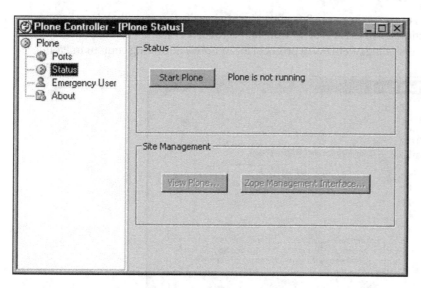

Figure 2-5. *The Plone Controller: You can quickly start and stop Plone through the Status page.*

■Tip You can also start/stop your Zope instance from the "Zope instance" Windows service that will be installed.

When Plone has started, you can access the Plone site by clicking the View Plone button. This starts a browser and accesses the Plone site; you should then see the Plone welcome page. Note that the address in the browser is http://localhost/; this is the address to access your Plone site. Clicking the Zope Management Interface button starts a browser and accesses the management interface. The address in the browser for this is http://localhost:8080/manage, which gives you access to the underlying application server. When you click the Manage button and access Plone, it will ask you for your username and password. This is the username and password you added in the installer.

Configuring the Server on Windows

The configuration for Plone is contained in a text file that you can edit to configure your Plone instance. You can change the ports Plone listens to, the log files it uses, and a whole host of other options. On Windows, some of the key features are available through the Controller and the graphical user interface (GUI).

As discussed earlier, to access the Controller, select Start ➤ Programs ➤ Plone ➤ Plone. The first page you will see is the Status page, which allows you to stop or start Plone. On the left of the Controller are a few other screens that we will now discuss.

Changing the Ports

The Plone Ports page, as shown in Figure 2-6, allows you to specify the ports that Zope listens on for incoming connections such as HTTP, File Transfer Protocol (FTP), and Web-Based Distributed Authoring and Versioning (WebDAV, a protocol for remotely authoring content in Plone).

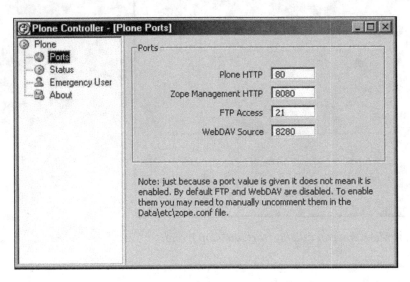

Figure 2-6. *The Plone Controller, where you can set the Plone ports*

The following are the four fields on the Ports page:

- *Plone HTTP*: This field specifies the port to access Plone for the user. The default is port 80, the standard default for a web server. Although this port is not required, without it you won't be able to access Plone with a web browser. If this port is enabled and Plone is running, the View Plone button will be enabled on the Status page.

- *Zope Management HTTP*: This field specifies the port to access the ZMI for the root of Zope (you will be asked to enter the administrative username and password you set during the installation). The default is port 8080. If this port is enabled and Plone is running, the Zope Management Interface button is enabled on the Status page.

- *FTP Access*: This field specifies the port to access Plone via FTP. The default is blank, meaning that this is not enabled; if you want to enable this, the usual port is 21. You can use FTP to transfer large files to and from Plone.

- *WebDAV Source*: This field specifies the port to access Plone via WebDAV. The default is blank, meaning that this is not enabled; if you want to enable this, insert a value. With WebDAV, you'll be able to perform tasks such as mapping your Plone server to a Windows drive letter.

As mentioned, when installing Plone, you will want to ensure that no other server is listening on the same port as Plone—servers such as IIS, Apache, and Personal Web Server (PWS) could be listening to port 80.

Starting Plone in Debug Mode

Up to this point, you have started and stopped Plone in production mode. This is the fastest way to run Plone, and it is recommended for production machines. This means you should use it only when you actually use the CMS. For developing add-ons in Plone or debugging problems, you will need to start Plone in debug mode. This mode is the recommended way of running Plone when you are developing products and skins, as you will do in later chapters. This method is not the default because it causes Plone to run about ten times more slowly than normal.

To start Plone in debug mode, select Start ➤ Programs ➤ Plone ➤ Development ➤ Plone Debug, and a command prompt will appear; all the log information will be printed to this window. To test that Plone is running, start a browser and go to `http://localhost/`; if Plone is installed successfully, you will see the Plone welcome screen.

■Note The Plone installer for Windows automatically registers a system service that prepares Plone so that it automatically starts on Windows startup. As we mentioned before, you also have at your disposal a user-friendly interface for starting and stopping Plone: the Status page of the Plone Controller.

Installing Plone on Mac OS X

The installer automates the installation of Plone on Mac OS X, so it isn't a hard task. You will need administrator access on the computer on which you want to install the CMS. You can download this installer from `www.plone.org/download`. Click "Get Plone for Mac OS X" to start the download of the installer; once it is completed, you will get a window similar to the one shown in Figure 2-7.

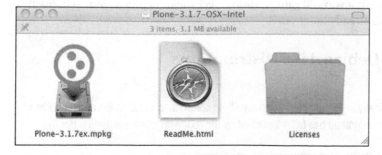

Figure 2-7. *Starting the Plone installation: You will see the Plone installer, the README.txt file, and a folder containing license information.*

Now double-click the installer to decompress the archive. The installer goes through the usual steps for installing software. Click the Continue and Go Back buttons at the bottom as necessary; most of the steps are self-explanatory. The installation takes about five minutes, depending upon the speed of your computer. When the installation has finished, you will find a new folder called Plone in the Applications folder of your Mac (if you didn't change the destination folder during installation). Plone isn't started by default. You will find the instructions you need in the README.html file in the zinstance folder (/Applications/Plone/zinstance); it contains a lot of useful information about running and managing your Plone installation, including how to start Plone.

You should first, as the file says, review the settings in /Applications/Plone/zinstance/buildout.cfg; then adjust the ports Plone uses before starting the site, if necessary; and then run /Applications/Plone/zinstance/bin/buildout to apply settings.

To start Plone, issue the following command in a terminal window:

```
/Applications/Plone/zinstance/bin/plonectl start
```

To stop Plone, issue the following command in a terminal window:

```
/Applications/Plone/zinstance/bin/plonectl stop
```

To test whether Plone has worked, use a browser to go to http://localhost:8080/. You should see the Plone welcome page. Click the link "View your Plone site" and use the password you set up during installation for your admin user to log in, and you can start working!

Installing Plone on Gnu/Linux

You will see now how to install Plone on UNIX-like operating systems. There are many UNIX-like distributions—the most well-known are Debian, Ubuntu, CentOS, and Fedora. For installing Plone on these systems, there are various installation methods at your disposal. You can use the specific package manager utilities of your distribution, you can use the Unified Installer, or you can use a more generic buildout method that helps you automatically install and deploy your Plone-based applications.

We will cover all three installation methods in-depth based on specific distribution package manager utilities available on Debian-like or Red Hat/Fedora/CentOS–based distributions and based on more specific Zope/Plone tools such as zc.buildout or Unified Installer.

If you want, you can also install Zope and Plone directly from the source code, as you can commonly do for other software. To do so, you need to be somewhat familiar with these kinds of tasks. If you do it this way, what you will gain is control over the directory layout, dependencies, and versions, as we have already mentioned.

Ubuntu and Other Debian-Like Distributions

Note In this book and specifically in this chapter, when we show commands to run in the command line, we will use the # character if the command has to be launched by the root user or by using sudo (for the distributions that use this).

For Ubuntu- and Debian-like distributions, there is a package available on the default repositories. You only have to type this command, and the setup will start:

```
# apt-get install plone3-site
```

During this installation, a window will pop up asking you to define a Zope user and the port of the HTTP server (other servers are disabled by default; you can enable them by editing zope.conf). Take note of the data you entered: this user will be the administrator of your Zope instance, and its password will be necessary for entering the ZMI.

After the end of the process, Zope will automatically start. You have to connect to the ZMI on http://localhost:8081/manage (if you haven't changed the HTTP port) and add a Plone site (see the "Adding a Plone Site" section later in the chapter for details). You can start and stop the Zope daemons with the script in /etc/init.d/zope2.x (as usual, you can use the update-rc.d command to define whether the daemon starts on boot). If you need to configure your Zope instance, the configuration file is available in /etc/zope2.x/plone-site/zope.conf.

Tip The Zope utilities for Debian-like distributions such as Ubuntu are available in /usr/lib/zope2.x/.

Installing on Fedora and Red Hat/CentOs

The standard repository doesn't contain a Plone 3 package, but luckily one is available from RPM Fusion (a popular third-party repository). You have to add this repository using the instructions at http://rpmfusion.org/Configuration.

For Fedora 10, you have to add the following repository:

```
# rpm -Uvh http://download1.rpmfusion.org/free/fedora/➡
rpmfusion-free-release-stable.noarch.rpm
http://download1.rpmfusion.org/nonfree/fedora/➡
rpmfusion-nonfree-release-stable.noarch.rpm
```

Then you can install your Plone site using yum:

```
# yum install compat-plone3-3.1.4-2.fc10
```

Next, you must define a Zope administrator with the following:

```
# zope ctl adduser username password
```

The username and password entered will belong to the Zope administrator and will be used to access the ZMI. The Zope server is stopped by default. You can start it with

```
# service zope start
```

and you can stop it with

```
# service zope stop
```

If you want to automatically start your Zope instance on startup, you can use `chkconfig`. For example, the following command starts Zope if you boot your system on run levels 3 and 5 (shell mode and graphic mode):

```
# chkconfig -level 35 zope on
```

The configuration file is in `/var/lib/zope/etc/zope.conf`. Now you can access the ZMI from `http://yourpcname:8080/manage` and add a Plone site (see the "Adding a Plone Site" section later in the chapter).

Tip All the Zope tools for the Fedora distribution are in `/usr/lib/zope/`.

If you want to customize the default behavior of Zope, you can modify the `zope.conf` configuration file. For example, you can change the port of your Zope web server in the `http-server` section under the label `address`. Other options are very well commented in the file and don't need further explanations. This is true not only for Fedora but for most other distributions as well.

Installing with the Unified Installer

Not all platforms have a package to quickly install Plone. Besides, package distributions have a major drawback: they are managed by distribution managers and are never updated. For these reasons, Plone developers have created the Unified Installer, available on `http://plone.org/products/plone`—click "Get Plone for Linux/BSD/Unix" to download it.

This package uses the same technology that lies behind `zc.buildout` to install the latest version of Plone on every Linux/BSD/OS X/UNIX/Solaris distribution, and it creates the same environment as `zc.buildout`. It provides you with Plone, Zope, and Python packages and an installation script that does all the dirty work for you. The Unified Installer comes with three different installation options:

- *Install as root or normal user*: Installing Plone as root user (with the `sudo` command) is recommended for a production Plone system, since it gives the software a new specific user with limited rights that will run Plone commands. For testing or developing Plone on your computer, you may prefer installing it as a normal user, since you won't have to worry about identities and rights.

- *Install as a ZEO (Zope Enterprise Objects) Cluster, or a stand-alone Zope server*: The ZEO installation allows several Zope client processes to share a common database server process. This allows you to configure the client/server architecture in order to optimize process workload.

- *Install the full kit, or just a single running instance*: A stand-alone Zope installation provides you with a simple way of doing things, and it's easier to understand. It is probably the best choice for development, for a simple environment, or if you want to quickly start discovering Plone.

Finally, you can still choose whether to install everything together or set everything up by yourself. Before starting installing, you should check whether you already have the following packages on your platform:

- GNU Compiler Collection (GCC).

- G++, the C++ extensions for GCC.

- GNU Make, the fundamental build-control tool.

- GNU Tar. This is the version of tar on all Linux, BSD, and OS X platforms but not Solaris.

- The bzip2 and gzip decompression packages. gzip is nearly standard; some platforms will require that bzip2 be installed.

When you are sure you have everything, you can start installing! The first step is to place the tarball into a convenient directory (e.g., your home folder), and unpack it:

```
tar zxf Plone-3.VERSION-UnifiedInstaller.tar.gz
```

Note Replace *VERSION* with the Unified Installer version you downloaded.

After that, you can move to the created directory:

```
cd Plone-3.VERSION.UnifiedInstaller
```

Now commands will depend on your installation preferences.

Note If you chose to install Plone as root, you should now switch to the super user, or remember to precede the following commands with sudo.

If you want to install Plone as a ZEO cluster (the best choice for production and complex development), use the following command:

```
./install.sh zeo
```

If you prefer a stand-alone Zope installation, use this:

```
./install.sh standalone
```

So, everything is done now. You can relax and take a look at the installation process, which should be working smoothly. If an error occurs, though, don't panic. Just do the following:

- Double-check that you've installed all of the previously listed packages.

- Carefully read the error message and try to understand what is missing.

- Take a look at README.txt file, especially the "Platform Notes" section; you can find a lot of useful information there.

Tip If you still can't figure out the problem, ask for help on the #plone IRC channel. You can always find people there to help you out. You can also go to http://plone.org/support, where you can take a look at the dedicated forums. You can also find useful information in the FAQs, at http://plone.org/documentation/faq.

If everything worked fine, you've successfully installed Plone on your machine. Welcome! You still have to take note of a couple of things before having fun with Plone. At the end of the installation, you will find some useful information in the README.txt file about how to start Zope and Plone, and you will also have to take note of your admin password, which will be available in adminPassword.txt.

If you have installed Plone as root, your Plone instance will be in /opt/Plone3.x/zinstance/. If you have installed Plone as a normal user, you will find the same directory, Plone-3.x/zinstance/, in your home directory. You can start your Zope instance with

bin/plonectl start

and stop it with

bin/plonectl stop

The ZMI is available at http://localhost:8080/manage, and your Plone site is available at http://localhost:8080/Plone. If you need to configure Zope, check the "Managing Your Buildout" section later in the chapter.

Installing Plone with zc.buildout

zc.buildout is a tool that lets you easily deploy a Zope installation with a set of products. It has been developed by the Zope Corporation and works on every operating system that Plone supports. The buildout installation is composed of recipes, written in the configuration file buildout.cfg.

The buildout script builds your Zope instance and helps keep the products you have chosen updated. To use this installation, your system will have to fulfil the following prerequisites:

- Python 2.4 (and sources)
- Python Imaging Library (PIL; see www.pythonware.com/products/pil)
- ElementTree (an XML-parsing library; see http://effbot.org/zone/element-index.htm)
- A C compiler

Tip On Debian GNU/Linux or Ubuntu you have to run the following command:

```
# apt-get install build-essentials python2.4 python2.4-dev python-imaging
```

On Red Hat, Fedora, and CentOs, you have to add RPM Fusion among your repositories (see http://rpmfusion.org/Configuration), as follows:

```
# yum groupinstall "Development Tools"
# yum install compat-python24 compat-python24-devel
```

The first step is to install Easy Install, a Python module bundled with setuptools that lets you automatically download, build, install, and manage Python packages. You can download it from http://peak.telecommunity.com/dist/ez_setup.py using your favorite browser, or you can download it using the command-line utility wget:

```
$ wget http://peak.telecommunity.com/dist/ez_setup.py
```

Then you have to launch the following:

```
# python ez_setup.py
```

Tip If your default Python version is not 2.4.x, you must specify python2.4 in place of python every time you need to call the Python interpreter. For example:

```
# python2.4 ez_setup.py
```

If you need to know which version of Python you are using, you have to launch the Python interpreter with python -V, and check the version.

Next, you can use Easy Install to install ZopeSkel:

```
#easy_install ZopeSkel
```

ZopeSkel is a collection of skeletons for quickly starting Zope projects such as buildout environments or new development packages. ZopeSkel includes the Paster utility, which is what we will use to show how to create your new buildout and install your environment:

```
$ paster create -t plone3_buildout myproject
```

After this command, you have to provide the following information about your Zope instance:

- The path of your Zope installation. Use this only if you have Zope installed and you want to share it between multiple buildouts (leave this answer blank if you want to install Zope).

- The path of your Plone products (if you want to share the same set of products between your buildouts, you can input the path where these products are installed). Again, leave this answer blank if you want to install the products listed in buildout.cfg.

- The Zope administrator username.

- The Zope administrator password.

- The port that the Zope HTTP server will use.

- Whether you want to start Zope in debug mode (the server outputs debug messages to your console).

- If verbose security has to be enabled (the server outputs various information about accesses on your Zope instance).

After you answer these questions, the directory myproject will be created. The following code shows you some example results of the answers to the questions:

```
$ paster create -t plone3_buildout myproject
Selected and implied templates:
  ZopeSkel#plone3_buildout  A buildout for Plone 3 projects

Variables:
  egg:      myproject
  package:  myproject
  project:  myproject
Enter zope2_install (Path to Zope 2 installation; leave blank to fetch
one) ['']:
Enter plone_products_install (Path to directory containing Plone
products; leave blank to fetch one) ['']:
Enter zope_user (Zope root admin user) ['admin']:
Enter zope_password (Zope root admin password) ['']: admin
Enter http_port (HTTP port) [8080]:
Enter debug_mode (Should debug mode be "on" or "off"?) ['off']:
Enter verbose_security (Should verbose security be "on" or "off"?)
['off']:
Creating template plone3_buildout
Creating directory ./myproject
  Copying README.txt to ./myproject/README.txt
  Copying bootstrap.py to ./myproject/bootstrap.py
  Copying buildout.cfg_tmpl to ./myproject/buildout.cfg
  Recursing into products
    Creating ./myproject/products/
    Copying README.txt to ./myproject/products/README.txt
```

```
  Recursing into src
    Creating ./myproject/src/
    Copying README.txt to ./myproject/src/README.txt
  Recursing into var
    Creating ./myproject/var/
    Copying README.txt to ./myproject/var/README.txt
-----------------------------------------------------------
Generation finished
You probably want to run python bootstrap.py and then edit
buildout.cfg before running bin/buildout -v

See README.txt for details
-----------------------------------------------------------
```

To bootstrap the buildout to get the standard zc.buildout tools, run

```
$ cd myproject
$ python bootstrap.py
```

This step is needed only once. You are now ready to build the system. Simply run

```
$ ./bin/buildout
```

This may take a long time, depending on the speed of your computer and Internet connection. It will download and build Zope, download and install Plone, and configure the two and all the products specified in buildout.cfg.

When it is finished, you can start Zope by running

```
$ ./bin/instance start
```

and you can stop it by running

```
$ ./bin/instance stop
```

Tip You can also use $ ./bin/instance fg, which will output all debug information to the shell.

Now you can access the ZMI at http://yourpcname:8080/manage and add a Plone site (see the "Adding a Plone Site" section later in the chapter).

The Buildout Directory Tree

Let's now take a look at the content of the buildout directory. First of all, you have the buildout configuration file (buildout.cfg), which we will explain shortly. You also have the bootstrap.py file used before to set up the buildout. Finally, you also have some directories:

- \bin: Recipes place their executables in this directory. By default, it contains the buildout command. The commands to start and stop your Zope instance are also found here.

- \develop-eggs: This directory contains links to any development eggs specified in buildout.cfg.

- \downloads: This directory contains the packages fetched by the buildout.

- \eggs: This directory contains the "new-style" products used by Plone (the new pre-ferred way to package Plone products is to use Python eggs, which we will talk about in the "Adding an Add-on Product" section). This way permits the reuse of products between Plone and other Python projects.

- \parts: This is the directory where your recipes are built.

- \products: Place your source here if you are developing an old-style Plone product.

- \src: This directory contains your projects if you are developing a new-style Plone product.

- \var: This directory contains the zodb database file and the log files.

Managing Your Buildout

Now let's take a look at the default buildout.cfg file:

```
[buildout]
extensions=buildout.eggtractor
parts =
    plone
    zope2
    productdistros
    instance
    zopepy


# Add additional egg download sources here. dist.plone.org contains archives
# of Plone packages.
find-links =
    http://dist.plone.org
    http://download.zope.org/ppix/
    http://download.zope.org/distribution/
    http://effbot.org/downloads
    http://dist.plone.org/thirdparty/


# Add additional eggs here
# elementtree is required by Plone
eggs =
    elementtree
    PIL
    pisa
    html5lib
    pyPDF
    BeautifulSoup
```

```
# Reference any eggs you are developing here, one per line
# e.g.: develop = src/my.package
develop =

[plone]
recipe = plone.recipe.plone>=3.1.1,<3.2dev

[zope2]
recipe = plone.recipe.zope2install
url = ${plone:zope2-url}

# Use this section to download additional old-style products.
# List any number of URLs for product tarballs under URLs (separate
# with whitespace, or break over several lines, with subsequent lines
# indented). If any archives contain several products inside a top-level
# directory, list the archive file name (i.e. the last part of the URL,
# normally with a .tar.gz suffix or similar) under 'nested-packages'.
# If any archives extract to a product directory with a version suffix, list
# the archive name under 'version-suffix-packages'.

[productdistros]
recipe = plone.recipe.distros
urls =
nested-packages =
version-suffix-packages =

[instance]
recipe = plone.recipe.zope2instance
zope2-location = ${zope2:location}
user = admin:admin
http-address = 8080
#debug-mode = on
#verbose-security = on

# If you want Zope to know about any additional eggs, list them here.
# This should include any development eggs you listed in develop-eggs above,
# e.g. eggs = ${buildout:eggs} ${plone:eggs} my.package
eggs =
    ${buildout:eggs}
    ${plone:eggs}

# If you want to register ZCML slugs for any packages, list them here.
# e.g. zcml = my.package my.other.package
zcml =

products =
    ${buildout:directory}/products
    ${productdistros:location}
    ${plone:products}
```

```
[zopepy]
recipe = zc.recipe.egg
eggs = ${instance:eggs}
interpreter = zopepy
extra-paths = ${zope2:location}/lib/python
scripts = zopepy
```

The first part of this configuration file (i.e., under [buildout]) contains the system-wide settings. Part of it is a list of operations to do in order. Every part listed here corresponds to a list of options that appears after the [buildout] part, preceded by the name of the option between square brackets. Every part has a recipe—the recipe is an installation or configuration script that runs using the parameters described in the same part. By default, every recipe is downloaded from the sites described in the [buildout] section.

Tip The Python Package Index (PyPI) web site contains a lot of different recipes; visit http://pypi. python.org to take a look. For example, you can automatically compile and install mandatory software dependencies from source, perform shell commands, and many other things. You can find extensive documentation about zc.buildout at http://pypi.python.org/pypi/zc.buildout.

The buildout command (in the directory \bin) uses the buildout.cfg file in the current directory as an argument. It checks whether your configuration matches the configuration in the buildout.cfg file. If necessary, it then downloads, builds, and configures the missing packages. If an update is out, it allows you to update the relevant product.

Tip If you need to modify some configuration parameters, you have to do this in buildout.cfg; otherwise, the next time you will launch the buildout command, your changes will be overwritten. For example, if you want to change the HTTP port, you have to change http-port in the [instance] part of buildout.cfg and launch ./bin/buildout. This way, the system will update the zope.conf file with the correct port. If you change the zope.conf file directly, the next time you launch buildout, your changes will be overwritten.

By default, buildouts and recipes will try to find the newest versions of distributions needed to satisfy requirements. This can be very dangerous for production environments, as well as time-consuming. The buildout newest option can be used to suppress this default behavior.

Tip If you don't need to update your installed products, you can run `buildout` in offline, nonupdating mode using the following:

```
$ ./bin/buildout -No
```

To get a full explanation of the various options available, run this:

```
$ ./bin/buildout --help
```

Another way to avoid the update of installed products is to add the following option to the `[buildout]` section of your `buildout.cfg` configuration file:

```
newest = false
```

Adding a Plone Site

Once you have installed Plone from source, you need to create an instance of Plone. To do this, you will need to log into the ZMI and add a Plone site. You can access this by going to the URL for the management interface, which is normally `http://localhost:8080/manage` (this port may change depending upon your installation). You will need the manager's username and password created during the Zope installation to access the ZMI.

You can add all types of objects via the drop-down list in the top-right corner, as shown in Figure 2-8. Scroll down the list until you find Plone Site, and then click Add.

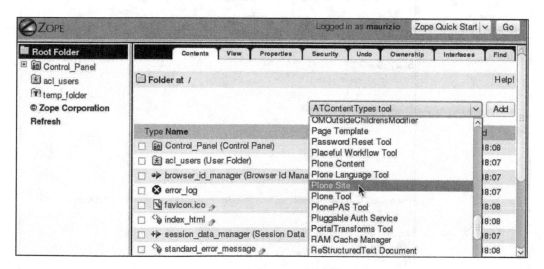

Figure 2-8. *Adding a Plone site: Use the Add drop-down menu in the ZMI.*

After selecting the Plone Site option, a form will display that prompts for some more information (see Figure 2-9):

- *Id*: This is the unique ID of the Plone site (e.g., enter **Plone** or **Site**—throughout this book, we often use mysite).

- *Title*: This is the title of the Plone site (e.g., enter **My Site**).

- *Description*: This is a description of the portal that members will see in e-mail messages or search engine results. Don't worry too much about this; you can always change it later in the Plone control panel.

■**Tip** Remember that search engine optimization (SEO) is a very important issue for web sites; Plone by default has an outstanding search engine visibility, but your help is important, too—so don't forget to add these kinds of details before publishing your site.

- *Extension Profiles*: This is a list of extension profiles through which you can install a Plone site with complex customizations added by default. You normally don't need to select anything here unless you have specific reasons and know what you are doing. Otherwise, just leave it at the default.

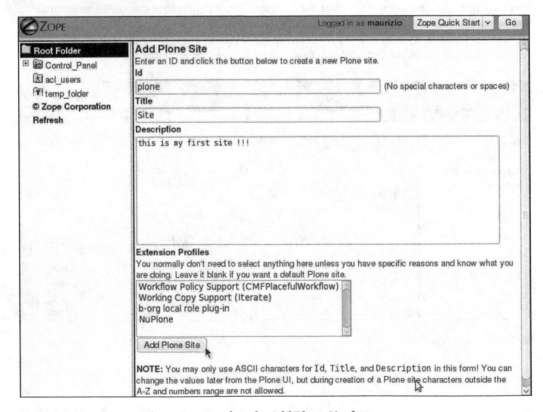

Figure 2-9. *To add your Plone site, complete the Add Plone Site form.*

After clicking the Add Plone Site button, your Plone site will be created. This may take a minute or two on slower machines because a great deal of processing occurs. The screen will then redirect you to the Plone welcome page.

Installing an Add-on Product

Finally, you will see how to integrate an add-on product in your Plone site. As we mentioned in Chapter 1, add-on products are modules that can give your Plone site additional functionalities and are made for integrating in Plone architecture.

How you'll choose to install an add-on product depends on a few factors:

- The way Zope was installed (from source or with zc.buildout)
- Whether you're installing a traditional Zope 2 product
- Whether you're installing a product packaged as a Python egg

Depending on which kind of installation method you used for your Plone instance and on which kind of package you need to integrate, the installation method of the package can vary. This inconvenience is being fixed by developers in newer versions of Plone and add-on products, because most new Plone add-on products are now packaged as Python eggs, but for now we need to pay attention to this issue.

As mentioned, Python eggs are the now-standard way to package and distribute all Python software. Using the buildout method gives you some advantages, since you can install both Zope 2–style and egg-based Products. If the buildout method is available for your installation, it is the recommended way to manage add-on product installation.

We will now show how to install egg-based add-on products through the buildout method. We will also show how to install Zope 2–style products with the buildout method, since many add-on products are still released this way.

Installing a Traditional Zope 2 Product

To install a traditional Zope 2 product, you can modify your buildout.cfg configuration and update the [productdistros] section. You just have to add the exact URL of the product tarball you want to integrate in your instance, as follows:

```
[productdistros]
recipe = plone.recipe.distros
urls =
    ...
    http://.../MyProduct-1.1.tgz
nested-packages =
version-suffix-packages =
```

Last, you need to launch the buildout script that will download the MyProduct package for you, because, as always, if you change buildout.cfg, you must rerun buildout:

```
$ ./bin/buildout
```

After you restart your Zope instance, you should see a new product available in the Add-on Products section of the Plone control panel. You can then install it in your Plone site and configure it as you like (see the "Adding/Removing Products in Your Site" section in Chapter 4).

Note There are other installation methods you can use through the buildout. For example, you could also manually download and unpack the tarball in the `Products` folder of the buildout and then restart the Zope instance. See the following documentation: `http://plone.org/documentation/tutorial/buildout/ installing-a-third-party-product`.

You can find more details on alternative installation methods at `http://plone.org/documentation/ tutorial/third-party-products`.

Installing a Product Packaged As an Egg with Buildout

Installing an egg-based product is very easy. You just have to properly update `buildout.cfg`, and the egg with all its dependencies will be automatically downloaded from the Python Package Index (the repository of software for the Python programming language). To do so, update the [`buildout`] section, and indicate the egg product to be installed:

```
[buildout]
...
eggs =
  ...
    my.egg
```

It is important to know that Zope will not automatically upload the `configure.zcml` file for packages outside the `Products` namespace, so you will have to update the [`instance`] section, as follows:

```
[instance]
...
zcml =
...
    my.egg
```

Then rerun the buildout script:

```
$ ./bin/buildout
```

After you restart your Zope instance, you should see a new product available in the Add-on Products section of the Plone control panel.

Summary

In this chapter, you have seen how to install Plone on different operating systems and with different methods. If you've followed the section appropriate for your OS, you will have successfully created your first Plone site!

Next, you'll learn how to use this powerful CMS, starting with how to add, modify, and manage content and then continuing with the basic configuration of the Plone user interface.

■ ■ ■

## CHAPTER 3

Managing Content with Plone

One of Plone's greatest advantages is that it has a very intuitive interface and easy-to-use tools; you can add and edit content with it even if you don't have any specific technical background. Let's prove this together, starting with what we first see when we are in front of Plone and the elements of the main interface, and continuing with how easy it is to create and organize content with Plone.

If you are going to work with Plone, the first thing to do is log in. This will let you enter the CMS and will give you the power to act in it.

Note The aim of this chapter is to present the CMS to beginners—that is, people that don't know Plone or have already approached it but need a generic and complete overview. If you are already familiar with Plone, you can either breeze through or skip this chapter altogether.

Also keep in mind that in this chapter we will see how Plone 3.0 works straight out of the box. Therefore, all the examples we will talk about and all the screenshots we will use to better understand the functioning of Plone could be a little different from what you may experience when working on a site that has been customized (e.g., by managing portlets or choosing a special workflow), or on another version of Plone.

Logging in As a New User

First, we need to get to our Plone site user interface. If you are on Windows, you can use the Plone Controller to start Plone and view the user interface (see Chapter 2 for more details), or simply type **http://localhost** into your browser (it won't work if your Plone instance is not running yet). If you work on a Mac, type **http://localhost:8080** into your browser and click the "View your Plone site" link. If you work in a Linux environment, also type **http://localhost:8080**. (Of course, these URLs will be valid only if you haven't changed certain basic configurations—for example, the ports.)

If you have personally installed Plone, you should have the username and password that came with the installation. This user has the role of an administrator, which allows you to log in and alter any content.

If you are not the manager of the Plone site, you may have received a username and a password from the site owner. The login procedure will be the same. To log in, you can either use the "Log in" box at the left of the page, as shown in Figure 3-1, or the "Log in" link at the top right, as shown in Figure 3-2.

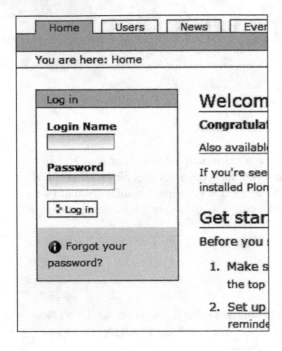

Figure 3-1. *The "Log in" box, where you can enter your username and password to log into your Plone site*

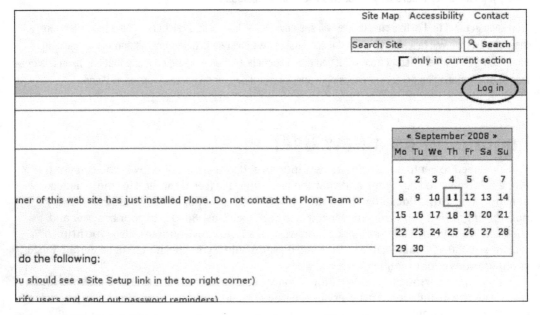

Figure 3-2. *The "Log in" link—another way to log into your Plone site*

The only thing you need to do is enter your username and password and click the "Log in" button.

Note Usernames and passwords are case-sensitive.

If you forget your password, don't worry. Click the "Forgot your password?" link near the login form and follow the instructions, and Plone will help you solve your problem!

If you don't have an account on the Plone site yet, click the Register link in the top-right corner of the page, as shown in Figure 3-3.

Note The Register link will be available only if the webmaster has enabled the self-registration feature. You'll see more about this in the "Managing Security Settings" section of Chapter 4.

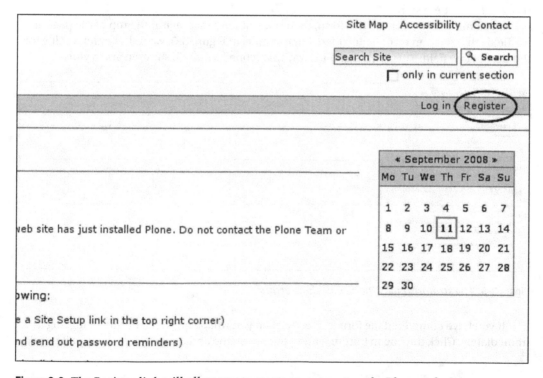

Figure 3-3. *The Register link will allow you to create an account on the Plone web site.*

This will take you to a registration form to complete, as shown in Figure 3-4.

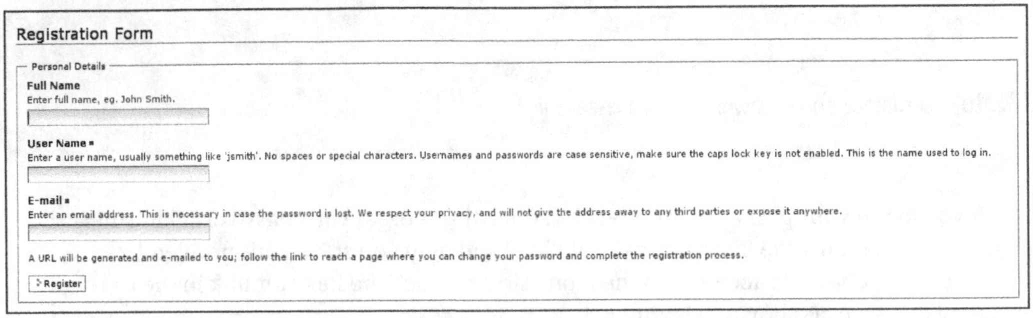

Figure 3-4. *The Registration form you have to complete to join the site*

For most fields, the gray help text beneath the field name indicates what you should enter. The fields with a little red box next to the text are required fields.

To complete the form, fill in at least the required fields, which are the ones with the little red square you see alongside the field title. Once you have completed this form, click Register to submit your information. Plone will create an account on the server for you, and you will be recognized by the system.

If you make any errors on this form, then you will see a message at the top of the page and the fields that have an error highlighted. For example, in Figure 3-5, we didn't enter a value for the User Name field. This is the standard way that Plone forms show errors to you.

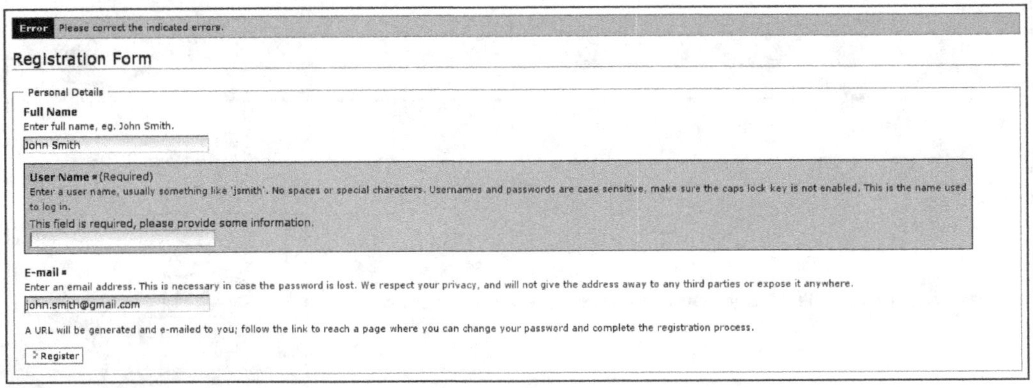

Figure 3-5. *The standard way Plone will show errors*

If you have completed the form correctly, then you will be given the option of logging in immediately. Click the Log In button, enter your username and password, and you will be in!

A First Look at the Plone Interface

Now that you're logged in, you'll notice a link with your username near the top right of the screen and a green header strip with tabs in the middle area.

First, let's see how the Plone interface looks globally (see Figure 3-6).

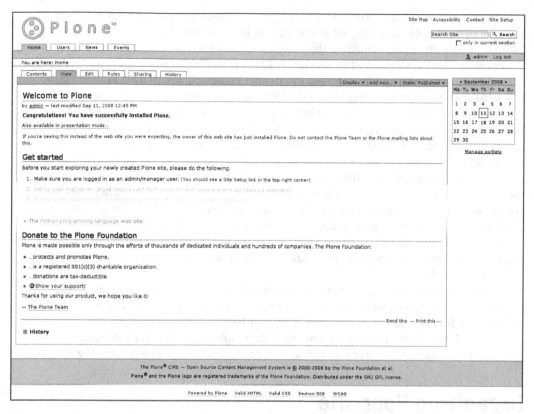

Figure 3-6. *The Plone interface as you will see it the first time you log in (a part of the panel has been cut to make the image more readable)*

At the top left is the Plone logo; clicking it will take you to the home page, no matter where you are within the site. At the top right are some links:

- *Site Map*: This presents an overview of the available contents on this site.

- *Accessibility*: This takes you to a page that gives you information about the accessibility of the site, and lets you choose the size of the text characters.

- *Contact*: This takes you to a form you can fill out if you want to contact the site administrator; anonymous visitors have the capability of doing this as well.

- *Site Setup*: This takes you to the Plone control panel, which offers a variety of options for the site administrator; we will go through it in detail in Chapter 4.

Below this first top section is a header strip that gives you some location and login info. The tabs starting from the left part of the screen (Home, Users, etc.) are the main areas of the site (folders you create in the root of the site). On the right of this header strip is a link to your username (we will discuss the function of it later in this chapter, in the "Setting Up Your Dashboard" and "Setting Up Your Preferences" sections), and a "Log out" link.

Below this strip on the left is a very useful feature that gives users a way to keep track of their location within the site: *breadcrumbs*. Breadcrumbs are a series of links back to each previous item in the site, showing each item's location in the site hierarchy.

The main part of the screen is occupied by the left column, a central area, and the right column. However, if you just logged in and you are in the root of the site, you won't see this column. In any other part of the site, the navigation portlet is contained in the left column and the calendar portlet is contained in the right column. If you've already created and published some content, you will see other portlets in this column as well, set up by default in Plone. (We will explain how to manage them in the "Managing Portlets" section of Chapter 4.)

The central area is your main working area. The green strip with tabs and options menus allows you to create, edit, organize, and manage content. The green tabs on the left part of the strip (Content, View, etc.) give you different views of the content and let you edit and configure various settings. On the right of the strip are three menus: The Actions menu lets you copy, cut, and paste objects in the folder you are in, and delete and rename items. The Display menu, which you will see only for folders and particular content types like collections, lets you change the way of viewing the contents. The State menu lets you manage the workflow status of the content (we will go through this in more detail later in the chapter).

The footer gives you information about Plone and the foundation that supports the project. Below that are a few more links, leading you to some information regarding Plone standards-compliance.

If you are the manager of the site, you will see all the options available in all its parts; if you are not the manager, what you see will depend on the permissions you have in the different areas of the site. In some of them, you may only have the right to view the content—in this case, you will not see the green strip. The way Plone shows content to different users is one of the most powerful features of it! You will soon appreciate this as you begin working with Plone.

Organizing Your Site

There are many platforms, such as Blogspot or MySpace, that allow you to easily create web content, but do not offer capabilities for organizing elements into groups or hierarchies and for managing contents inside their containers. Plone is a big step ahead! With Plone, you can organize web content in the same way you organize your documents, files, programs and other items on your local PC. In other words, the method of storing and organizing items in Plone is very similar to a normal file system, except that the folder and its content exist inside Plone.

A folder can contain any type of content, content can be copied and pasted between folders, and of course folders can contain other folders. That gives you the ability to create a neat hierarchy of items and give logical structure to your site.

The folders you initially create in the root of the site (that is the Home tab) will be the main sections of your site; you'll see them in the navigation header strip as new tabs, and you'll see them in the navigation portlet.

To add a folder to your site, go to the section where you want to add it (it can be Home or another section/folder) and select Folder from the "Add new" drop-down menu. This will add a folder and take you to the edit properties page for that form. A folder has just two rather simple attributes that a user can edit: *title* and *description*. We will discuss these attributes for documents, but they are the same for folders. Folders have different green tabs that represent different views and functions, but we will talk about them later; what is interesting for us right now is the Contents tab.

The Contents tab will take you to the contents of a folder and let you organize them, allowing you or other users with the appropriate permissions to perform a variety of tasks, such as moving, renaming, deleting, publishing, and changing the order in which the contents are listed. As shown in Figure 3-7, you will also see a simple table of the folder contents.

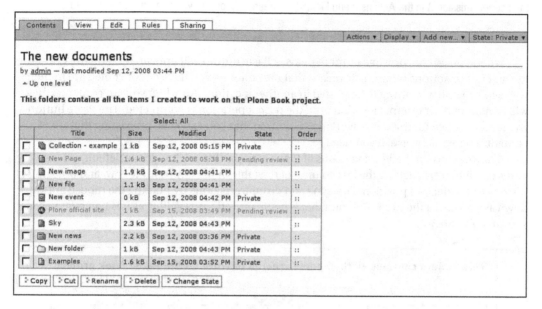

Figure 3-7. *The Contents tab, which gives you information about the items contained in a folder and lets you perform some tasks*

Each row of the table shows the following:

- The title of the item (plus an icon)
- Its size
- When it was last modified
- Its current workflow status
- Order selectors

On the left are check boxes for selecting the items you want to change/organize. Across the bottom is a series of options: Copy, Cut, Rename, Delete, and Change State.

These functions are all pretty self-explanatory, and you can apply them to multiple objects at once by clicking several check boxes.

For example, to quickly rename a piece of content, toggle the check box of that item, and then click Rename. This will open the rename form and allow you to rename the title of each item in that list (see the note in the "Editing a Page" section later in the chapter to understand what this operation is for). Click Save to have the changes take effect. The Cut and Copy buttons allow you to copy or move content between different folders. The Delete button allows you to delete the item from Plone.

Note The actions of Cut, Copy, Delete, and Rename are also available for any content type (according to the user permissions) in the Actions menu located on green strip on the View and the Contents tabs.

When you cut or copy one or more items, a Paste button will appear, both on the Contents tab and in the Actions menu. This means that the contents you have cut or copied are in the web site's memory, waiting to be pasted in another location. But when you cut contents, they will remain in their original location until the paste operation is completed. The Paste button will remain active for the entire working session, so that you can keep on pasting that set of contents somewhere else, if you need to.

A new feature in the latest versions of Plone is the ability to change the default order of items in a folder by clicking the last column of the table in the appropriate row, and dragging the row to the desired position. Dragging and dropping is done by holding the mouse button down as you move the item. The item that is being moved turns yellow as it is being moved, as shown in Figure 3-8.

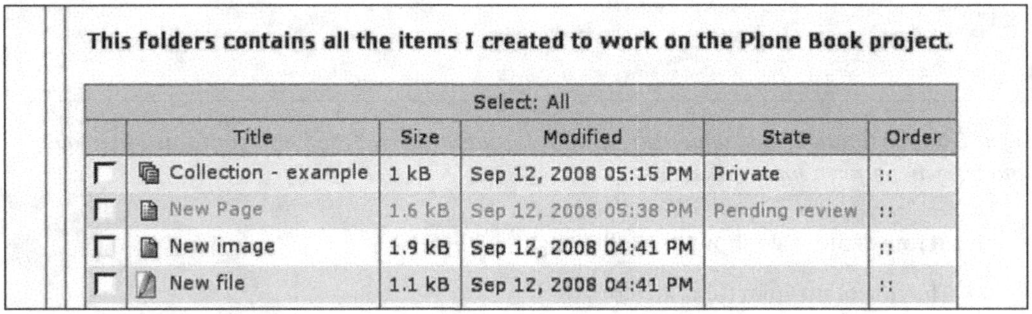

This folders contains all the items I created to work on the Plone Book project.

		Title	Size	Modified	State	Order
				Select: All		
☐	🗐	Collection - example	1 kB	Sep 12, 2008 05:15 PM	Private	::
☐	📄	New Page	1.6 kB	Sep 12, 2008 05:38 PM	Pending review	::
☐	🖼	New image	1.9 kB	Sep 12, 2008 04:41 PM		::
☐	📄	New file	1.1 kB	Sep 12, 2008 04:41 PM		::

Figure 3-8. *Reordering items in the Contents panel: Just click the item you want to move, and drag and drop it into the new position.*

When the mouse button is released, the item stays where it was dropped.

The following features will appear in the folder contents only when certain things happen:

- If the content has an expiration date set and it has expired, you will see the word "expired" appear in red next to the title of the item.

- If the server has an external editor installed, you will see a pencil next to the item that you can click to edit with it.

- If the content is locked, you will see a lock icon appear next to the content.

Just like on your hard drive, if you copy, move, or delete a folder, all the contents of the folder will also be moved, copied, or deleted. Organizing your contents in a Plone site is, therefore, very easy; if you are used to managing documents on your local machine with directories and folders, you won't have any problem organizing your Plone site, because it works the same way.

However, there is another useful way to organize your content—particularly content that's spread all over a site: it involves a more sophisticated content type, called a *collection*. A collection searches your Plone site and finds all objects that match certain criteria, allowing you to group lots of disparate content. We will talk about this feature later in the "Gathering Disparate Elements into Coherent Collections" section of this chapter.

Setting Up Your Dashboard

After you have logged in, you can click your username in the member bar in the top-right corner to set up your dashboard and your preferences.

Each user has a personal dashboard—a page of the site that they can customize as they wish. If you haven't set up your dashboard, this will be empty for now. To configure it, click the green Edit tab; Figure 3-9 shows you the panel that will appear.

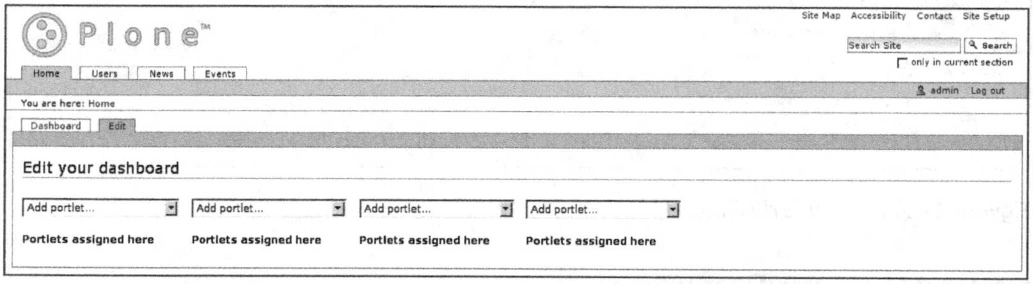

Figure 3-9. *Editing your dashboard: You can add different portlets according to your needs.*

You will be able to add *portlets*—that is, discrete rectangular areas that contain list views of news, events, recently changed items, and such. You control which portlets you view in your dashboard and where they are placed; use the drop-down menus to select which portlets you want to add and where.

For some types of portlets, you will be asked to set some more options; for example, if you choose the Add RSS Portlet option, a panel will appear requiring you to choose the number of items to display, enter a URL for the RSS feed, and specify a feed reload time (see Figure 3-10).

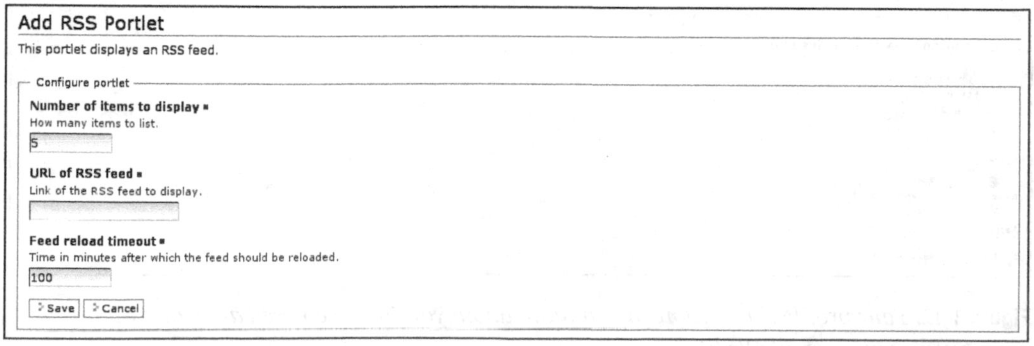

Figure 3-10. *Adding an RSS portlet on your dashboard*

Set up your dashboard so that it's most useful for you. To see how your dashboard appears, return to the View tab (Figure 3-11 gives an example of how it might look).

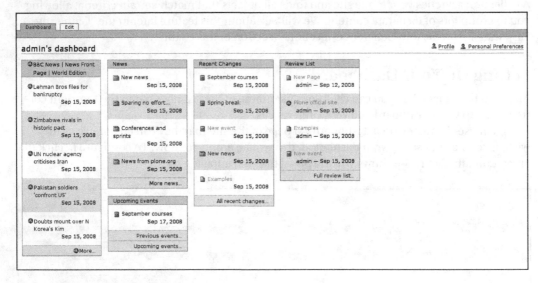

Figure 3-11. *An example dashboard*

Setting Up Your Preferences

In your dashboard (which you can reach by clicking your username link on the right part of the header strip), you will notice a few links in the top-right corner. Clicking Profile leads you to a panel that shows all the recent content you've created/edited (see Figure 3-12).

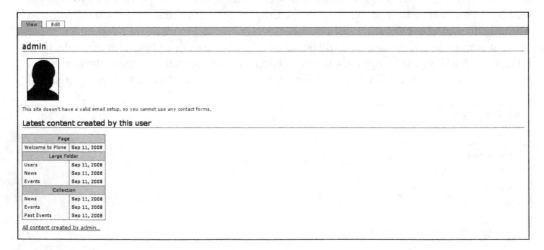

Figure 3-12. *Your profile shows some information about you (if you entered any), and all the recent items you've created/edited.*

Clicking the Edit tab lets you enter some information about yourself, including a photo or other image, as shown in Figure 3-13.

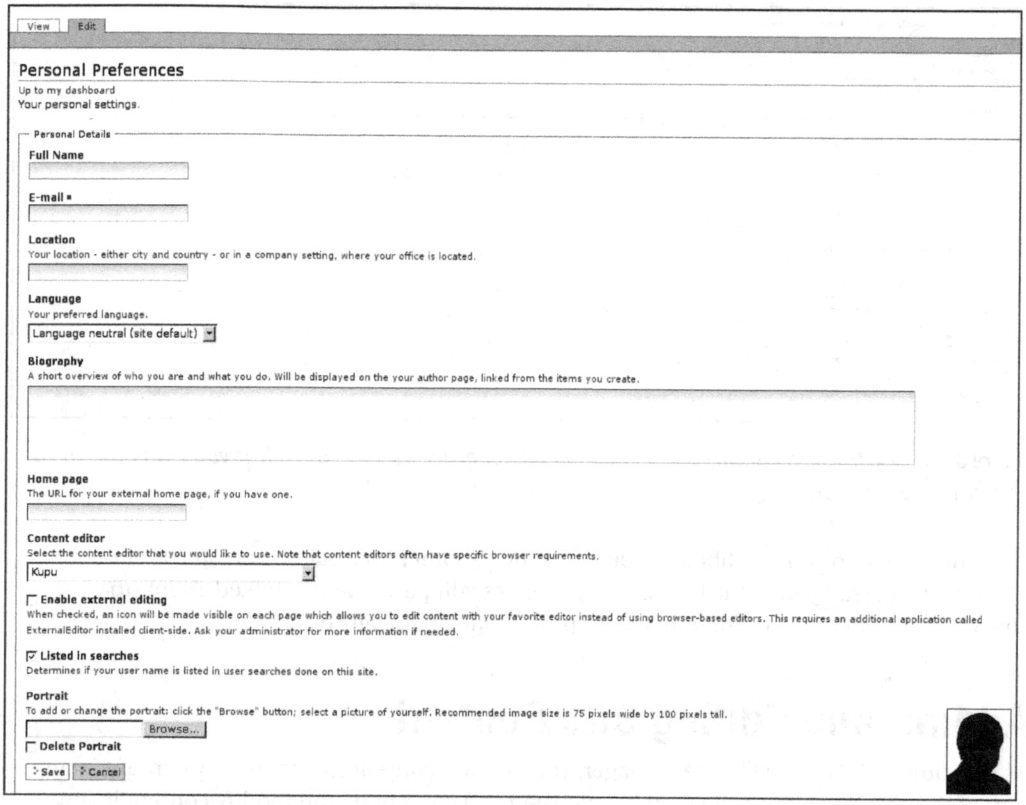

Figure 3-13. *Editing your profile*

Most of the fields are self-explanatory, but let's talk about the most interesting ones:

- The "Content editor" field lets you choose through a drop-down menu the content editor you would like to use. The default setting is to use Kupu, a visual editor that lets you edit web pages with a nice graphical interface. The other option that's always available is "Basic HTML Textarea editor," which is good if you are accustomed to writing web pages using HTML. If your Plone site is provided with other editors, you will see them as options in this drop-down menu. Remember that content editors often have specific browser requirements.

- The "Enable external editing" field lets you enable an external editor if one has been installed in the Plone site. As the description below the option says, if you check it, "an icon will be made visible on each page which allows you to edit content with your favorite editor instead of using browser-based editors."

When other users click your username link (it usually appears under the title of items you have personally created), they will be able to see some of the information you entered, together with your photo and a table listing all the latest content you've created. If you are an authenticated user, you will also see a box called "Feedback for author" above that table; this box contains a form for sending the user a message, as shown in Figure 3-14.

Figure 3-14. *The form to contact other members to let other users know what you think about the content they created*

Going back to your dashboard, you will notice another link, called Personal Preferences. Clicking it will lead you to the Personal Preferences edit panel we just talked about (the one you access by clicking the Edit tab in your profile, shown in Figure 3-13).

Adding and Editing Site Content

As mentioned, if you are the site manager, you can add content to and modify content in any part of the site; if you are a site member, you can add content to and modify content in any folder where the site administrator has given you the right to do so.

There are a number of distinct types of content that you can add, and each can be viewed/ edited in different ways. For this reason, Plone references each type of content differently. Out of the box, Plone provides the following content types:

- *Collection*: This is a grouping of contents that can be located in different parts of the site, according to certain criteria you set. See the "Gathering Disparate Elements into Coherent Collections" section of this chapter.

- *Event*: This is an upcoming event, meeting, conference, or other event.

- *File*: This is a piece of content such as a movie, sound clip, text file, spreadsheet, compressed file, or anything else you can upload.

- *Folder*: This is like a folder on a hard drive—a container you can put content into so that it is easy to find later.

- *Image*: This is an image, such as a GIF or JPEG file.

- *Link*: This is a link to another item; it can be internal or external to your web site.

- *News Item*: This is a document about new information (e.g., a press release); it is normally shown under the News navigation tab.

- *Page*: This is an item that presents some static information to the user. This is the most common type of content added and most closely represents a typical web page.

Let's go through the features of these content types using the page content type as an example, showing in detail how to add and edit documents easily and quickly. Using these basic content types, you can build a dynamic site through a browser without any programming. Isn't that great? That's the power of the Plone CMS from the end user's point of view.

Actually, you can add and edit content in a Plone site in many ways other than just through a web browser. You can access Plone via File Transfer Protocol (FTP), Web-Based Distributed Authoring and Versioning (WebDAV), and scripts as well. But for now, we will just deal with the web browser interface.

Adding and Editing Pages

First, ensure you are logged in, because only logged-in users can add content.

If you are able to add content to a folder, then the folder will show up with the green border around the top. If the green border doesn't appear, then you won't be able to add content; the green strip contains the actions you can perform in the current location. In the top-right corner of the green border, you will see a drop-down menu called "Add new." Click it to open a drop-down list of items to add. To add a new page, select Page, as shown in Figure 3-15.

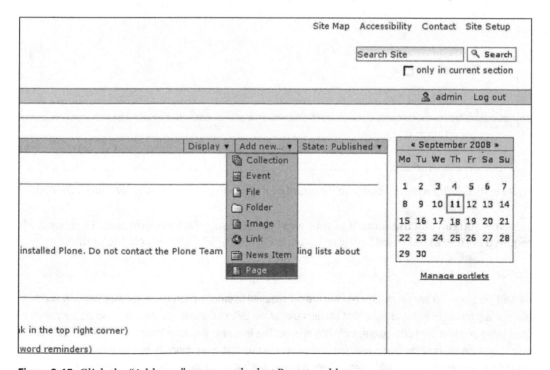

Figure 3-15. *Click the "Add new" menu and select Page to add a new page.*

Editing a Page

Once you have clicked to add a new page, you will be taken directly to the Add Page panel, as shown in Figure 3-16.

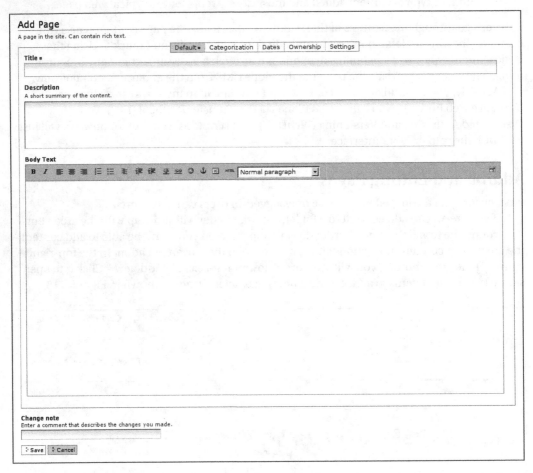

Figure 3-16. *Editing a page: Thanks to the visual editor, creating a web page is very easy with Plone.*

Now you can edit the content in your web browser using the form provided. The only field required is Title, as indicated by the red square. Fill in this field with a meaningful title.

Note In Plone 3.0 and later versions, you are not required to enter a short name for your items. A *short name* is a group of letters and signs that become part of the URL of the web content. You can create your titles using any keyboard characters, including spaces. The first time you save the item, Plone will convert your title to the short name (using near-equivalents of the title that you provided), so that it will respect the restrictions that concern web addresses. Therefore, you won't need to worry about short names! If you wish to change the short name of an item, you can use the Actions menu in the green strip and select the Rename option.

The second field to fill in is the description, which is optional. However, it is always a good idea to include one; it gives the reader a brief, quick indication of the content of the item, and it will appear in the content listings and in search results.

The largest field you see is the body text, where you can create the content of your page. Plone makes this operation very easy thanks to a visual editor. The one Plone implements by default is Kupu, which allows you to do WYSIWYG (what you see is what you get) editing, meaning that when you make a change, you see the effect immediately. Plone will automatically take care of the HTML, similar to how some word-processing software works. That means that if you're used to working with an office suite, you won't have any problem editing content with Plone.

The last field is called "Change note," and allows you to store helpful memos describing changes to content as you make them. This is particularly useful for pages that are going to be worked on by several people.

Once you have finished editing your document, click the Save button to commit your changes. You will be returned to the View tab where you can see how the document will be shown to users; to edit it again, click the Edit tab.

If you don't provide the correct input on the edit form, when you save the document you will be returned to the edit page and your errors will be highlighted. At this point, your changes won't have been applied—you must correct the mistakes and click Save again before the changes will be committed.

The View tab shows the document you have created. You will see that the title, description, and content are all shown in slightly different styles. Right below the title of the page is a byline that contains information about the author of the document, including the date the page was last edited.

Setting Page Metadata

Any piece of content can have any number of properties assigned to it. These properties are known as *metadata* and provide information such as keywords, copyrights, and contributors to an item.

This entire set of properties is optional and is usually used only if there are special requirements for the content, especially since this information isn't normally shown to the person viewing the content. However, this data can be very useful for enabling certain features of Plone—above all, for searching or categorizing the content. Once you get familiar with metadata, you will discover how helpful some of it is.

You can edit the item metadata through the set of gray tabs that appear in the Add Page panel, as shown in Figure 3-17.

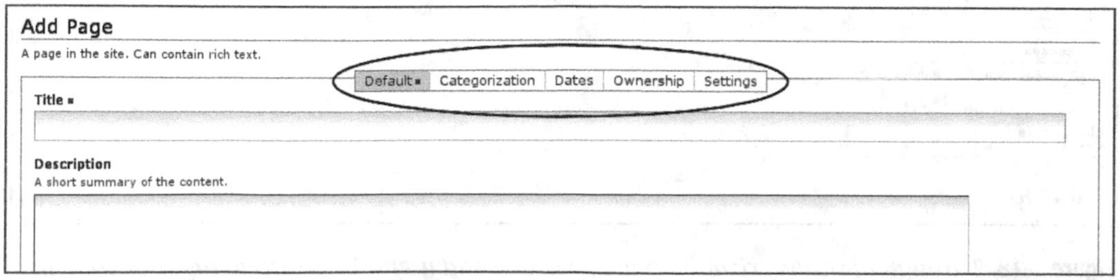

Figure 3-17. *The gray tabs for setting metadata*

Let's go through all the available tabs.

Default

This is the normal edit panel, where you can change the content of the fields just discussed.

Categorization

In this panel (shown in Figure 3-18), you can add categories (keywords) to the item by selecting them from the existing ones (if there are any), or by typing new values in the "New categories" field. (Once you insert a new category, it will appear in the "Existing categories" list the next time you enter the Categorization panel). By default, there are no keywords in the Plone system, and only site administrators may add new keywords—other users will be able to select among them.

Below these two fields is a field called Related Items and an Add button (you won't see this option for folders). This is for selecting other items you want to link to the one you are editing. If you click the Add button, a new window will appear that will let you choose from the existing content in your site. Take advantage of this option, as it can be very useful. You can let your visitors know about content that shares the same topic, and give them more information and details.

The Location field lets you specify a geographic location associated with the item.

The Language choice is the language in which the document is written; the default is the site default language.

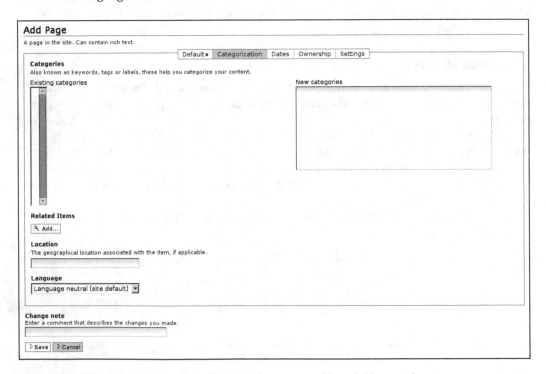

Figure 3-18. *Through the Categorization panel, you can add useful keywords to tag your content.*

Dates

In this panel (shown in Figure 3-19), you can set a publishing date and an expiration date for the item. This allows you to set a time slot during which the item will be available to all users. The item will be automatically published on the date you indicate and will no longer be visible after the expiration date you choose.

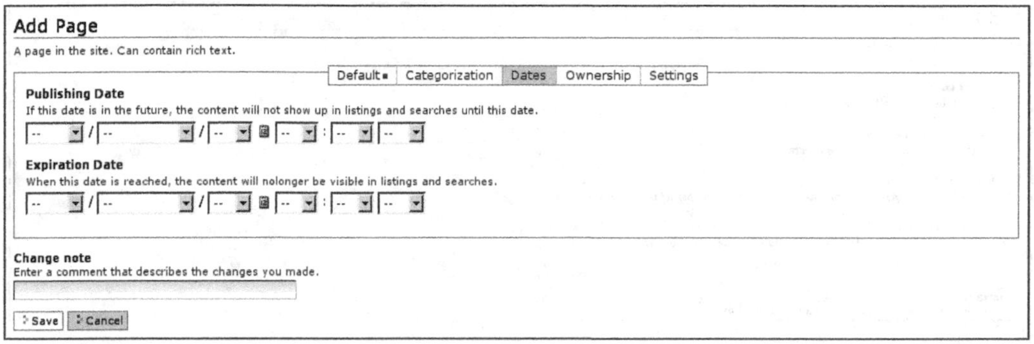

Figure 3-19. *On the Dates panel, you can change the publishing and expiration dates of your content according to your needs.*

Ownership

This panel (shown in Figure 3-20) contains three different fields for adding information about the creators of, contributors to, and copyright of the item.

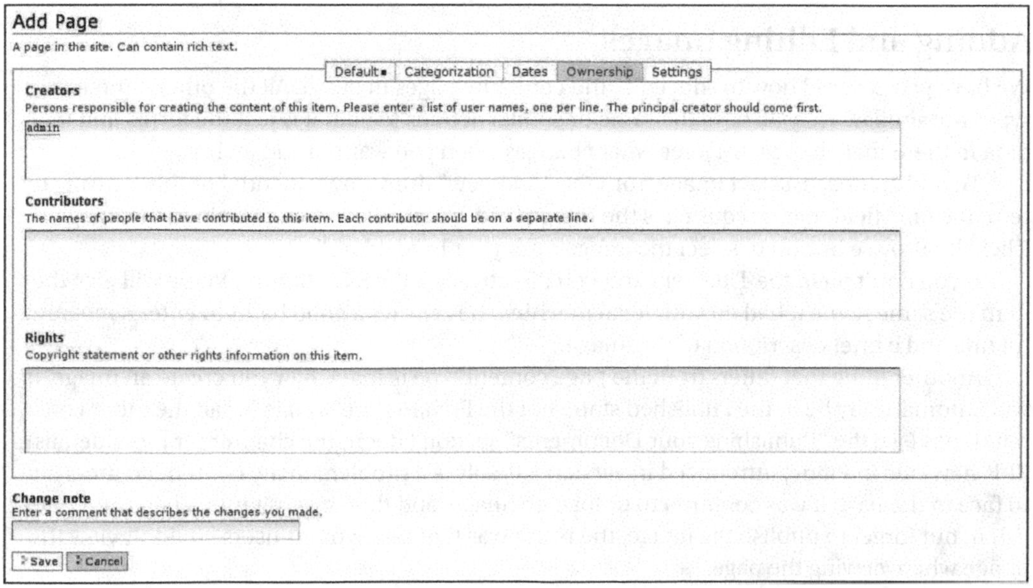

Figure 3-20. *On the Ownership panel, you can change the author of the content or add other contributors and copyright information.*

Settings

This panel (shown in Figure 3-21) normally presents four options. A brief description is provided for each of them, so we won't describe them in detail here. (However, we will talk about the "Allow comments" option in more detail in the "Commenting Content" section later in the chapter).

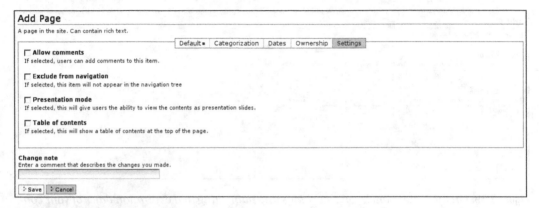

Figure 3-21. *On the Settings panel, you can set some useful options about your content, like allowing users' comments and excluding the item from navigation.*

■Note These settings can vary a bit from content type to content type.

Adding and Editing Images

We have just covered how to add, edit, and configure pages in detail. All the other content types are similar. They all have the same or similar actions to edit; it is just the forms and the data in them that change. Let's see what changes when you want to add an image.

To add an image, select Image from the "Add new" drop-down menu. For this type of content, the only field that is required is the Image field, which allows you to upload the image. Click the Browse button to select the image from your hard drive.

If you don't fill in the Title field and you directly click the Save button, Plone will give the item the same name it had on your local machine. It is always a good habit to enter a meaningful title and a brief description of the image.

Another thing that differs from the page content type is that when you create an image, it will automatically be in the Published state, not the Private state, as it is for all the other content types (see the "Publishing your Documents" section later in the chapter for more details). This new rule in Plone, introduced in version 3.0, solves a problem many content creators had to face in the past: it was common to upload an image, and then insert it into a page and publish it, but forget to publish the image; the result was that anonymous users couldn't view the image when viewing the page.

So, you won't see the State menu on the green strip for images; but you can always change the state of this item by clicking the Contents tab of the folder containing it and using the "Change state" button.

The image content type has an additional green tab near the Edit tab called Transform. This will take you to a panel that shows the image and a drop-down menu with some options; these will let you transform the image a bit—basically to rotate it or flip it around the vertical or the horizontal axis. Click the "Execute" button to make the transformation effective.

You can't edit images directly; instead, you can edit the image on your hard drive using a graphics program such as Adobe Photoshop or GNU Image Manipulation Program (GIMP). Once complete, clicking the Edit tab allows you to upload your new image into Plone (toggling the "Replace with new image:" option and uploading it again). If you do a lot of image manipulation, you can add an external editor, a tool that lets you edit images using a program without having to upload and download them (to do so, you need to install and configure your favorite external editor in Plone, but we suggest doing this only if you're a skilled developer).

Note You probably won't need to edit your image on your hard drive or with an external editor if you just want to manipulate the size of it to insert it in a page. That is because when you upload an image, Plone will automatically rescale it to a variety of sizes, ready to be used in your content. So, when you insert an image into your content, a Size drop-down list will provide a choice between many image sizes and formats (as shown in Figure 3-22), and you won't need to use an external image-editing application to crop or change the size of an image.

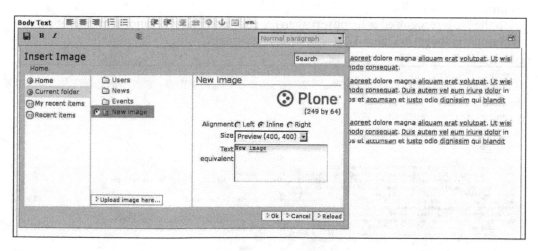

Figure 3-22. *A drop-down menu lets you choose among different image sizes.*

Adding and Editing Files

The file content type refers to any arbitrary file that can be uploaded from your hard drive. To add a file, select File from the "Add new" drop-down menu. The Add File panel will appear, as shown in Figure 3-23.

Add File
An external file uploaded to the site.

| Default■ | Categorization | Dates | Ownership | Settings |

Title

Description
A short summary of the content.

File ■

Browse...

> Save   > Cancel

Figure 3-23. *Editing a file: You can insert a title and a description, and you can browse your PC to find the file you want to upload.*

As with images, you can browse your hard drive by clicking the Browse button to find the file you want to upload. You can upload any sort of item, including a plain-text file, a Microsoft Word document, a Microsoft Excel spreadsheet, an executable program, an Adobe Acrobat document, and so on.

If the file is recognized as being text, then the content of the file is shown in the web page; an example is shown in Figure 3-24.

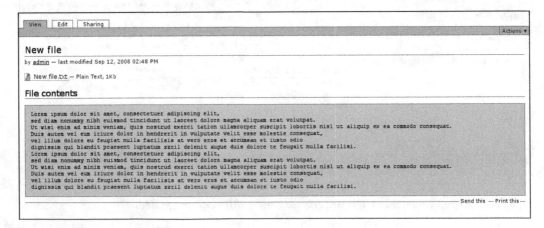

Figure 3-24. *File content types containing plain text will show their content.*

Otherwise, the file is downloadable and users must download it to their local hard drive and edit it there. Afterward, they can upload it again to the system. Files on a Plone web site are treated simply as files, and will show up in contents lists for folders.

Note Most file formats, including Word documents and PDF files, are searchable. That means you can index their content, which will be considered when you perform a search!

Adding and Editing Events

An event is usually something that will happen in the future; it can be a conference, a party, any kind of meeting—that will depend on what your site is about. This content type is for informing people about these kinds of appointments.

You can add events to Plone, and they will show up on the calendar. To add an event, select Event from the "Add new" drop-down list. An event has more information than most Plone objects; however, most of it is self-explanatory; you can see part of the editing panel in Figure 3-25.

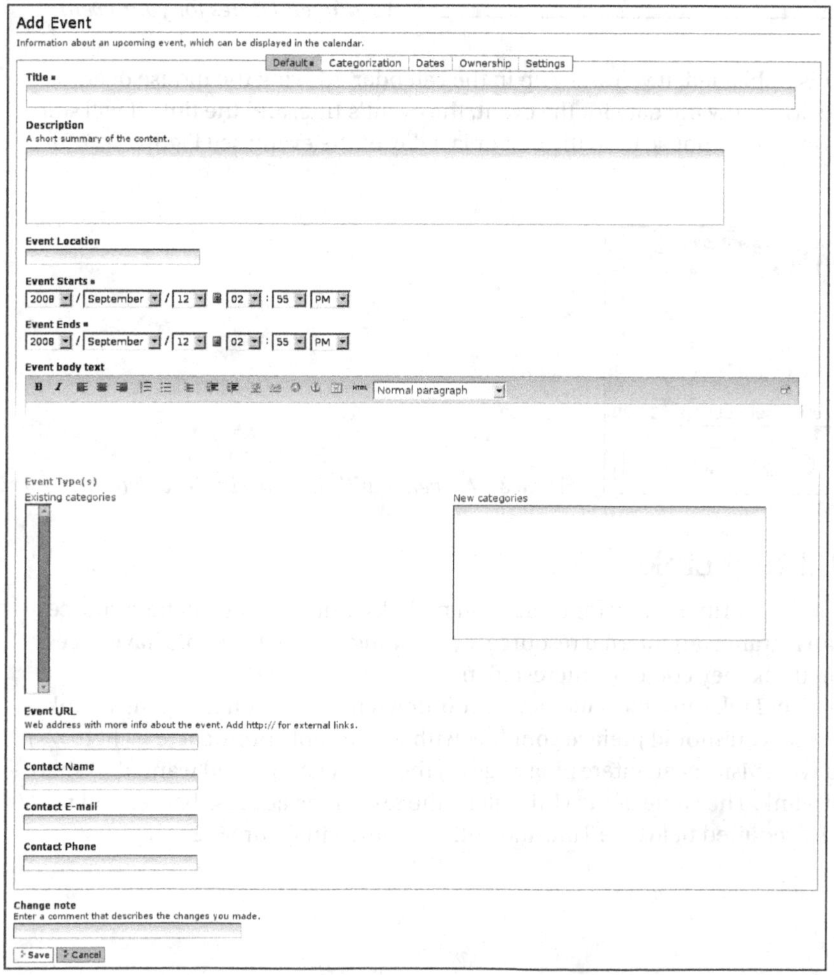

Figure 3-25. *Editing an event*

There are three required fields: Title, Event Starts, and Event Ends. Events can span multiple days or be in the past—as long as the start date is before the end date. To enter a date, select the appropriate dates from the drop-down menu or click the date icon to open a graphical date picker, as shown in Figure 3-26.

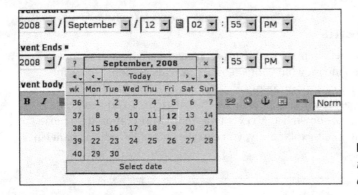

Figure 3-26. *The pop-up calendar makes it easier to choose start and end dates for your event.*

Once the event is published, it will show up in the calendar. Moving the mouse over the item in the calendar will show the date for the event, the event's title, and the time it will start or end, depending on if your mouse is on the first or last day of the event; see Figure 3-27 for an example.

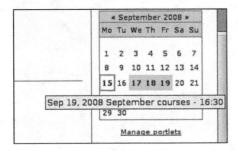

Figure 3-27. *Events will show up in the calendar.*

Adding and Editing Links

Link content types are the primary way for users to share links. These URLs can be resources on the Internet or an intranet, an internal resource, or anything to which visitors have access on the Web and you think they could be interested in.

To add a link, select Link from the "Add new" drop-down menu. If you are going to link to an Internet resource, you should preface your link with the suitable protocol (e.g., http://). For instance, if you were visiting an interesting page on the BBC web site and wanted to share this, you could add a link. The value of the URL will be the text in the address bar (e.g., http://news.bbc.co.uk). The required fields are Title and URL, as shown in Figure 3-28.

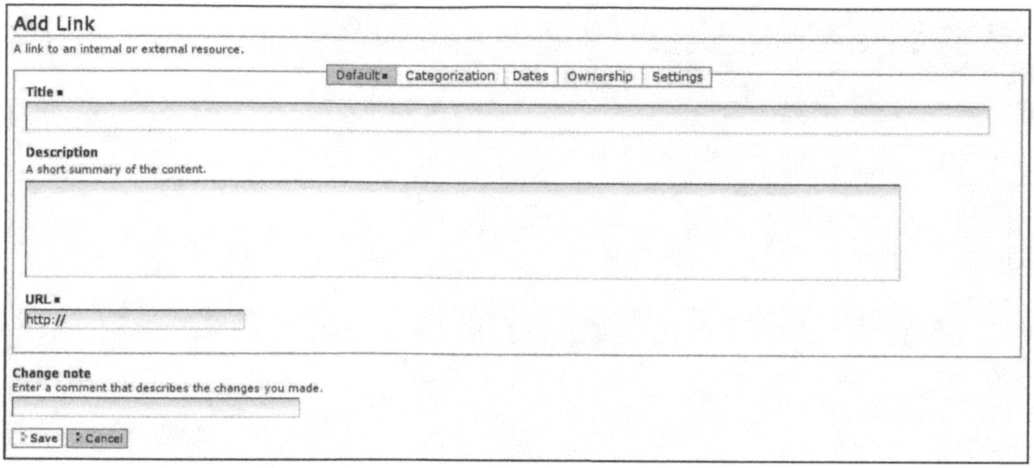

Figure 3-28. *Editing a link: You have to insert a title and a web address; you can also add a description and a comment about the changes you made.*

Adding and Editing News Items

News items are commonly used on web sites to display news that is of interest to the reader. Actually, a news item contains the same information as a document. Usually news items are contained in the news section of the site, but you can add a news item in any folder. News items, when published, will appear in the News portlet (if you didn't eliminate it through the Manage portlets panel—we will talk more about this in the "Managing Portlets" section of Chapter 4) no matter where they are stored.

To add a news item, select News Item from the "Add new" drop-down menu. You will see that the edit panel (shown in Figure 3-29) is very similar to the page edit panel—the only real difference is that at the end of it there are two additional fields to add an image (by clicking the Browse button and selecting a file on your hard drive) and a caption for it.

The image you upload through the Image field will be automatically resized and positioned at the top right in the body text. You can always decide to insert more images within the body text, using the appropriate icon on the visual editor to add them. You are free to insert as many images as you want in the body text, placing them where you wish. Look at Figure 3-30 for an example: the image in the top-right corner is the one we uploaded through the Image field; the one on the left has been inserted in the body text, using the "Add image" icon in the visual editor.

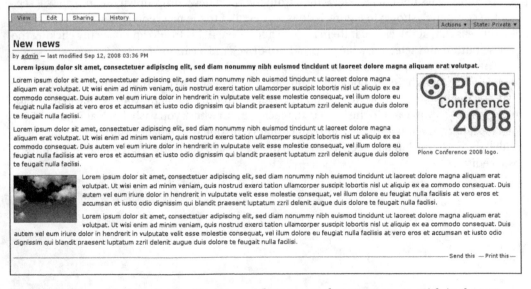

Add News Item
An announcement that will show up on the news portlet and in the news listing.

Default ■ Categorization Dates Ownership Settings

Title ■

Description
A short summary of the content.

Body Text

B *I* | ≣ ≣ ≣ | ≣ ≣ | ≣ ≡ | ↺ ⤵ ⊡ | HTML | Normal paragraph ▾

Image
Will be shown in the news listing, and in the news item itself. Image will be scaled to a sensible size.

Browse...

Image Caption

Change note
Enter a comment that describes the changes you made.

Save   Cancel

Figure 3-29. *The Add News Item panel is similar to the Add Page panel, except you can also add an image that will be shown in the news listing and in the news item itself.*

View   Edit   Sharing   History

Actions ▾ State: Private ▾

New news
by admin — last modified Sep 12, 2008 03:36 PM

Lorem ipsum dolor sit amet, consectetuer adipiscing elit, sed diam nonummy nibh euismod tincidunt ut laoreet dolore magna aliquam erat volutpat.

Lorem ipsum dolor sit amet, consectetuer adipiscing elit, sed diam nonummy nibh euismod tincidunt ut laoreet dolore magna aliquam erat volutpat. Ut wisi enim ad minim veniam, quis nostrud exerci tation ullamcorper suscipit lobortis nisl ut aliquip ex ea commodo consequat. Duis autem vel eum iriure dolor in hendrerit in vulputate velit esse molestie consequat, vel illum dolore eu feugiat nulla facilisis at vero eros et accumsan et iusto odio dignissim qui blandit praesent luptatum zzril delenit augue duis dolore te feugait nulla facilisi.

Plone Conference 2008 logo.

Lorem ipsum dolor sit amet, consectetuer adipiscing elit, sed diam nonummy nibh euismod tincidunt ut laoreet dolore magna aliquam erat volutpat. Ut wisi enim ad minim veniam, quis nostrud exerci tation ullamcorper suscipit lobortis nisl ut aliquip ex ea commodo consequat. Duis autem vel eum iriure dolor in hendrerit in vulputate velit esse molestie consequat, vel illum dolore eu feugiat nulla facilisis at vero eros et accumsan et iusto odio dignissim qui blandit praesent luptatum zzril delenit augue duis dolore te feugait nulla facilisi.

Lorem ipsum dolor sit amet, consectetuer adipiscing elit, sed diam nonummy nibh euismod tincidunt ut laoreet dolore magna aliquam erat volutpat. Ut wisi enim ad minim veniam, quis nostrud exerci tation ullamcorper suscipit lobortis nisl ut aliquip ex ea commodo consequat. Duis autem vel eum iriure dolor in hendrerit in vulputate velit esse molestie consequat, vel illum dolore eu feugiat nulla facilisis at vero eros et accumsan et iusto odio dignissim qui blandit praesent luptatum zzril delenit augue duis dolore te feugait nulla facilisi.

Lorem ipsum dolor sit amet, consectetuer adipiscing elit, sed diam nonummy nibh euismod tincidunt ut laoreet dolore magna aliquam erat volutpat. Ut wisi enim ad minim veniam, quis nostrud exerci tation ullamcorper suscipit lobortis nisl ut aliquip ex ea commodo consequat. Duis autem vel eum iriure dolor in hendrerit in vulputate velit esse molestie consequat, vel illum dolore eu feugiat nulla facilisis at vero eros et accumsan et iusto odio dignissim qui blandit praesent luptatum zzril delenit augue duis dolore te feugait nulla facilisi.

—— Send this — Print this —

Figure 3-30. *You can add an image to represent the news, and as many as you wish in the text.*

Inline Editing

There is another way to modify content: inline editing. Thanks to this feature, you can click any editable part of an item to do a quick update, correct a spelling error, or change a date on an event.

The normal procedure for editing content involves clicking the Edit tab, and thus reloading the entire page; inline editing is a quicker way to edit; it's powered by Ajax, and it's very useful for reviewing content and making small corrections.

Notice that when you pass the mouse over the editable part of the item, a subtle box will outline the editable text. You just have to click inside it and you will be able to edit that part of the item, as shown in Figure 3-31.

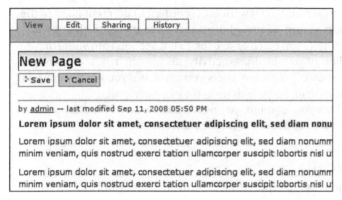

Figure 3-31. *An example of inline editing*

Remember to click the Save button, and your changes will be committed.

Automatic Item Locking and Unlocking

If you are working on an item that other people have the right to edit, you probably want to let them know that you are editing it so that you can prevent other users from manipulating the content at the same time. Plone takes care of that as well!

When you click the Edit tab for an item, that item immediately becomes locked. This means that when another user who also has the permission to edit that content goes to it, they will be shown a message saying that the item is locked. The message specifies the name of the user editing the content and when they started working on it. See Figure 3-32 for an example.

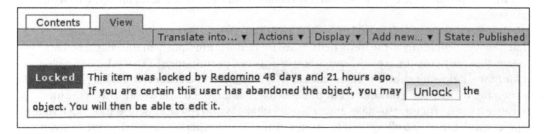

Figure 3-32. *The system informs you that the item is locked.*

Clicking the Unlock button in the message allows you to unlock the content so that you can edit it (e.g., if you realize the other user is not really working on it or the message says that the item was locked several days ago).

Managing and Sharing Your Content

You've already seen how to add content to your site and organize it, but we still have to discuss some important features of Plone, such as publishing your content, restricting types in a folder, applying different views to a folder, and using the versioning features. We'll also discuss another characteristic that makes Plone a very powerful tool: the possibility of managing a web site in collaboration with one or more other users.

You can share the permission to see/edit/review/publish content in different parts of the site with just one user you trust, with a group of contributors that have specific skills, or with all the members of the site. For example, you can manage the Event section with your friend, the Products folder with the suppliers of your business activity, and so on. In other words, you can take advantage of the collaboration of how many users you want, but you are the one who chooses which contents to share with who, and which tasks they can perform.

But before you learn how to share your content, you need to know how Plone manages the visibility of objects, so let's start talking about the publication states.

Publishing Your Documents

One important thing to understand is how the publication control system works.

▪Note As we mentioned at the beginning of this chapter, we are assuming you're using a noncustomized Plone; therefore, the workflow set up for it will be the default one—that is, the simple publication workflow.

At any point in time, each item of content in your Plone site is in a particular state. This state describes its permissions and roles within the Plone site. By having items in different states, it is possible to apply different security to each item of content. For example, sometimes an item may take a week or two to prepare and involve multiple revisions; so it will pass from the Private state to Pending, maybe to the Private state again, and so on. Eventually you will want to publish the content so that it is visible for all users and shows up in the navigation and search.

When a document is created, it is given an initial state, called Private (the only item that behaves differently is the news item, as we mentioned previously in the chapter). This means that only you, the creator, and users with special permissions in that folder, can view it for now—it doesn't show up in searches or in the navigation tree for normal users. In fact, by default, content isn't automatically published and available to the world. This is useful because it gives you time to make any necessary changes and updates before showing it to the whole world, but it also allows you to make it available to particular users who you've given permission to.

To change the state of an item, you can use the State menu (in the upper-right corner of the green strip) for any content type (except for images, as mentioned). Click it and
a drop-down menu will appear, as shown in Figure 3-33.

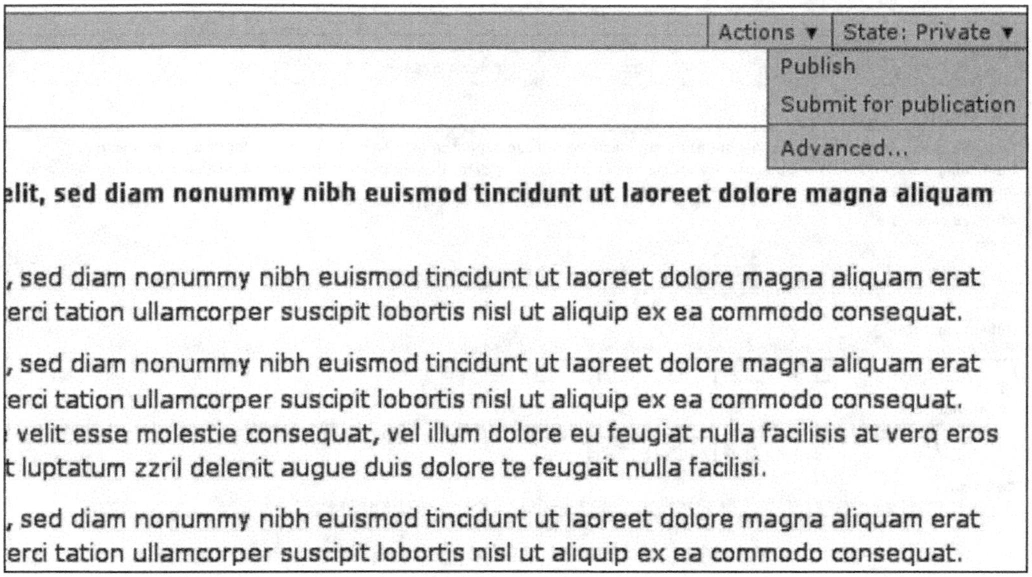

	Actions ▼	State: Private ▼
	Publish	
	Submit for publication	
	Advanced...	

lit, sed diam nonummy nibh euismod tincidunt ut laoreet dolore magna aliquam

, sed diam nonummy nibh euismod tincidunt ut laoreet dolore magna aliquam erat
erci tation ullamcorper suscipit lobortis nisl ut aliquip ex ea commodo consequat.

, sed diam nonummy nibh euismod tincidunt ut laoreet dolore magna aliquam erat
erci tation ullamcorper suscipit lobortis nisl ut aliquip ex ea commodo consequat.

velit esse molestie consequat, vel illum dolore eu feugiat nulla facilisis at vero eros
t luptatum zzril delenit augue duis dolore te feugait nulla facilisi.

, sed diam nonummy nibh euismod tincidunt ut laoreet dolore magna aliquam erat
erci tation ullamcorper suscipit lobortis nisl ut aliquip ex ea commodo consequat.

Figure 3-33. *The State menu: According to your permissions, you will see the available workflow
transitions. In this case, you can publish the item or submit it for revision.*

The options available in this menu will change according to the permissions you have for
that item and the current state of the item. The current state of an item is shown after the word
"State" in the menu, and the different states correspond to different colors.

But let's see all the options to understand how they work:

- *Publish*: Choosing this option will put the item in the Published state, in which the item
  is available on the web site to all users and anonymous visitors. If you are the site manager, this option will be available in the publication menu; users without the manager
  role for that content won't see this option. The color for the Published state is blue.

- *Submit for publication*: Selecting this option will put the item in the Pending for Review
  state, in which the item is waiting for the approval of a user with the role of reviewer
  (this concept will become clearer when we talk about roles and permissions in Chapter 4,
  in the "Managing Users and Permissions" section). The color for the Pending review
  state is light orange.

- *Send back*: When an item is in the Published state, if you click the State menu you will
  see different options available, one of which is "Send back." If you select this option,
  the item will be sent back to the Private state. The color for the Private state is red.

- *Retract*: Selecting this option will change the state either to Private or Public Draft,
  according to the type of workflow that was configured for the Plone site (see the "Type
  Settings" section of Chapter 4). The color for the Public Draft state is green.

Special workflows configured in your Plone site could have more and different options and workflow states (such as "In progress," "Open for submissions," etc.; see Chapter 7).

The last option in the State drop-down list is Advanced. Clicking this will open a form for changing the status of an object, as shown in Figure 3-34.

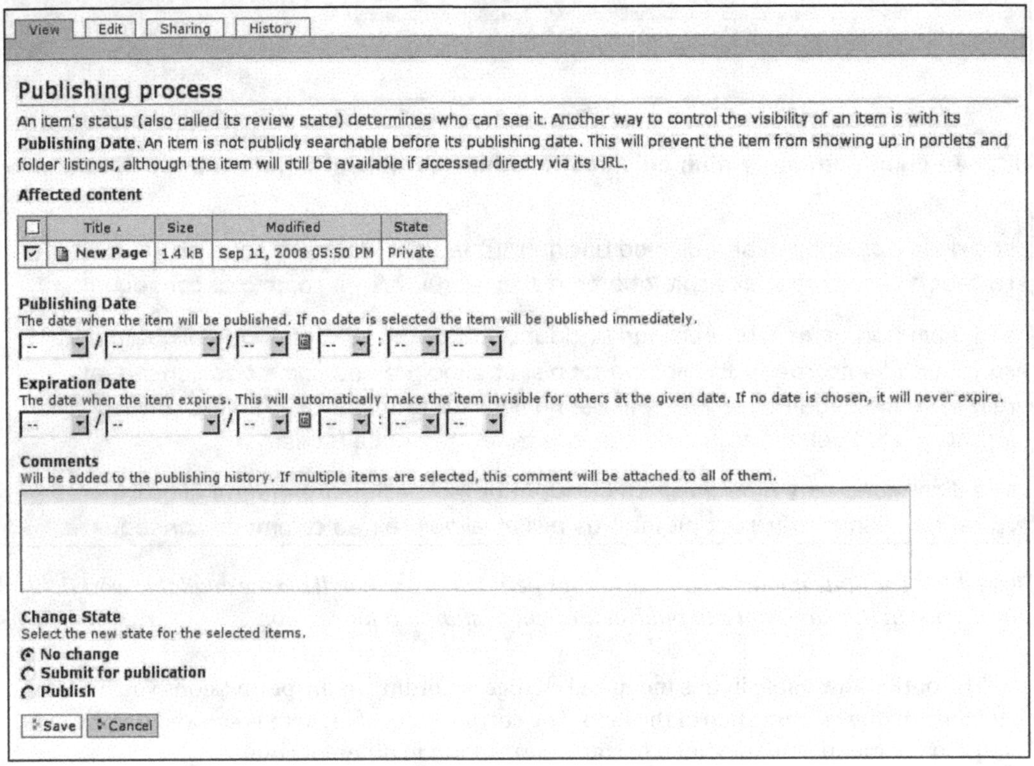

Figure 3-34. *The advanced options for the publishing process*

You can set a publishing date and an expiration date (just as you can by clicking the gray Dates tab in the edit panel, as explained previously). You can add comments that will be added to the publishing history and change the state of the item, choosing from the available options; this list will vary according to the role of the user and the type of workflow of the site, as mentioned.

For folders, there is an extra field, "Include contained items"; if you check that box, the state changes will affect all the items the folder contains and any subfolders and other contained items; if you don't check it, the state change will affect the item only. It is a very useful option to easily change the availability of an entire section of a web site.

The publication state of objects is very important—always remember to publish the content you want to be visible to the rest of the world! Also, certain content types, such as news items and events, will not initially appear on the web site as you expect—for example, contents in side portlets and events in the calendar will not appear until you publish them.

The Publication State History

In the View panel of any item, if you or another user have changed the state of it at least once, a History button will appear on the bottom of the panel. Clicking it will open a window, showing the publication history of the item, as shown in Figure 3-35.

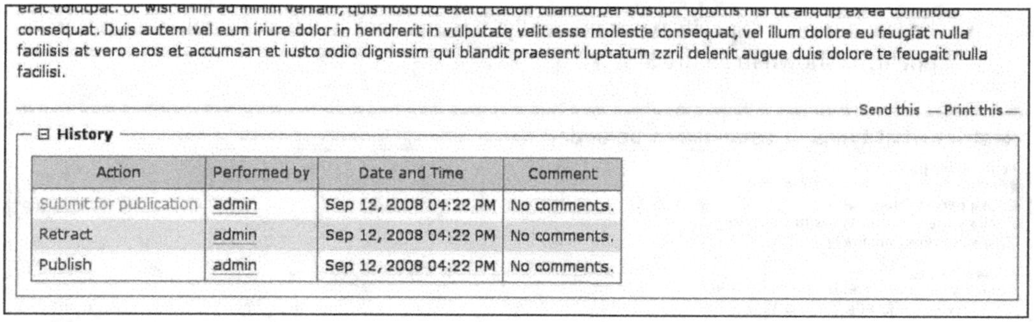

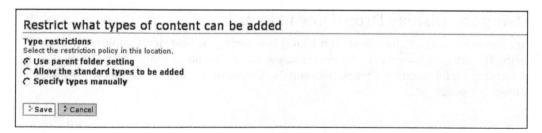

Figure 3-35. *The publication history of an item: You can check who performed which state changes for your item.*

You can therefore see all the state changes that occurred, examining the workflow state, the user that made the change, the date the change occurred, and the comments that user eventually added in the Comments field in the Publishing Process panel.

Restricting Content Types in a Folder

Another useful feature for managing content in a Plone site is restricting content types in a folder. It is a way to control content creation in certain parts of the site if many users have the right to add content in it and you want to set some rules.

To use this feature, select the last option in the "Add new" drop-down list, called Restrictions. A panel with three options will show up, as shown in Figure 3-36.

Figure 3-36. *The panel that lets you restrict content types for folders*

- By default, the "Use parent folder setting" option is checked (this option doesn't exist for parent folders, of course; in this case, the default option is the second one). This means that the folder inherits settings from the folder that contains it.

- The second option, "Allow the standard types to be added," means that all content types can be added to that folder.

- The last option is "Specify types manually"; if you check it, a list of available types will appear, as shown in Figure 3-37.

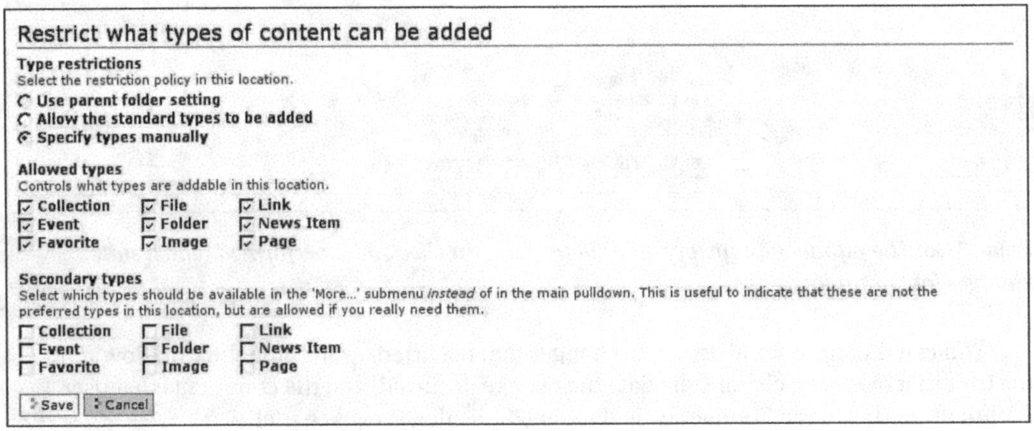

Restrict what types of content can be added

Type restrictions
Select the restriction policy in this location.
○ **Use parent folder setting**
○ **Allow the standard types to be added**
⦿ **Specify types manually**

Allowed types
Controls what types are addable in this location.
☑ **Collection**   ☑ **File**   ☑ **Link**
☑ **Event**   ☑ **Folder**   ☑ **News Item**
☑ **Favorite**   ☑ **Image**   ☑ **Page**

Secondary types
Select which types should be available in the 'More...' submenu *instead* of in the main pulldown. This is useful to indicate that these are not the preferred types in this location, but are allowed if you really need them.
☐ **Collection**   ☐ **File**   ☐ **Link**
☐ **Event**   ☐ **Folder**   ☐ **News Item**
☐ **Favorite**   ☐ **Image**   ☐ **Page**

Save   Cancel

Figure 3-37. *You can specify what content types are allowed in folders.*

The first set of check boxes lets you decide which content types can be added to that folder. By default, as you can see in Figure 3-37, all types are allowed. You can set up your folder by toggling on and off the different types. The second set of check boxes, called "Secondary types," allows you to choose types that are allowed, but are not *preferred*; meaning that they will appear in the More submenu instead of the main drop-down in the folder's "Add new" menu.

Using the Display Drop-Down Menu

Another important task for a content manager is choosing the best view for folders and contents. To manage the view of folder contents, you use the Display drop-down menu on the green strip for folder content types, between the Actions menu and the "Add new" menu, as shown in Figure 3-38.

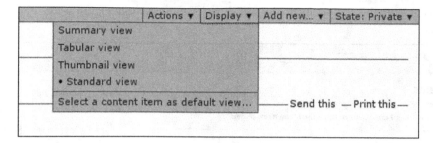

Figure 3-38. *On the Display menu, you can choose the view for your item.*

This menu allows you to choose how the folder displays its contents to web site visitors. The available options are

- *Standard view*: This is the default option; the folder will show its contents as in Figure 3-39.

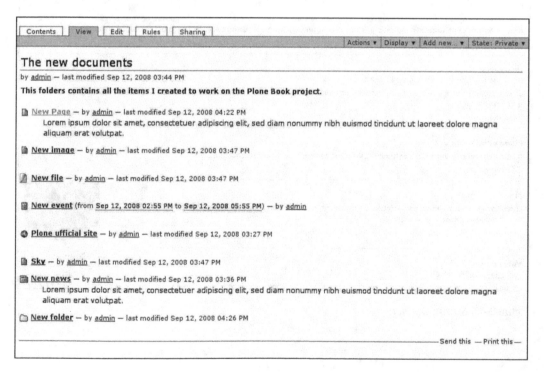

Figure 3-39. *Standard view*

- *Summary view*: With this option, the folder will show its contents as in Figure 3-40.

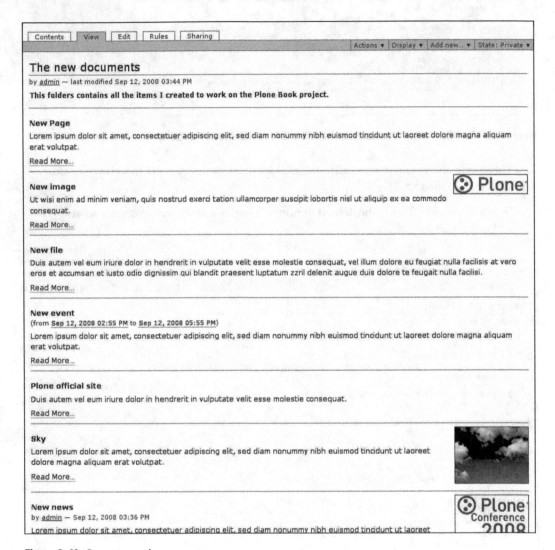

Figure 3-40. *Summary view*

- *Tabular view*: If you choose this option, the folder will show its contents as in Figure 3-41.

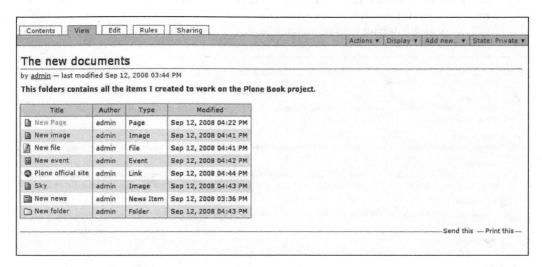

Figure 3-41. *Tabular view*

- *Thumbnail view*: If you choose this option, the folder will show its contents as in Figure 3-42.

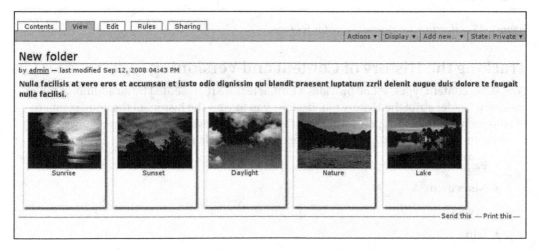

Figure 3-42. *Thumbnail view*

- *Select a content item as default view*: If you choose this option, a panel with a list of items contained in that folder will appear, as shown in Figure 3-43. Not all content types are included in this list (e.g., folders are not available). You can choose one item from the list—for example, a page with some text that presents that section—and this will become the default view for that folder.

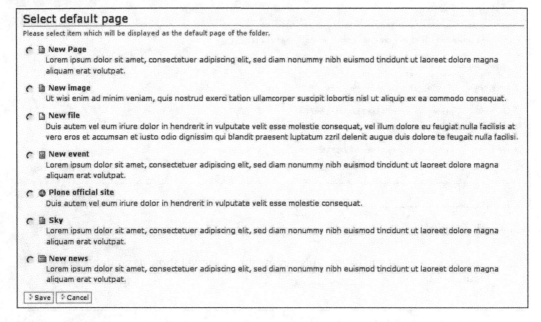

Figure 3-43. *Selecting the default page for folders*

Tracking the History of Content and Versioning

Fore some content types, Plone provides a further feature represented by an additional tab on the green header strip: the History tab. It allows you to view the history of the item, compare the different versions of it, preview previous versions, and revert to previous versions.

The content types that have this feature enabled, by default, are

- Pages
- News items
- Events
- Links

The site administrator can decide to enable or disable the versioning feature through the site setup (you will see how to do this in the "Type Settings" section of Chapter 4).

Click the History tab to access the Revisions panel, shown in Figure 3-44.

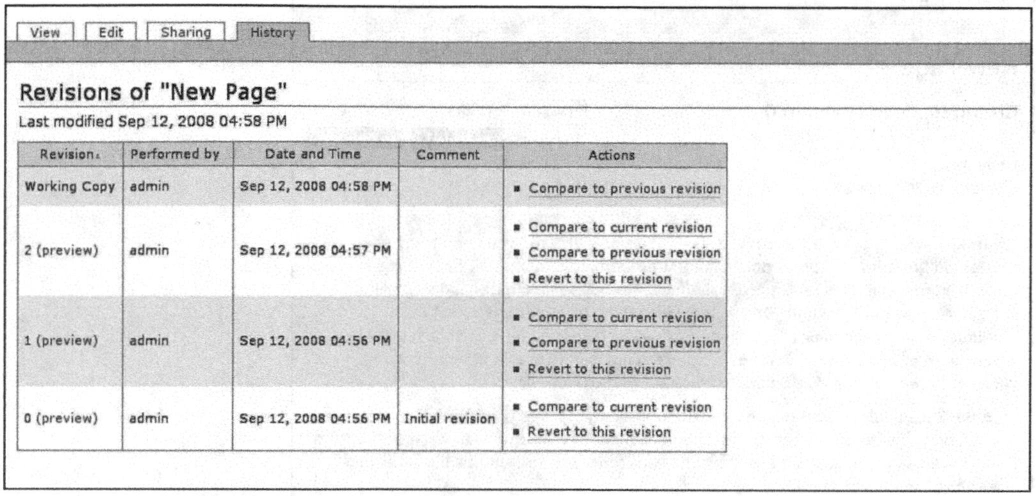

| View | Edit | Sharing | History |

Revisions of "New Page"
Last modified Sep 12, 2008 04:58 PM

Revision	Performed by	Date and Time	Comment	Actions
Working Copy	admin	Sep 12, 2008 04:58 PM		■ Compare to previous revision
2 (preview)	admin	Sep 12, 2008 04:57 PM		■ Compare to current revision ■ Compare to previous revision ■ Revert to this revision
1 (preview)	admin	Sep 12, 2008 04:56 PM		■ Compare to current revision ■ Compare to previous revision ■ Revert to this revision
0 (preview)	admin	Sep 12, 2008 04:56 PM	Initial revision	■ Compare to current revision ■ Revert to this revision

Figure 3-44. *On the History tab, you can view all the previous versions of your item, compare them, and revert to an old revision.*

A new version is created every time a user with the right to edit saves it. So, the length of the table you will see depends on how many saves have been made.

The first row of the table, by default, is the current version; clicking the column heading will change the listing order. Notice that the first column (Revision, showing the different versions of the item) is formed by links you can click (except for the first row, since it is the current version). You can quickly view any of the previous versions by clicking the corresponding link—the item will show up right underneath the version history.

The Comment column shows any text that was entered in the "Change note" field (at the bottom of the Edit panel) by the user who made the changes. If this field was left blank, it may be filled in automatically in some cases—for example, when depending on the state changes the user made.

The last column, called Actions, allows you to compare a version to the previous or current one, as well as revert to a specific version.

Clicking "Compare to previous/current revision" in the left column will lead you to a new panel, shown in Figure 3-45.

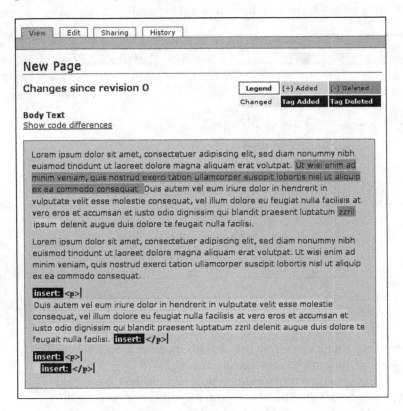

Figure 3-45. *Comparing a previous version to the current one*

The changes that occurred will be highlighted, following a legend you can look over in the top right of the panel:

- Added content is highlighted in light green.

- Added tags are highlighted in dark green.

- Deleted content is highlighted in light red.

- Deleted tags are highlighted in dark red.

- Text that has been changed is highlighted in yellow.

If you click the "Show code differences" link, you can view the changes in the code; a new panel will appear, the two versions will be placed side by side, and the legend just mentioned will be used to show the changes.

The versioning feature is useful for keeping track of all the changes you or other users make to a document—above all if many people work on it. It also gives you the option of going back to a previous version and viewing it by clicking the Revision column. If for any reason you decide that the item has to be reverted to that version, just click the "Revert to this revision" link in the Actions column. For example, perhaps one of your collaborators changed a document you wrote a week ago, entering details you don't want to display to everybody yet? You don't need to retract the publication of the item—just use the versioning feature and click the "Revert to this revision" link corresponding to the version you want to restore!

Sharing Your Content

Through the Sharing tab, which you will find near the Edit tab on the green strip of any content type, you can share your content with other authenticated site users so that multiple people can collaborate with the management of that item/section of the site (of course, if you are not the site manager or creator of that item/section and you don't have the appropriate permissions, you won't see this tab).

Click the Sharing tab and the Sharing panel will appear, as shown in Figure 3-46.

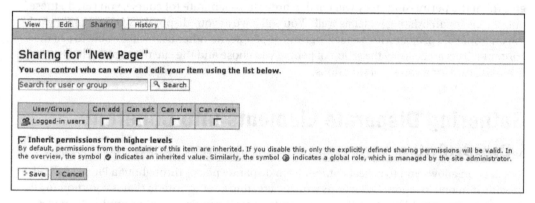

Figure 3-46. *The Sharing tab: You can give local permissions to different users or groups.*

The table below the search box provides a list of all the users that have some rights for that item. If you are the site manager and you haven't shared this item yet, you will see only one entry in it—"Logged-in users"—with none of the check boxes checked. You should use this line only if you want to share the item with *all* users of the site.

Using the search box on top of the panel, you can type the name of a user or a group (we will talk more about users and groups in the "Managing Users and Permissions" section of Chapter 4) and click the Search button; if Plone finds the user or group you were searching for, this will be added to the table, and you can proceed with the assignment of permissions, which are represented by the columns of the table:

- *Can add*: Users (or groups) with this permission can add new content items. These users will be able to edit the items they create as well.

- *Can edit*: Users (or groups) with this permission can edit that item. When this permission is granted on a folder, users will be able to edit not only the folder (its title and description), but any items in the folder. However, the user is not allowed to delete any of the content.

- *Can view*: Users (or groups) with this permission can view the item; that means that they can view it even if it is in the Private state, but they cannot make any changes.

- *Can review*: Users (or groups) with this permission can publish the item; that means that they will see the Publish option in the State menu and can publish directly.

Click the Save button to make the changes effective.

Note A very important thing to consider is that changes made through the Sharing tab will override the default workflow permissions that were configured for the site (we will talk about workflows in detail in Chapter 7).

Through the Sharing tab, you can very quickly create a reserved area: to do so, create a new folder, click the Sharing tab, and leave "Inherit permissions from higher levels" checked. Then choose the users or groups you want to share the contents of this reserved area with, and give them the permissions they will need in order to collaborate (of course, you can do these operations for an existing folder as well). You will have at your disposal a whole area for working on a specific project with a specific group of people; no other user will be able to see the content of this area—only the group of people you chose and the site managers. This is a very useful feature for a variety of situations.

Gathering Disparate Elements into Coherent Collections

A collection allows you to collect content from disparate places throughout a Plone site and provide it in one location. Collections work by creating a set of criteria that is common to all the objects you would like to gather. These criteria can be various—for example, all images or all news items with "Plone" in the text, all items with a certain creation date, or all items with a specific value (keyword) and/or another specific value, and so on.

You can make any combination of criteria you want—the possibilities are endless and can fit any kind of need. Besides, you can set many other features, such as the number of items to display or the order of the listed items. Collections can be used for a remarkable variety of purposes; many use cases will probably occur to you as you get to know the power of collections!

Plone produces RSS feeds for collections as well. With these, you can track updates on specific content that matches certain criteria. You can also use collections just for the purpose of generating a specific RSS feed—for example, for keeping track of all news that talks about a specific topic, or of content that a specific user creates in a certain area. To use this feature, just click the "RSS feed" link at the bottom of the View panel for the collection. But let's start with how to create a collection.

Adding a New Collection

To add a new collection, select this option from the "Add new" drop-down menu. You will see the Add Collection panel, as shown in Figure 3-47.

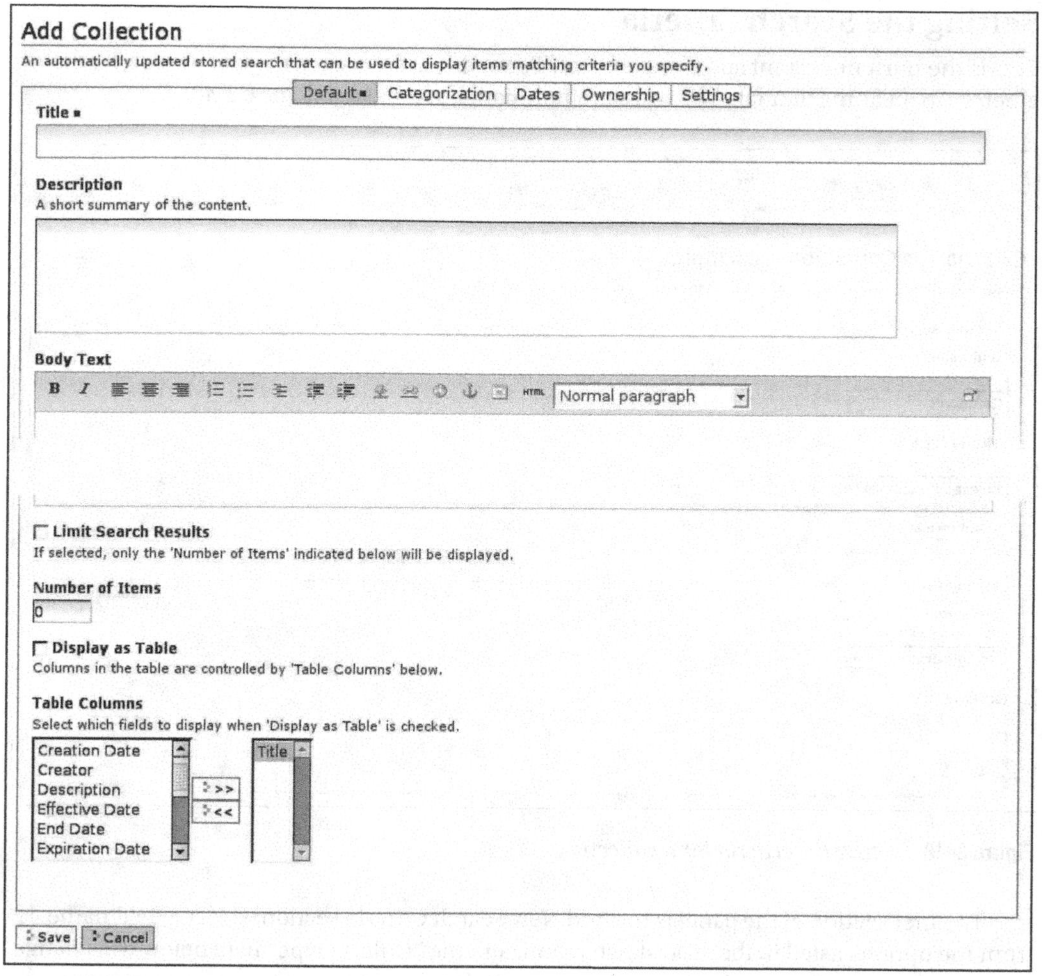

Add Collection

An automatically updated stored search that can be used to display items matching criteria you specify.

| Default ■ | Categorization | Dates | Ownership | Settings |

Title ■

Description

A short summary of the content.

Body Text

B *I* ≡ ≡ ≡ ≡ ⋮≡ ⋮≡ ⋮≡ ⋮≡ ⋮≡ ⋮ ⋯ ○ ⋃ ⋈ HTML Normal paragraph   ▼

☐ **Limit Search Results**

If selected, only the 'Number of Items' indicated below will be displayed.

Number of Items

0

☐ **Display as Table**

Columns in the table are controlled by 'Table Columns' below.

Table Columns

Select which fields to display when 'Display as Table' is checked.

Creation Date		Title
Creator		
Description	>>	
Effective Date	<<	
End Date		
Expiration Date		

Save   Cancel

Figure 3-47. *Editing a collection*

This panel will help you create your collection, preparing the container; but the most important part of it will be the setup of criteria, which you will see in the next section.

The only field that is required is the title. You can add a brief description and some body text to explain the purpose of the collection or provide other important information.

The Limit Search Results option allows you to set a limit of results to be displayed; if you check this box, you should enter a number in the Number of Items field below. The Display as Table check box lets you decide whether you want the results to be displayed in a table, and the Table Columns field below allows you to select which fields to display in the table: just click the item you want to add (this will be represented by a new column in the table) and click the arrows that point to the left box, which contains the fields that are already included (they have to be highlighted, as Figure 3-47 shows).

Setting the Search Criteria

This is the most important and complex part. To set the criteria, click the Criteria tab on the green strip, near the Edit tab. You will see a new panel, as shown in Figure 3-48.

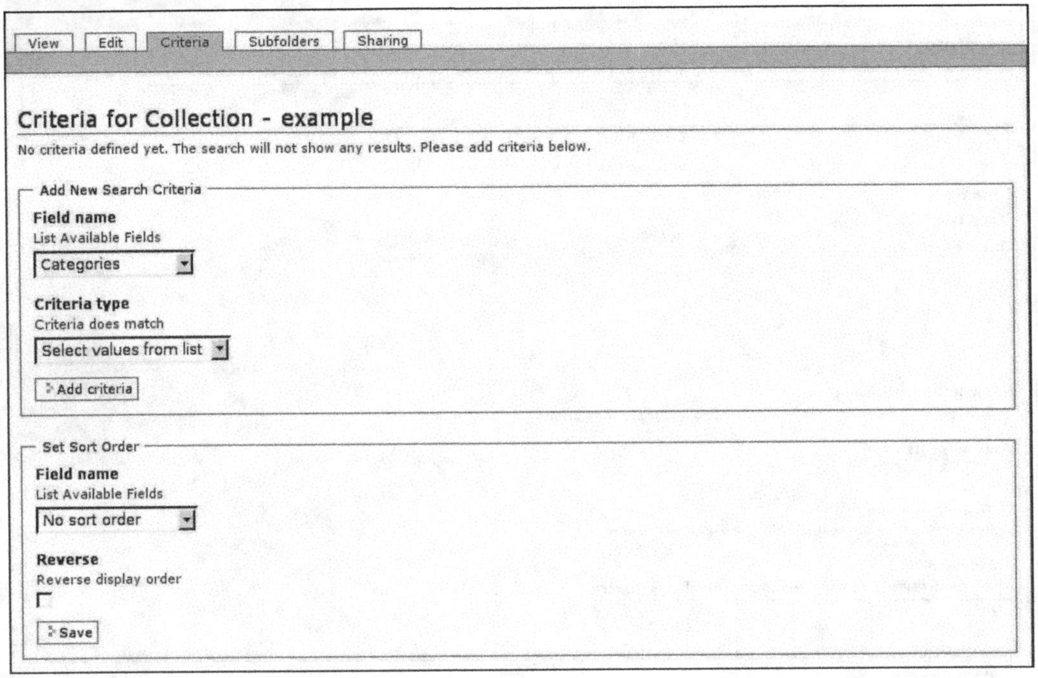

Figure 3-48. *Setting the criteria for a collection*

The first section of the panel is the Add New Search Criteria section; select a field name from the options listed in the drop-down menu, and the "Criteria type" field below will change accordingly. Use this second field to select the criteria type you wish to apply. For example, if you choose Categories from the "Field name" drop-down menu, you will be given three options in the "Criteria type" field:

- *Select values from list*: This option allows you to select the values you want to set as criteria from a list (which will show all the categories you've already added for your content within the site—Figure 3-49 gives you an example). If you choose this option, you will then be asked to choose the operation used to join the different values—"or," the default option, means that an item, to be included in the collection, has to have at least one of the selected categories (it can have more than one, but one is enough); "and" means that the item must have all the selected categories.

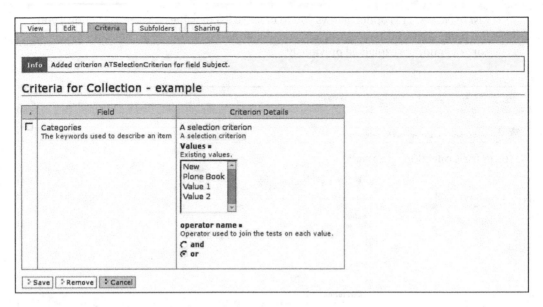

Figure 3-49. *Choosing categories from a list*

- *Text*: This option allows you to enter a simple string criterion in a text field (Figure 3-50 shows you the panel that will show up).

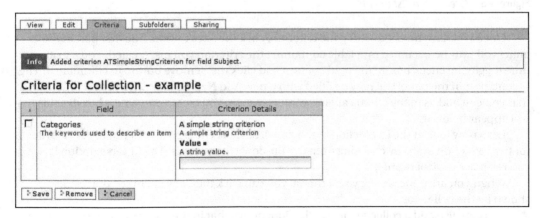

Figure 3-50. *Entering a simple string criterion*

- *List of values*: This option allows you to create a list of values (Figure 3-51 shows you the panel that will show up); again, you will be asked to choose an operator name—"or" or "and," as explained previously.

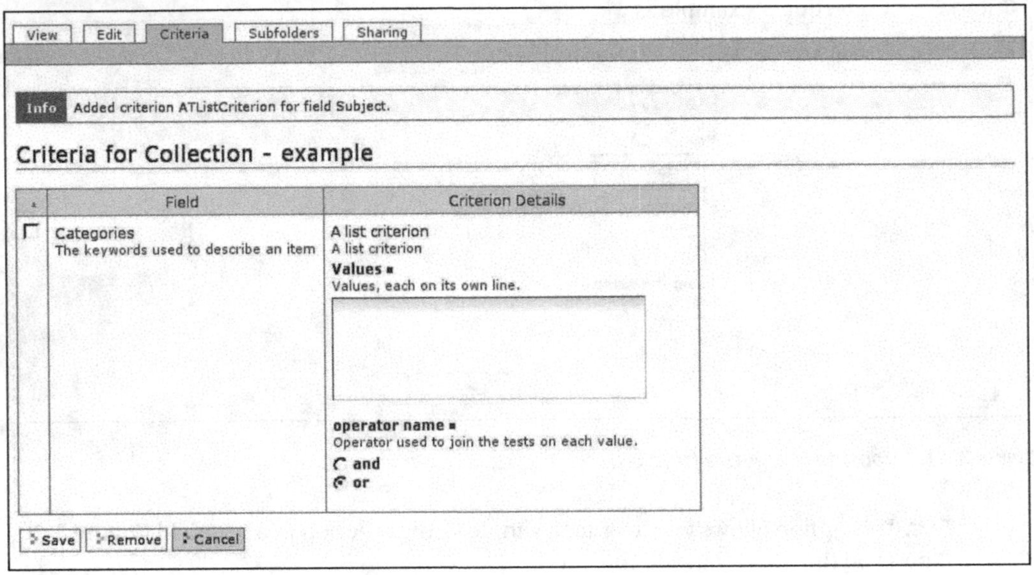

Figure 3-51. *Creating a list of values*

Once you have finished setting the criterion, click the Save button. The first part of the panel will now be occupied by a table containing the criterion you just created. You can at any time toggle the check box on the right column and click the Remove button to eliminate it. The second part of the panel will now be filled with a new Add New Search Criteria box: that means that you can add as many criteria as you want; each time you create one, a new box like this will appear below it.

Let's now look at the last section of the panel, Set Sort Order. It allows you to set an order for the collection items by choosing from a drop-down list of fields. The Reverse option lets you reverse the display order.

When you are done setting your criteria, you can click the View tab to see the results shown by the collection.

You can also add a collection to a collection; notice that in the View panel, in place of the "Add new" menu in the top green strip, there is an "Add collection" option. Clicking it will allow you to create another collection that will search results within the collection that contains it.

The best way to learn how collections work is to perform some tests and try adding different types of collections. You will find that collections are a very powerful tool and a great feature for organizing your content without affecting the existing hierarchical structure of your site.

Finding Content in Your Site

Plone automatically sets up searching and navigation for users, so it is easy for everyone to find the content you have added.

Plone contains a powerful search engine system based on Zope's ZCatalog. This search engine allows content to be cataloged in multiple ways and to be queried efficiently and quickly. The "Understanding the Portal Catalog" section of Chapter 5 covers the internals of how this works and how it can be queried.

Also, searches in Plone are simplified by a powerful feature, LiveSearch, which we will talk about later in this chapter.

When you are searching for content, the results will be shown to a user according to the content publication state and the permissions the users were granted.

At the top of the page in your Plone site, a search box provides an easy way to do simple textual searches, similar to a search engine. For example, enter **Tuesday** to find all content that contains the word *Tuesday*. A result of all matching content will display.

The list of results you will get presents contents with a title (plus an icon to help you identify the content type), description, and byline with the name of the author, the date that the content was last edited, and a rate of relevance (see Figure 3-52 for an example).

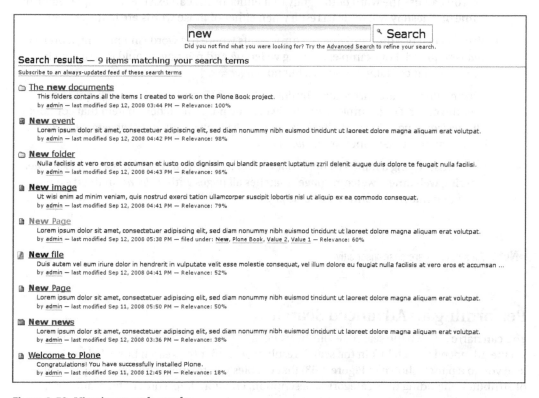

Figure 3-52. *Viewing search results*

Large sites may have a lot of results, so only 20 results display at a time. You can go through all the results by using the navigation bar at the bottom of the search result pages.

Under the title of the result page you will notice a link that reads "Subscribe to an always-updated feed of these search terms." This will let you set an RSS for all the contents that match the terms you entered, so that you will be aware of matching contents that will be created in the future.

The search feature provides quite sophisticated search, with features similar to most search engines. You can make this simple query quite complex. For example, you can use the following options:

- *Globbing*: You can use an asterisk to signify any letters. For example, entering **Tues*** matches *Tuesday* and *Tuesdays*. You can't use the asterisk at the beginning of a word, though.

- *Single wildcards*: You can use a question mark anywhere to signify one letter. For example, entering **ro?e** matches *rope*, *rote*, *role*, and so on. You can't use the question mark at the beginning of a word, though.

- *And*: You can use the word *and* to signify that both terms on either side of the *and* must exist. For example, entering **Rome and Tuesday** will return a result when both those words are in the content.

- *Or*: You can use the word *or* to signify that either terms can exist. For example, entering **Rome or Tuesday** will return a result when either of those words are in the content.

- *Not*: You can use the word *not* to return results where the word isn't present; a prefix of *and* is required. For example, entering **welcome and not page** would return matches for pages that contained *welcome*, but not *page*.

- *Phrases*: Phrases are surrounded by double quotes (") and signify several words one after the other. For example, entering **"welcome page"** matches an item that contains *This welcome page is used to introduce you to the Plone Content Management System*, but not an item that contains just *welcome*.

- *Not phrase*: Using a minus (-) prefix allows you to specify a "not" phrase. For example, entering **welcome -"welcome page"** matches all pages with *welcome* in them except those that match the phrase *welcome page*.

■**Note** All searches are case-insensitive.

Performing an Advanced Search

You can narrow down the search results by using an advanced search, which is accessible via the Advanced Search link in the search result page, under the search box. Clicking it will lead you to a panel (shown in Figure 3-53) that enables you to query content using a number of attributes, including title, categories, description, creation date, content type, author, and even review state.

You may want, for example, to search in the description or title only. Options for this are presented on the advanced search form. Any search result will match the input (if given) of all the fields; the results will be an intersection of all the terms.

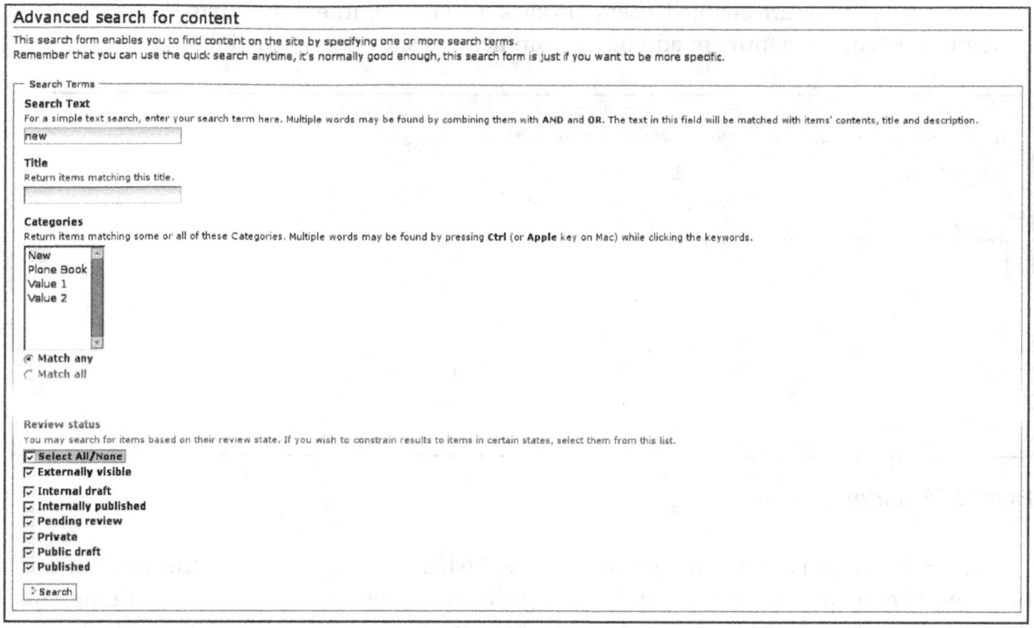

Figure 3-53. *The advanced search options*

The LiveSearch Feature

LiveSearch is a powerful feature that incorporates Ajax scripting technology to make searches quicker and more effective. It finds matches as soon as you begin typing, so that the results for a search are instant, appearing below the search box (but without changing the current page) and changing every time you type or delete a new letter in the search box.

The search results are narrowed as you type more letters, and you don't have to leave your keyboard to navigate to the content you are interested in. You just have to select it in the LiveSearch box as soon as it appears among the results.

Commenting Content

Feedback from users is a vital part of any web site. By allowing users to add comments, you ensure that users can give feedback, correct typographical errors, and otherwise discuss the content.

You can enable discussions in one of two ways:

- You can turn on the discussion feature by clicking the gray Settings tab in the item's Edit panel and checking the "Allow comments" option.

- You can also turn on the "Allow comments" option for certain content types (perhaps just for news items, or for all of them if you like) through the site setup options (we will talk about setting this option in the "Type Settings" section of Chapter 4) or through the ZMI (Zope Management Interface, the back-end management interface of Plone—we'll discuss this further in Chapter 5).

Once discussions are enabled, users can click the Add Comment button to discuss the content, which opens a form for adding the comment, as shown in Figure 3-54.

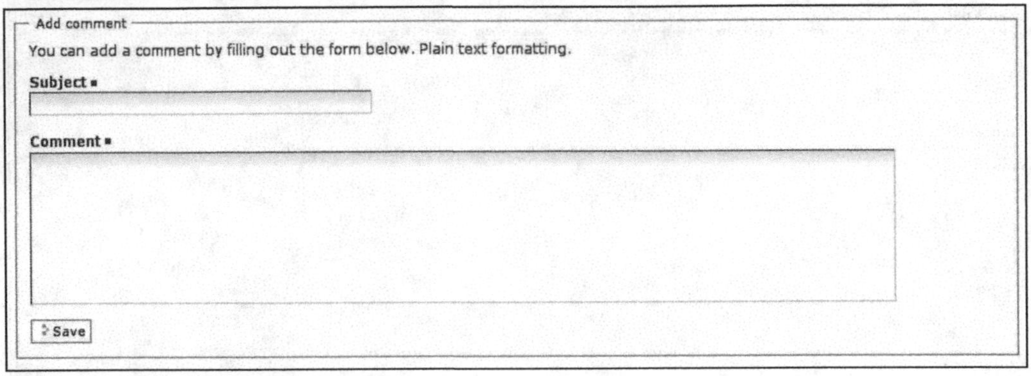

Figure 3-54. *Adding a comment*

Enter the subject and text of the comment, and when you are done, click the Save button; both fields are required. The text is entered as plain text, so just type away as usual. Comments don't go through any workflow, so comments show up as soon as they have been added.

Once a comment has been entered, it can be replied to, forming a threaded list of comments on an item. To reply to a comment, click the Reply button underneath it. If you want to post a comment on another topic, use the Add Comment button (not the Reply button).

If you are the site manager, you will see another button—the orange Remove button. As the site manager, you can remove any replies or threads—for example, if you think that the discussion is inappropriate.

■Note Disabling replies doesn't remove the comments; it just stops them from being shown; so reenabling comments will show the existing comments again.

Summary

In this chapter, you saw how the Plone interface looks and how to start interacting with it. You learned how to create and manage content, how to organize the different sections and objects contained in them, and how to change the publication state of the items you've created. You also saw how to search content within the site and how to add comments. That means you are now able to manage a site based on Plone completely autonomously!

Was it a hard task? Surely not. The power of Plone, as we have said time after time, lies in its ease of use and intuitiveness. You can go forward and start seeing how to configure and customize the settings of your Plone site through a browser, without writing a single line of code. Are you ready? Let's go on!

CHAPTER 4

■■■

Administering a Plone Site

After you have figured out how to add and edit content, you will want to start customizing your site. This chapter explains how to perform simple customizations in Plone using the options available to administrators. These customizations are all configuration options you can make through the Web.

All the parts of a Plone site are designed to be easily changed and customized; for example, you can manage security, users, and groups. The boxes in the left and right columns, which are called *portlets*, can be added, hidden, moved, and so on. You can also change the content rules so that Plone will automatically act certain ways in response to various triggers.

The first and most useful place to look for administering your Plone site is the Plone control panel, which offers a variety of options for the site administrator. In this chapter we will go through all its parts in detail. But remember, to perform the customizations described in this chapter, you need to be logged in with the manager role.

Main Site Setup

You can access many of the administration functions of a Plone site, including the name and description of your site, user and group administration, and any errors that occur within your site, through the Plone control panel. To do so, click the Site Setup link at the top-right corner of the site, as shown in Figure 4-1.

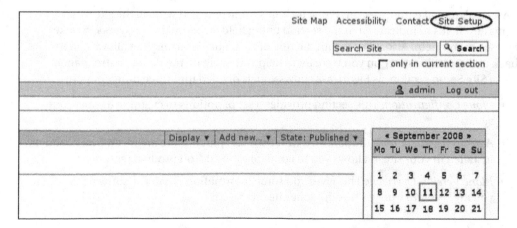

Figure 4-1. *The Site Setup link, which lets you enter the Plone control panel*

The term *control panel* is common, so don't confuse it with the Zope Management Interface (ZMI) control panel that shows the low-level ZMI options. Actually, we could describe the Plone control panel as a more user-friendly interface for some of the functions provided in the ZMI; it's shown in Figure 4-2.

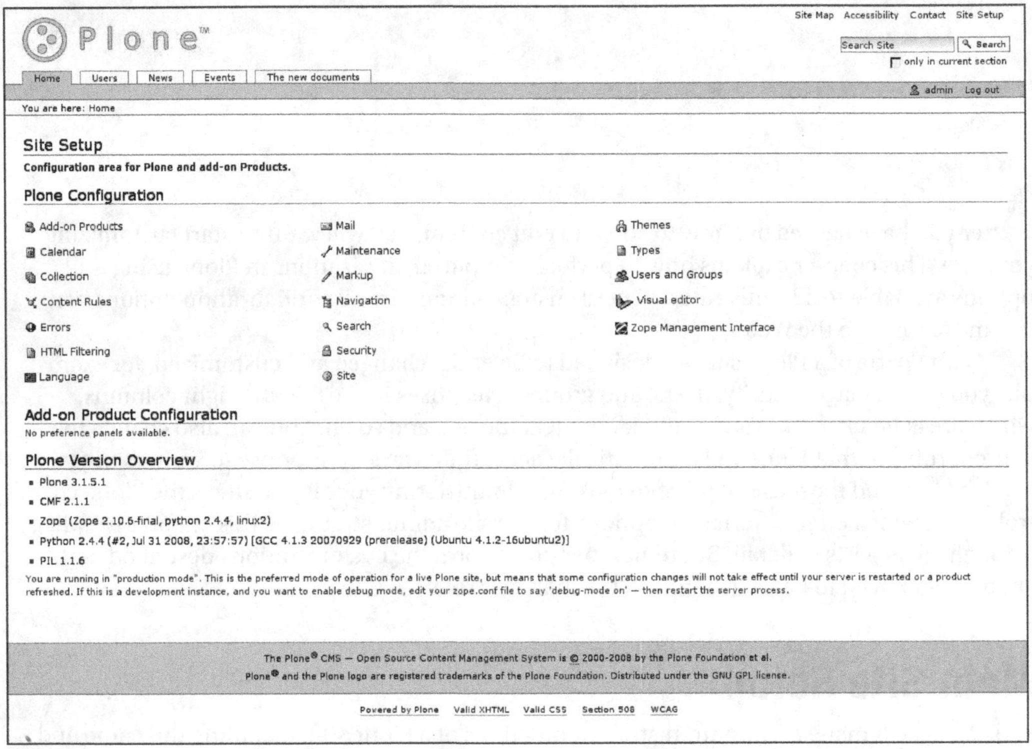

Figure 4-2. *The Plone control panel, where you can access all the configuration panels to set up the different aspects of your web site*

As usual, to make things easier, Plone includes some gray text with all the site setup sections and fields to indicate what the section or the field is for and how it works, so take advantage of this help. Also, underneath the title of each panel is a link that allows you to go back to the previous section you were in, to help you navigate the Plone control panel.

The Site Setup section, as Figure 4-2 shows you, is divided into three different parts:

- *Plone Configuration*: This section provides a set of options to customize your Plone site.

- *Add-on Product Configuration*: You won't see this part if there are no add-on products installed in your site. It allows you to configure the add-on products settings.

- *Plone Version Overview*: This gives you some information about the software versions you are using to work with your Plone site.

We will start by showing the simplest configuration options you can manage through the Plone control panel, presented in the first part of it, and then move on to the more complex ones in the following sections.

Managing Your Site Settings

The main site-wide settings are gathered in the Site Settings panel, which will show up if you click Site on the Plone control panel. Figure 4-3 shows the Site Settings panel.

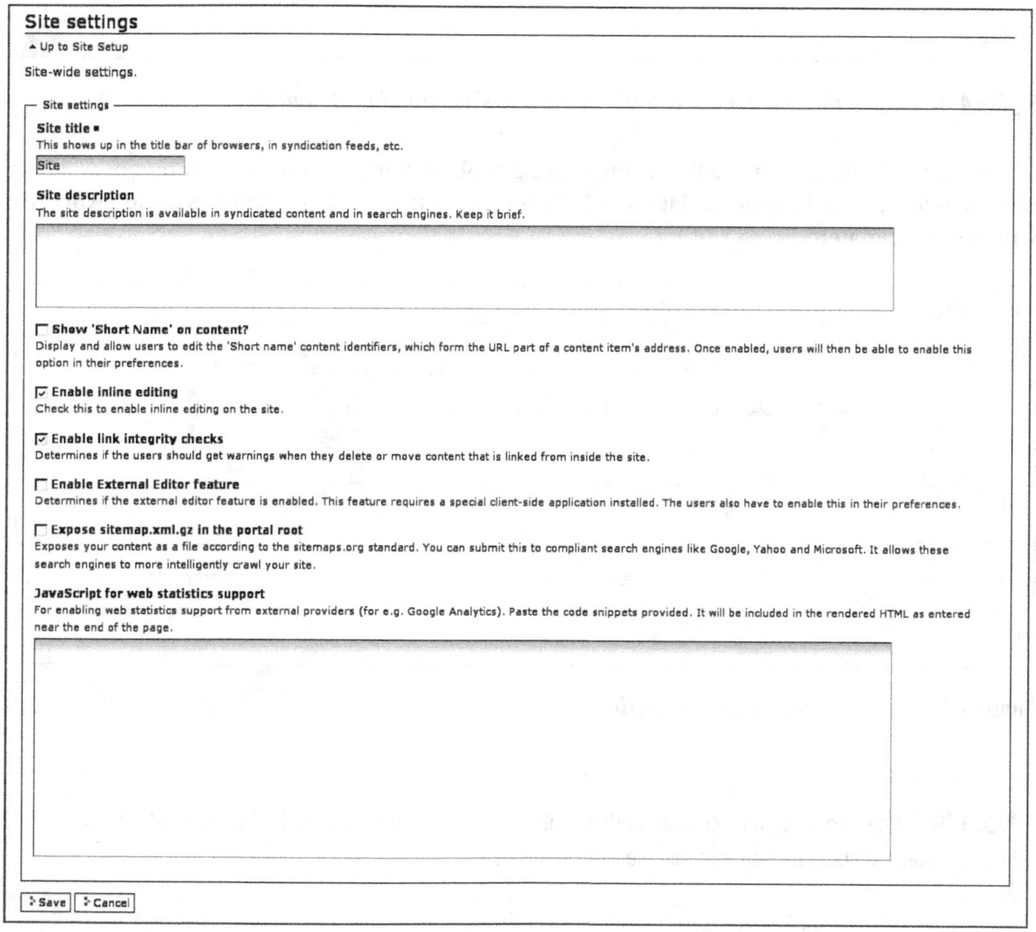

Figure 4-3. *The Site Settings panel, where you can enter a title and a description for the entire site and set some useful options like exposing the site map and enabling/disabling the inline editing feature*

The Title field contains the site title, which will show up in the title bar of visitors' browsers, in syndication feeds, and such. You can add a description of your site as well; this will show up in search engines results, so take care to write something meaningful, clear, and brief.

The "Show 'Short Name' on content?" option concerns short names (also known as IDs—these were discussed in Chapter 3). You can check this box if you want to add better control over short names: enabling the option will allow all the site members to choose the "Allow editing of Short Names" option in their personal preferences, as shown in Figure 4-4.

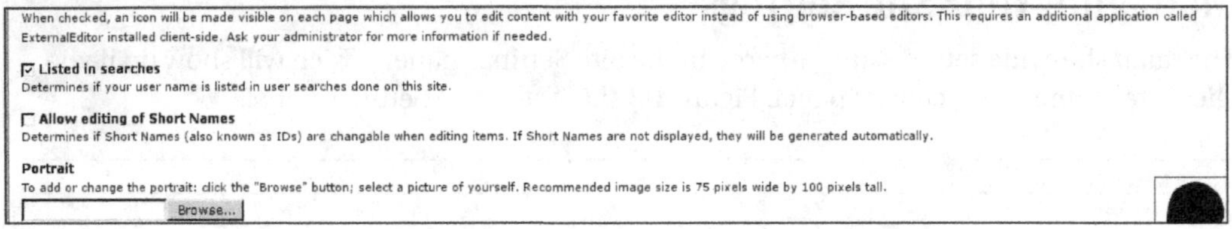

When checked, an icon will be made visible on each page which allows you to edit content with your favorite editor instead of using browser-based editors. This requires an additional application called ExternalEditor installed client-side. Ask your administrator for more information if needed.

☑ **Listed in searches**
Determines if your user name is listed in user searches done on this site.

☐ **Allow editing of Short Names**
Determines if Short Names (also known as IDs) are changable when editing items. If Short Names are not displayed, they will be generated automatically.

Portrait
To add or change the portrait: click the "Browse" button; select a picture of yourself. Recommended image size is 75 pixels wide by 100 pixels tall.

Browse...

Figure 4-4. *A new option will be available in the users' personal preferences.*

If a user decides to enable the "Allow editing of Short Names" option, short names will be changeable when editing items. Figure 4-5 shows what a user who enabled this option will see when editing an item.

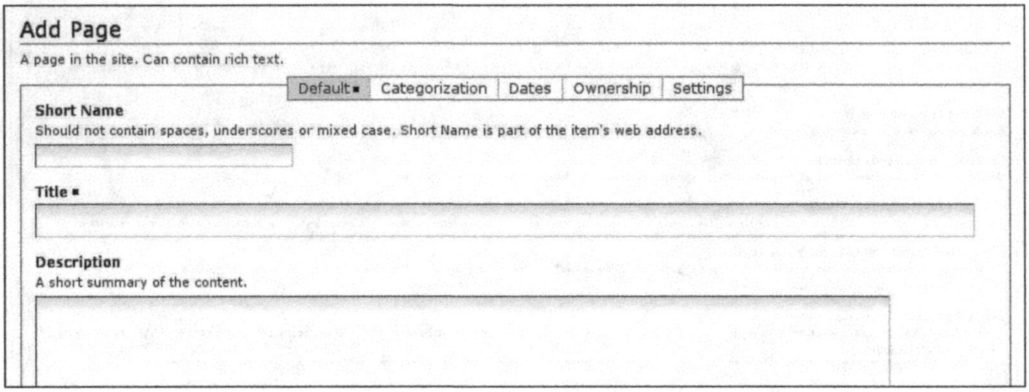

Add Page

A page in the site. Can contain rich text.

Default■ | Categorization | Dates | Ownership | Settings

Short Name
Should not contain spaces, underscores or mixed case. Short Name is part of the item's web address.

Title ■

Description
A short summary of the content.

Figure 4-5. *Editing short names manually*

Note Short names have to be created with specific rules. If you are not sure that all your site members will know them, it could be better to disable this option.

The "Enable link integrity checks" option is checked by default. This means that when you delete an item in your site, the system will show you a warning message if this item is internally linked to some other content (Figure 4-6 shows you an example).

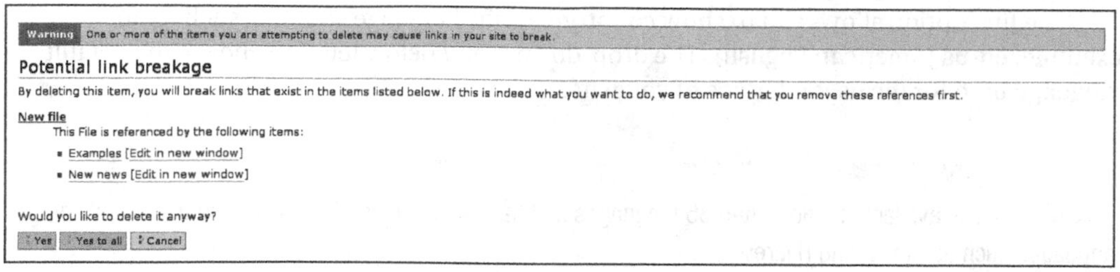

Figure 4-6. *The system will warn you if you risk breaking internal links.*

This is a useful feature, since it allows you to consider all the contents that will be affected by your decision to break the link, enabling you to eliminate or change the internal links that won't work any more once you have deleted the item they refer to. If for any reason you want to disable this feature, just uncheck this option.

The following option will enable the external editor feature; of course, you will have to install a special client-side application to use an external editor. Besides, individual users will have to enable this feature in their personal preferences.

The "Expose sitemap.xml.gz in the portal root" option creates a file called `sitemap.xml.gz` that contains all your site content listed as URLs; the file will automatically update every time a change occurs and will allow search engines to more intelligently crawl your site.

The last field is a text field that you will use if you decide to enable statistics support from external providers (some of them are available for free on the Web, like Google Analytics). Those will probably ask you to copy and paste a code segment into the bottom of your content to enable the service. This text field is the right place to paste this code; Plone will take care of including it in the rendered HTML.

Managing Language Settings

To configure the language of your site, click Language in the Plone control panel. Figure 4-7 shows the Language Settings panel.

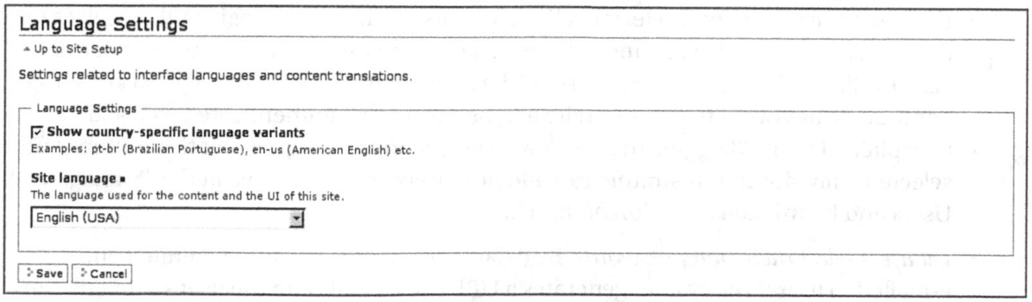

Figure 4-7. *The Language Settings panel*

The first option allows you to show country-specific language variants, such as, for example, en-us (American English). The drop-down menu below lets you choose the default language used for the user interface of your site.

■**Note** Plone is available in more than 35 languages and handles Chinese, Japanese, and even right-to-left languages such as Arabic and Hebrew!

Managing Security Settings

To configure the security settings of your site, click Security in the Plone control panel. Figure 4-8 shows the Security Settings panel.

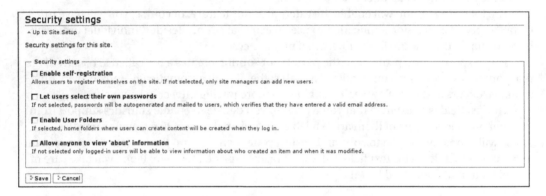

Figure 4-8. *The Security Settings panel*

You can enable/disable the four different options presented by this panel by checking/unchecking their check boxes and clicking the Save button. The options are as follows:

- *Enable self-registration*: If selected, all site visitors will be able to register themselves on the site. A Register link will appear on the header strip for anonymous users, near the "Log in" link. Clicking Register, users will be asked to fill out a form; they will get a username and a password to enter the site and perform some authenticated web activity, as explained in the "Logging in As a New User" section of Chapter 3. If this option is not selected, only site administrators can add new users, as you will see in the "Managing Users and Permissions" section of this chapter.

- *Let users select their own passwords*: By default, passwords are autogenerated and e-mailed to users. The system generates a URL and e-mails it to the user so that he can reach a page where he can change his password and complete the registration process. This proceeding has a second aim as well—to verify that users have entered a valid e-mail address. If you select this option, you will be able to choose the password for the user you are adding, and the username and password will be communicated to the user via e-mail.

- *Enable User Folders*: If selected, a personal folder for each user will be created; this folder is set up with particular security so only that member (and administrators) can add and edit content in that folder. Users will be able to access their personal folder by clicking the My Folder link in the header strip in the upper-right corner of the site, as shown in Figure 4-9.

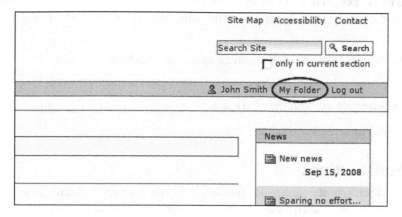

Figure 4-9. *The My Folder link will appear if you enable the appropriate option. All users will have a personal folder at their disposal.*

- *Allow anyone to view 'about' information*: If selected, everyone, including anonymous visitors, will be able to see information about who created an item and when it was modified; if not selected, only logged-in users will.

Managing Theme Settings

To configure some of the settings that affect the site's look and feel, click Theme in the Plone control panel. Figure 4-10 shows the Theme Settings panel.

Theme settings

⌃ Up to Site Setup

Settings that affect the site's look and feel.

— Theme settings —

Default theme ■
Select the default theme for the site.

| Plone Default ▾ |

☐ **Mark external links**
If enabled all external links will be marked with link type specific icons. If disabled the 'external links open in new window' setting has no effect.

☐ **External links open in new window**
If enabled all external links in the content region open in a new window.

Show content type icons ■
If disabled the content icons in folder listings and portlets won't be visible.

| Always show icons ▾ |

[▷ Save] [▷ Cancel]

Figure 4-10. *The Theme Settings panel, where you can choose the look of your web site and manage how external links and content type icons behave.*

The first drop-down menu allows you to select the default theme for the site (we will talk about how to drastically change the site look in Chapter 6). The second option, "Mark external links," lets you decide whether you want all the external links to be marked with link type–specific icons. The third one, "External links open in new window," if selected, makes all external links in the content region open in a new window; but for it to be enabled, the previous option has to be checked. The last option allows you to decide whether the content icons in folder listings and portlets are visible and to whom. The drop-down menu shows the available options:

- *Always show icons*: All users, even anonymous visitors, can view the icons.

- *Only for users who are logged in*: Only authenticated users can view the icons.

- *Never show icons*: No one can view the icons.

Always remember to save your changes.

Managing Mail Settings

Configuring the mail settings of your site is important for many reasons, including sending passwords to your site members. To configure these settings, click Mail in the Plone control panel. Figure 4-11 shows the Mail Settings panel.

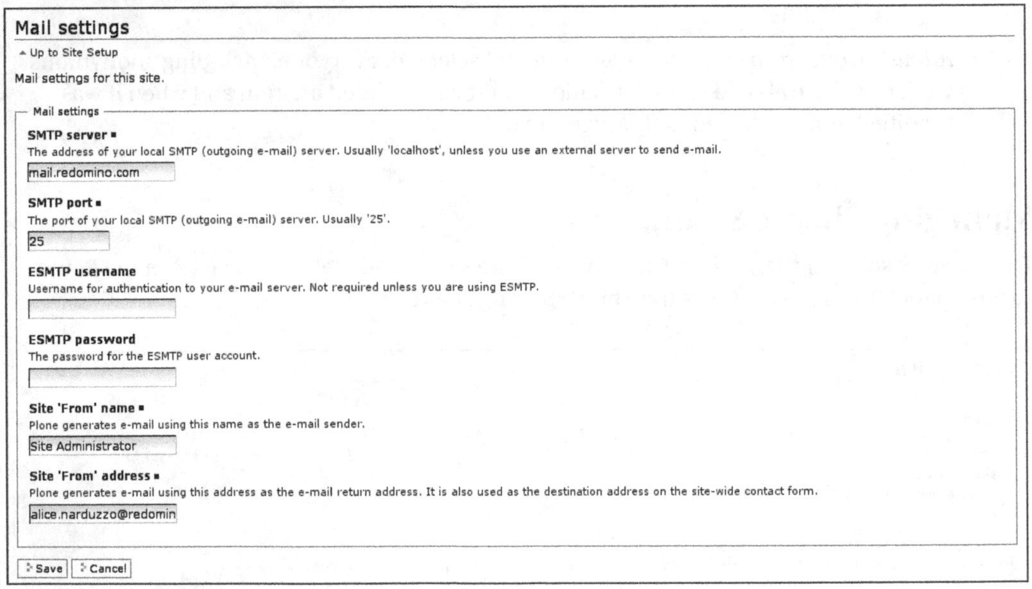

Figure 4-11. *The Mail Settings panel*

You are required to set the address of your local SMTP server and its port. The two following fields are not required, unless you are using ESMTP. In this case, enter the username and password for the ESMTP user account.

Finally, set the last fields: the "Site 'From' name" e-mail sender name will show up as the e-mail sender in every e-mail that Plone will generate, and the "Site 'From' address" is the e-mail return address that will be used in every e-mail and as the destination address on the site-wide contact form.

Managing the Site Maintenance Options

To set the Zope server and site maintenance options, click Maintenance in the Plone control panel. Figure 4-12 shows the Maintenance panel.

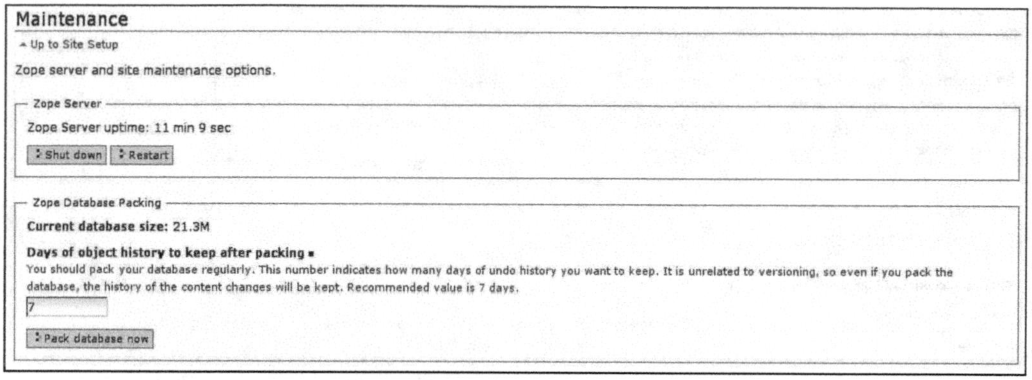

Figure 4-12. *The Maintenance panel*

You can shut down and restart the Zope server, using the corresponding buttons, and view the Zope server uptime.

The Zope Database Packing section shows you the current database size and allows you to set the days of object history to keep after packing; as the field description says, the number you set indicates how many days of undo history you want to keep. It is unrelated to versioning, so even if you pack the database, the history of the content changes will be kept. The recommended value is seven days.

Note It's a good habit to pack your database regularly.

Using the Error Log

The error log catches errors that may occur in a Plone site; these are things such as Page Not Found (404) errors, unauthorized errors, and so on.

This isn't designed to trap errors from forms. For instance, if a site user doesn't enter a required field in a form, then this won't be reported; this isn't an error since it is captured by the validation framework (see the "Logging in As a New User" section of Chapter 3 and Figure 3-5 for more details about errors from forms). This error log is designed to catch internal server errors that may occur.

Click Errors in the Plone control panel to see the errors reported by the Plone site. Figure 4-13 shows the Error Log panel.

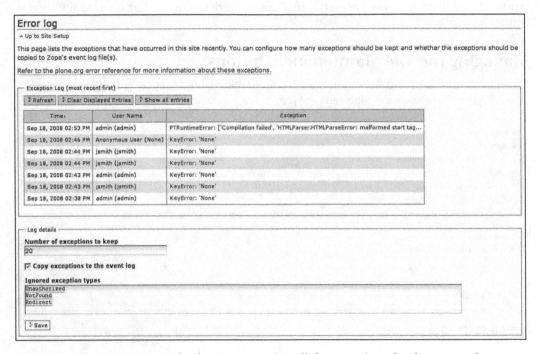

Figure 4-13. *The Error Log panel, where you can view all the exceptions that have recently occurred in your site*

A table shows you the time the error occurred, the user who viewed the error, and a description of it. You can log each exception and view it on the screen. This means that if a user is visiting your site and an error occurs, you can go to the error log and see what happened. Just click any exception log (this section will be empty if no error occurred), and a page will describe in detail the error. This log page will include a complete Python traceback and the incoming request, as shown in Figure 4-14.

Note Remember that for any problem you may run into during your work, you can always count on the Plone community! A way to find help is the Plone Chat Room. Check the Support section on Plone.org (`http://plone.org/support`).

Figure 4-14. *The Exception Details panel (a part of the panel has been cut to make the image more readable)*

When a user reports an error, the system will warn her with a message (Figure 4-15 is an example), reporting an entry number to identify the error. The user can also click the link provided in that page to directly contact the site administrator to inform her about the error or ask for help or explanations.

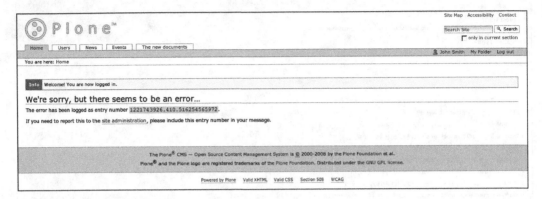

Figure 4-15. *The error message that a user will see*

If an error is raised and you are a site administrator, you will get a custom error page with a link to view the entire error description page, rather than the standard page shown in the figure. The following standard error types occur:

- *Unauthorized*: This occurs when a user doesn't have the right to perform a function.

- *NotFound*: This occurs when the item a user is trying to access doesn't exist.

- *Redirect*: This is an error that can raise an HTTP redirect.

- *AttributeError*: When an object doesn't have this attribute, this error is raised.

- *ValueError*: This occurs when a value given is incorrect and isn't caught correctly by the validation or other framework.

The Exception Log section shows all the most recent errors; to see all of them, click the "Show all entries" button. You can also use the Refresh button to refresh the list and the Clear Displayed Entries button to clear the list.

The "Log details" section allows you to set up some settings:

- *Number of exceptions to keep*: These are the exceptions to keep in the active log on the screen. The default is 20.

- *Copy exceptions to the event log*: This copies each exception to the file-based log file. Not doing this means that no permanent record will be kept for exceptions. The default is that this is selected.

- *Ignored exception types*: This is a list of exception types to ignore (entries must be entered one per line). The default is Unauthorized, NotFound, and Redirect.

The link "Refer to the plone.org error reference for more information about these exceptions" will lead you to the error reference section of the Plone.org site, where you can find useful information to solve problems that have occurred in your Plone site.

Navigation Settings

To configure how navigation is constructed in your site, click Navigation on the Plone control panel. Figure 4-16 shows the Navigation Settings panel.

Navigation Settings

▲ Up to Site Setup

Lets you control how navigation is constructed in your site.

Note that to control how the navigation tree is displayed, you should go to "Manage portlets" at the root of the site (or wherever a navigation tree portlet has been added) and change its settings directly.

┌─ Navigation details ──

☑ **Automatically generate tabs**
By default, all items created at the root level will add to the global section navigation. You can turn this off if you prefer manually constructing this part of the navigation.

☑ **Generate tabs for items other than folders.**
By default, any content item in the root of the portal will be shown as a global section. If you turn this option off, only folders will be shown. This only has an effect if "Automatically generate tabs" is enabled.

Displayed content types
The content types that should be shown in the navigation and site map.

☑ Collection	☑ Folder	☑ News Item
☑ Event	☑ Image	☑ Page
☑ Favorite	☑ Large Folder	
☑ File	☑ Link	

┌─ ☐ Filter on workflow state ───
The workflow states that should be shown in the navigation tree and the site map.

☐ **Externally visible**

☐ **Internal draft**

☐ **Internally published**

☐ **Pending review**

☐ **Private**

☐ **Public draft**

☐ **Published**

[↻ Save]

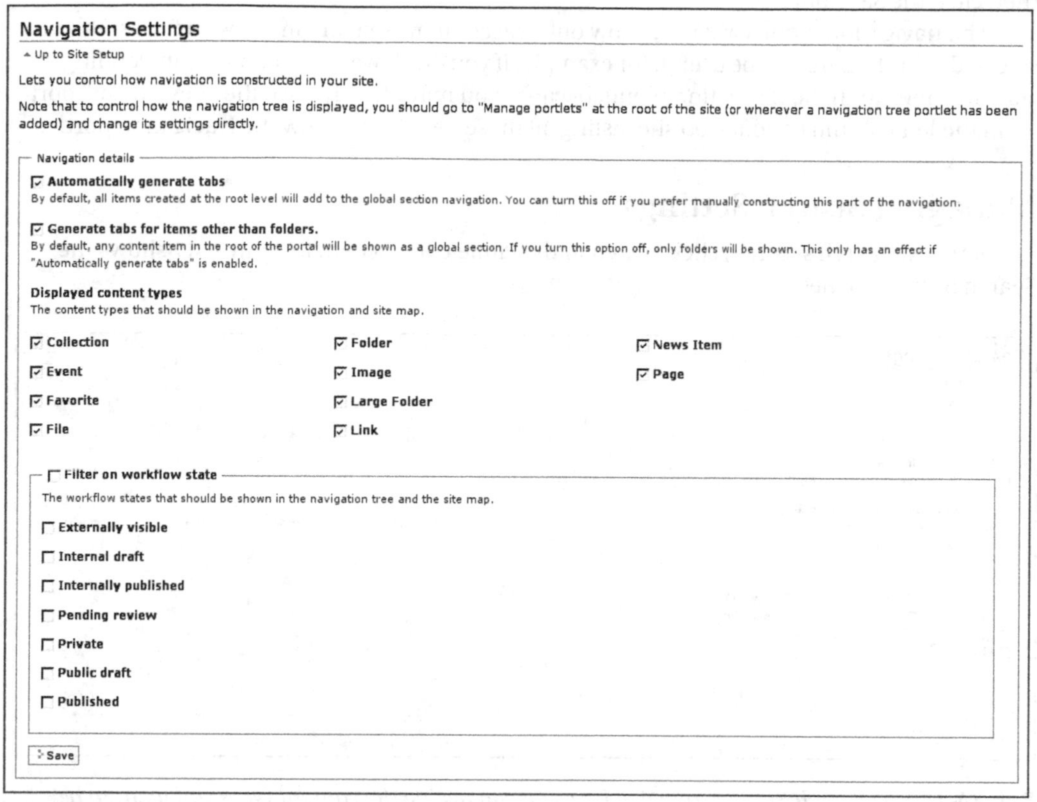

Figure 4-16. *The Navigation Settings panel*

The first two options let you control the generation of tabs in the global section navigation—that is, the tabs in the main light blue header strip, which correspond to the global section of your site.

The gray help text beneath the two options clearly explains how to use them:

- *Automatically generate tabs*: By default, all items created at the root level will add to the global section navigation. You can turn this off if you prefer to manually construct this part of the navigation.

- *Generate tabs for items other than folders*: By default, any content item in the root of the portal will be shown as a global section. If you turn this option off, only folders will be shown. This has an effect only if "Automatically generate tabs" is enabled.

The "Displayed content types" section allows you to decide which content types can be shown in the navigation tree and in the site map. Most of the options are already selected by default.

The last section of the Navigation Settings panel, "Filter on workflow state," allows you to filter the content to be shown in the navigation menus according to the workflow state (usually, content in the navigation menus is shown according to the user's permissions). To do so, check the "Filter on workflow state" option, select the workflow states in the list below, and then click the Save button.

The navigation menus will now show only the contents that are in the workflow states you selected. This feature can be useful, for example, if you don't want the contents in Pending state to show up in the navigation menu, because you may already have the "Review list" portlet in the left column of your web site, listing all those items just below the Navigation portlet.

Managing Search Settings

To set up the search settings, click Search in the Plone control panel. Figure 4-17 shows the Search Settings panel.

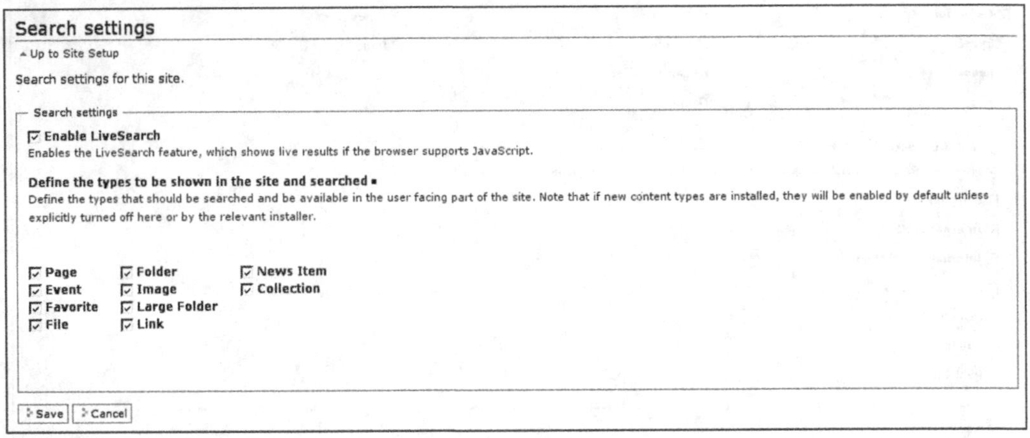

Figure 4-17. *The Search Settings panel, where you can decide the content types you want to be shown in search results*

The first option allows you to enable/disable the LiveSearch feature (which we discussed near the end of Chapter 3).

The list of options below it represents all the available content types in your site. Check all the ones you want to be available in searches. Of course, the results that will be available in searches depend on the user's permissions as well. For example, if you toggled the page content type in the Search Settings panel and some pages in the "private" state match the search criteria a user used, those pages won't appear in the search results if the user doesn't have the permission to view them (this concept will become clearer when we talk about workflow, roles, and permissions in the "Managing Users and Permissions" section in this chapter). This is one of the best examples of how Plone cleverly manages security!

Adding/Removing Products in Your Site

As we will thoroughly talk about later, you can customize your Plone site through a variety of add-on products that allow you to add new features to your site to meet almost any need and serve different purposes.

If you or your site administrator has installed add-on products, the Add/Remove Products panel is the place where you can enable and disable these products in your site. To go to it, click Add-on Products in the Plone control panel. Figure 4-18 shows the Add/Remove Products panel.

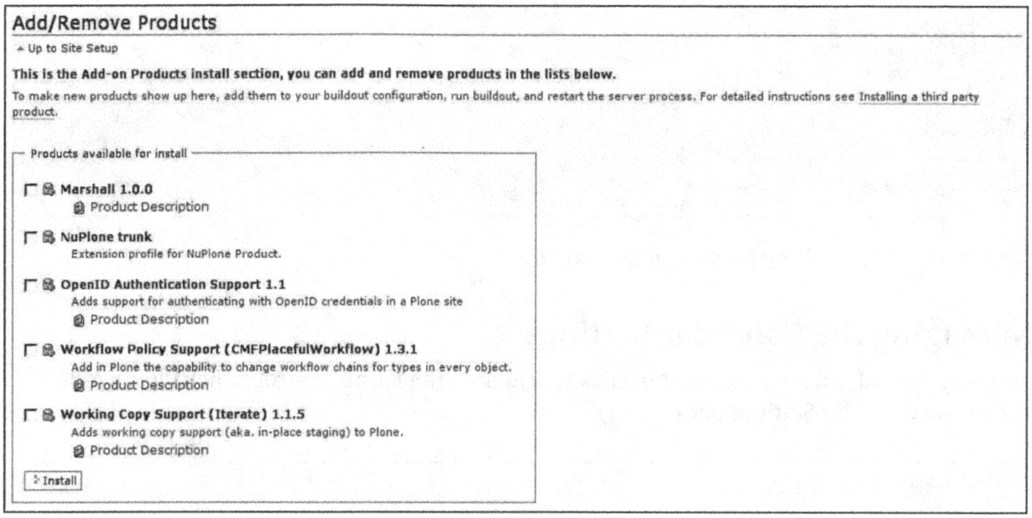

Figure 4-18. *The Add/Remove Products panel*

You will see a list of all products available (meaning that they have already been installed on the file system). To add one of them to your site, check its check box, and click the Install button.

The product will be now placed in the right part of panel, which contains the list of products that have already been added to the site. To uninstall one of them, check its check box, and click the Uninstall button. The product will return to the left part of the panel, in the "Products available for install" list. Notice that below each product name there is a Product Description link—this will lead you to a page that describes the product and its features.

In the Installed Products list (on the right side of the Add/Remove Products panel), there is an additional link, called Install Log, below each product; it will lead you to some information about the installation/uninstallation processes that occurred for that product. Figure 4-19 shows you an example.

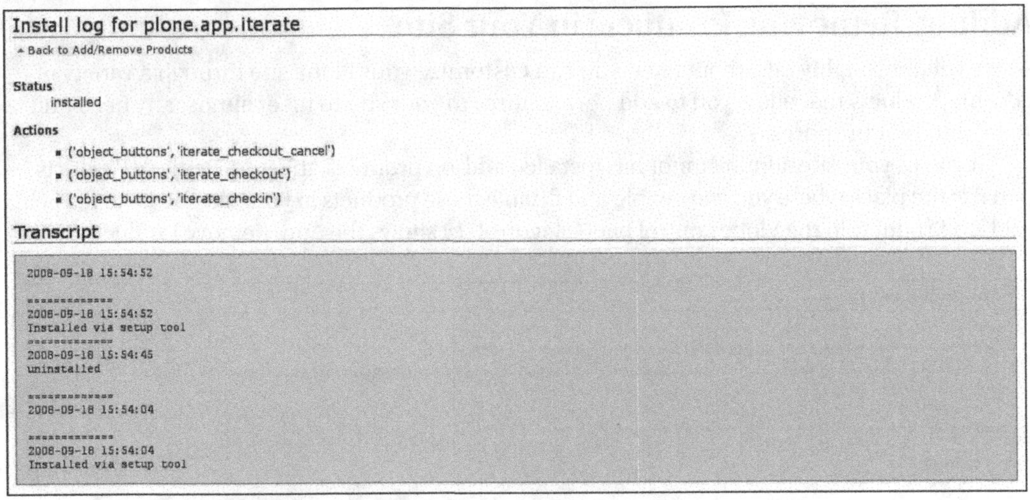

Figure 4-19. *The install log for an add-on product*

Managing the Calendar Settings

To set up the calendar configuration, click Calendar in the Plone control panel. Figure 4-20 shows the Calendar Settings panel.

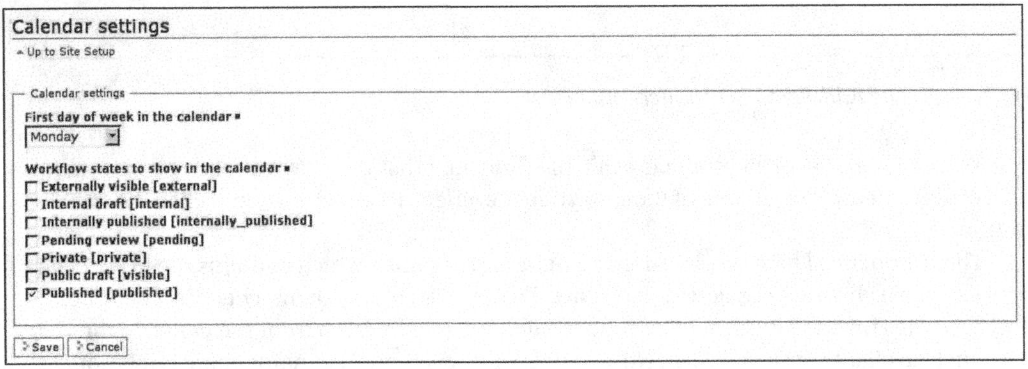

Figure 4-20. *The Calendar Settings panel*

The first option you can set up is the day of the week you want to show first on the site calendar.

The list below that shows all the different workflow states that you can display in the calendar. Events in these workflow states will be highlighted in the calendar, as shown in Chapter 3, in Figure 3-27. The "Published [published]" option is already selected—that is why when you publish an event, it automatically shows up in the calendar. If you, for example, check the "Pending review [Pending]" check box, all the events with this workflow state will show up in the site calendar.

Managing the Collection Settings

To set up the collection configuration, click Collection in the Plone control panel. Figure 4-21 shows the Collection Settings panel.

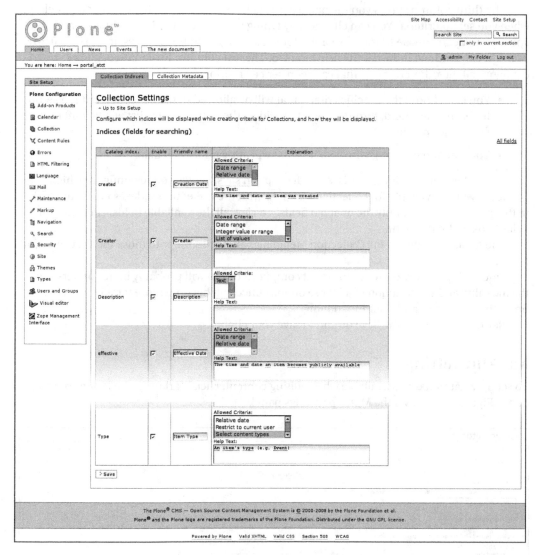

Figure 4-21. *The Collection Settings panel (a part of the panel has been cut to make the image more readable)*

Notice that this section is composed of two panels, Collection Indexes and Collection Metadata. Use the green tabs in the header strip to view them. The Collection Indexes panel, as its description says, allows you to configure which indexes will be displayed while creating criteria for collections and how they will be displayed.

The table in this panel shows you only the fields enabled for collection criteria. If you want to view all the fields available, click the "All fields" link at the top right. You can enable or disable all the different entries presented in the table through the corresponding check box in the second column.

The third column shows you the name of the field as it appears in the collection panel when you set up criteria. You can change it by typing it in the text field where the name appears; you can choose a "friendly name" for it, as the column header says, in order to help users quickly understand what the field refers to. The last column, Explanation, allows you to configure all the different fields that can represent a criterion for collections:

- You can choose the specific criteria that will be allowed in the collection criteria setup for each single field, through the list provided; the entries of this list will be different from field to field.

- You can add or change the help text that will appear for each field.

The Collection Metadata panel, as its description says, allows you to configure which metadata will be available for collection views. As with the Collection Indexes panel, the table in this panel shows you only the enabled fields. To view all the available fields, click the "All fields" link at the top right.

The table columns on the Collection Metadata panel are similar to those for the Collection Indexes panel.

Since this part of the site setup is a bit complicated, you will probably better understand the meaning and the function of all these options once you become more familiar with collections, their features, and their functioning.

Remember to click the Save button to save your changes.

Markup Settings

To set up what markup is available when editing content, click Markup in the Plone control panel. Figure 4-22 shows the Markup Settings panel.

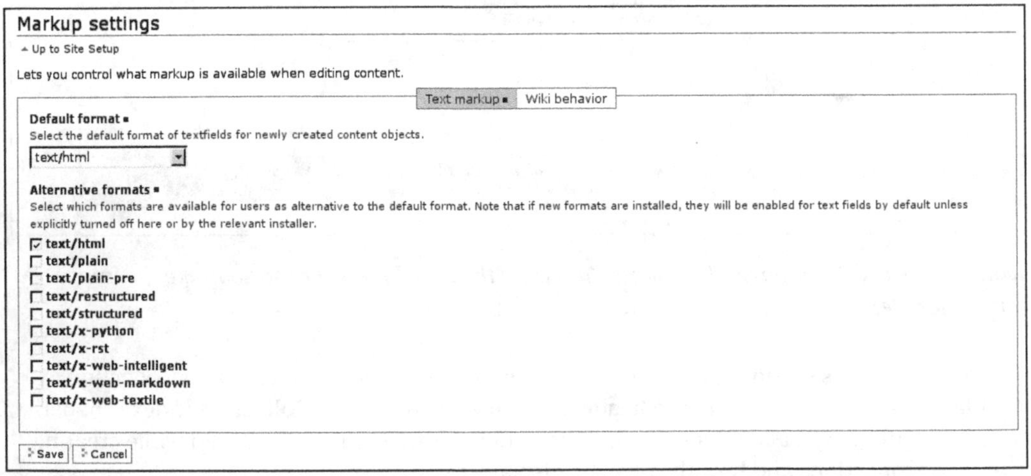

Figure 4-22. *The Markup Settings panel*

Notice that there are two sections: "Text markup" and "Wiki behavior." The first one has a little red square next to it, meaning that configuring its setting is required. You will be asked to choose the default format of text fields for newly created content objects, through a drop-down list, and select which formats are available for users as alternatives to the default format. As the field description says, if new formats are installed, they will be enabled for text fields by default unless explicitly turned off here or by the relevant installer.

Click the "Wiki behavior" tab, and you will be able to choose one or more content types to turn wiki behavior on. The available options are

- Page

- Event

- News item

Remember to click the Save button.

Type Settings

To manage the workflow, visibility, and versioning settings for the content types of your site, click Types in the Plone control panel. Figure 4-23 shows the Type Settings panel.

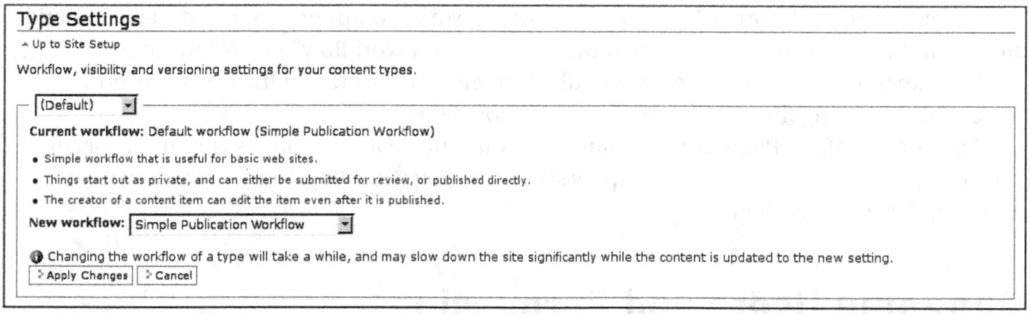

Figure 4-23. *The Type Settings panel, where you can manage different settings for each content type*

Through the first drop-down menu, you can choose a content type. As soon as you choose one, some options will appear (depending on the content type you selected). In Figure 4-24, we selected the page content type.

Some gray text will briefly describe the content type. Below that, you can choose whether the content type will be globally addable (which means whether you can add it in any part of the site); whether you want to allow comments on it (see the "Commenting Content" section in Chapter 3); and whether it will be visible in searches.

You can then decide the versioning policy for that specific content type. The Automatic option is selected by default. This option will leave the versioning behavior as explained in the "Tracking the History of Content and Versioning" section of Chapter 3. If you select "No versioning," this function will be disabled, and if you select Manual, you will have more control over versioning.

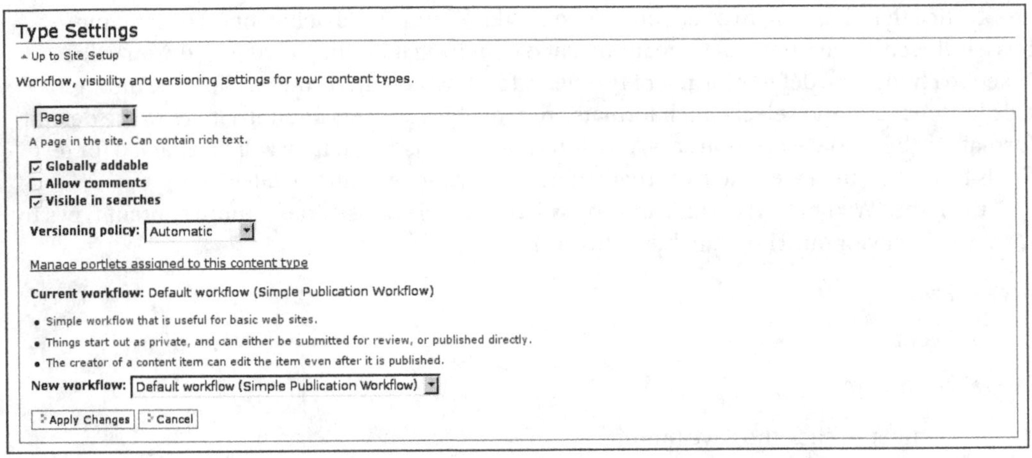

Figure 4-24. *The Type Settings panel for the Page content type*

The "Manage portlets assigned to this content type" link, as you will see in the "Using the Block/Unblock Portlets Controls" section later in this chapter, lets you manage portlets that will be displayed for that specific content type.

You can then get information about the current workflow applied to the content type and choose another workflow by selecting it through the "New workflow" drop-down menu.

You can also globally change the workflow by selecting Default in the first drop-down menu and then using the "New workflow" drop-down menu.

This section of the Plone control panel is very useful because it allows you to act specifically on particular content types and apply specific settings for them; again, freedom is an important keyword for Plone!

Managing Users and Permissions

As we already started to mention, Plone has a powerful and fine-grained security model. It provides a myriad of options for security at all levels, so each object can have custom security for a user, a role, a group, and so on.

The security for Plone is so powerful and multifaceted that it can be quite hard to debug and manage. However, getting the security right might be the most important aspect of your Plone site setup.

One of the most common tasks you will need to perform as an administrator of a Plone site is dealing with site members, and a security breach in your site is probably the most serious blunder you can make. For this reason, we will cover Plone security quite comprehensively—focusing on managing users and groups through the Plone control panel in this chapter, managing security and workflows through Zope in Chapters 7 and 8, and creating custom member profiles in Chapter 12.

In this chapter, we will mainly cover the user terminology and key interfaces with which your users will interact, as well as how to add and edit users and groups through the Plone interface—a first step in the "security" topic in Plone.

Users, Roles, and Groups

Before seeing how to manage users and their permissions, we'll try to clarify the concepts of users, roles, and groups in Plone.

Each person visiting a Plone site is referred to as a *user*. The user may or may not be authenticated by Plone, and users who are not authenticated are called *anonymous users*. Users who are authenticated are logged into an existing user account.

Anonymous users are the lowest level of users in that they usually have the most restrictions. Once users log in, they gain the roles their accounts give them. A user is identified by a short identifier—for example, John. By default, no users are created for you in Plone, except the one added to Zope by the installer to give you administrator access. The name of that user is whatever you set up in the installer—usually Admin.

A Plone site has a series of *roles*, which are logical categorizations of users. Instead of setting every user's permissions individually, each role is assigned permissions individually. Every user can be assigned zero to many roles; for example, a user can be a member and a manager. Each role is identified by a simple name—for example, Member.

A Plone site has five predefined roles, split into two groups: assignable roles and nonassignable roles. *Assignable roles* are roles that you can grant to users. *Nonassignable roles* are roles you don't grant specifically to a user but that occur within a Plone site. For example, you don't assign the anonymous role to a user.

The following are the nonassignable roles:

- *Anonymous*: This role refers to a user who hasn't logged into the site. This could be a user who has no account or who has merely not logged in yet.

- *Authenticated*: This role refers to any user who is logged into the site, whatever their role. By definition, a user is either anonymous or authenticated; the two are mutually exclusive. Because the authenticated user doesn't provide much in the way of granularity, it isn't recommended for most applications.

The following are the assignable roles:

- *Owner*: This is a special role given to users when they create an object. It applies to a user for that object only; the information is stored on the object. You don't normally explicitly assign someone as an owner; Plone does that for you.

- *Member*: This is the default role for a user who has joined your site. Anyone who joins using the Register button in the Plone interface has this role.

- *Reviewer*: This is a user with more permissions than a member but less than a manager. Reviewers are users who can edit or review content entered by a member; however, they can't change the site's configuration or alter a user account.

- *Manager*: Managers can do almost anything to a Plone site, so you should give this role only to trusted developers and administrators. A manager can delete or edit content, remove users, alter a site's configuration, and even delete your Plone site.

Somewhat different from the users and roles is the concept of *groups*. A role indicates the set of permissions the user with that role is granted, while a group is a logical categorization of users. You can grant an entire group a certain role in a certain section or in the whole site. For example, the marketing department may be one group, and the engineering department may be another group. Each user can belong to zero to many groups, and groups can be part of other groups. Groups are optional; you don't need to use them, but the Plone team found them useful enough to integrate them. Site administrators can use the groups in any way they choose, such as to group a department or a certain class of users. By default, three groups are created for you: administrators, reviewers, and authenticated users.

Managing Users Through the Web

Using the Plone interface you can easily add new users, alter user information, change their roles, and so on. Click Users and Groups in the Plone control panel. The Users and Groups section will show up, with three green tabs on the header strip; the first tab presents the Users Overview panel, as shown in Figure 4-25.

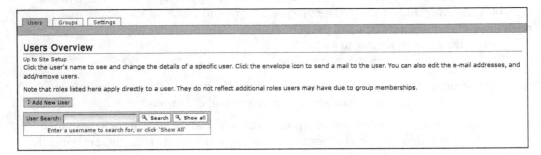

Figure 4-25. *The Users Overview panel, where you can look for different users and change some settings about their accounts and roles*

Adding New Users

To add a new user, click the Add New User button. A registration form will appear, as shown in Figure 4-26.

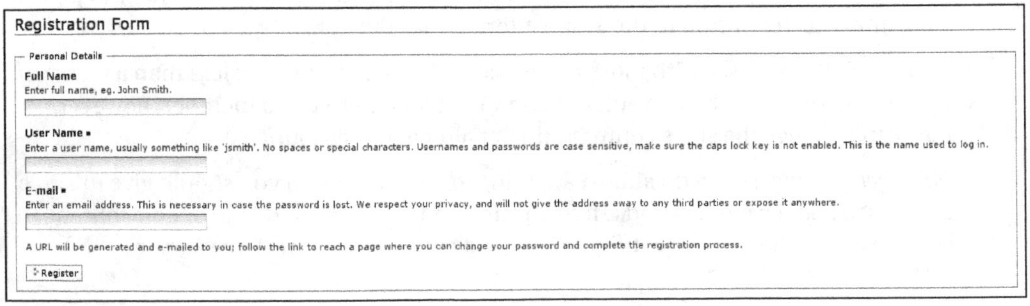

Registration Form

— Personal Details —

Full Name
Enter full name, eg. John Smith.

User Name ■
Enter a user name, usually something like 'jsmith'. No spaces or special characters. Usernames and passwords are case sensitive, make sure the caps lock key is not enabled. This is the name used to log in.

E-mail ■
Enter an email address. This is necessary in case the password is lost. We respect your privacy, and will not give the address away to any third parties or expose it anywhere.

A URL will be generated and e-mailed to you; follow the link to reach a page where you can change your password and complete the registration process.

‡ Register

Figure 4-26. *Adding a new user*

Complete the form with the appropriate information in the three fields, following the gray help text underneath each of them. Then click the Register button.

A new URL will be generated and sent to the e-mail address you entered in the E-mail field. The user will have to follow the link they received to complete the registration process; they will land on a page like the one shown in Figure 4-27.

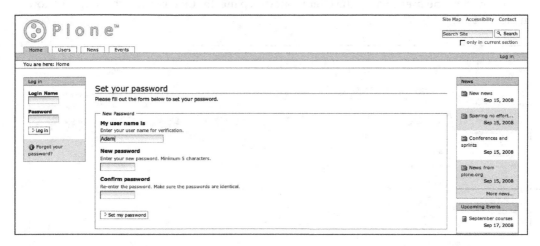

Figure 4-27. *Setting a new user's password*

The user will be able to set their own password and then directly log into the site.

■**Note** To make the registration process work, you have to correctly configure the mail settings for your Plone site (see the "Managing Mail Settings" section earlier in the chapter).

Changing Users Details

To change a user's details in the User Overview panel (see Figure 4-25), you can search for a specific user by entering their username in the User Search box and clicking the Search button, or you can click the "Show all" button that is next to the Search button to view the list of all the site members.

In both cases, you will see a table with the username in the first column and their e-mail address in the second (if you searched for a specific user and the system found it, the table will simply have a single entry). Additionally, there will be a central column showing the available roles, a column for resetting the user's password, and a column for eliminating the user.

To assign new roles to a user, just check/uncheck the corresponding check boxes in the Role column in the appropriate row, and then click the Apply Changes button. The roles you assign here will refer to the entire site and will apply directly to a user; they do not reflect additional roles users may have because of group memberships.

You can also send e-mail to a user by clicking the envelope icon, or you can change their e-mail address by typing a new one in the text field next to the icon.

The Reset Password column is very useful if you need to change your site members' passwords for security reasons. Just select the usernames whose passwords you want to change by checking the corresponding check boxes in the Reset Password column, and click the Save button. From that moment, users won't be able to use their previous passwords to log in, and they will receive an e-mail with a link to click in order to reset their passwords.

If you click the user's name, the User Properties panel for that user will show up, as shown in Figure 4-28.

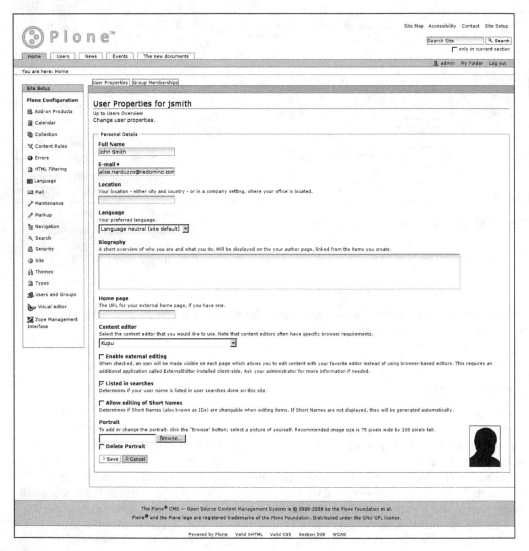

Figure 4-28. *The User Properties panel, where you can edit a user's profile*

This panel is very similar to the Personal Preferences panel each user can access by clicking Profile in their personal dashboard (see the "Setting Up Your Preferences" section in Chapter 3). Since you're the site administrator, of course, you have the right to change all the information about the user.

On the header strip, you may have also noticed the Group Membership tab. We'll discuss its characteristics in the following section, when we talk about groups.

Managing Groups Through the Web

Click the Groups tab in the Users and Groups section of the Plone control panel, and the Groups Overview panel will appear, as shown in Figure 4-29.

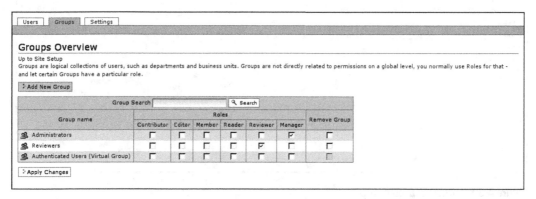

Figure 4-29. *The Groups Overview panel, where you can add and manage groups and their roles*

Through this panel, you can manage the groups of users in your site and add new ones. A table shows you all the existing groups in your site, presenting their names, their roles, and a column with check boxes to delete them.

As we mentioned before, three groups are created by default: *administrators*, a group of users with the role of manager; *reviewers*, a group of users with the role of reviewer; and *authenticated users*, a virtual group, because all users with an account in the site are authenticated users. That means that assigning a specific role to the authenticated users group will give all site members the permissions configured for that role.

Note The roles you assign to a group will affect all the users and groups in the site that are part of it. To give a group permissions for a specific site area or single item, use the Sharing tab of the corresponding folder or other content (revisit the "Sharing Your Content" section of Chapter 3 for details on this).

Adding New Groups

To add a new group, click the Add New Group button. The Create a Group panel on the Group Properties tab will appear, as shown in Figure 4-30. Note that there are two other tabs in the green header strip: Group Members and Group Portlets; we will talk about these soon.

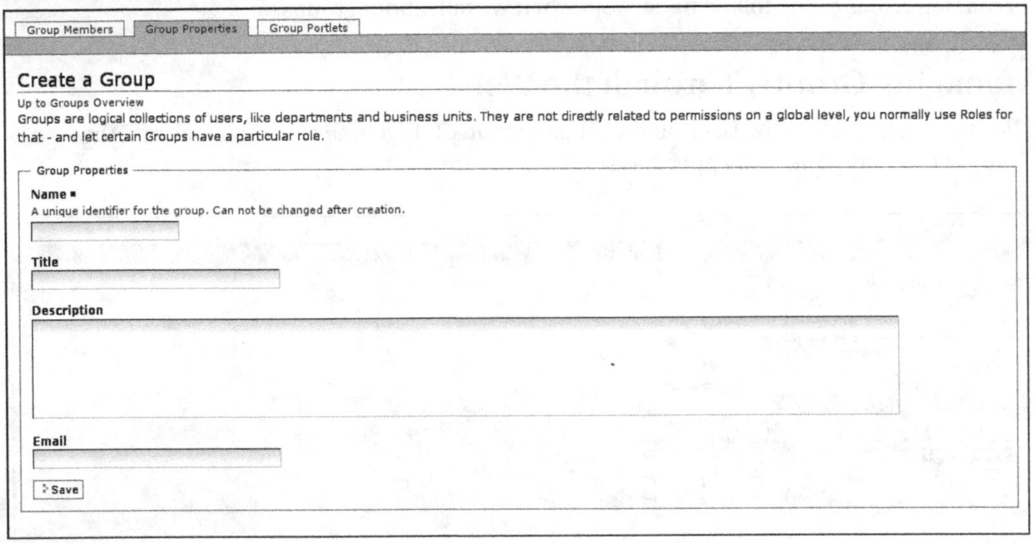

Figure 4-30. *Adding a new group*

You now have to fill out the form on this page—the only required field is the name for the group. Choose this carefully, because you will not be able to modify it after creation. You can then enter a title, a description, and an e-mail address for the group. When you have completed the form, click the Save button.

You will return to the Groups Overview panel. Notice that the new group you just created shows up in the table.

Changing Group Details

To change the roles assigned to a group, use the check boxes in the Roles column, and then click Apply Changes. Use the Remove Group column on the right to eliminate one or more groups.

To change a group's details, click its name in the left column of the table. You will be taken to the Group Members tab (see Figure 4-31), which will allow you to configure the group.

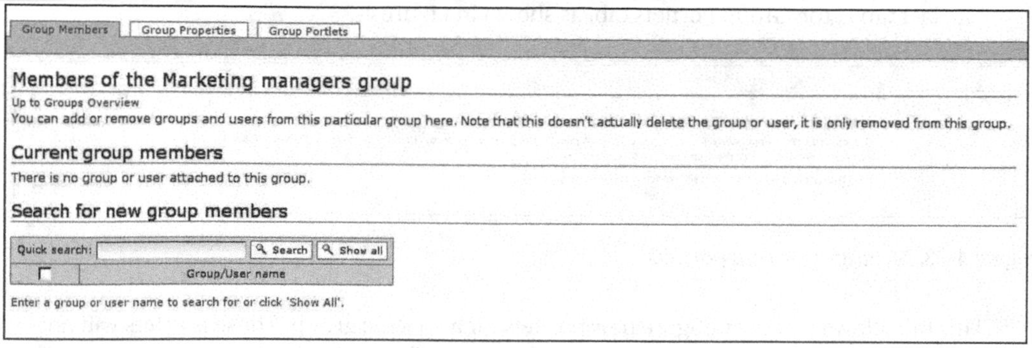

Figure 4-31. *Managing members and details of a group*

If you just created the group, no users will be part of it. This is the case for the default groups created by Plone as well. If the group is already populated, you will see a table listing all the users or groups that are part of it in the "Current group members" section. The left column of the table shows each member's e-mail address; you can click it to send a message to that user or group of users.

To delete a member, check the check box in the right column, and click the "Remove selected groups/users" button.

To add a new member, you can either use the search box or the "Show all" button in the "Search for new group members" section. Select one or more users or groups you want to add to that group, and click "Add selected groups and users to this group."

You can also change a user/group's group membership by clicking the user/group in the "User name" column of the table and clicking the Group Membership tab. Figure 4-32 shows you the panel that will appear.

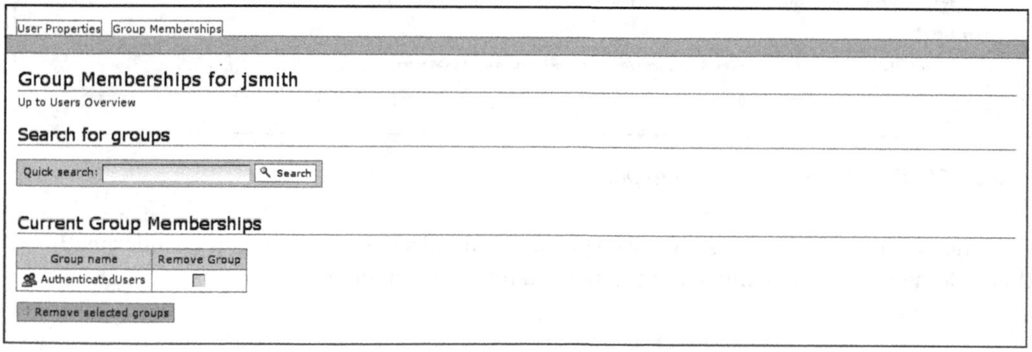

Figure 4-32. *Managing a user's group memberships*

The last tab is the Group Portlets tab, as shown in Figure 4-33.

Figure 4-33. *Managing group portlets*

This tab allows you to configure new portlets for a specific group. These portlets will normally be rendered below the context portlets, which are the portlets that have been set for the various sections of the site. You can use the "Add portlet" drop-down lists on the left and right sides of the page to manage the portlets (we will discuss this further in the "Managing Portlets" section of this chapter, so don't worry if it doesn't sound clear yet). For example, you might add a "Review list" portlet for the reviewers group or a "Recent items" portlet for a group whose members are interested in being updated about new content within the site.

User/Group Settings

Click the Settings tab in the Users and Groups section of the Plone control panel, and the User/Groups Settings panel will appear, as shown in Figure 4-34.

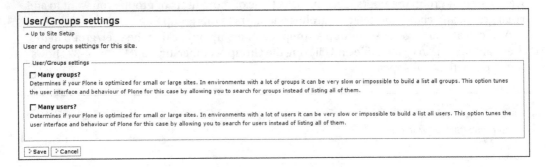

Figure 4-34. *The User/Groups Settings panel*

The two available options are self-explanatory, thanks to the gray help text underneath them. Remember to click the Save button if you make any change.

Configuring the WYSIWYG Editor

Plone features an integrated visual editor called Kupu, an open source client-side WYSIWYG editor. Kupu is tightly integrated with Plone and, like Plone, is standards-compliant and browser-independent. Besides, Kupu can be easily customized through the Web via the Plone control panel. Figure 4-35 shows the Kupu Configuration panel.

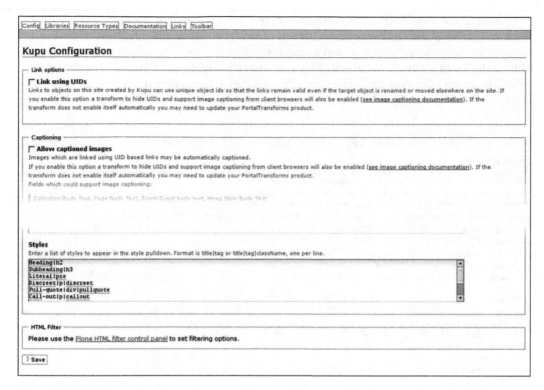

Figure 4-35. *The Kupu Configuration panel (a part of the panel has been cut to make the image more readable)*

The Kupu Configuration panel is quite wide, but don't worry; that is just because you can configure many settings, which won't be a hard task.

You've probably already noticed that there are six tabs. Let's go through all of them.

Main Configuration

The Kupu Configuration panel presents different sections. Each of them includes an explanation, so you shouldn't have any problem understanding what each is for.

A very useful feature is the "Link using UIDs" option, which will keep links from breaking. If you choose this linking mechanism, you will be able to link items through their UIDs rather than their relative paths so links won't break even if the target object is renamed or moved elsewhere on the site.

The Styles box allows you to manage styles for tables and paragraphs. Since a table/paragraph style consists of a name, the HTML element it applies to, and optionally a CSS class name, you will have to know all of these to add custom styles. You can also remove styles from the listing contained in the two text areas, called Tables and Styles, in the Styles box, simply by deleting the lines you don't need.

Library Configuration

Click the Libraries tab to view the Kupu Libraries panel, as shown in Figure 4-36.

Libraries are static or dynamic collections of resources, defined by the system at a deeper level; they provide abstract locations for objects of any type. For example, you usually use a library when you insert an image into a page content type: when you click the "Insert image" icon on the Kupu toolbar, a panel will appear, as shown in Figure 4-37; thanks to a specific library, this panel shows all the images already uploaded in the system that you can choose from.

Figure 4-36. *The Kupu Libraries panel*

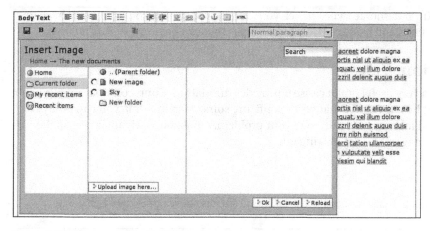

Figure 4-37. *An example of a library*

Kupu Resource Types

Resource types are the way Kupu distinguishes objects. Managing the settings on the Kupu Resource Types panel is advisable only if you have a good grasp of resource types. Figure 4-38 shows what the panel looks like.

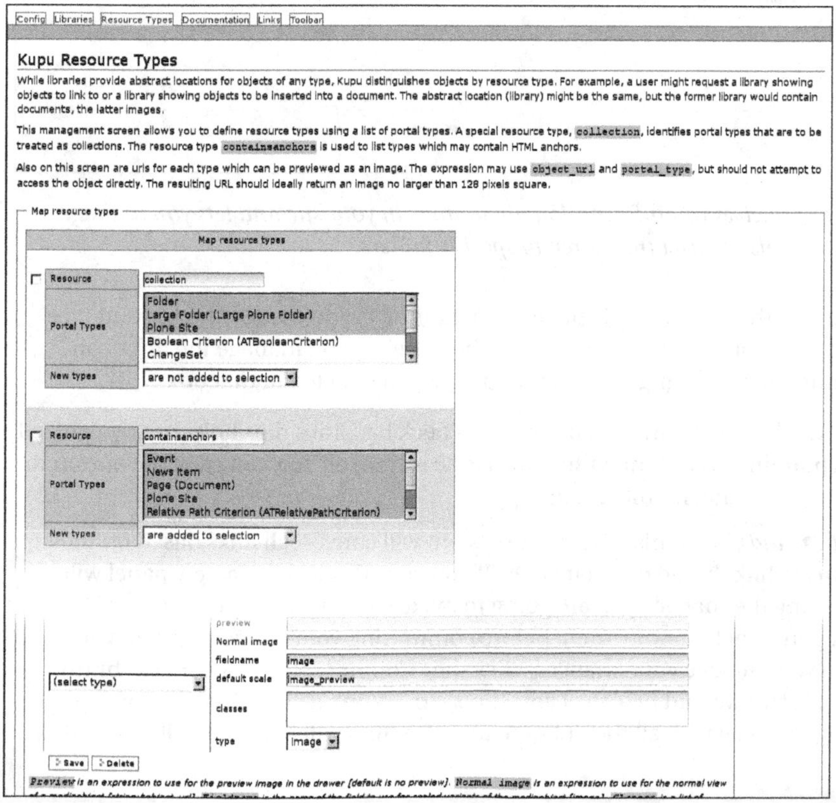

Figure 4-38. *The Kupu Resource Types panel*

Through the Kupu Resource Types panel, you can also choose which portal types have to be treated as collections and manage URLs for the types that can be previewed as an image.

Documentation

Documentation is a very useful tab because it provides tutorials on Kupu configuration. When you can't figure out how to set up, change, or configure something in Kupu, you can always come to this tab and look for the solution to your problem. A linkable navigation box on the left will help you find what you are looking for.

Links

This tab will help you manage links within your Plone site, as shown in Figure 4-39.

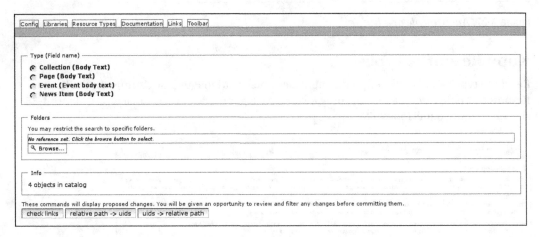

Figure 4-39. *The Links tab gives you information about links in your site and lets you manage their behavior. You can also restrict the search to specific folders.*

The first section on the Links tab, "Type (Field name)," lets you choose the content type you want to work on. The buttons at the bottom of the panel let you manage the links contained in all the items corresponding to the content type you selected in that box:

- *check links*: Clicking this button allows you to check bad links (i.e., links not recognized by Kupu as pointing to content within this Plone instance). You can click the button to see the broken links and modify them.

- *relative path ➤ uids*: With this button, the system will convert all links based on their relative paths to links based on their UIDs. If you click this button, a new panel will appear, showing the changes you are going to make so that you can check them and ensure that you want to modify them before committing your changes. When you are sure you want to save your changes, click the "Commit selected changes" button (remember that, as we said before, if you choose the "Link using UIDs" option in the Kupu Configuration panel, all the links created after that will automatically use UIDs).

- *uids* ➤ *relative path*: With this option, the system will convert all links based on their UIDs to links based on their relative paths. If you click this button, a new panel will appear that will work in much the same way as that for the "relative path ➤ uids" option.

The Folders section lets you restrict the search of links to manage to specific folders through a Browse button. Click it, and a new window will appear, where you can select a folder by navigating through your site's hierarchy or using the search box. If you select a specific folder, the changes you commit will affect only its content.

The section on the Links tab named Info gives you some useful information. depending on what kind of task you are performing. For example, if you select a specific folder, the Info box will tell you how many links the system has found in that folder, so you can be aware of the particular links that will be affected by the changes you commit.

Toolbar Configuration

The Toolbar tab lets you configure the toolbar that site members see when they're editing content. The toolbar can be highly customized; for example, you can show certain buttons only to particular users or groups, add certain functions for trusted site members, build a custom toolbar for users with specific permissions, and so on.

The first part of the panel allows you to control the visibility of all buttons together, and the second one allows you to act on the button individually. To do so, you need to know the expressions for limiting the visibility of buttons. For example, to limit the visibility of the "Insert image" button, go to the "Image drawer" button, which should be active, and insert the following expression in the text field next to it:

```
python:member and member.has_permission('Manage portal', portal)
```

This hides the "Insert image" button for users who don't have the "Manage portal" permission so that only administrator users can add images (perhaps because we don't trust the artistic tastes of our users enough).

Managing HTML Filtering

Plone has a system that removes specific tags embedded in content saved as HTML. For example, if you paste code for embedding videos, slide shows, or music players from web sites such as Flickr, YouTube, or MySpace, you will not be able to see them, because Plone does not allow this type of content.

There are several HTML filters available on Plone sites that in general act in union; the main ones are the Kupu HTML filter, Safe HTML, and mxTidy.

Plone filters HTML tags that are considered security risks. But it also does this to prevent broken or incorrect code from having a negative impact on page layout.

Note Plone's HTML filtering system is above all a security system. Plone filters out the tags that are used for HTML embedding because they can be abused and used to create escalation attacks. Therefore, we suggest that you make changes to this only if you absolutely trust all members of your site.

From version 3.0 onward, the main HTML filtering settings have been moved from the ZMI into the Plone user interface. You can now manage tags, attributes, and styles; remove them from the filtering system; and create custom ones through the Plone control panel.

To access the HTML filter settings, click HTML Filtering in the Plone control panel. Figure 4-40 shows the HTML Filter Settings panel.

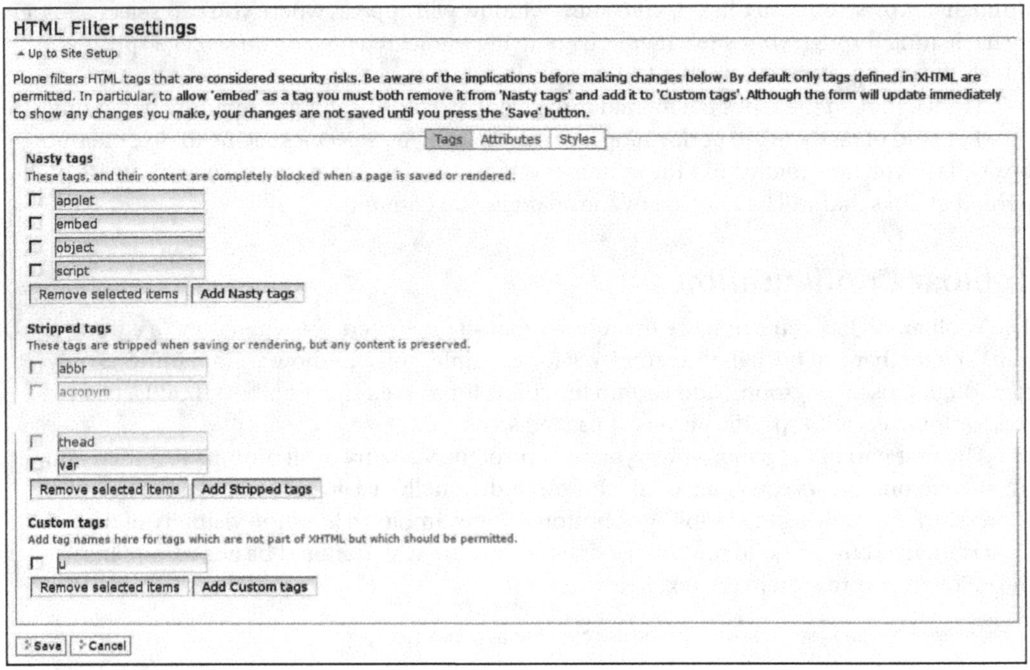

Figure 4-40. *The HTML Filter Settings panel*

This panel presents three tabs, for controlling the configuration of tags, attributes, and styles, respectively.

Tags

The Tags tab allows you to configure three different types of tags:

- *Nasty tags*: These are tags and content that are completely blocked when a page is saved or rendered. This means that if you create or paste code that contains these tags, the system will eliminate not only the tags but also the content within it.

- *Stripped tags*: These are tags that are stripped when saving or rendering, but any content is preserved. This means that the system will eliminate those tags but not the content they contain.

- *Custom tags*: These are new tags that are not part of XHTML but that should be permitted. You can specify which tags you'd like to permit by writing their names in the text field in the "Custom tags" section.

You can add and remove tags from the filtering system by checking/unchecking their check boxes and clicking the "Remove selected items" and "Add Nasty/Stripped/Custom tags" buttons under each of the three parts of the panel.

Let's go through an example so you can better understand how to use the HTML Filter Settings panel. Imagine you want to add a Google map on a page of our site to indicate to site visitors the location of a building. To do so, you can copy the code that Google Maps offers you and paste it in the HTML code of the page. But, as we said, by default the map will not be displayed. To solve this, follow these simple steps:

1. Go to the HTML Filter Settings panel by clicking HTML Filtering in the Plone control panel.

2. Remove "object" and "embed" from the "Nasty tags" list.

3. Remove "object" and "param" from the "Stripped tags" list.

4. Add "embed" and "iframe" to the "Custom tags" list by clicking the "Add Custom tags" button and using the text field that appears.

5. Click the Save button, and return to the page where you pasted the map. Refresh the page, and the map will show up.

Attributes

Click the Attributes tab to manage the attribute settings. This panel consists of two sections:

- *Stripped attributes*: This section deals with attributes that are stripped from any tag when a page is saved or rendered.

- *Stripped combinations*: Through this section, you can choose a combination of tags and attributes so that those attributes will be stripped only for certain tags.

You can add and remove attributes from the filtering system by checking/unchecking their check boxes and using the "Remove selected attributes" and "Add Stripped attributes" buttons under each section of the panel.

Styles

Click the Styles tab to manage the style settings. This panel lets you control which kinds of styles are permitted for the style attributes. The panel consists of two parts:

- *Permitted styles*: This section deals with CSS styles that are allowed in style attributes.

- *Filtered classes*: This section provides a text field where you can add classes that you don't want to allow in class attributes.

You can add and remove classes by checking/unchecking their check boxes and using the "Remove selected items" and "Add Permitted styles" buttons. However, be careful and notice that in the "Permitted styles" section, you are adding/removing classes that *are* allowed, not filtered, which is the opposite of how the Tags and Attributes tabs work.

Managing Portlets

Portlets have been mentioned several times already throughout the book, but here we'll go into greater depth about them. Portlets are user interface components that are displayed in a web site. For example, the calendar you may see in the right column of a Plone web site (see Figure 4-41) is a portlet, as is the navigation menu you see in each section. In Plone, you can quickly and easily manage the portlets displayed in your site (moving, eliminating, and changing them) using only the Plone user interface.

On most pages of your site, if you are logged in with a manager role, you will see a "Manage portlets" link in the left and right columns of the screen, as shown in Figure 4-41. (This may depend on the layout of your page if you have already customized it.)

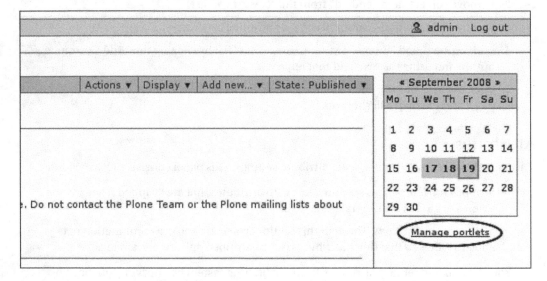

Figure 4-41. *The "Manage portlets" link*

By default, some portlets are set for you in the left and right columns; you will see them only if there are already published contents to populate them (e.g., the News portlet will be shown only if there are already some published news items on your site).

Managing and Adding Portlets

To manage the portlets for the entire sites, go to the Home folder, and click the "Manage portlets" link. The folder underneath will inherit all the settings. If you want to show different portlets in a specific area, go to that folder, and click the "Manage portlets" link from there (you can either add other portlets more than the ones set in the Home folder or override those settings, as we'll show you soon). In both cases, a panel similar to the one shown in Figure 4-42 will appear.

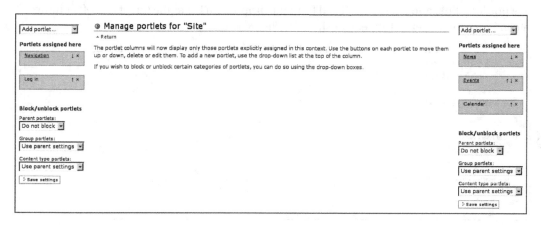

Figure 4-42. *The Manage Portlets panel*

You can manage portlets in the left and right columns separately. The portlets that are already set up in these sections are shown in light blue boxes under the title "Portlets assigned here" (see Figure 4-43). You can eliminate a portlet by clicking the red *x* in the top-right corner of each box, and you can change its position (up or down) by using the arrow to the left of the red *x*.

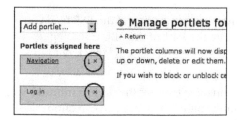

Figure 4-43. *Moving and removing portlets*

You can add a new portlet by selecting an option from the "Add portlet" drop-down menu, which lists all the portlets available in your site.

If the portlet you have selected requires configuration, a screen that allows you to fill in this information will appear. Once you complete the configuration, a new light blue box will appear in the Manage Portlets panel, indicating that the new portlet has been added.

Next, we'll walk through an example so you can better understand how to configure portlets. Imagine you want to add the RSS Feed portlet in the left column in all sections of the site to offer site visitors a quick overview on the latest BBC headlines. To do so, click the "Manage portlets" link, and choose RSS Feed from the drop-down list at the top of the left column. A configuration panel will appear, as shown in Figure 4-44.

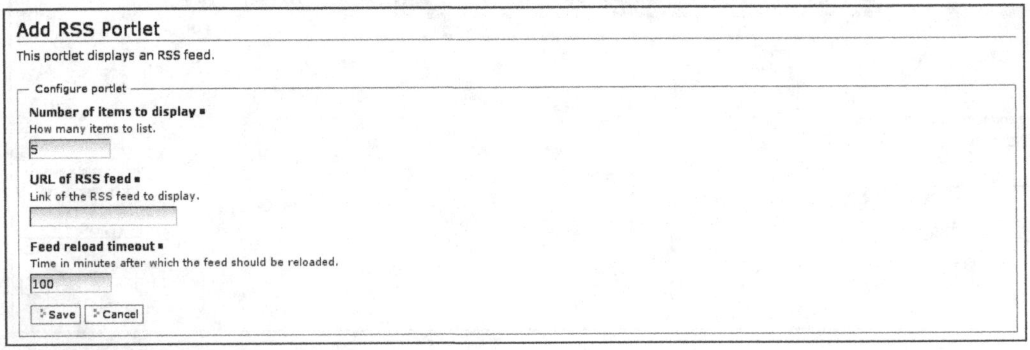

Figure 4-44. *Adding an RSS Feed portlet*

You now have to set up your new portlet, which is done via the following sections on this panel:

- *Number of items to display*: This is a text field where you have to enter the number of entries you want to display in the portlet; the default value is 5, but you can choose any number of items you want.

- *URL of RSS feed*: This is a text field where you have to paste the link of the RSS feed you want to display; in this case, you can copy and paste the URL of the BBC front page news RSS feed: http://newsrss.bbc.co.uk/rss/newsonline_world_edition/front_page/rss.xml.

- *Feed reloaded timeout*: This is a text field where you have to enter the time in minutes after which the feed should be reloaded; the default value is 100, but you can choose any number of minutes you want.

Click the Save button, and the result will look approximately like the example in Figure 4-45.

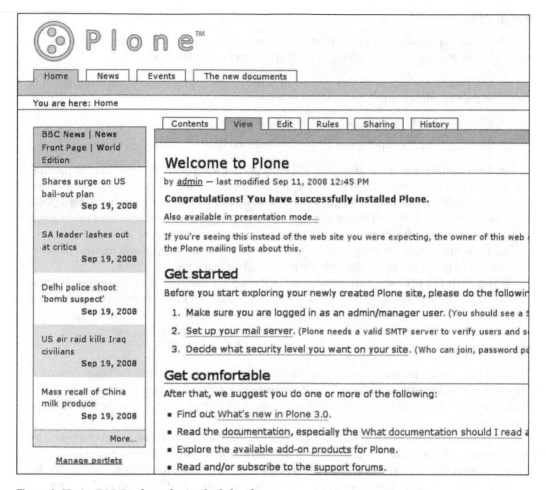

Figure 4-45. *An RSS Feed portlet in the left column*

You can always return to the configuration panel of a portlet by clicking its name in the light blue box.

Using the Block/Unblock Portlets Controls

To manage portlets at the folder level or even for individual pages, you can use the last section shown in both columns, titled "Block/unblock portlets."

We'll run through an example to better explain how you can manage portlets in different parts of your site. Suppose you created a folder called "New documents," where you work on new ideas collaborating with other users, and you want to add (only in that area of the site) a portlet in the left column that shows all the recent changes that happen in your site. Let's go through the different options.

Parent Portlets

This drop-down menu lets you control the inheritance of portlets from parent folders (i.e., the folders above the current one). The options in this menu are as follows:

- *Use parent settings*: With this option, all of the parent folder settings are inherited; this is the default option.

- *Block*: This option blocks all inherited folder settings.

- *Always show*: This option overrides any inherited blocks.

In this example, you'll eliminate the RSS Feed portlet you added in the site in the previous example and replace it with the Recent Changes portlet. To do so, you need to go to the "New documents" folder, click the "Manage portlets" link, and choose Block from the "Parent portlets" drop-down list of the left column in order to block the inheritance from the folders above it. Remember to click the "Save settings" button to commit your changes.

You can then choose Recent Changes from the "Add portlet" drop-down menu, choose the number of items to display through the panel that appears, and click Save.

If you return to your site, you will see that in the left column, the "New documents" folder will show the Recent Changes portlet, while it will show the RSS Feed portlet in any other area of the site.

Group Portlets

Through the "Group portlets" menu, you can set different portlets for different user groups. This means that you can show a certain set of portlets to a specific group of users, or you can create a custom group of users with certain interests and display a particular set of portlets for just this group.

To manage portlets for different groups, you first have to create some group portlets. To do so, go to the Users and Groups section in the Plone control panel, select a group in the Groups Overview panel, and click the Group Portlets tab. Then use the Manage Group Portlets panel that will appear, as described earlier in the "Managing and Adding Portlets" section of the chapter.

The options for and mechanisms of the "Group portlets" menu are the same as the "Parent portlets" menu, but they concern group portlets.

Content Type Portlets

Through the "Content type portlets" menu, you can configure portlets for different kinds of content types. This means that you can have a certain set of portlets every time you view an item representing a specific content type. For example, you can set specific portlets for news items so that every time you view news, you will have specific portlets at your disposal.

To configure portlets for content specific types, you need to click Types on the Plone control panel, choose the content type from the drop-down list at the top of the Type Settings panel, and then click the "Manage portlets assigned to this content type" link, as shown in Figure 4-46.

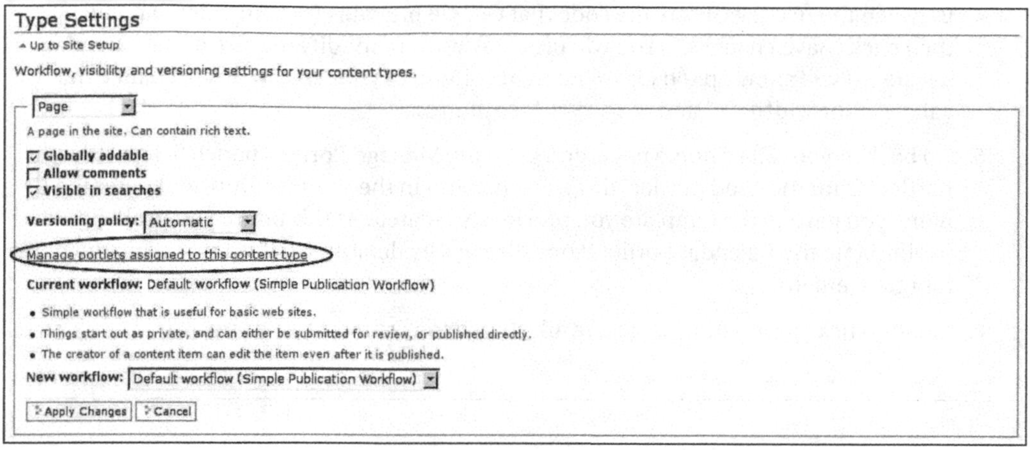

Figure 4-46. *The "Manage portlets assigned to this content type" link for the page content type*

The Manage Portlets panel for the content type you chose will show up, and you can add the portlets you want using the "Add portlets" menu. The portlets will show up only when you view items of that specific content type.

To further customize the portlets displayed for specific content types, you can use the "Content type portlets" drop-down menu. You can, for example, block the inheritance from parent folders so that only the portlets you specifically set for certain content types will show.

The options for and mechanisms of the "Content type portlets" menu are the same as the "Parent portlets" menu, but they of course concern content type portlets instead.

Using Classic Portlets

"Classic portlet" is one of the options on the "Add portlet" drop-down list, and it allows you to add a portlet created for earlier versions of Plone or to add a customized portlet you created in the custom folder in the portal_skins tool through the Zope Management Interface (ZMI). We haven't covered this back-end interface yet, but we will go through it in Chapter 5, and we will talk about the portal_skins tool in Chapter 6.

Here's an example that will better explain how the "Classic portlet" option works. Suppose you want to add a Google calendar to your site and show it in the right column.

To do so, you will need to create a new template for your portlet through the ZMI (if you don't feel comfortable with it yet, you may choose to go through Chapters 5 and 6 first, before performing this task). To do so, follow these steps:

1. Go to the custom folder in the portal_skins tool, and select "Page template" from the Add drop-down menu in the top-right corner.

2. Give an ID to your new template, and click the Add button.

3. Click the template you just created, delete the code from the field that will appear, and replace it with the following code:

```
<div metal:define-macro="portlet">  </div>
```

4. Between the two tags, paste the code that Google provides for your calendar, and then click "Save changes." (You will probably want to modify the size of the calendar, because it will show up too big in the right column of your site; to do so, change the values in the `width="x"` and `height="x"` attributes.)

5. Go back to your site's home page, and go to the Manage Portlets panel. Select "Classic portlet" from the "Add portlet" drop-down menu in the right column, and enter the ID name you gave to the template you previously created. At this point, you probably want to eliminate the Calendar portlet Plone displays by default. Do this by clicking the red *x* for that element.

6. Finally, click "Save settings." The result should look similar to Figure 4-47.

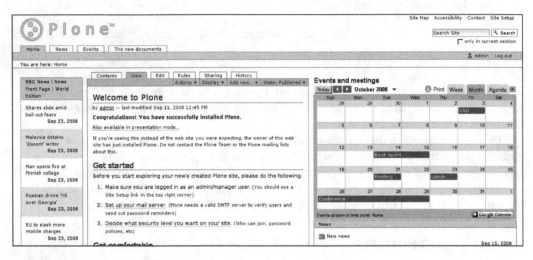

Figure 4-47. *Your Google calendar in the right column of the site*

Managing Automatic Rules

From version 3.0 onward, you can create rules that are assigned to one or more folders and triggered when content in a given folder is added, removed, or changed.

This feature offers a variety of opportunities and allows you to deeply customize your Plone site behavior. You can create your own rules, match as many conditions as you want for the rule to be triggered, and perform as many actions as you want. It's not easy to put all the potential of this feature into words; it's much easier to experience this tool's power by experimenting with it.

To create and manage content rules, click Content Rules on the Plone control panel, and the Content Rules panel will appear, as shown in Figure 4-48.

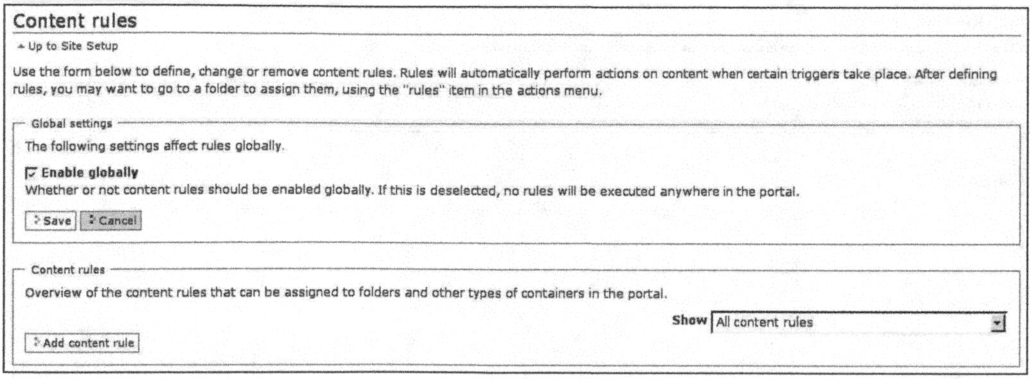

Figure 4-48. *The Content Rules panel, where you can create new content rules according to your needs*

The first section of the panel, "Global settings," contains an important option that lets you decide whether content rules should be enabled globally; this option is checked by default. If you deselect it, no rules will be executed anywhere in the portal. (Remember to click the Save button if you make a change.)

There are no rules created by default, so if you haven't created any yet, the "Content rules" section won't show anything except the "Add content rule" button. Otherwise, this section will show all the rules you have created. You can click any rule to see how it acts and make changes to it. You can enable, disable, or delete one or more rules by checking/unchecking their check boxes in the table that will appear when you will have one or more content rules and using the Enable, Disable, and Delete buttons. Additionally, you can show only certain types of rules by selecting the types of rules you want to display from the Show drop-down menu at the top-right corner of the "Content rules" section.

Creating a New Rule

Let's see how to create a new rule. Click the "Add content rule" button, and the Add Rule panel will appear, as shown in Figure 4-49.

You then have to enter a title and choose which kind of event will trigger your rule (this is the only required information on this panel). Optionally, you can enter a description to help members understand how the rule works and what it is for. The Enabled option is checked by default; uncheck it if you don't want your new rule to be enabled for now. The "Stop executing rules" option lets you decide whether execution of further rules should stop after the rule you are creating is executed. When you are finished setting up the rule, click the Save button, and you will be returned to the Content Rules panel.

Once you have added a new content rule to the table, you have to set its conditions and actions. Let's do it together! Click the rule, and a configuration panel will appear, as shown in Figure 4-50.

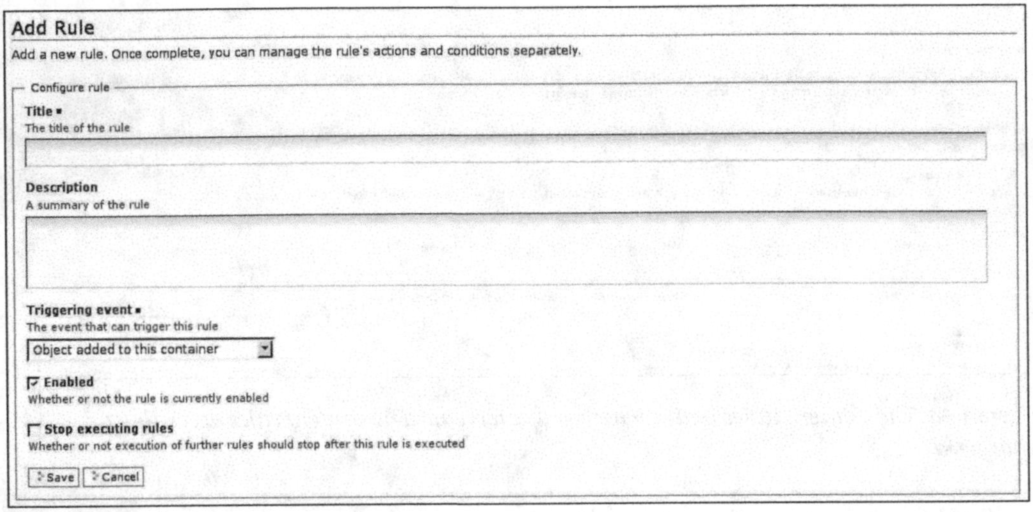

Add Rule

Add a new rule. Once complete, you can manage the rule's actions and conditions separately.

┌─ Configure rule ───
│
│ **Title ▪**
│ The title of the rule
│
│ [   ]
│
│ **Description**
│ A summary of the rule
│
│ [   ]
│ [   ]
│
│ **Triggering event ▪**
│ The event that can trigger this rule
│ [Object added to this container   ▼]
│
│ ☑ **Enabled**
│ Whether or not the rule is currently enabled
│
│ ☐ **Stop executing rules**
│ Whether or not execution of further rules should stop after this rule is executed
│
│ [Save] [Cancel]
└───

Figure 4-49. *The Add Rule panel*

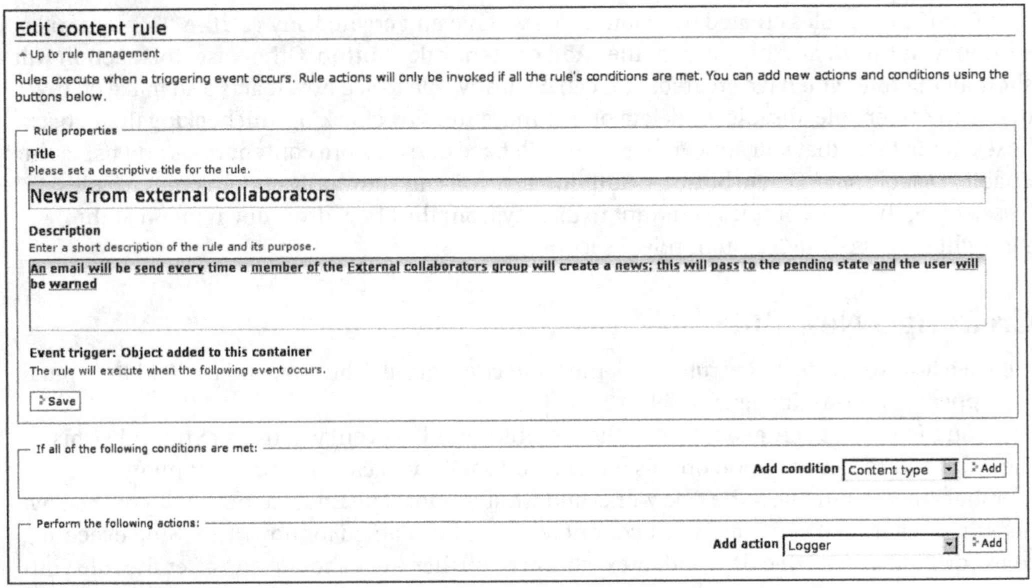

Edit content rule

▲ Up to rule management

Rules execute when a triggering event occurs. Rule actions will only be invoked if all the rule's conditions are met. You can add new actions and conditions using the buttons below.

┌─ Rule properties ──
│
│ **Title**
│ Please set a descriptive title for the rule.
│
│ [News from external collaborators   ]
│
│ **Description**
│ Enter a short description of the rule and its purpose.
│
│ [An email will be send every time a member of the External collaborators group will create a news; this will pass to the pending state and the user will]
│ [be warned   ]
│
│ **Event trigger: Object added to this container**
│ The rule will execute when the following event occurs.
│ [Save]
└───

┌─ If all of the following conditions are met: ────────────────────────────────
│   **Add condition** [Content type ▼] [Add]
└───

┌─ Perform the following actions: ───
│   **Add action** [Logger ▼] [Add]
└───

Figure 4-50. *Setting conditions and actions for your new content rule*

In the "Rule properties" section, you can modify the title and the description of the rule if you'd like. This section also reminds you of the kind of event that will trigger the rule. Note that you can't change this once it has been set. (This is the most important element of the rule; it's what characterizes the rule—so if you want to change it, it probably means you should create a different rule.)

The second section, "If all of the following conditions are met," is self-explanatory. This is where you can create one or more conditions for the rule to be performed. Use the drop-down menu to choose the type of condition, and a new configuration panel will appear, depending on the condition you select. You can match as many conditions as you want. Use the Edit or Remove buttons that appear next to the conditions you added to manage or delete them, and the arrow buttons to move conditions up or down. The conditions available by default are

- *Content type*: This condition makes the rule apply only to a certain content type or certain content types. You will be able to select the content types through the menu that will appear. You can select more than one content type by keeping the Ctrl key pressed while selecting the options.

- *File extension*: This condition makes the rule apply only if the target is a file with a particular extension. If you choose this condition, you'll be given a text field in which to enter the extension.

- *Workflow state*: This condition can restrict rules to objects in particular workflow states. If you choose this condition, a panel will appear where you will be asked to set one or more states through a workflow state list; keep the Ctrl key pressed to select more than one state.

- *Workflow transition*: This condition can restrict rules to execute only after a certain transition. If you choose this condition, a panel will appear, and you will be asked to select one or more options through a Workflow transition list; keep the Ctrl key pressed to select more than one state. This condition will be available only for certain types of content rules (depending on what you set as the event that will trigger your rule).

- *User's group*: This condition can prevent a rule from executing unless the current user is a member of a particular group. If you choose this condition, a panel will appear, and you will be able to select one or more groups from the Group name; to select more than one group, keep the Ctrl key pressed while selecting the options. You can therefore create rules that apply only for actions performed by specific group users; for example, you can monitor the actions of users you don't completely trust, and you can even create special groups of users and then create special rules for them.

- *User's role*: This condition can prevent rules from executing unless the current user has a particular role. If you choose this condition, a panel will appear, and you will be able to select one or more roles from the Roles list; to select more than one role, keep the Ctrl key pressed while selecting the options. You can therefore create rules that apply only for actions performed by users with specific roles.

The "Perform the following actions" section lets you add actions that must be performed by the rule when the conditions configured for it are met. Use the "Add action" drop-down menu to choose the type of action to be performed. A new configuration panel will show up, depending on which action you select. You can match as many actions as you want. Use the Edit or Remove button that will appear to manage or delete them, and use the arrows to move conditions up or down. The conditions available by default are

- *Logger*: This action will output a message to the log system; you can, for example, log content modifications in the event log of your Zope instance, which is the tool that registers events that occur in your Plone instance. You can set the logger name (by default, Rule_log is already set, but you can enter a more specific name—anything that will help you remember the type of actions you want to monitor), the logging level (leave it set to its default), and the message of the log (you can follow the suggestion offered by default in the text field and replace &e with the triggering event and &c with the type of context).

- *Notify user*: This action will create a message for the user. You must enter a sentence for the message (e.g., "A copy of this item has been stored in the 'Archive' folder") and the type of message to be created. When all the conditions set for that rule are met, the system will show the user a message, as Figure 4-51 shows (we chose the Info message type).

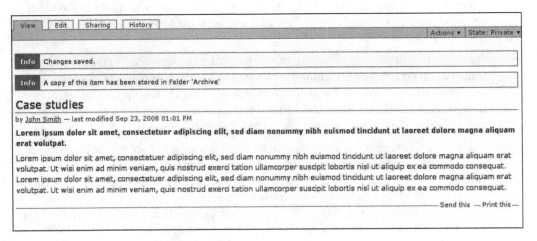

Figure 4-51. *You can set a message to notify the user.*

- *Copy to folder*: This action will create a copy of an item (depending on the conditions you set) to a different folder. If you choose this action, a new panel will appear, and you will be able to select a target folder where a copy of the item will be created. To indicate the target folder, you can enter a path relative to the portal root in the "Target folder" text field and click the Search button to navigate through the different folders.

- *Move to folder*: This action will move an item (depending on the conditions you set) to a different folder. If you choose this action, a new panel will appear, and you will be able to select a target folder where the item will be moved. To indicate the target folder, you can enter a path relative to the portal root in the "Target folder" text field or click the Search button to navigate through the different folders. It's probably a good idea to add a complementary action (Notify user) to this one so that the user will be warned that the item she created will not appear in the folder she was in, because the rule moved it to the target folder.

- *Delete object*: This action, as the name says, deletes an item (depending on the conditions you set).

- *Transition workflow state*: This action will trigger a workflow transition on an object, meaning that the item (depending on the conditions you set) will automatically pass to another workflow state. You will be asked to choose a workflow transition from the drop-down list that will appear. You can, for example, select "Submit for publication" so that the reviewer group can review the items in order to publish them.

- *Send mail*: This action will generate an e-mail that will be sent to one or more addresses. You will be asked to enter a subject, one or more addresses where you want to send the message, and the text of the message. You can, for example, receive a message every time content is published to check everything that becomes visible to the public.

When you are viewing a rule that has already been assigned, you will see a fourth box, called Assignments, that lists the items for which that rule is assigned. You can click the item's name to go directly to it.

Assigning Rules

After you define your rules, you will have to go to the folder or item where you want to apply them to assign them. Don't worry, this task is very easy and gives you the freedom to apply or disable the rule wherever you want! To do so, use the Rules tab on the green strip. The panel shown in Figure 4-52 will show up.

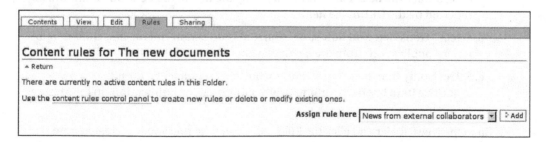

Figure 4-52. *Assigning rules to a folder*

Use the "Assign rule here" drop-down menu to select a rule, and add it by clicking the Add button. (The menu will show you, of course, the rules you've previously defined through the Content Rules panel in the Plone control panel.)

A table will show you the rules (if any) that are already active in that item. Use the buttons below the table to manage them: Enable, Disable, "Apply to subfolders," "Apply to current folder only," and Unassign.

Here's an example that will better explain how the content rules work. Suppose you want to create a rule so that every time a news item is created in the News folder by a member of a certain group (we will suppose you created a group called External Collaborators for members you don't know in person), you will receive an e-mail about it so that you will be able to monitor the activity of that group's members in the News folder. You also want the rule to put the news in the Pending state and notify this fact to the user.

Let's do it together, step-by-step:

1. You have to add a new content rule. To do so, click Content Rules on the Plone control panel to bring up the Content Rules panel, and click the "Add content rule" button at the bottom of the second section.

2. You now have to complete the rule's properties. Enter **News from external collaborators** for the title, and write the following brief description: **An e-mail will be sent every time a member of the External Collaborators group will create a news; this will pass to the Pending state and the user will be warned.** Finally, choose the event that will trigger this rule: "Object added to this container. Click the Save button.

3. Click the rule you just created to set the conditions and actions for it:

   a. Select "Content type" from the "Add condition" menu, and choose News Item from the menu that appears.

   b. Select "User's group" from the "Add condition" menu, and choose the External Collaborators group from the menu that appears.

   c. Select "Send mail" from the "Add action" menu, and complete the form that appears. Enter **Info 'My site'—New news** for the subject, your e-mail as the e-mail recipient, and **A new news item '${title}' was created by a member of the External Collaborators group; the item automatically passed to the Pending state. Check here: ${url} to see the text of the news item.** in the Message text field. In this case, ${title} will be dynamically replaced by the title of the item, and ${url} will be replaced by the URL of the item.

   d. Select "Transition workflow state" from the "Add action" menu, and choose "Submit for publication" from the menu that appears.

   e. Select Notify from the "Add action" menu, and complete the form that appears. Enter **The item has been automatically submitted for publication.** in the Message text field.

4. Go to the News folder and click the Rules tab. Select the rule you just created from the "Assign rule here" drop-down menu, and click the Add button. That's it!

Summary

In this chapter, you have started to configure and customize your Plone web site. You have seen how to use the Site Setup section; how to add and manage users and groups; how to add, eliminate, and move portlets; and how to create content rules.

As a site administrator, you should now have all the skills you need to manage a web site, its content, and the users who contribute to populate and manage it. We surely haven't covered all the features that make Plone so powerful and flexible, but we've given you a broad overview.

In Part 2 of this book, "Configuring Plone," you'll learn more about the structure of Plone, and you'll start exploring the backstage of your web site. You'll see how the Plone architecture is structured, and you'll begin to use the ZMI to configure some aspects of your site.

PART 2

...

Configuring Plone

In the first part of the book, you learned how to work with Plone's front-end user interface; you are now able to add and manage content and to administer a Plone site, performing simple customizations and managing users and groups. It is now time to put your hands on the back end of the system. You will learn how to configure Plone, its graphical design, and its authentication system.

Objectives

In this second part, you will see what lies behind Plone, and you will go through some basic concepts about the structure and logic of Plone. In addition, you will see how to get around the Zope Management Interface, the place where you can deeply customize your application, even if you are not a programmer; you will see how to manage and create new content types and how to search and index them. You will then learn how to change the look and feel of a Plone site; how to manage security and workflows; and how to integrate with other services, such as LDAP and relational databases, for user authentication.

References

If you need further information about how to configure Plone, here some of the most useful places you can find about Plone's back-end interface:

- **The Zope Book** (www.zope.org/Documentation/Books/ZopeBook)
- **Zope Developer's Guide** (www.zope.org/Documentation/Books/ZDG/current)
- **Martin Aspeli's** *Professional Plone Development* (Packt Publishing, 2007)
- www.w3schools.com
- http://plone.org/documentation

CHAPTER 5

■ ■ ■

Behind the Scenes

This chapter covers two main areas. First, we will explain some basic concepts about the technologies behind Plone, specifically, concepts that will help you better understand how your Plone site works "behind the scenes" and how you can customize it. Second, we'll give you some practical information about how to configure, search, and index new content types in the context of the important concepts of acquisition and the Template Attribute Language.

The first area of this chapter will introduce some technical concepts and other features inherited from the application server Zope. If you already are comfortable using the application server Zope that lies behind Plone, you may want to jump to other practical chapters, but if you are interested in discovering why Plone is so powerful and easily extensible, you should read this chapter in its entirety.

Understanding Object-Oriented Web Development

Plone, as you have started to see through the previous chapters, is a powerful CMS that gives you freedom and flexibility. It allows you to organize content through your browser just as you would in a file system directory. For example, you can create some main areas in the root of your web site and then create a hierarchy of subfolders to organize them. Each item you add in your site can be a different type of object (folder, document, image, link, and so on).

But what lies behind the scenes? And what is an *object*? Plone is built over Zope, an application server written in Python and widely based on object-oriented programming techniques. If you are unfamiliar with the concept of objects, don't worry, because there isn't much to know. An object is just a "thing" that encapsulates some behavior. Each different type of object has methods that you can call on the object. An example is a computer mouse. A computer mouse could have methods such as move, click, and right-click. In Plone, every document is an object of a particular type. This means that the document is not just a static bit of text. It is something a little more complicated and far more useful—it's a software object that possesses an object identity that can be accessed programmatically through Plone. So, to be more specific, objects are collections of code and data wrapped up together, and they are published by Zope's publishing engine. However, as you will see in this chapter, the Zope architecture adds another concept when it publishes your object: acquisition. What do we mean by *acquisition*? In a standard object-oriented environment, an object inherits its behavior from its parent. In Plone and Zope, an object also inherits behavior from its container, which is also an object. An object goes through a container hierarchy to figure out how to get its behavior. Since acquisition is a concept that comes from the Zope application server, for more information you can refer to the Zope Book, and we'll discuss acquisition in more depth in the "Object Publishing and Acquisition" section in this chapter.

Object-oriented programming is a common pattern to build modern applications. Its main goals are to be easy to understand and to provide well-known design patterns and the ability to reuse portions of code. Plone inherits these advantages and many others from Zope and the programming language Python. For starters, no code and templates are mixed together. Instead, the presentation, logic, and content (data) will always be separate. If you are a developer, you probably already understand the importance of this, and it will become even clearer as we move ahead. If you would like to know more about object-oriented development, you can visit http://www.zope.org/Documentation/Books/ZopeBook/2_6Edition/ObjectOrientation.stx.

Doing Through-the-Web Development: The ZMI

Developing "through the Web" simply means working through a browser. With Zope, you can develop new features for your Plone site, adding pieces of code directly from your browser through the Zope Management Interface (ZMI). The ZMI is the basic interface that gives you access to Plone's underlying Zope interface. You can add, edit, or delete objects in the ZMI hierarchy with just a few clicks.

How do you access the ZMI? There are two ways to access it:

- Adding /manage to the URL of your site (this operation will lead you to the Zope Management Interface of the section you were in, so you should probably do it from the root)

- Clicking the Site Setup link you find in the top-right corner of the Plone interface and then clicking the Zope Management Interface link

The ZMI for your Plone site should look like Figure 5-1.

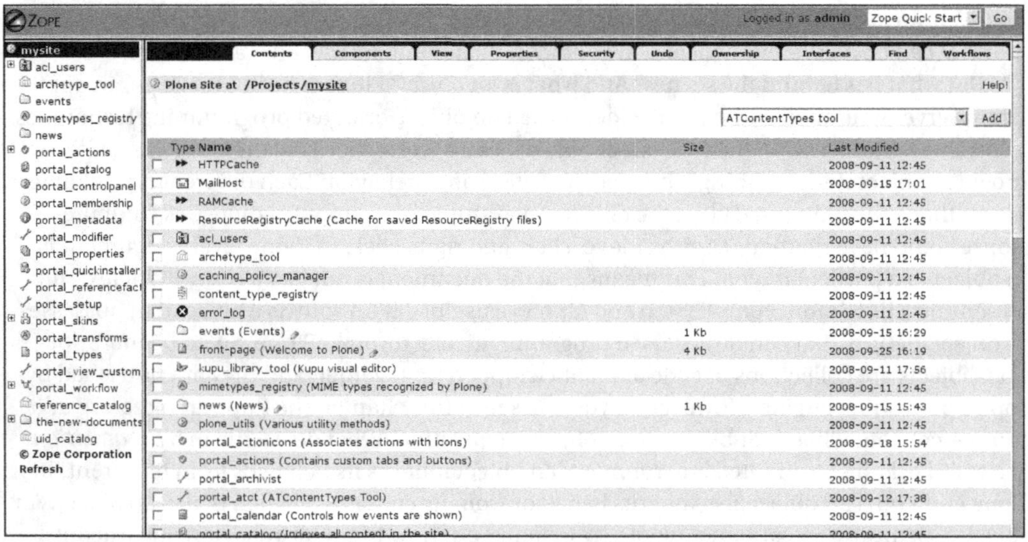

Figure 5-1. *The ZMI of a typical Plone site (part of the screenshot has been cut to make the image more readable)*

Once you are in the ZMI, you can click a particular object, and you will see several management tabs that will lead you to different configuration forms, as shown in Figure 5-2. Common tabs are View, Edit, and Security, but each type of object can have different tabs depending on how the object can be configured.

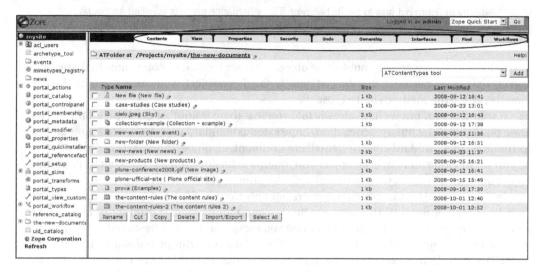

Figure 5-2. *The different tabs you can click to access different configuration forms*

As you can imagine, it is easy to use only a browser to develop new features through the ZMI, which allows you to dispense with the FTP deployment that other frameworks usually require. But working through the Web also has some disadvantages. For example, if you manually customize your site by adding a bunch of scripts and templates and you want to use them elsewhere, it may be difficult and annoying to apply your changes to other sites because you will need to apply changes manually. And, what happens if you miss some configuration? That is why in Plone developing through the file system can sometimes be the best way to operate.

File system development, in contrast to through-the-web development, means that all your behaviors are wrapped up in a Python package containing your code and templates, and if you want, you can keep all the features covered by several automatic tests. This is very important because if someone changes something in the code, you will be alerted. Last, but not least, it is easy to distribute your code. The installation process merely requires extracting the code and putting it in particular places of the Zope instance. We will talk about file system development in Chapter 9.

Understanding Object Publishing and Acquisition

Object publishing and acquisition are low-level concepts that Plone inherits from the application server Zope. If you are not a developer, you can probably jump to the later sections of this chapter. But if you are interested in better understanding how object publishing works, you should continue with this section (in fact, you can even deepen your knowledge by reading the sections of the Zope Book that tackle these topics).

> **Note** Acquisition is a very important and nonintuitive aspect of Plone. To reiterate, in a standard object-oriented environment, an object inherits its behavior from its parent. In Plone and Zope, an object also inherits behavior from its container, which is the object that contains it. An object goes through a container hierarchy to figure out how to get its behavior. This inheritance process is called *acquisition*.

In Plone, you are actually publishing objects that are located in Zope; most of them are objects that are persisted in the object database. On these objects you can get services by directly calling the methods that expose them.

It sounds clear, but we have already told you that there is another concept adopted in the Zope publishing machinery: acquisition. Zope extends standard object-oriented programming techniques. In a standard object-oriented environment, an object inherits its behavior from its parent. In Plone and Zope, an object also inherits behavior from its container, that is, the object that contains it, as we mentioned at the beginning of this chapter.

In Zope, an object can inherit behaviors not only from itself and its parent classes but also from its container parents! Thus, you can apply a template or call a Python script in a particular context by acquisition. For example, when you request a Uniform Resource Locator (URL) from Plone, an object in the environment is called. Plone does this by translating the URL into a path. So, if the URL is /mysite/login_form, Plone breaks that URL down into a path and looks up each of those objects in the database. It finds the Plone object and then a login_form object inside the Plone object. Looking up this path is called *traversal*; essentially, Zope traverses across those objects and then calls the last one in the path.

When Zope calls the login_form object, the object is executed in its context. The term *context* is something you will hear a lot of in Plone. It is merely the current context of the object being executed. In this case, it is /mysite. The context changes a lot as you move through a Plone site. If you called the URL /mysite/Members/login_form in a browser, then the context would be /mysite/Members. The main idea is that you can put an object in the root of a Plone site, and any object can get to it through acquisition.

Just as with standard object-oriented programming, you can also override an object through acquisition, for example by putting an object with the same ID as another object in your Plone site into a different folder for the same site. This use case is very useful because it allows you to modify entire sections by adding only one object to the folder tree.

Let's imagine you are managing a web site of a company. All the pages of the web site display a particular banner (for example a red banner) on the top of the screen. Say you want to have a different banner in one particular section instead of the default one in the root of the portal.

Take the following hierarchy:

```
banner.jpg (background red)
      |_ Technologies
            |_ Wood technology
                  |_ ...
            |_ Plastic technology
                  |_ ...
            |_ ...
```

If you want to show a different banner in the "Wood technology" and "Plastic technology" sections, you just have to put a different banner.jpg into the respective folders, because the closest banner.jpg takes precedence. Look at the following example:

```
banner.jpg (background red)
     |_ Technologies
            |_ Wood technology
                   |_ banner.jpg (background brown)
                   |_ ...
            |_ Plastic technology
                   |_ banner.jpg (background blue)
                   |_ ...
            |_ ...
```

In this case, you have a common banner in the entire site, but for each technology section you will have a different banner without writing any Python code, without writing any templates, and without adding if statements. So, nontechnical users can easily override this image without writing any code and wasting time!

Although this probably makes sense right now, acquisition can get quite complicated, especially when looking through the context hierarchy (which can occur). If you want to learn more about it, you can read Zope lead developer Jim Fulton's excellent discussion of acquisition at http://www.zope.org/Members/jim/Info/IPC8/AcquisitionAlgebra/index.html.

Managing Content Types Through the ZMI

You saw in Chapter 3 all the content types you can add, by default, in a Plone site: pages, images, news items, and so on. But you can also create custom content types through the ZMI. Do you want a document object to have different tabs at the top? Do you want a document object to be manipulated differently, look differently, and even be called something completely different? No problem—you can change your instance of Plone through the Web.

The definition for creating a content type is usually dictated by the requirement that users need to add, edit, and control these objects. It can be tempting to start creating a content type for every type of object, but as with all development, you need to be careful. Would it be possible to use one content type instead of two, with only minor differences? Knowing how to figure this out will come from experience, but the next few chapters will certainly help.

Configuring Content Types

So, your Plone site contains content types, but how does the Plone site know how they are configured? The answer is that attributes, methods, security, and skins of any of the content types are defined on the file system in Python and associated code. This information is enough for Plone to understand how to use the product. The only exception to this, as you have seen, is the workflow, which is normally defined externally from the content type. Some products have their own workflow that is added to the content type for its behavior.

Each content type in Plone has a setting in the portal_types tool. Although each content type in the portal_types tool has only one setting, that type can have an unlimited number of objects in your database. The configuration is looked up when needed, so if you change the configuration, you will automatically update all the objects of that type in the database.

To access the registration information, go to the ZMI (in the root, which is www.mysite.com/manage), and click the portal_types tool. You will be presented with a list of all the content types registered in this Plone site, as shown in Figure 5-3. Most of these content types are recognizable as something you would add through the Plone interface with a few exceptions, such as Plone Site, TempFolder, and so on.

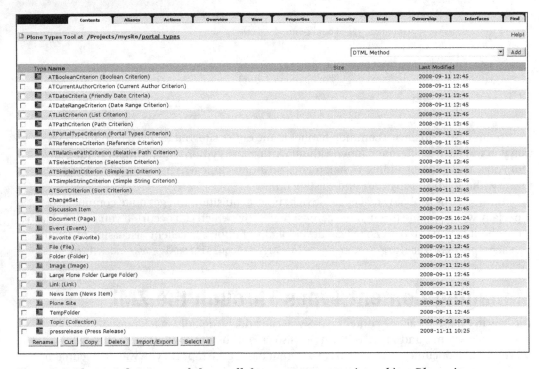

Figure 5-3. *The* portal_types *tool shows all the content types registered in a Plone site.*

Each of these objects is an instance of factory type information, which is the name for a particular type of configuration. Click any of these objects to access the type's information (see Figure 5-4 for an example); for example, when you click Event, you get the local copy of the information about the content type. You can alter this through the Web to change its configuration. The following are the values you will see if you open the configuration form for a content type:

- *Title*: This is a title for the content type.

- *Description*: This is the description that appears for this content type. This is used if you go to the folder contents and click Add without selecting a content type to add; a list of all the content types organized by descriptions will appear.

- *i18n Domain*: This is for internationalization and localization.

- *Icon*: This is the ID of the icon that's used for this content type.

- *Product metatype*: This is the metatype for this content type. This matches up the Plone content type with a Zope metatype.

- *Product name*: This is the product name where this metatype is defined.

- *Product factory method*: This is the method that's called by the product factory to create this piece of content.

- *Initial view name*: This isn't used in Plone.

- *Implicitly addable*: This indicates whether this content can be added to Plone. If this is selected, then it can be added, unless explicitly specified otherwise.

- *Filter content types*: If this content type is a folder, then enable this to filter the content types that can be added by users to this folder object.

- *Allowed content types*: If this content type can contain other items and "Filter content types" is enabled, only the types of content specified in this list will be allowed.

- *Allow discussion*: This indicates whether users can add comments to this content type.

- *Default view method*: This indicates the default template.

- *Available view methods*: This is the list of available view methods on the current type in the menu Display shown in the green bar of Plone.

- *Fall back to default view*: This option, if selected, implements a fallback to default view; that is, if a selected view (i.e., a template) does not exist, the system will return the default view instead of a NotFound error.

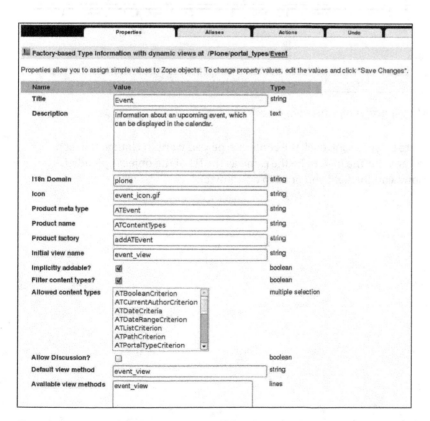

Figure 5-4. *The type's information panel for the Event content type (the last part of the panel has been cut)*

We will now cover some of the aspects of this registration information in a bit more detail, including showing some examples.

Changing Icons for a Content Type

To see just how simple it is to change the details of your content, let's look at a simple example: how do you change the icon for a content type? Say you don't like the icon that appears to identify a certain content type. It is a pretty simple matter to upload a new image and then make sure that the value for the icon is set in the form described previously.

Note Icons work best if they have a transparent background and they are 16 pixels wide and 16 pixels high.

To change the icon for a content type, you can follow these simple steps:

1. Click portal_skins, click "custom," and add a new image with an ID (for example mynewsitem_icon.gif), as shown in Figure 5-5.

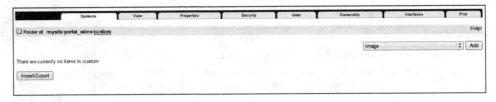

Figure 5-5. *Adding a new image to change a content type icon*

2. Then in the portal_types tool, click the content type you want to change the icon of, and set the value for the icon to be the same as the ID of the object uploaded (Figure 5-6 shows you the field you need to customize).

To test that the icon has changed, go to the Plone interface, and look for where the object may appear; for example, do a search or look at the Add New menu (see Figure 5-9 later in this chapter for an example).

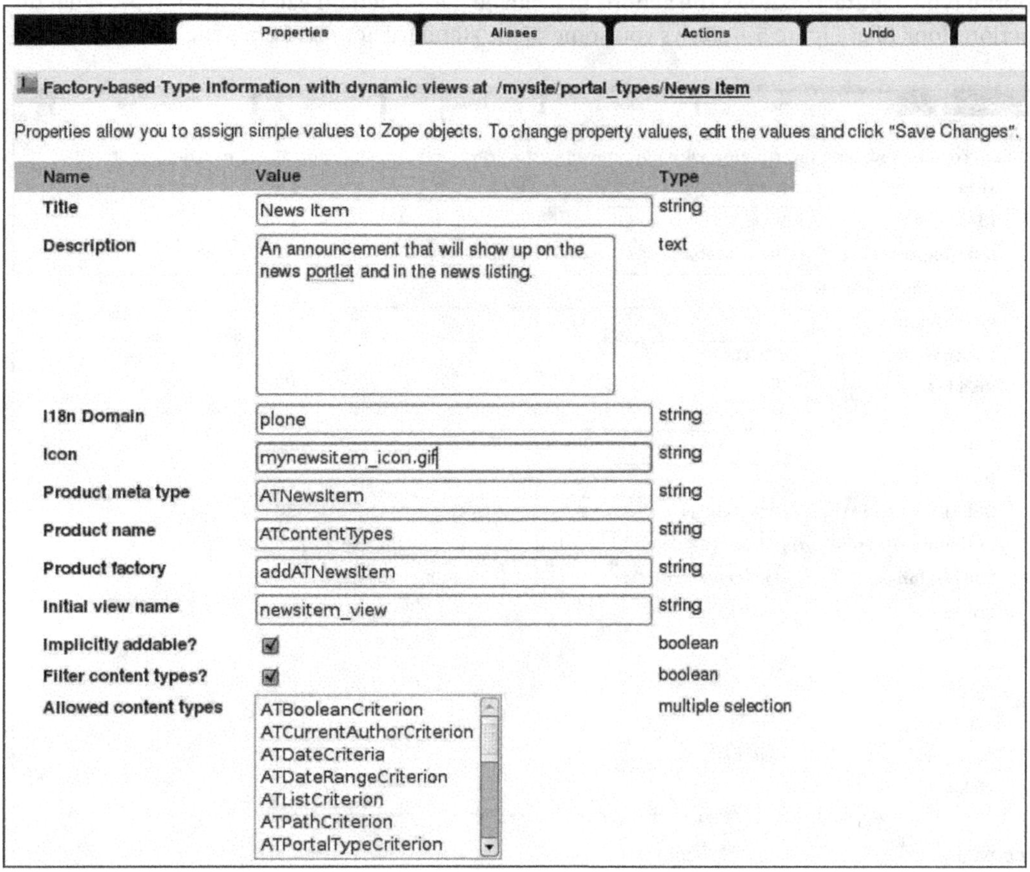

	Properties	Aliases	Actions	Undo

Factory-based Type Information with dynamic views at /mysite/portal_types/News Item

Properties allow you to assign simple values to Zope objects. To change property values, edit the values and click "Save Changes".

Name	Value	Type
Title	News Item	string
Description	An announcement that will show up on the news portlet and in the news listing.	text
I18n Domain	plone	string
Icon	mynewsitem_icon.gif	string
Product meta type	ATNewsItem	string
Product name	ATContentTypes	string
Product factory	addATNewsItem	string
Initial view name	newsitem_view	string
Implicitly addable?	☑	boolean
Filter content types?	☑	boolean
Allowed content types	ATBooleanCriterion ATCurrentAuthorCriterion ATDateCriteria ATDateRangeCriterion ATListCriterion ATPathCriterion ATPortalTypeCriterion	multiple selection

Figure 5-6. *Change the value for the Icon field of the content type.*

Looking at Actions

Actions in Plone are activities that can be performed upon content items. When you are look-ing at the content type configuration in `portal_types`, you will see an Actions tab on each portal type. Figure 5-7 shows the actions that can be performed on each content type. What do actions look like? Figure 5-8 shows you some of the standard actions for a page.

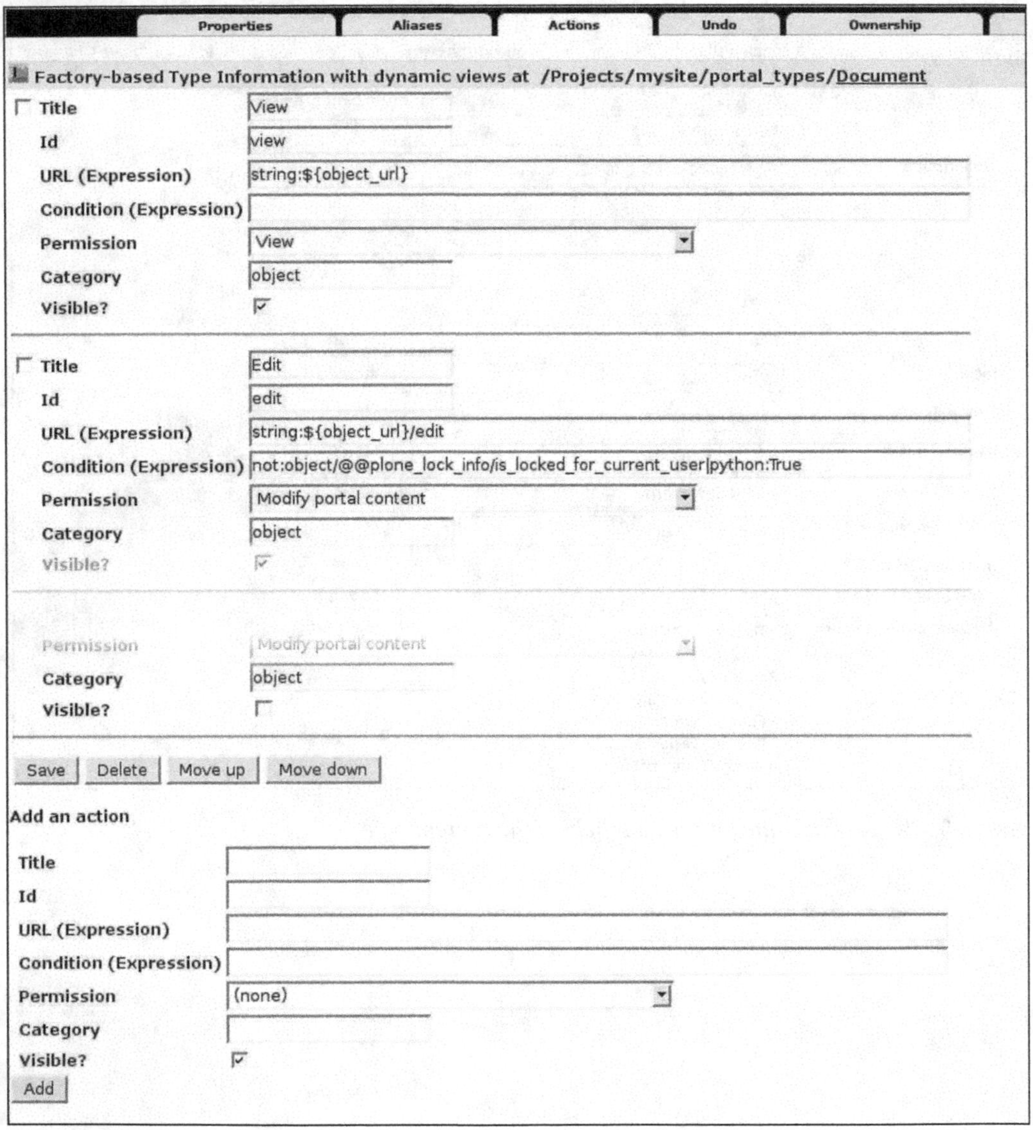

Figure 5-7. *The ZMI panel that shows you the actions for the Page content type*

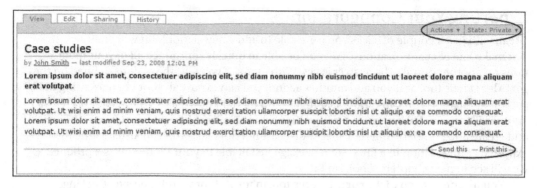

Figure 5-8. *Some of the actions you can perform in the Page content type*

As we mentioned earlier, actions are stored on tool objects. Many of the tools contain actions, but you really don't have a great way to search for the location of an action. If you want to change a particular action on your Plone site, you have to find the tool that stores it. The following tips help you find an action:

- If you are looking for an action such as viewing or editing a piece of content, then it is on the particular content type in the `portal_types` tool.

- If you are looking for an action for the site, then it is in the `portal_actions` tool.

- If you can't find the action so far, look in a related tool; for example, joining and logging in are in `portal_membership`.

- If you can't find the action you are looking for after trying the previous tips, go to `portal_actions` to see the list of tools and look through all the action providers.

Plone looks up the actions for content types in the following manner:

- For an object, all the actions are queried.

- For each action, conditions, permissions, and visible properties are checked; if they pass, then the action will be returned.

- Each action will be shown in the user interface, usually in the form of tabs at the top of the content or at the top of the site.

- The URL for this action is the URL of the object with the actual action appended to the end.

Once you have found the action, you can then customize it as much as you like. For instance, if you want to add a new action as a green tab for a document, you have to go and find the correct place (for actions that have to appear as a green tab for the content type, you would have to add the category `object_tabs`). Normally actions are used as tabs in Plone, but since they can be called programmatically, they could be used in any way.

Exporting Your Configuration

Great, with just a couple of clicks you were able to add a new action! But what happens if you make lots of customizations? Will you be able to quickly reproduce all of your modifications on another portal? The answer is yes. With Plone, if you edit the actions defined on the portal_actions tool or if you add another action, you can export all your changes using the portal_setup tool. You can export a configuration (better known as a *profile*), import it into another Plone site, back up your configuration when all works fine with just a couple of clicks, and create and compare different snapshots. Last but not least, you can also include the exported configuration in a file system package installable in your Plone site as a product, as we will see in next chapters. Cool, isn't it?

You just need to go to the portal_setup tool in the ZMI of your Plone site. Clicking the Export tab, you can export all the available steps or just those steps related to the tools involved in your customizations. Clicking the button, you will be asked to download a compressed file containing the XML files describing your configuration. Once you've saved the tar.gz file locally, you can go to another Plone portal and, through its portal_setup tool, import your configuration: to do so, click the Import tab, go to the end of the panel, use the Browse button to upload the saved tarball, and then click the Import uploaded tarball button. You should have correctly imported the changes.

Generally, you can export all of the "handmade" configurations on the ZMI using the portal_setup tool, not just portal_actions! So, if you change some settings in portal_skins, portal_properties, portal_workflows, and so on, no matter—with Plone, you can save, export, and reproduce your setup easily on another Plone site.

So, what does a profile look like? Here is the XML code representing the default Plone configuration for portal_actions:

```xml
<?xml version="1.0"?>
<object name="portal_actions" meta_type="Plone Actions Tool"
   xmlns:i18n="http://xml.zope.org/namespaces/i18n">
 <action-provider name="portal_workflow"/>
 <action-provider name="portal_types"/>
 <action-provider name="portal_actions" />

 ...
 <object name="object" meta_type="CMF Action Category">
  <property name="title"/>
  <object name="folderContents" meta_type="CMF Action" i18n:domain="plone">
   <property name="title" i18n:translate="">Contents</property>
   <property name="description" i18n:translate=""/>
   <property name="url_expr">
    string:${globals_view/getCurrentFolderUrl}/folder_contents
   </property>
   <property name="icon_expr"/>
   <property name="available_expr">object/displayContentsTab</property>
```

```
 <property name="permissions">
  <element value="List folder contents"/>
 </property>
 <property name="visible">True</property>
 </object>
...
```

Creating a New Content Type from an Existing Type

You may need to create a specific type of document in your web site for which none of the default content types in Plone suits you requirements. Maybe you need to add press releases to your site; previously, you usually just used a news item, but now you would like to apply a different workflow on it and have a different look, say adding a footer that shows up automatically when you create a new item. How can you do this easily?

The answer is that you can repurpose a content type. *Repurposing* is taking the information for an existing content type and creating multiple, slightly different copies of the same type. So, repurposing may be a quick and simple option to work in this case (or any similar cases)!

A big drawback of this approach is that you can't really change much beyond the actions, the skins, and some of content type settings. So, before you proceed down this path, please be aware that you are limited to these points; you can't add new fields or attributes, for example. If you want to do more, check out how to write content types in the next two chapters.

Say for now you want to make a press release type that is like a news item but does the following:

- It has the name Press Release in the drop-down list.

- It has a different icon.

- It has a different workflow from a news item.

- It has a different view.

- It keeps the same data structure as a news item.

- It retains the news item type.

For this example, we'll show how to take the factory-based type information for a news item, load it into the portal_types tool, and then call it Press Release. This will allow you to reuse all the existing code and information while giving you new options.

In the ZMI, access portal_types, and complete the following steps:

1. The simple way to repurpose an existing type such as the default news is copying and pasting the default news item in portal_types, then renaming the pasted item to Press Release, and finally configuring it properly.

2. How to change an icon was discussed earlier in this chapter; simply upload the image into your custom directory and then alter the Icon property in the `portal_types` page for the new Press Release content type. The result will be something similar to what you can see in Figure 5-9.

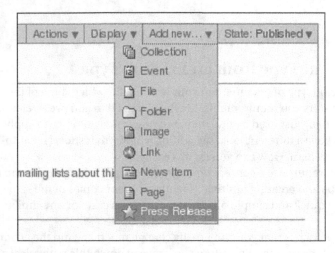

Figure 5-9. *You can easily change the icon of a content type; the new icon will be shown, for example, in the Add New menu.*

3. If you go to `portal_workflow`, you can see that each content type has its own workflow. Because this is now a new content type, you can now change the workflow for press releases only. Perhaps press releases require an extra stage of review, or they, when published, send e-mails to certain users. You can now make a new workflow, as you will learn in Chapter 7, and assign it to your press release.

4. Adding a new view means customizing the `newsitem_view` page template and renaming it to something meaningful, such as `pressrelease_view`. You may want to alter that file to add some information about the company at the bottom of the page. For example:

```
<h2>About the Press area</h2>
<p>This news is made by our press area staff</p>
```

5. After you have saved your changes to your new page template, return to the settings for the press release in `portal_types`, and go to the Actions page. Change the action for viewing a press release from pointing to `newsitem_view` to pointing to `pressrelease_view`. Now whenever you view a press release, that view page will display, as shown in Figure 5-10.

In this case, we have added a Press Release object, and the footer about the press area staff is in the template so that users don't need to remember to type this in every time.

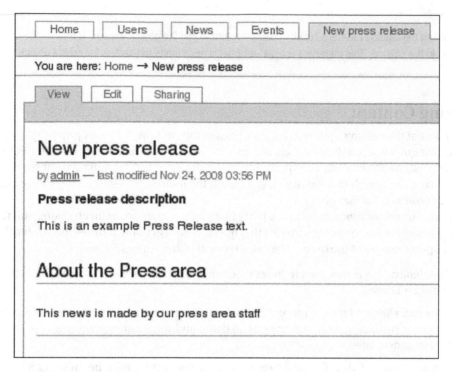

Figure 5-10. *The view of our new Press Release content type: it shows the footer we added in the content type configuration. The user will not have to add this information each time, but it will be shown when the item is saved.*

Understanding the Portal Catalog

You have seen how to search for content in Plone, but we will now go into detail and show how the underlying categorization and searching of content occurs. The portal_catalog tool stores all of this information, which is a slightly different and extended version of the underlying ZCatalog tool. You will find an excellent online reference for ZCatalog at http://zope.org/Documentation/Books/ZopeBook/2_6Edition/SearchingZCatalog.stx.

The catalog provides three key elements to a Plone site:

- It creates indexes of content.

- It holds metadata about the content in the index.

- It provides a search interface to quickly examine the content of your Plone site.

Between all of the different objects present in your Zope site, only the actual instances of your content types are cataloged. Zope objects, tools, and other objects aren't placed in the catalog. For this reason, the catalog tool is closely tied to the content types and their usage. You can access the catalog by accessing the portal_catalog tool in the ZMI.

Note When the catalog returns a result, it doesn't return to you the object; instead, it returns the metadata stored in the catalog. This metadata is a series of fields or columns for each value on the object.

Indexing Content

The first part of the catalog's job is to build indexes of the content. An index primarily provides a method for quickly and efficiently searching the content. For this reason, the content of the index isn't designed to be clear or to make sense; it is designed for fast and efficient searching instead. When you search in a Plone site, you search the indices, and the catalog will return matching result sets for that query.

An index queries a Plone object for a particular value, a method, or an attribute, and then it indexes whatever that object returns for that query. How it actually indexes the content depends upon the type of the index. The main types of indices are as follows:

- *DateIndex*: This is designed to index dates and lets you do searches based on DateIndex dates and times.

- *DateIndexRange*: This is a more efficient implementation of DateIndex for cases where you have two dates, such as start and end dates, and you want to perform lots of searches within those dates.

- *KeywordIndex*: This will return a result if any of the keywords in the index match the given query. This is ideal for searching subjects or keywords on objects.

- *ZCTextIndex*: This index provides full-text searching capabilities efficiently on pieces of text. It supports a large number of features, discussed in detail later.

You can see what indexes are defined in a catalog by clicking `portal_catalog` and selecting the Indexes tab. This will give you a list of all the indexes defined in your Plone site. The columns are the name of the index, the type, the number of hits, and when the index was last modified.

If you are ever unsure of the contents of an index, then you can see the contents of the indexes in the ZMI. Click `portal_catalog`, and select Catalog, and this will list every object cataloged at this time. Click an object, and a window will pop up with the contents of the index and the metadata. The metadata comes first, so scroll down to see the indices.

To add, remove, or alter the indices, return to the Indexes tab. Use the usual Add drop-down box to add a new index or remove an index. If you want to run a reindexing of a particular index, then select the indexes in the left, and click the Reindex button. If you add an index to the catalog, it isn't populated, meaning you then need to click the Reindex button to ensure that there is some content in your index.

Note If you have a large site, this indexing can be quite long and processor-intensive, so you should avoid doing this during peak load times.

How an Object Is Indexed

Content types are indexed automatically because they inherit from a class called PortalContent, which inherits from a mix-in class called CMFCatalogAware. The CMFCatalogAware class handles all the code to ensure that when you add, edit, cut, copy, delete, or rename an object, the catalog and workflow are kept up-to-date.

Essentially, the object is passed to the catalog, and the appropriate instruction for the catalog is called (index, remove from index, and so on). The catalog then runs through each index and for each index queries the object by looking for attributes or methods on the object. For most indices, the attribute or method looked up is the same name as the index. For example, for the index name Title, CMFCatalogAware would look for an attribute or method named Title and populate the index with the result and then repeat the process with each of the metadata columns.

Two exceptions to this process are the FieldIndex and TopicIndex types. When you add a FieldIndex, you can specify that the index examine a different value than the name of the index. For example, you could make an index with the ID getVersion, which looks at the value of version.

As you will see later, some indices have advantages over others, so it can be useful to have two different indices pointing to the same value.

TopicIndex is a different type of index in that it builds up a series of sets at the time the content is indexed. If you wanted to do a lot of searches for multiple conditions, then you cannot query with normal catalog searches. For example, if you want to search only for images that have a title with more than 30 characters, then you could add a search for o.portal_type == 'Image' and len(o.Title()) > 30. To do this, you need to create a TopicIndex and then click the index from the Indexes tab; you can even add multiple expressions to build up an index. At this time, TopicIndex indices aren't used anywhere in Plone.

Searching or walking through the directory tree waking up the objects from the ZODB is slow and inefficient. As you will see in this chapter, it is better to use the portal_catalog tool, querying one or more indices and retrieving a list of small objects named *brains* (see the "Using Search Results" section in this chapter).

How Do You Reindex All the Content on Your Plone Site?

The CMFCatalogAware mix-in class also provides two useful methods for reindexing a particular object: reindexObject and reindexObjectSecurity. With reindexObject, you can refresh all indices without any parameter or pass a list of indices that need to be refreshed. The method reindexObjectSecurity instead refreshes security-related indices for the given object.

If you have made a large number of code-level changes, put in a new product, or renamed or moved your root Plone object, then you may need to reindex all the content on your site. In the ZMI, click portal_catalog, click Advanced, and click Update Catalog. This will run the process of updating your catalog.

■**Caution** This is an even more task-intensive than reindexing just one index, and it can take a very long time and use a lot of memory and processing power if you have a large database.

Searching the Catalog

Of course, the biggest question is how to search the catalog and use the results. The first of these tasks depends upon the indices, so we cover each of the indices and show how to search them. The second of these tasks involves manipulating the results, so we'll show you how to do this too.

All of the following examples are in Python because it is the best way to search a catalog. We also show a quick example of how to hook this into a page template. We strongly recommend using Python for manipulating the catalog because it really is the best way to do things; it allows you the greatest flexibility without having to worry about the syntax.

In general, you achieve searching by calling the method searchResults on the portal_catalog object and passing through a series of keyword parameters. A couple of reserved keywords exist, but the rest are mapped directly to the indices of the same name.

So if you wanted to search the SearchableText index, you would pass a keyword parameter for SearchableText through to the search method. The reserved keywords are as follows:

- sort_on: This is the index to sort the results on, assuming that the index allows sorting (full-text indexes don't allow sorting).

- sort_order: This allows a reverse or descending sort on a certain parameter; if not specified, the default is ascending.

- sort_limit: This is an optimization hint to make sorting a little quicker, returning only the number of items that you want.

So, a general search for the first five published items ordered by date looks something like this:

```
context.portal_catalog.searchResults(
    review_state = "published",
    sort_order = "reverse",
    sort_limit = 5,
    sort_on="Date"

)
```

The search will return the intersection of the index results, so this will find the first five items that are published, in reverse date order. You can't do searches that are the union of results; you could do multiple results and then add the results together, but this is a rather unusual case.

If you perform a search with no values, then the entire contents of the catalog are returned. By default, all searches add values for effective and end dates, ensuring that you see content only between these times, unless the user calling the search has the "Access inactive portal content" permission.

Searching a Field or Date Index

To search a FieldIndex index, pass through the value of the field. Any hits that match will be returned; for example, to search for all the images in a site, use the following:

```
results = context.portal_catalog.searchResults(
    Type = "Image"
)
```

A field index can take a range of objects as well, and the index will attempt to find all the values in between by performing a comparison of the values. This range could be between two dates, two numbers, or two strings; it really depends upon the value of FieldIndex. You do this by passing a dictionary to the index, rather than just a string. The dictionary should contain two values: a list called *query*, which contains the values to be tested, and a *range*, which defines a range of the values. The range is a string of one of the following:

- min: Anything larger than the smallest item
- max: Anything smaller than the largest item
- minmax: Anything smaller than the largest and bigger than the smallest

For example, to find all events that have an end time greater than now (in other words, anything in the future), use the following:

```
from Products.CMFCore.utils import getToolByName
from DateTime import DateTime
portal_catalog = getToolByName(context, 'portal_catalog')
now = DateTime()
results = portal_catalog.searchResults(
        Type = "Event"
        end = { "query": [now,],
                    "range": "min" }
)
```

To search on a range, such as all news items in December, you would need to calculate the start and end dates for the month. From those dates, you can then construct the following query:

```
start = DateTime('2009/12/01')
end = DateTime('2009/12/31')
results = portal_catalog.searchResults(
        Type = "News Item",
        created = { "query": [start, end],
                        "range": "minmax" }
)
```

Date indices work in the same manner as field indices, and often you'll see dates placed inside field indices, which works just fine.

Searching a KeywordIndex

By default, a KeywordIndex returns all the values that match in the keyword index. Subject is the only KeywordIndex; this is the keyword that a user has assigned to an object through the Properties tab of the Plone interface. To search for all items with the keyword *Africa*, use this:

```
results = context.portal_catalog.searchResults(
        Subject = "Africa"
)
```

Similar to a FieldIndex, a KeywordIndex can be passed a more complicated query, with several objects and an and/or operator ("or" is the default). This allows you to find all objects that have almost any combination of keywords. To find all objects that have the subject *Africa* and *sun*, use the following:

```
results = context.portal_catalog.searchResults(
        Subject = { "query": ["Africa", "sun"],
                        "operator": "and" }
)
```

Searching a PathIndex

A path index allows you to search for all objects in a certain path. It will return every object below a current location, so if you ask for all objects in Members, it will return everything in everybody's home directories. For example, for all objects that have Members in their path, use this:

```
results = context.portal_catalog.searchResults(
        path = "/Plone/Members"
)
```

If you want to further restrict this, you can do so by passing through a level parameter that sets where you expect the value to be. The level is a number representing its position in the path, from the left when splitting it up by forward slashes. For example, in the previous code, Plone is level 0, Members is level 1, and so on. Similarly to KeywordIndex, you can pass through an and/or operator. To get all objects in the /Plone/Members/danae folder and the /Plone/testing/danae folder, use the following:

```
results = context.portal_catalog.searchResults(
        path = { "query": ["danae"],
                "level" : 2 }
)
```

Searching a ZCTextIndex

ZCTextIndex is the most complicated of all indexes and takes a whole host of options. Each one requires a lexicon; fortunately, Plone creates and configures all this out of the box.

If you click portal_catalog, select the Contents tab, and click plone_lexicon, you can see the default configuration of the lexicon. Clicking the Query tab will show you all the words that are in the lexicon built out of your Plone site content.

The ZCTextIndex is searched using the format we described in Chapter 3. It takes terms for searches like those you can use in Google or other search engines. At its most basic, you can search for any term (note that this is case insensitive), like so:

```
results = context.portal_catalog.searchResults(
        SearchableText = "space"
)
```

But you can also search for all of the following, as you already saw in Chapter 3:

- *Globbing*: You can use an asterisk to signify any letters. For example, entering **Tues*** matches *Tuesday* and *Tuesdays*. You can't use the asterisk at the beginning of a word, though.

- *Single wildcards*: You can use a question mark anywhere to signify one letter. For example, entering **ro?e** matches *rope*, *rote*, *role*, and so on. You can't use the question mark at the beginning of a word, though.

- *And*: You can use the word *and* to signify that both terms on either side of the *and* must exist. For example, entering **Rome and Tuesday** will return a result of when both those words are in the content.

- *Or*: You can use the word *or* to signify that either terms can exist. For example, entering **Rome or Tuesday** will return a result of when either of those words are in the content.

- *Not*: You can use the word *not* to return results where the word isn't present; a prefix of *and* is required. For example, entering **welcome and not page** would return matches for pages that contained *welcome*, but not *page*.

- *Phrases*: Phrases are grouped with double quotes (" ") and signify several words one after the other. For example, entering **"welcome page"** matches *This welcome page is used to introduce you to the Plone Content Management System*, but not any content that contains just *Welcome*.

- *Not phrase*: You can specify a phrase with a minus (-) prefix. For example, entering **welcome - "welcome page"** matches all pages with *welcome* in them, but not ones that match the phrase *welcome page*.

Using Search Results

So, you have some results, but now what do you do with them? The first thing a lot of people do is look at the results and assume that it is a list of the objects that were cataloged. Well, it isn't; rather, it's a series of catalog brains. These *brains* are actually lazy objects that contain the metadata columns defined earlier. You can access any of these columns as if they were attributes. For example, to print all the IDs of result objects, use the following:

```
results = context.portal_catalog.searchResults()
for result in results:
    print result.getId
return printed
```

In this example, getId is the name of a metadata column, so it will display the value for getId that the catalog had for that object.

If you try to access a value that doesn't exist as a metadata column, then you will get an AttributeError. The following are a few methods available from a catalog brain:

- getPath: This returns the physical path for this object inside Zope.

- getURL: This returns the URL for this object with virtual hosting applied.

- getObject: This returns the actual object.

- getRID: This is a unique ID for the object in the catalog, and it changes each time the object is uncataloged. It is for internal purposes only.

So, if you wanted to get the object for each result, you can do so, as you will see in the following example. However, there is a reason the catalog doesn't do this: it's expensive (in terms of computation) because it involves waking up an object from the database (and all the objects in between) and making lots of security checks. If you can, try to make your metadata contain the right information, you will have a much faster application. Obviously, sometimes metadata can't contain everything, but it's worth considering in the design. To get each object, use the following:

```
results = context.portal_catalog.searchResults()
for result in results:
    object = result.getObject()
    print object
return printed
```

Since you have a Python list of these brains, it's now straightforward to manipulate the results in a manner that you see fit. To find out how many results were returned, you can just call the length function (in Python, len()) on the list, like so:

```
results = context.portal_catalog.searchResults()
print "Number of results", len(results)
return printed
```

To get just the first ten items, use a Python slice, like so:

```
results = context.portal_catalog.searchResults()
return results[:10]
```

To do further filtering, you could manually filter the whole list, like so:

```
results = context.portal_catalog.searchResults()
for result in results[:10]:
    # Title returns a string so we can use the find method of
    # a string to look for occurrence of a word
    if result.Title.find("Plone") > -1:
        print result.Title
return printed
```

To get a random object from the catalog, use the random module, like so:

```
import random
results = context.portal_catalog.searchResults()
r = random.choice(results)
object = r.getObject()
return object
```

Tying It All Together: Making a Search Form

In the previous discussion, we showed you how to get some results out of the catalog, and we used Script (Python) objects to demonstrate that. But you are probably asking yourself, how can I do this from a page template?

Now we will talk about the page templating system commonly used in Plone: Zope Page Templates (ZPT). It generates valid XML and allows you to create dynamic web pages for Zope web applications. Zope Page Templates use the Template Attribute Language (TAL), which consists of special tag attributes. But TAL is not the topic of this chapter; we will introduce it in Chapter 6; for details about ZPT, you can take a look at the Zope Book (http://www.zope.org/Documentation/Books/ZopeBook/2_6Edition/ZPT.stx).

We will assume you have the results from a catalog query and loop through them in a page template using tal:repeat. This is how a lot of portlets are put together; the published and events portlets just do both queries and then show the results.

Those portlets embed the query in a page template either by calling it directly:

```
<div tal:define="results python:➥
here.portal_catalog.searchResults(portal_type="Event")">
```

or by calling a separate Script (Python) object that returns the results. For example, in the following, the script is called getCatalogResults:

```
##parameters=
kw = {}
# enter your query into the kw dictionary
return context.portal_catalog(**kw)
```

In a page template, you would get the results in the following manner:

```
<div tal:define="results here/getCatalogResults">
```

After doing this, you need to loop through the results using the standard tal:repeat syntax. So you can access each metadata column directly in the TAL by making a path expression to the column. You could get the title from the metadata by calling result/Title. The following code is an example page that loops through the contents of getCatalogResults and displays each item in a simple unordered list:

```
<html xmlns="http://www.w3.org/1999/xhtml" xml:lang="en-US"
      lang="en-US"
      metal:use-macro="here/main_template/macros/master"
      i18n:domain="plone">
<body>
<div metal:fill-slot="main">
<ul tal:define="results here/getCatalogResults">
    <li tal:repeat="result results">
        <a href=""
           tal:attributes="href result/getURL"
           tal:content="result/Title" />
        <span tal:replace="result/Description" />
    </li>
</ul>
</div>
</body>
</html>
```

One property of the searchResults method is that if you don't pass any parameters to the function, it will look them up from the incoming request. So if you wanted to allow a form to post parameters to your results, then all you have to do is change the previous results line to the following:

```
<ul tal:define="
    results python: here.portal_catalog.searchResults(REQUEST=request)
    ">
```

Now you can redo your query and append any index to the URL. For example, if you called this page template testResults and appended ?Type=Document to the end of the URL of your browser, only the documents in your site would appear. The following is a form to call your page template:

```
<html xmlns="http://www.w3.org/1999/xhtml" xml:lang="en-US"
      lang="en-US"
      metal:use-macro="here/main_template/macros/master"
      i18n:domain="plone">
<body>
<div metal:fill-slot="main">
  <p>Select a content type to search for</p>
  <form method="post" action="testResults">
    <select name="Type">
      <option
        tal:repeat="value
python:here.portal_catalog.uniqueValuesFor('portal_type')"
        tal:content="value" />
        </select>
        <br />
        <input type="submit" class="context">
    </form>
</div>
</body>
</html>
```

This script uses a method called uniqueValuesFor on the catalog, which will return all the unique values that exist for an index. This lets you perform a task such as populating a little drop-down box in a form, which is a pretty useful thing to have.

Note Since you can pass in almost any request values, you can set up a search form that would pass this information through to the search form. This is what the search and advanced search pages do. For instance, you will note that if you go to a Plone site and search for *beer* in the search box, your URL will now have Searchable-Text=Beer.

At this point, it becomes an exercise in HTML and page templates to make the pages as complicated as you would like. Of course, the best place to look for all this is in the actual templates of Plone, which give lines upon lines of great examples. All the portlets you are familiar with in Plone (such as the calendar, events, related, and so on) are all built using catalog queries to determine what to show.

Taking Advantage of the ZCA: Searching by Interfaces

As you will see in later chapters, Plone takes advantage from the Zope Component Architecture. One of the main concepts of the ZCA are interfaces. Interfaces are something like contracts; an interface can be used for marking objects (marker interface) or to tell you whether the object promises to have some behaviors described in the interface itself.

Objects may provide one or more interfaces, but . . . why are we talking about interfaces now? It's because this information is indexed by the `portal_catalog` tool into the `object_provides` keyword index. This way, we can gain flexibility by getting rid of `portal_type` catalog queries and with a more generic interface using the `object_provides` index (this will be clearer in the example we are about to describe).

Let's imagine a common use case. Many times catalog queries are made by `portal_type`, but what happens if you want to replace a component with a different one in order to get a better and faster implementation? Or if in your application you want to let both types of objects coexist? Normally, you would modify all catalog queries in your Python code; the resultant code would not be reusable and generic. But by using the ZCA instead, you will most likely not be required to modify any existing (and well-working) code at all!

For a more specific example, imagine a survey application for an e-learning web site. Users log in and fill out the survey. When the user submits his answers, the results are stored in a `Result` object type in the survey object itself. The objects of the `Result` type provides the `IResult` interface, and this object could be used for storing results, comparing different results for the same survey, compiling statistics, and so on. After a couple of months, the site will already have a lot of users and survey submissions, but you may need to have a new result object that is not a stand-alone object but instead is able to contain other objects, such as a folder (in Plone slang we call it a "folderish" object), for instance because you need to handle survey attachments with a particular workflow management and some extra features along with that workflow.

The solution in this case is quite simple. You only need to create a new folderish result type that will provide the same interface `IResult`; for instance, the `ResultFolder` type. So, `ResultFolder` promises to behave just as it's described in the `IResult` interface; other components of the application already know how to deal with this object because it has the same behavior of the old type `Result`. After writing a new factory component, newly created results will be of the `ResultFolder` type. You get all of this without making any change in the existing code, plus you can use and compare old and new type of objects!

And what about user portlets and search interfaces for result types based upon catalog queries? No changes are needed to your existing, tested, and well-working code!

How is it possible? Because all catalog queries are based on the `object_provides` index instead of the `portal_type` one, all catalog queries will search for objects that provide the `IResult` marker in its interface. It doesn't matter if the new type of result has a different `portal_type`.

Catalog queries made by interfaces are similar to the following:

```
from Products.CMFCore.utils import getToolByName
from Products.Quiz.interfaces import IResult
portal_catalog = getToolByName(context, 'portal_catalog')
results = portal_catalog.searchResults(object_provides=[IResult.__identifier__,])
return results
```

Basically, instead of searching for portal_type, we use interfaces that let you gain in flexibility. If the existing catalog queries are similar to the previous one, no changes are needed to your code!

The Python code of the previous example returns a list of all brains in the entire portal of objects, and every single brain in that list corresponds to an object that provides the IResult interface. As shown in this chapter, you probably want to filter the results by creator or review state.

Note If you try to use the previous code, it will not work. IResult cannot be imported because the Quiz package doesn't exist; it is only an example!

Finally, here's a real example taken from plone/portlet/collection/collection.py:

```
class ICollectionPortlet(IPortletDataProvider):
    """A portlet which renders the results of a collection object.
    """
    ...
    target_collection = schema.Choice(title=_(u"Target collection"),➥
            description=_(u"Find the collection which provides➥
            the items to list"),required=True, source=SearchableTextSource➥
            Binder({'object_provides' : IATTopic.__identifier__},➥
            default_query='path:'))
    ...
```

The source of target_collection is built using an object_provides index query. So, if you create a new type that inherits from ATTopic and provides the same interface as IATTopic, this portlet will work fine also with your new type, without any changes.

Summary

In this chapter, you made a big leap forward: you went from the user side to the configuration side. You started to see what lies behind Plone and how to manage objects and features in a deeper layer of the system, the Zope Management Interface. We usually work on the ZMI only when we need to perform tasks we can't perform through the Plone user interface.

After you learned how to access the ZMI, you tackled some concepts that Plone inherits from the application server Zope, such as object publishing and acquisition, and you saw how to manage content types through the ZMI and how searching and indexing work in Zope and Plone.

You can now move on to customizing the look and feel of Plone, managing Plone skins, working with templates and CSS, and working with JavaScript and KSS. The next step is customizing your Plone site aesthetically—it's time to pretty up your site!

■ ■ ■

## CHAPTER 6

Customizing Plone's Look and Feel

It is now time to think about the look and feel of your site. If you want to manage your Plone site's visual appeal, you have to know first of all how the Plone user interface is put together. A Plone site's visual aspects are made up of a collection of page templates, style sheets, components, and configuration settings that together comprise a Plone theme.

In this chapter, we will cover all the key definitions and theme elements that comprise a site. We will define terms such as *skins* and *layers*. Then we will cover customizing the Plone user interface, concentrating on the power that Cascading Style Sheets (CSS) brings to the site developer. We will run through the key variables and show how you can change them.

We will then go on to briefly discuss the integration of JavaScript, a scripting language widely used for client-side web development, with Plone and then conclude with some techniques using KSS, a wonderful new technology for building dynamic, engaging web sites using JavaScript, Ajax, and other technologies, but without using JavaScript directly.

Changing the Entire Site's Look Quickly

If you don't know much about CSS or user interface design in general, don't worry—you can change your Plone site's look with just a few clicks using a ready-to-use Plone theme. There is only one skin available by default in a standard Plone installation—NuPlone—but there are many available on http://plone.org/products. You can choose your favorite by typing **theme** in the search box and taking a look at the results that appear. You will then have to download and install the package and then enable it in the Site Setup area, in the Add-On Products section.

We'll show what you need to do to change the entire site's look using a different prepackaged theme. For simplicity, we will apply the NuPlone theme, which, as just mentioned, is available by default in Plone. But this step will be the same for any other theme product, as long as you correctly download and install it in your Plone instance.

You just need to go to the Plone control panel, click Add-on Products, select the NuPlone product, and click the Install button, as shown in Figure 6-1.

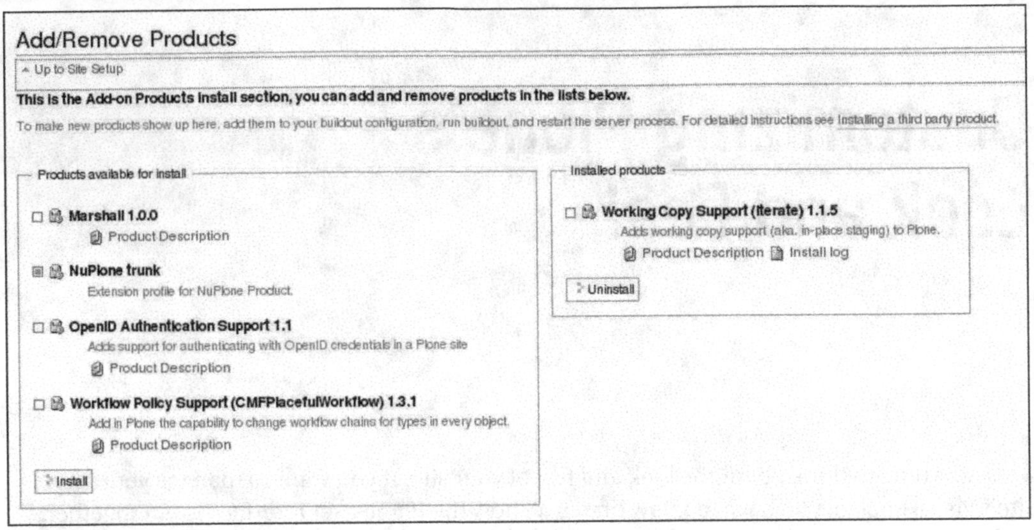

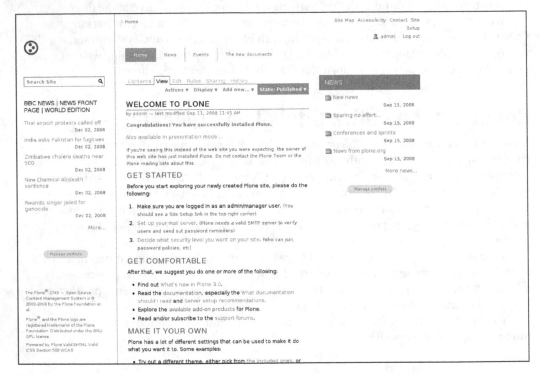

Figure 6-1. *Installing the NuPlone product in your Plone site will completely change its look.*

That's it! You'll immediately notice that the visual aspects of your site have changed, as shown in Figure 6-2.

Figure 6-2. *The standard Plone home page with NuPlone, a theme product available by default in your Plone installation*

To change the theme of your site back to the default, go to the Plone control panel, click Themes, and change the default theme through the "Default theme" drop-down menu. Simply select "Plone default," and your site's look will go back to the original one.

Introducing Plone Skins

A *skin* determines exactly how any document is displayed to the user, including the images and styles surrounding the content. A skin groups many elements, including static items (such as images) and dynamic pieces (such as scripts), wraps each piece of content, and presents them in a certain manner. A skin is also the place where you will put style sheets and JavaScript.

Your Plone site must have at least one skin that will be used as the default, but it can have as many skins as the site developer wants. A user may optionally flip between skins, should the site developer want to allow the user to do so. The default Plone skin is the one you see on http://plone.org, with the familiar blue and green interface. But Plone doesn't have to look at all like this—its look is entirely up to you. For example, take a look at some of the sites listed at http://plone.net/sites, which offer many possible custom looks.

The templates and other elements that compose a skin are registered on a tool named portal_skins. One of the advantages of this structure is that Plone's templating system allows you to completely separate presentation, logic, and data, and to reuse code. In other words, if you want to modify the look and feel of your entire site, you don't have to modify each individual page. Usually, you'll have to modify just a couple of templates or CSS files.

When we say "reuse" code, we mean that you'll have to write it only once. For example, you can change the structure of all the pages of your portal by modifying just one base template. For instance, one of the most commonly used base templates is main_template. It provides the logical structure for all the pages of the portal, and it is invoked by all templates. If you customize main_template, all other templates will be affected.

Thus, if you want to change only the visual aspects of your pages (such as the size and color of certain titles), you need to modify only one CSS file. If you want to do structural modifications, you can simply customize main_template, and all the views of your portal will be affected.

Using Layers Within a Skin

A skin is divided into logical collections of templates and scripts called *layers*. Altering these individual collections allows a user to easily add components to a skin or remove them. The layers are represented in a skin by a hierarchical list of folders. Each layer matches the name of a folder, and each folder contains the skin elements.

The order of the layers in that list is the key factor to how Plone finds the elements. Remember the concept of acquisition from Chapter 5? This is a very important construct for Plone, so it is worth repeating: in a standard object-oriented environment, an object inherits its behavior from its parent. In Plone and Zope, an object also *acquires* properties and behaviors from its parents. So, when an element, such as logo.jpg, is requested from the skin, the skin looks through the layers to find the element. The skin starts by looking at the first layer assigned to that skin (by default, the first layer that is considered is custom). If the skin can't find the element in the first layer, it moves to the second layer. (To find out which is the second layer that will be considered, look at the Properties tab of the portal_skins tool, "Layers (in order of precedence)." We will talk about it in a moment.) It continues looking through the list of layers until it finds the element for which it's looking. If it can't find the element, then a 404 error is raised and returned to the browser.

By allowing higher layers to take precedence over lower layers, developers and administrators now have the ability to customize and manipulate their sites in a programmatic fashion through the layers. For instance, if you don't like a particular element of a Plone skin, you can customize the result by moving that element up a layer so that it will have precedence on the element you don't like.

You can sort your skins and layers in Plone with the `portal_skins` tool, shown in Figure 6-3. To access the `portal_skins` tool, go to the ZMI and click "portal_skins."

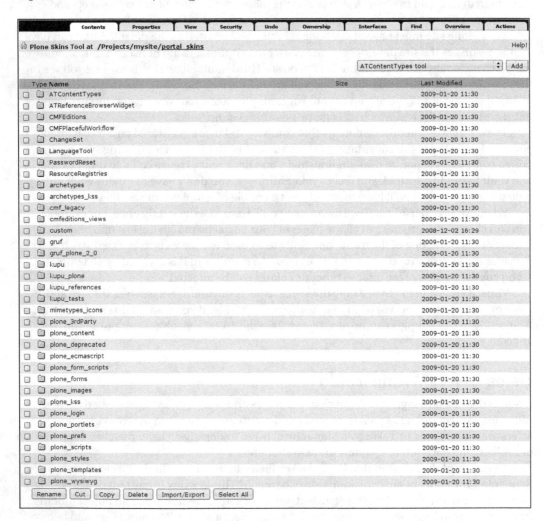

Figure 6-3. *The portal_skins tool, which allows you to manage skin elements and customize the look of your site*

Clicking the Properties tab at the top of the `portal_skins` tool brings up all the skins and layers that compose your site's look, as shown in Figure 6-4.

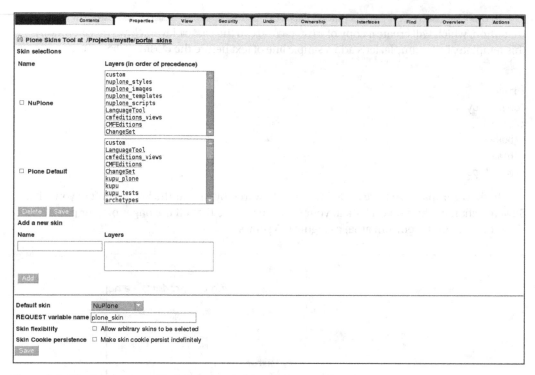

Figure 6-4. *The Properties tab of the portal_skins tool*

The list of these layers in the Properties section may seem intimidatingly long. However, this hefty number of layers gives you a large degree of flexibility and reuse.

Let's take a look at how these skins are displayed. Each skin displays on the left, with a text area to the right displaying all the layers within that skin. Each layer is the name of a folder or a File System Directory View (FSDV) from the Contents tab. An FSDV is a new object in Plone that allows you to directly access skin elements defined in the file system, instead of having to go through the Zope object database, as usual. FSDVs make development and customization easier. By reading objects directly from the file system, it's much easier for developers to write and edit the code that produces the site.

Your First Customization

Let's return to the Contents section of the portal_skins tool: most of the folders that you can see point to areas of the file system. If you click an element contained in one of the folders in the portal_skins tool, a Customize button will appear. Click it, and you will be able to change the code of the element; this operation will create a modified copy of that element in the custom layer, which by default is the layer on the very top, taking priority over all other layers.

Let's walk through a very simple example. Search for main_template in the portal_skins tool. On the Find tab in the portal_skins tool, type **main_template** in the "with ids" field, and click the Find button. Zope will show you a list of items that match your query search. The element highlighted with a red * means that it is the item on top of a given skin.

In our case, main_template is placed in portal_skins - plone_templates. Click the Customize button, which will create a copy of main_template in the custom layer. Now you can modify this template. For example, let's add a simple line of text before the closing </body> tag:

```
...
<div>
Powered by me
</div>
</body>
</html>
</metal:page>
```

In this example, you have added the text "Powered by me" at the bottom left of your site. Save the changes, and take a look at your site: you will see that all the pages of your portal show this text in the bottom area, as Figure 6-5 shows.

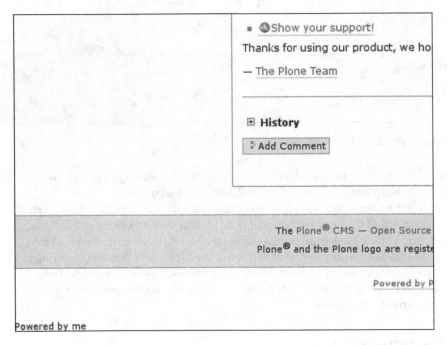

Figure 6-5. *By customizing main_template, you can add items to all the pages in your portal.*

■**Note** If you delete the customized main_template version contained in the custom layer, all pages of your portal will go back to the default version provided by Plone in the plone_templates layer. So, don't worry if something goes wrong when you are customizing an element of Plone—if you want to revert it, simply delete the customized element in the Custom folder.

Templates and CSS: Customizing Your Plone Skin

To really customize the look and feel of your Plone site manually, you need to know how skins work. This will come with experience, but we'll try to give a quick overview. The main stars are templates, CSS, and Python scripts. Templates define the structure of the site's visual aspect; CSS defines the way that pages display those visual aspects (colors, font, and layout); and Python scripts give the logic.

There are two ways for templating Plone: ZPT and DTML. Document Template Markup Language (DTML) is commonly used by Plone to generate dynamic CSS and JavaScript files, while Zope Page Templates (ZPT) is the page generation tool commonly used in Plone. We will introduce those concepts, but if you want to create dynamic views with Plone, you will need to get used to working with the ZPT language template. DTML was widely used in legacy Zope applications, but nowadays it's used only for non-HTML text like JavaScript and CSS dynamic files. You'll see here how to edit CSS in Plone. By simply overriding Plone's existing styles, you can make consistent changes.

DTML and ZPT

In the `portal_skins` tool, there are a few DTML files. One of these is `CMFPlone/skins/plone_styles/mobile.css.dtml`:

```
...
body {
    font-family: <dtml-var fontFamily>;
    background-color: &dtml-backgroundColor;;
    color: &dtml-fontColor;;
    margin: 0;
    padding: 0;
}
table {
    font-size: 100%;
}
a {
    color: &dtml-linkColor;;
    background-color: transparent;
}
...
```

As you can see, settings like `font-family` for the body are defined dynamically. The DTML engine will replace `<dtml-var fontFamily>` with the correct value given dynamically from the `fontFamily` variable; it's the same for the shortened syntax `&dtml-backgroundColor;;`, and so on. (Don't be confused by the double semicolons; they exist just because the syntax `&dtml-backgroundColor;` will be replaced with the value that is "dynamically" appropriate. So, for example, if `&dtml-backgroundColor;` means white, then it will become white;.) The generated CSS code will look like this:

```
body {
    font-family: "Lucida Grande", Verdana, Lucida, Helvetica, Arial, sans-serif;
...
```

This example is quite simple, but it's useful for understanding how DTML works. DTML allows you to do many things, but since nowadays its usage is quite limited, it is easy to acquire the skills you need for working with it. If you want to gain a wider and more complete overview of DTML, visit http://zope.org/Documentation/Books/ZopeBook/2_6Edition/DTML.stx.

The actual style sheet that does most of the work, plone.css, has a number of variables in it that are populated using DTML. The DTML syntax for plone.css is actually pretty simple. How are values filled dynamically by the DTML? Each variable relates to a corresponding attribute in a property sheet, which you can customize. To access this property sheet, click the portal_skins tool in the ZMI, then click plone_styles, and finally click base_properties. In the base_properties object you will find the default values used by dynamic CSS files. DTML replaces the DTML variables with the proper values you indicated in base_properties.

You can customize this object by changing the values that are set by default. Customizing the base_properties object in this way will change all of the generated CSS. You can, for example, change fonts, font sizes, backgrounds, colors, and border settings.

Now try to add a basic customization for your portal. Customize the default base_properties object by changing the value for the fontColor property from Black to Red, and see what this looks like in your Plone interface.

Note If nothing changes, check your browser cache settings and purge the cache of Plone in the portal_css tool if needed. In order to do this, navigate to portal_css and click Save, or use debug/development mode to avoid saving every time you change something. Remember not to use debug/development mode when managing public web sites, since it will make everything much slower.

Like DTML, ZPT allows you to create dynamic pages for the Web, but with a different syntax. As you have just seen, DTML is not a valid HTML-like markup language.

ZPT works around the limitations of DTML. Using ZPT, you will be able to collaborate with designers without any problems, since ZPT can be rendered well by WYSIWYG tools. ZPT is indeed a valid HTML-like markup language. Using ZPT, designers can produce an HTML template using their favorite WYSIWYG editor, and programmers can easily create a dynamic model using the same template. For these reasons, ZPT is the preferred tool for writing HTML views, because they are similar to HTML and make possible a better separation of logic, presentation, and data.

Let's play with ZPT in a couple of simple examples. Go to the Custom folder in the portal_skins tool, and add a page template from the Add menu of the ZMI. Type **home_view** as the ID, and click the Add and Edit button. Zope will prompt for you a default ZPT code; keep it like it is and save it.

Now try to apply this view to the objects contained in your portal. It is as simple as appending the /home_view string to the end of the URL in your browser. You will see a simple page that shows you the title of the current object and the identifier of the page template (home_view).

If you apply this page template to different objects, what is displayed on your screen will change depending on the context: the result changes, properly showing the correct title.

If you take a look now at the ZPT code you just added, you should see something like this:

```
...
    <h2><span tal:replace="here/title_or_id">content title or id</span>
        <span tal:condition="template/title"
                tal:replace="template/title">optional template title</span></h2>
...
```

This ZPT code will be replaced with dynamic HTML like this:

```
...
    <h2>Site
    </h2>
...
```

The `replace` statement means that the dynamic statement `here/title_or_id` will replace the element. So, if you have

```
<span tal:replace="here/title_or_id">content title or id</span>
```

you get as a result

```
Site
```

The `content` statement is slightly different. A `content` statement will not replace the entire HTML element, but rather only its content:

```
<span tal:content="here/title_or_id">content title or id</span>
```

The rendered HTML result of the preceding code will be

```
<span>Site</span>
```

You can also use conditions, use loops on items, define variables, and so on, for creating dynamic pages; for more details about basics features of Zope Page Templates, see the Zope Book chapters about ZPT, where you can find more instructions about condition elements and about how to change attributes: `http://www.zope.org/Documentation/Books/ZopeBook/2_6Edition/ZPT.stx`.

You can also define and call macros from other templates in order to reuse templates. In fact, `main_template` comprises the skeleton of the Plone page and defines a lot of macros that are reusable by other templates.

Managing Viewlets

As mentioned, Plone is geared toward object-oriented and Zope 3 programming techniques, and this is true also for presentation components such as views and forms. Views in Plone are not only simple dynamic HTML but also instances of Python classes.

Common presentation components used in Plone are views, forms, portlets, and viewlets. We will talk about views and forms in the following chapters; here, we will introduce the concept of *viewlets*. A viewlet is responsible for rendering a section of a page. All viewlets are registered in a *viewlet manager*, which is a container of viewlets that you can hide or display. You can change the display order of registered viewlets in the viewlet managers or plug new custom viewlets without having to modify any existing template, as you will see later.

You may wonder why things get so complicated. Wouldn't it be better to keep things simple with ZPT templates and procedural Python scripts? There's a couple of good reasons not to. First of all, by using viewlets, you can take advantage of object-oriented programming techniques, thus writing better and more reusable code. Second, with Python code in viewlets, you can write Ajax components with KSS, which can do a lot of cool things. You can create a complex assignment system of portlets or viewlets, build a set of configurable and reorderable portlets or viewlets to manage your site, or, maybe in the near future, support dragging and dropping of visual components.

You have seen that the `main_template` used by Plone to render all pages provides a set of slots to fill in. But `main_template` also calls some viewlet managers that manage the rendering of their registered viewlets. Viewlet managers are something like containers of registered viewlets.

For example, the default page of Plone is split into different sections: the top area is rendered by a viewlet manager that calls the other viewlets.

How are viewlet managers called by `main_template`, and which viewlets and viewlet managers are available? If you take a look at the `main_template` code, you will find a lot of lines like this:

```
<div tal:replace="structure provider:plone.portaltop" />
```

This corresponds to a call to a viewlet manager. In this case, the `div` will be replaced with the HTML code rendered by the `plone.portaltop` viewlet manager. On this viewlet manager are registered a lot of viewlets that render the top area of our pages (logo, search form, etc.).

To get a deeper look at how viewlets are organized on the viewlet manager interface, take a look at `http://localhost/mysite/@@manage-viewlets` (see Figure 6-6).

Notice that within `plone.portaltop`, a lot of viewlets and viewlet managers are registered. You can hide some viewlets or viewlets managers, change the display order, and so on.

Note that you can do all this without customizing the `main_template`. One of the main problems encountered when customizing templates in `portal_skins` is that they sometimes cause conflicts with other add-on products. If we make some customizations to `main_template` and then install another product that provides a custom `main_template`, Plone can become broken as a result. Using viewlets instead, you can do basic configurations through a simple web interface, simply reordering or hiding elements, without customizing `main_template`.

You can now practice with this viewlet management interface and take a look at what happens after your updates.

Notice that all of your updates can be exported using the `plone_setup` tool. So, you can save your configuration, export it to an XML file, compare different snapshots, and then import the exported file into another Plone site. If you are a programmer, you will be able to include the exported XML file in your file system product—when your add-on product is installed, all your updates to viewlets will be automatically applied.

Try it: go to the `portal_setup` tool, click the Export tab at the top of the page, and then check the Viewlet Settings check box to export your viewlet settings. Finally, click the "Export selected steps" button to confirm and download the generated tarball containing your customizations.

Figure 6-6. *The viewlet structure of a Plone page allows you to manage viewlets.*

Extracting the downloaded tarball, you will find a viewlets.xml file containing your updates. In this example, we've exported an XML file that hides the plone.searchbox for the Plone Default skin. This way, Plone will not show the search box in the top-right corner.

```xml
<?xml version="1.0"?>
<object>
 ...
 <order manager="plone.portalheader" skinname="Plone Default">
  <viewlet name="plone.skip_links"/>
  <viewlet name="plone.site_actions"/>
  <viewlet name="plone.searchbox"/>
  <viewlet name="plone.logo"/>
  <viewlet name="plone.global_sections"/>
 </order>
 ...
 <hidden manager="plone.portalheader" skinname="Plone Default">
  <viewlet name="plone.searchbox"/>
 </hidden>
</object>
```

If you want, you can make other customizations and try to reimport your profile into another Plone site. It is as easy as clicking the Import tab of the `portal_setup` tool of another Plone site and uploading your compressed tarball. Note that there are other add-on products that provide a friendlier interface to manage viewlet. For example, take a look at the GloWorm add-on product (`http://plone.org/products/gloworm`).

Editing CSS

As already explained, in Plone, logic, layout, and data are always separated. It is always a bad idea to put style directly into templates, like in this example:

```
<table border="1">
...
</table>
```

or this:

```
<span style="color: Red;"> Text here </span>
```

In these examples, you get as a result a table with borders and a span with red text. Imagine spreading code like this throughout your pages: what will happen if you want to change the layout of all the tables or the color of all the titles? You will have to edit all the HTML pages of your site.

Alternatively, you should use CSS instead of styling pages directly in your HTML templates. CSS helps display basic HTML code. For example, if you want to change the color of a link or create a new style for all the pages in a site, you just need to edit a single CSS file.

Plone itself is widely based on CSS files, so you can style your site without editing HTML templates. Perhaps the easiest way to see exactly what the CSS does for a Plone site is to turn off style sheets in your browser. The difference is striking to say the least.

CSS files in Plone are registered on the `portal_css` tool. There are a lot of registered CSS sheets, and you can enable or disable those registered elements or add new CSS sheets. On each of these registered items, you can configure several options:

- *Title*: This allows you to set a title for your CSS sheet.

- *Condition*: This is useful, for example, if you need to enable a particular CSS sheet only under certain conditions.

- *Merging allowed*: This merges your item with other CSS sheets.

- *Caching allowed*: This makes your CSS sheet cacheable.

- *CSS Media*: This allows you to set the target media of your CSS sheet. The `all` option is used for all media type devices, the `screen` option is used for computer screens, the `print` option is used for printers, and so on (for more details, visit `www.w3schools.com/css/css_mediatypes.asp`).

- *rel*: This is filled with the value stylesheet by default, since it refers to the relationship between the document and the resource used for displaying page elements.

- *Render type*: This makes it possible for you to choose from three types of rendering for your CSS. This option affects how your CSS will be included in your pages; the default value is import.

- *Compression type*: This sets compression for your CSS (safe/full/none); compressing the CSS allows you to speed up the loading time of loads.

So, with the portal_css tool, you can register new CSS files and choose whether they will be merged altogether, whether they are cacheable, their media type, the method of rendering, the compression, and a condition. You can also reorder the items, overriding existing settings.

Conditions are particularly useful, for example, to force a certain CSS sheet to apply only when the context is an image (python:here.portal_type == 'Image'), or to switch your portal to RTL mode, which means right to left, for languages such as Hebrew and Arabic (using python:portal.restrictedTraverse('@@plone_portal_state').is_rtl()).

Examining Example Customization Snippets

So, what is the best way to customize the look and feel of your portal? This section will show some examples that demonstrate simple customizations you can make to your Plone site.

Note When working with CSS, you can use the debug mode option of the portal_css tool, but remember to avoid using it on web sites, since it slows down the interface of the whole portal.

As you may have already noticed, there are a lot of items registered in the portal_css tool. One of the items that is added by default is the ploneCustom.css item. This is the file where you can put your CSS changes. You should use this and override the relevant properties you want to change here, instead of customizing other registered CSS files like plone.css to avoid problems when upgrading Plone to newer versions. Writing your own plone.css makes sense only for very heavy customizations.

The ploneCustom.css file is reachable through the portal_skins tool (portal_skins/plone_styles); it is shown in Figure 6-7. As you can see, it contains not only CSS code but also DTML code. This allows you to obtain dynamic CSS code, which is useful because it provides some parameters from other tools like the base_properties tool (portal_skins/plone_styles/base_properties). In the ploneCustom.css file, you can change, for example, font types, font and background colors, and so on.

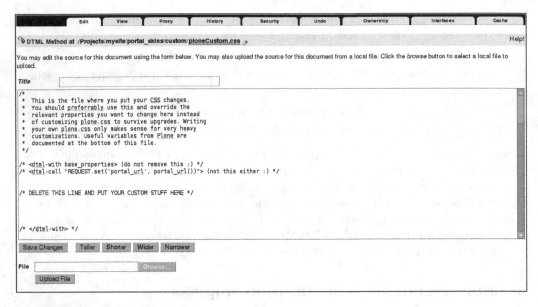

Figure 6-7. *Customizing the ploneCustom.css file*

All the settings in base_properties are dynamically looked up in ploneCustom.css. Of course, as you already know, you can customize the base_properties object by clicking the Customize button, and the new values will override the default ones.

Let's now practice customizing. You can customize the portal logo by providing a different image. To do so, go to the plone_images layer in portal_skins (portal_skins/plone_images) and customize the logo.jpg item. You can also customize other elements in this layer (e.g., arrows, object and action icons, etc.).

base_properties provides a set of basic graphical customizations. If you want to include more advanced graphics, you can customize ploneCustom.css, adding more advanced rules. For example, you can improve the readability of the pages of the portal by increasing the base font size of all text in base_properties. In order to achieve this, add these lines:

```
...
p {
    line-height:1.8em;
}
dd {
    line-height:1.8em;
}
ul {
    line-height:1.8em;
}
a:hover {
    background-color: Black;
    color: White;
    font-weight: bold;
}
...
```

Here we have increased the space between lines to 1.8 em. We have also changed the background color and the color of links when a hover event occurs. This way, people with visual impairments will have an easier time seeing the links.

Working with JavaScript

As with CSS, Plone also provides a registry tool for JavaScript: `portal_javascripts`. This tool is very similar to `portal_css`. Many of the options, such as debug/development mode, are basically the same.

Take a look at the `portal_javascripts` tool, and notice that all the JavaScript is registered by default. On each JavaScript script, you have the same options as with the CSS tool (e.g., "Inline rendering" and "Condition") You can put Python or TAL conditions here (TAL stands for *Tag Attribute Language* and is the standard attribute language used to create dynamic templates). A common use case is to include a JavaScript library for image content types in order to create special effects on single images (e.g., an image that enlarges when the mouse moves over it) or on photo galleries. What you would do is similar to that shown for `portal_css`. You just need to upload a JavaScript file in the `custom` layer of the `portal_skins` tool and register it in the `portal_javascripts` tool.

We will not go deeper into explaining how to work with JavaScript. The important thing to know is that if you want to add some JavaScript effects in Plone, you will have to register them in the `portal_javascripts` tool, and then you can customize the tools where you want to apply them.

KSS: Ajax Made Easy

Ajax stands for "Asynchronous JavaScript and XML." With Ajax techniques, you can create more interactive user interfaces for your web applications using asynchronous background calls to server procedures. As you've already seen, Plone has some useful Ajax features. These features are made with the Ajax framework Kinetic Style Sheets (KSS). KSS allows user interface development without writing any JavaScript or entirely rewriting a preexisting user interface.

KSS provides a set of commands from its own DOM-like inspector, which you can use if you want to write KSS plug-ins, and has both a client-side JavaScript library and server-side support. The main goals of KSS are

- Staying low-impact. If you have an old browser or JavaScript disabled, you can still work with Plone.

- Working easily with Ajax. You can write your Ajax components without knowing any JavaScript.

- Being widely based on object-oriented programming and built with Zope 3 technologies.

- Wide test coverage (which is intrinsically synonymous with quality; if developers change something in the KSS code, automatic tests can detect whether something goes wrong).

Many user interface components are sensitive to the KSS technology in Plone. Common use cases for KSS, for example, are the inline editing of Plone contents and orderable listings for folder contents.

But how does it work? Well, KSS is based on CSS selectors that describe dynamic behaviors and server actions. In other words, you declare a set of rules and events in a KSS file with a CSS-like syntax, like this:

```
#css_selector_id:click {
    evt-click-preventdefault: True;
    action-server: your_server_action;
    action-client: alert;
}
```

So, when a user clicks a "KSSified" element identified by a CSS-like selector, an asynchronous server action will be performed. The server action gets the element to be updated using a CSS selector, computes the HTML code on the server side, and then sends the resulting code back to the page that needs to be updated. These KSS files are registered on the portal_kss tool. With this tool, you can add your own new KSS style sheets. Let's look at how to implement two very popular features: inline editing and sortable folder lists.

When you use the inline editing feature in Plone by clicking a "KSSified" element (e.g., the Title field of a document), a server action replaces this element with a small edit form that lets you change the title without a page reload. This is very useful when you want to edit just one field of your object without loading the whole standard edit form.

Another more complex "KSSified" component of Plone is the folder contents view: if you click one of the headers of the folder contents table, the order of elements will change. How is this possible? Let's look at the details. Look at the foldercontents ZPT code to see how to make your list of items sortable depending on their workflow status. As shown in plone/app/content/browser/table.pt, the header of the State column is marked with the ID foldercontents-status-column since its items are sortable depending on their workflow status:

```
<th class="nosort column"
    id="foldercontents-status-column"> ➥
<tal:state i18n:translate="listingheader_status"
    >State</tal:state> </th>
```

In CMFPlone/skins/plone_kss/plone.kss, we register the click event on the State column for the server action foldercontents_update_table, as shown here:

```
#foldercontents-status-column:click {
    action-server: foldercontents_update_table;
    evt-click-preventdefault: True;
    foldercontents_update_table-pagenumber: currentFormVar('pagenumber');
    foldercontents_update_table-sort_on: "review_state";
}
```

Here, we render foldercontents_update_table passing two arguments: pagenumber and sort_on. foldercontents_update_table is registered in plone/app/content/browser/configure.zcml, as follows:

```
<browser:page
    for="*"
    class=".foldercontents.FolderContentsKSSView"
```

```
            attribute="update_table"
            name="foldercontents_update_table"
            permission="cmf.ListFolderContents" />
```

Also, it is handled by the update_table method, available on the Python class FolderContentsKSSView, which is defined in plone/app/content/browser/foldercontents.py. Let's now find this method and take a look at the FolderContentsKSSView class:

```
class FolderContentsKSSView(TableKSSView):
    table = FolderContentsTable
```

The update_table method is inherited by the Python class TableKSSView defined in plone/app/content/browser/tableview.py:

```
class TableKSSView(KSSView):
    '''Base class that can be used from a KSS view
    Subclasses only need to set the table property to a different
    class.'''
    table = None
    def update_table(self, pagenumber='1',
                sort_on='getObjPositionInParent', show_all=False):
        self.request.set('sort_on', sort_on)
        self.request.set('pagenumber', pagenumber)
        table = self.table(self.context, self.request,
                                  contentFilter={'sort_on':sort_on})
        core = self.getCommandSet('core')
        core.replaceHTML('#folderlisting-main-table', table.render())
        return self.render()
```

Here we can take a closer look at the method that takes care of updating the code. update_table gets the HTML code of the ordered table, sets the KSS command, and then replaces the folder contents table area with the computed HTML.

Finally, update_table calls the render method that lets KSS return the results of the actions performed on the command set.

Though quite complex, this example shows something interesting: you have built, with Plone, a complex Ajax user interface without writing a single line of ugly JavaScript code. This is a good thing because JavaScript is difficult to maintain and your code reusability is improved.

What Can You Do with KSS?

Plone 3 is shipped by default with KSS included, and it introduces more dynamic behavior that lets users improve their experience with Plone. Two of the most important KSS-powered features are inline editing and sortable folder contents views, as mentioned.

■**Note** If you use an old browser that doesn't support KSS, you can still use Plone, because it is designed to have an alternative interface for these kind of cases.

These are standard Plone features, but with KSS you can also build complex user inter-faces based on drag-and-drop.

Let's see a practical use case. You'll integrate the KSS-aware add-on Image Editor (http://plone.org/products/imageeditor) into your Plone site. This add-on provides an embedded image editor that lets you edit your previously uploaded images just using your browser. Thanks to this, you will be able to resize, cut, and manipulate images without having to download and edit them with an application before reuploading them to Plone. Download and install Image Editor to your Plone site. On all image content types, a Visual Transforms tab will appear that will allow you to edit images directly in your browser. Figure 6-8 shows you an example.

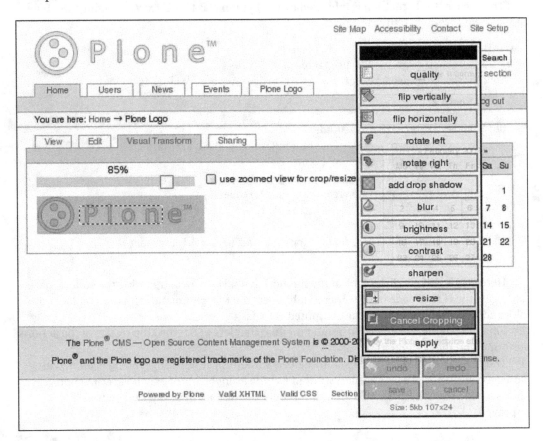

Figure 6-8. *Thanks to the embedded image editor, you can edit and transform images directly through the Plone user interface.*

How to Disable KSS in Plone

KSS is enabled by default for authenticated users. If for some reasons you want to disable it, go to the `portal_kss` tool, deselect all enabled KSS registered files, and then confirm by clicking the Save button.

If you want to disable only the inline editing feature and you have a Plone version higher than 3.1, you can go to the `portal_properties/site_properties` configuration tool and deselect the `enable_inline_editing` property, or you can use the Plone control panel to select Site Setup ➤ Site and uncheck the "Enable inline editing" option.

Summary

You will see throughout the book that the flexibility of Plone concerns the management of content, workflow and security, and users and groups; the creation of content rules; and the integration of extensions, databases, and other services. In this chapter, you started to see that you are free to design your interface's visual aspect as you want.

You have seen how to apply a ready-to-use Plone theme and that you can change your site's aspects very quickly without a lot of background knowledge. You were introduced to Plone skins and their functioning, and you began your first manual customizations. You then explored Plone templating, including working with DTML and CSS. Finally, you got an introduction to JavaScript and KSS.

In the next chapter, we will start talking about Zope security architecture, which is inherited by Plone. You will learn how to add new users and roles in Zope, how to set up existing workflows and create new ones, and how to implement and configure workflow policies. We will then dedicate one more chapter to security, dealing with advanced user management.

■ ■ ■

## CHAPTER 7

Managing Security and Workflows

Zope has a very powerful and granular security architecture, and Plone of course inherits this structure. This chapter shows how security settings are handled in the Zope application server. Most of the concepts in this chapter are related to Zope users and permissions management, but as you saw in Chapter 4's "Managing Users and Permissions" section, you can also manage users, groups, and permissions through the Plone interface. If you have to work with simple settings, you should always work at the Plone level and use its tools for user management, security, and permission settings instead of working in the ZMI.

This chapter also covers a topic related to security: workflows in Plone. Workflows let you define different behaviors for your objects in different logical states. In particular, you can alter permission settings for each logical state. You can manage users' permissions for reviewing, generate PDF documents, view and modify an item or just certain parts of it, and so on.

In Plone, you can create very simple workflows or build complex systems, which is a very important feature for a web application, because it allows people with different roles to interact well together. In this respect, Plone comes with a set of well-tested workflows available by default for common use cases. For example, with just a couple clicks, you can convert a section of your portal into a reserved area or create an intranet. You can also associate custom workflows to your objects, with different behaviors and security settings for each state.

Implementing Security in Zope

These are the main concepts in Zope's security architecture:

- Permissions
- Roles
- Users
- Groups

We went through these Plone concepts in Chapter 4's "Managing Users and Permissions" section. Basically, users can have one or more roles, and roles can be assigned by default or "acquired" from a particular context (for example, granting higher privileges in certain folders). Roles can also be granted to a particular group so that when a user becomes a member of that group, that user will "acquire" the group's roles. In this way, roles and groups are used for grouping similar users so that you can define security configurations once per group or role, instead of setting this configuration for each user of a certain type.

The security machinery checks whether a user can perform some operation by querying permissions. For each role, you can assign one or more permissions that grant or remove the ability to perform specific operations.

Let's start with the Security tab in the root of the ZMI so that you can see how to manage security settings. Figure 7-1 shows just a small part of the panel that will appear if you are in the root of Zope (`http://localhost:8080/manage`).

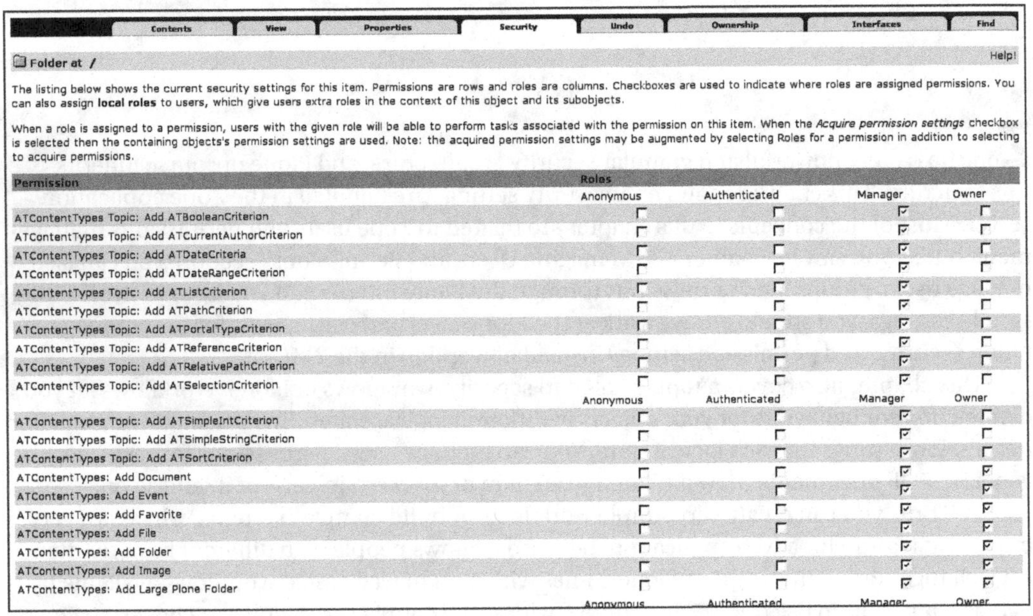

Figure 7-1. *Part of the security settings in Zope that will appear by clicking the Security tab in the ZMI*

As you can see, a lot of permissions are available by default; they're listed on the left side. You'll also see a couple of roles, listed in the top, middle, and bottom rows.

If you click the Security tab for your Plone site (instead of at the root of Zope), you can see the other roles that are available, as shown in Figure 7-2. These are the roles that are created by default in Plone.

You can grant each permission to one or more roles; you just have to select the check box in the appropriate column and row.

■**Note** Permissions are *contextual*, meaning that you can, for instance, grant a permission in the root folder of Zope, and in another folder you can override that permission setting. In this way, you can easily create different areas with different context-sensitive permissions. We'll go into this in just a moment.

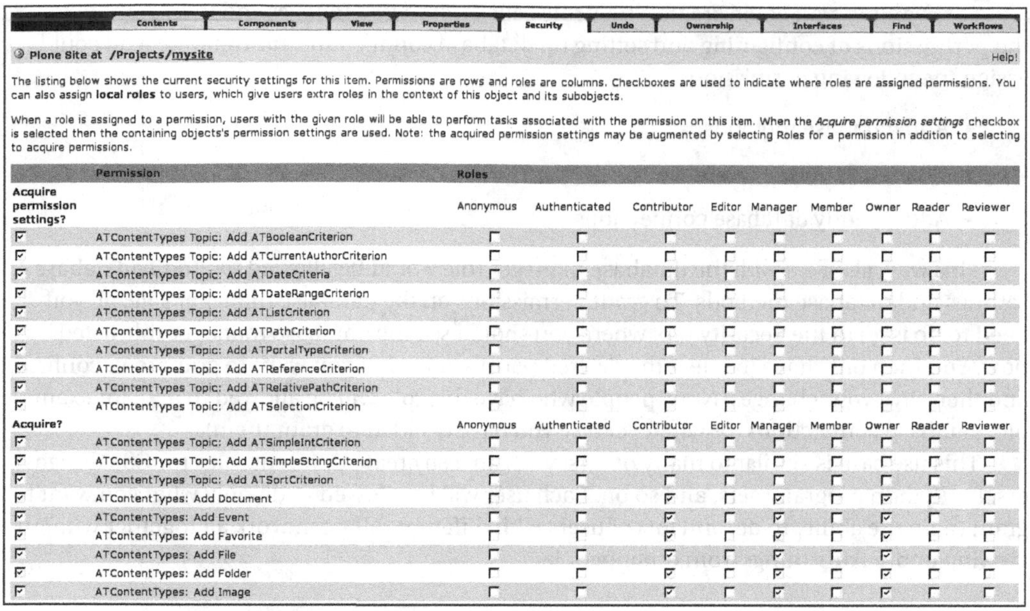

| Contents | Components | View | Properties | Security | Undo | Ownership | Interfaces | Find | Workflows |

🄯 Plone Site at /Projects/mysite   Help!

The listing below shows the current security settings for this item. Permissions are rows and roles are columns. Checkboxes are used to indicate where roles are assigned permissions. You can also assign **local roles** to users, which give users extra roles in the context of this object and its subobjects.

When a role is assigned to a permission, users with the given role will be able to perform tasks associated with the permission on this item. When the *Acquire permission settings* checkbox is selected then the containing objects's permission settings are used. Note: the acquired permission settings may be augmented by selecting Roles for a permission in addition to selecting to acquire permissions.

Acquire permission settings?	Permission	Roles									
		Anonymous	Authenticated	Contributor	Editor	Manager	Member	Owner	Reader	Reviewer	
☑	ATContentTypes Topic: Add ATBooleanCriterion	☐	☐	☐	☐	☐	☐	☐	☐	☐	
☑	ATContentTypes Topic: Add ATCurrentAuthorCriterion	☐	☐	☐	☐	☐	☐	☐	☐	☐	
☑	ATContentTypes Topic: Add ATDateCriteria	☐	☐	☐	☐	☐	☐	☐	☐	☐	
☑	ATContentTypes Topic: Add ATDateRangeCriterion	☐	☐	☐	☐	☐	☐	☐	☐	☐	
☑	ATContentTypes Topic: Add ATListCriterion	☐	☐	☐	☐	☐	☐	☐	☐	☐	
☑	ATContentTypes Topic: Add ATPathCriterion	☐	☐	☐	☐	☐	☐	☐	☐	☐	
☑	ATContentTypes Topic: Add ATPortalTypeCriterion	☐	☐	☐	☐	☐	☐	☐	☐	☐	
☑	ATContentTypes Topic: Add ATReferenceCriterion	☐	☐	☐	☐	☐	☐	☐	☐	☐	
☑	ATContentTypes Topic: Add ATRelativePathCriterion	☐	☐	☐	☐	☐	☐	☐	☐	☐	
☑	ATContentTypes Topic: Add ATSelectionCriterion	☐	☐	☐	☐	☐	☐	☐	☐	☐	
Acquire?		Anonymous	Authenticated	Contributor	Editor	Manager	Member	Owner	Reader	Reviewer	
☑	ATContentTypes Topic: Add ATSimpleIntCriterion	☐	☐	☐	☐	☐	☐	☐	☐	☐	
☑	ATContentTypes Topic: Add ATSimpleStringCriterion	☐	☐	☐	☐	☐	☐	☐	☐	☐	
☑	ATContentTypes Topic: Add ATSortCriterion	☐	☐	☐	☐	☐	☐	☐	☐	☐	
☑	ATContentTypes: Add Document	☐	☐	☑	☐	☑	☐	☑	☐	☐	
☑	ATContentTypes: Add Event	☐	☐	☑	☐	☑	☐	☑	☐	☐	
☑	ATContentTypes: Add Favorite	☐	☐	☑	☐	☑	☐	☑	☐	☐	
☑	ATContentTypes: Add File	☐	☐	☑	☐	☑	☐	☑	☐	☐	
☑	ATContentTypes: Add Folder	☐	☐	☑	☐	☑	☐	☑	☐	☐	
☑	ATContentTypes: Add Image	☐	☐	☑	☐	☑	☐	☑	☐	☐	

Figure 7-2. *Part of the security settings for your Plone site*

Adding New Roles

You can add new roles directly on the Security tab. In the "User defined roles" field at the bottom of the page, enter a name for your new role, and click the Add Role button, as shown in Figure 7-3.

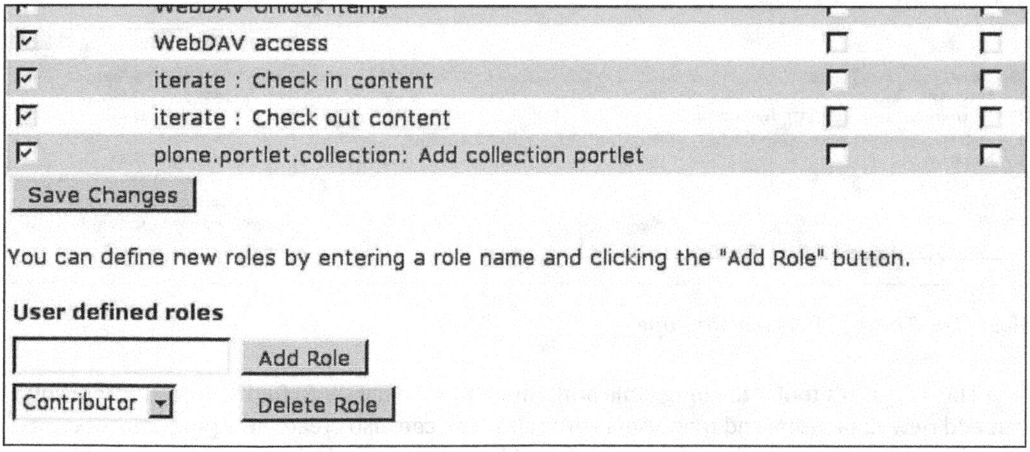

	WebDAV Unlock items		
☑	WebDAV access	☐	☐
☑	iterate : Check in content	☐	☐
☑	iterate : Check out content	☐	☐
☑	plone.portlet.collection: Add collection portlet	☐	☐

[Save Changes]

You can define new roles by entering a role name and clicking the "Add Role" button.

User defined roles

[_____]   [Add Role]

[Contributor ▾]   [Delete Role]

Figure 7-3. *Adding a new role*

For example, you could create a new role called *database manager* and then grant to it the permissions of configuring and setting up database connections; for example, you could assign the following permissions:

- Add database methods

- Change database methods

- Add Z gadfly database connections

This way, all users with the database manager role would be allowed to modify database settings and database methods. To grant permissions on the database manager role, all you need to do is go to the Security tab, where you should see the database manager role listed now. You then only have to select the desired permissions that you want to grant to it, confirm, and then save your changes. Now, people who have this role will be allowed to add, for example, database connections (or whatever else you have decided to grant them).

This use case is similar to many others; you can also create different roles for CSS designers, for Python programmers, and so on. Each user will be allowed to do only what you want to grant them the ability to do, and lots of users with different roles can work all together without viewing or breaking things from other people.

Understanding the Way Zope Stores Users' Information

Where does Zope store user information by default? Zope users will be stored by default in the `acl_users` tool (ACL, in computer sciences in general, stands for *access control list*). If you have an account on a Zope server and you try to log in, Zope will authenticate you through the `acl_users` tool. Figure 7-4 shows you what the `acl_users` tool looks like.

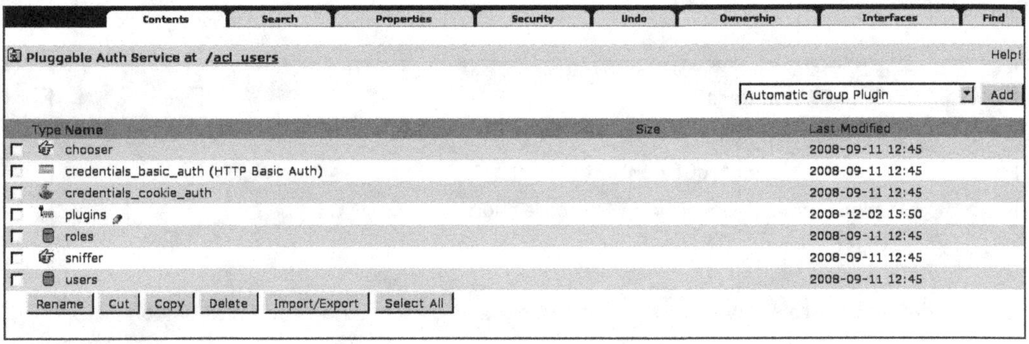

Figure 7-4. *The acl_users tool for Zope*

The `acl_users` tool is the pluggable authentication service (PAS) folder object, where you can add new Zope users and map users with roles. You can also create new plug-ins, for example, to manage user authentication through an LDAP server or other systems you already use.

If you want to create a new Zope user, you have to click Users in the `acl_users` tool and then click "Add a user." As a simple example, let's create a new user called *new_user* and assign it to have the manager role. Fill in the creation form, as shown in Figure 7-5, and then confirm by clicking the Add User button.

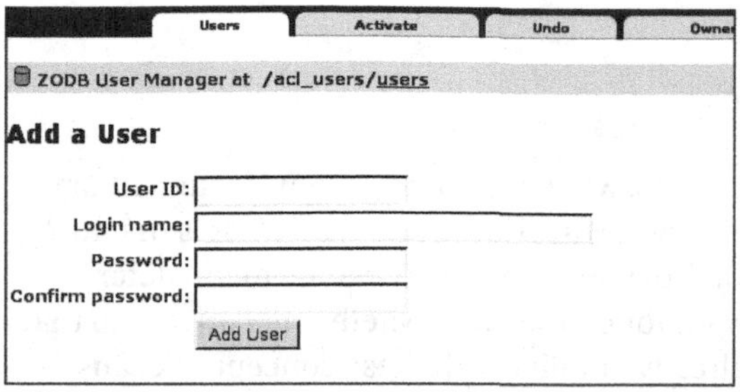

Figure 7-5. *Adding a new user in the acl_users tool*

You may grant to new_user higher privileges by changing the roles assignment. Click the Roles option in the Zope `acl_users` tool, and click the "?" link near the manager role. Here you can search for the new user you just created and enable it for the manager role, as shown in Figure 7-6.

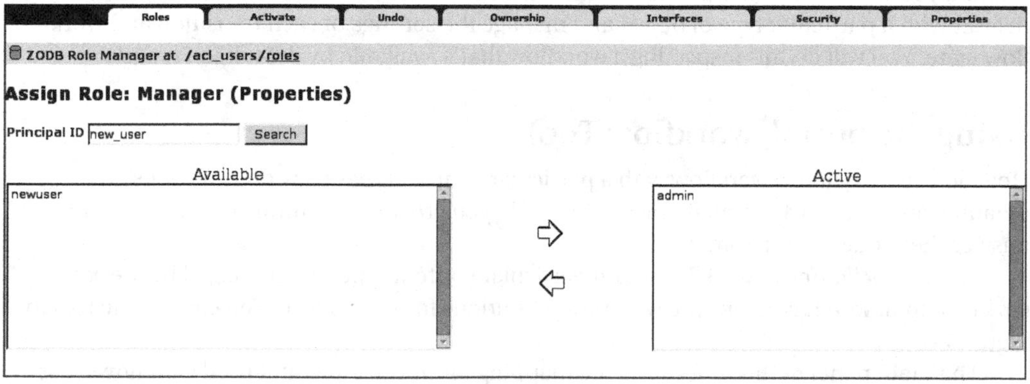

Figure 7-6. *Assigning the role of manager to your new user*

Now you have a new Zope user, new_user, with manager privileges.

In the root of Zope, you always have an `acl_users` tool, but you can also create one or more `acl_users` tools in certain folders contained in the Zope instance; then you can use those tools to store users or override the roles of existing users. That's how you create different areas with local Zope users so that they can authenticate only in that part of the application. For example, you could create accounts for developers only in a certain area (by creating an `acl_users` tool in the proper folder) so that developers can manage the code in one section but won't have the ability to view or manipulate code in other sections.

What you have just seen is only part of what you can do with Zope and users in Zope. If you are interested in finding out more information about Zope 2 security, you can take a look at the Zope Book at www.zope.org/Documentation/Books/ZopeBook/2_6Edition/Security.stx. But, as you probably already know, Plone introduces other advanced security features. Let's go through these new concepts now!

Using Plone Workflows

As you may have already noticed in previous chapters, when you create a new document or view a document as a logged-in user, you'll see the State drop-down menu. "What is that for?" you may ask. Well, it's for managing the "visibility" of your content. The State menu determines whether a page is published so that every visitor can see it or whether it's private so that only certain users can see it. You are probably already familiar with these concepts, because you met them in Chapter 3. So, the State drop-down menu allows you to trigger a state transition and put the item in another logical state. These state transitions compose what is known as *workflow*. This term in general refers to the series of actions that people will go through in an organizational structure. Thus, in content management, it is the step-by-step status that a piece of content will go through, depending on the organization's needs. We'll go more in-depth into workflows in just a moment.

The chain of actions that occurs on objects in Plone is managed by its workflow. In this section, you will see how it is possible, with a few clicks, to change the workflow associated by default with a particular type of object and manage the settings of each transition and workflow state. You will do this inspecting a workflow that's available by default in Plone.

Using the portal_workflow Tool

How do you associate a workflow with a particular content type? How do you choose the default state for a newly created object? Where do you create or customize workflows? We'll answer these questions in order.

First, associations of workflows with particular content types are managed by the portal_workflow tool, which contains the workflow definitions for your portal. You can see the tool in Figure 7-7.

The main panel of this tool shows the mapping for portal types and used workflows. For instance, as you can see, the Document (Page) content type is associated with the (Default) workflow, and the (Default) workflow is mapped to the simple_publication_workflow, since this is what is assigned by default. From here, it is possible to change the workflow mapping.

Don't worry if the workflow you choose doesn't have some states, because you can map them by changing the previous state to a new one that is available in the new workflow you want to enable! You can change the workflow mapping through the Plone interface as well; just enter the Plone control panel, and click Types. As you learned in Chapter 4's "Main Site Setup" section, through this panel you can change the default workflow, either for individual content types or for the entire web site. Whenever you change the associated workflow for an object, you will be prompted to assign a mapping so that you can migrate the old states to new states of existing objects; see Figure 7-8 for an example of changing states to equivalent ones in the new associated workflow.

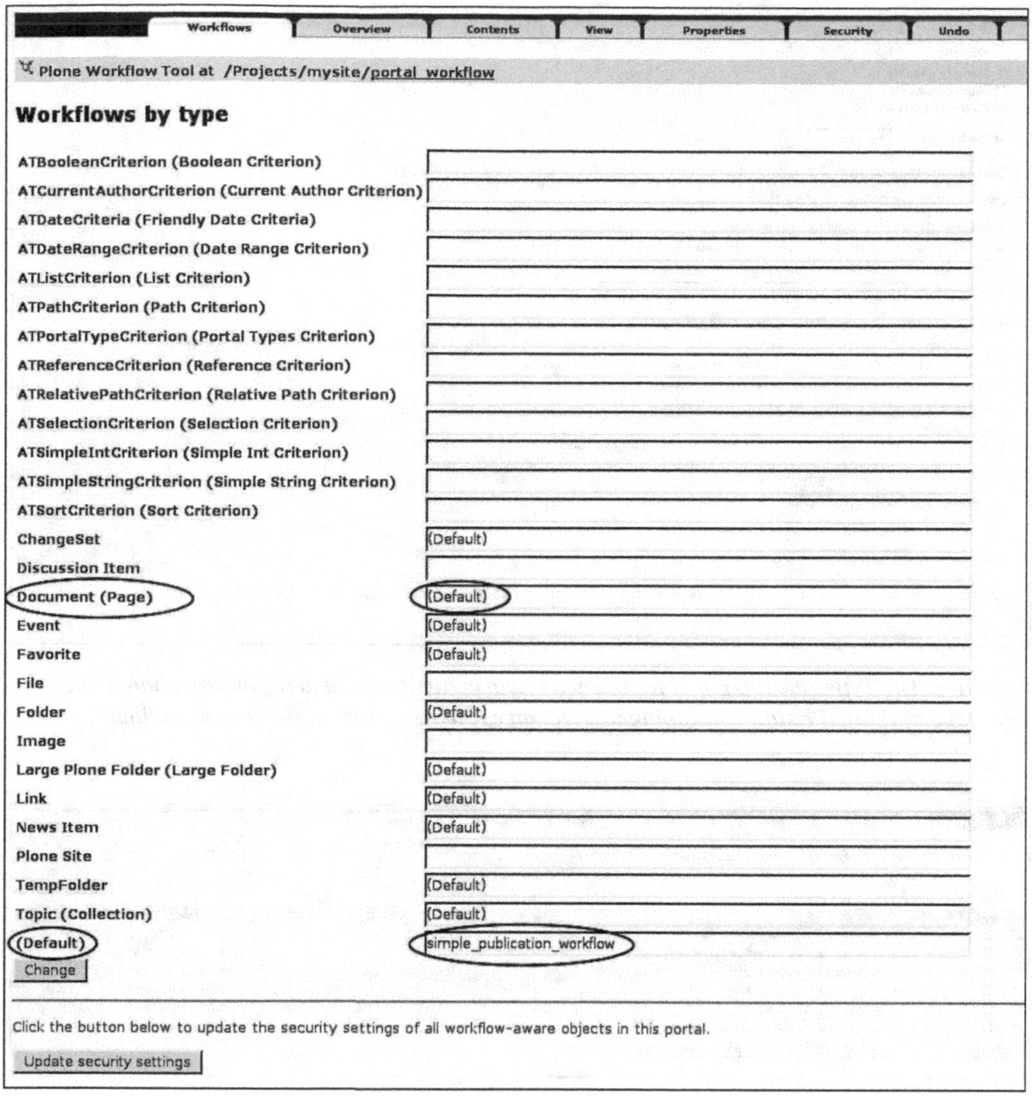

Workflows	Overview	Contents	View	Properties	Security	Undo

⚒ Plone Workflow Tool at /Projects/mysite/portal_workflow

Workflows by type

ATBooleanCriterion (Boolean Criterion)	
ATCurrentAuthorCriterion (Current Author Criterion)	
ATDateCriteria (Friendly Date Criteria)	
ATDateRangeCriterion (Date Range Criterion)	
ATListCriterion (List Criterion)	
ATPathCriterion (Path Criterion)	
ATPortalTypeCriterion (Portal Types Criterion)	
ATReferenceCriterion (Reference Criterion)	
ATRelativePathCriterion (Relative Path Criterion)	
ATSelectionCriterion (Selection Criterion)	
ATSimpleIntCriterion (Simple Int Criterion)	
ATSimpleStringCriterion (Simple String Criterion)	
ATSortCriterion (Sort Criterion)	
ChangeSet	(Default)
Discussion Item	
Document (Page)	(Default)
Event	(Default)
Favorite	(Default)
File	
Folder	(Default)
Image	
Large Plone Folder (Large Folder)	(Default)
Link	(Default)
News Item	(Default)
Plone Site	
TempFolder	(Default)
Topic (Collection)	(Default)
(Default)	simple_publication_workflow

Change

Click the button below to update the security settings of all workflow-aware objects in this portal.

Update security settings

Figure 7-7. *The portal_workflow tool in the ZMI*

The portal_workflow tool has many useful tabs and buttons you should note. One particularly important button you will find in the portal_workflow tool is the "Update security settings" button in the Workflows tab, which lets you update security settings. You should use it every time you change any security configuration, as you will see soon in this chapter. There's also a Contents tab that lets you see what workflows are defined in your portal, as shown in Figure 7-9.

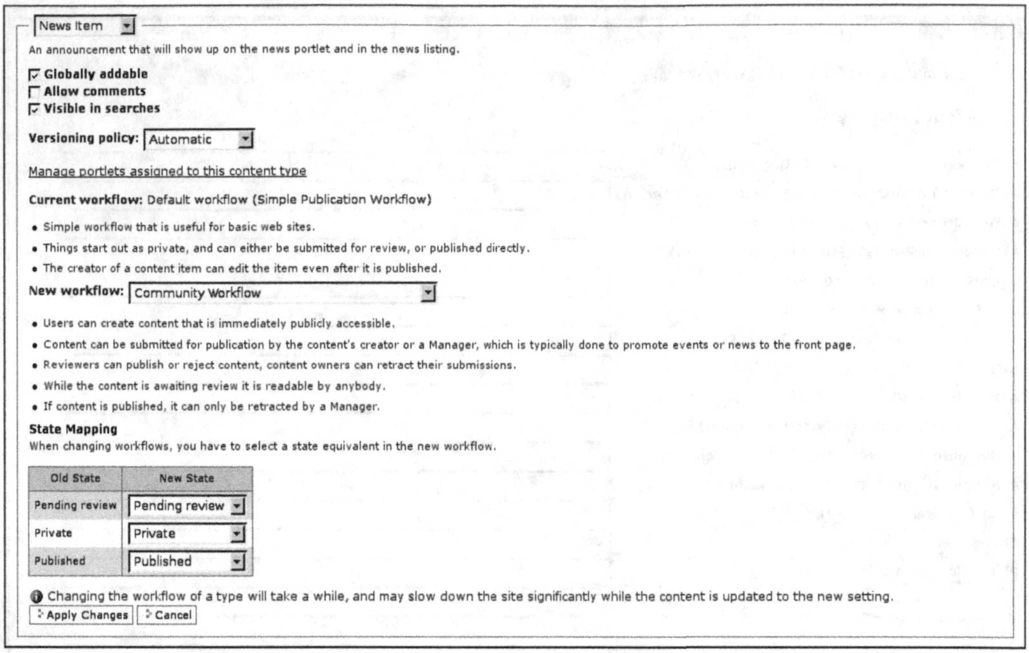

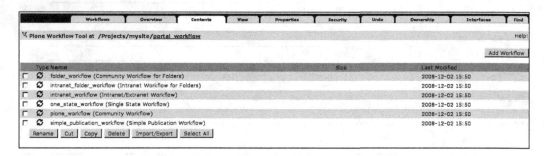

Figure 7-8. *The Type Settings panel for the news item content type, where you can change the workflow and use the state's mapping to select an equivalent state in the new workflow*

Figure 7-9. *The Contents tab in the portal_workflow tool*

Let's look more closely at the `simple_publication_workflow` so that we can show how to manage states, transitions, roles and permissions, groups, variables, and scripts.

Managing an Existing Workflow

As you can see in the Contents tab for the `portal_workflow` tool, one of the available workflows is the one we already talked about, the `simple_publication_workflow`, which is set by default for your site.

Other defined workflows are as follows:

- `folder_workflow`: This is for folders and used in conjunction with the Community workflow. It has no Pending state and allows the owner to publish the folder without approval.

- `intranet_folder_workflow`: This is an Intranet workflow for folders. It's normally used with the Intranet/Extranet workflow on folder types. It has only two states: Private and Internal Draft.

- `intranet_workflow`: This is an Intranet/Extranet workflow. It's an intranet workflow when content is accessible only if you are logged in. Its basic states are Internal Draft, Pending Review, Internally Published, and Private. It also has an Externally Published state, so you can make selected content available to people outside the intranet.

- `one_state_workflow`: This is a single-state workflow. This is essentially a workflow with no transitions but only a Published state.

- `plone_workflow`: This is a Community workflow. Users can create content that is immediately publicly accessible; content can be submitted for publication by the content's creator or a manager, which is typically done to promote events or news to the front page. Reviewers can publish or reject content, and content owners can retract their submissions. While the content is awaiting review, it is readable by anybody. Once content is published, it can be retracted only by a manager.

The Contents tab is also the place where you can create your own workflows, as you will see later in this chapter.

Click the `simple_publication_workflow` link, and a new panel will appear, as you can see in Figure 7-10.

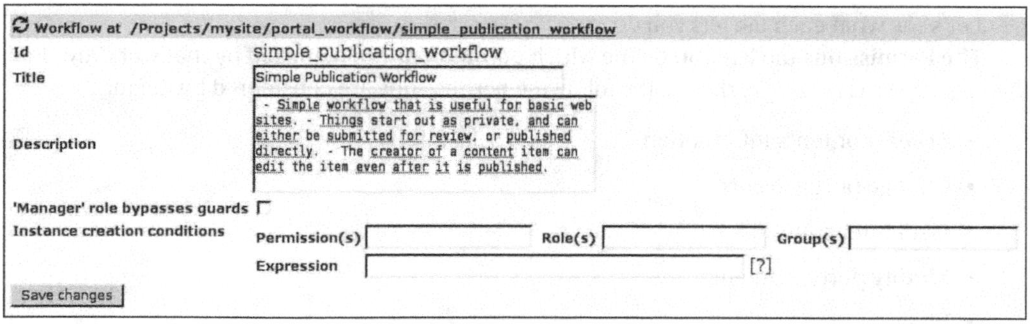

Figure 7-10. *Information about the simple_publication_workflow*

The `simple_publication_workflow` is useful for basic web sites. The description says it all: "Things start out as private, and can either be submitted for review, or published directly. The creator of a content item can edit the item even after it is published."

Before explaining the behavior of this workflow in detail, we'll introduce some basic concepts about how workflows are built.

The main concepts of state-based workflows are as follows:

- States
- Transitions
- Roles
- Permissions

In Plone there are also other features such as review lists, variables, or custom scripts after or before transitions.

A workflow defines one or more logical states and can be associated to a specific portal_ type. When you create a new document, it will be in the initial state defined by the associated workflow. At this point, if you have the correct rights, you can click a state transition, and change it to another logical state. In each logical state, users have different permission settings; in other words, the mappings for member roles vary. Each mapping looks like a matrix that establishes the relationships between roles and permissions for each state.

For each workflow defined in Plone, some useful configuration tabs are available in the ZMI:

- States
- Transitions
- Variables
- Worklists
- Scripts
- Permissions
- Groups

Let's see what each tab lets you do.

The Permissions tab lets you define which permissions are managed by that workflow. For the simple_publication_workflow, the following permissions are considered by default:

- Access contents information
- Change portal events
- List folder contents
- Modify portal content
- View

You can add other permissions to the previous list by using the "Add a managed permission" drop-down menu shown in Figure 7-11. You can also remove permissions by selecting the appropriate check box and clicking the "Remove selected" button.

The Permissions tab is available for each individual workflow state: click the States tab, choose a workflow state, and then click the Permissions tab. Here, you can create a custom permissions-roles mapping for each state, as you will see soon when we will talk about the States tab. In this way, you can grant or not grant permission to members, according to the kind of security settings you want to enable for your content. For instance, by default the anonymous role can view a published object but not hidden objects, only a user with the manager role can edit it, and the creator of it can't edit it (see Figure 7-12).

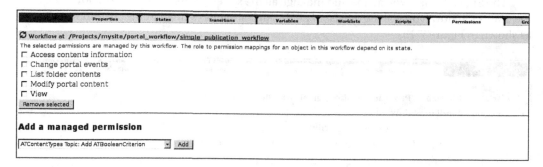

Figure 7-11. *The Permissions tab for simple_publication_workflow*

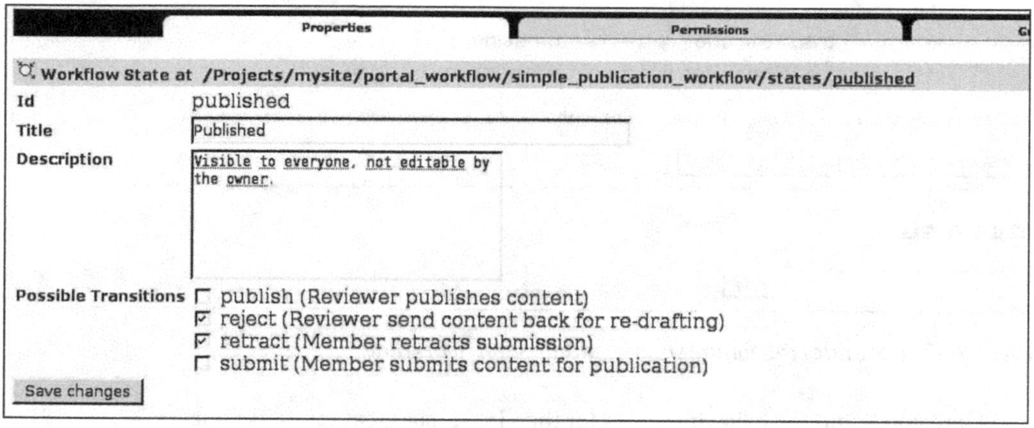

Figure 7-12. *The Permissions panel for a single state*

You can also protect single fields so that they can be viewed, modified, and so on, only by users with certain roles and permissions. But, to do so, you need to write some supplementary code, so we won't face this case here.

The Worklists tab lets you define one or more review chains. By default you will find a review queue for the Pending state.

The Scripts tab lets you include Python scripts in your workflow in order to run them before or after a particular transition. By default it is empty, and these scripts are written only by programmers, not end users (so don't worry about security issues).

The Variables tab lets you add new variables to include in the workflow history of your objects, and you can catalog this information. For example, you can add as variables the time when a transition was performed or comments about the last transition.

The Groups tab lets you set how groups are managed in your workflow. In particular, you can create a group-roles mapping for each logical state.

And now we will cover the most important configuration tabs for workflows: States and Transitions.

The States tab lets you define and manage all the states defined in your workflow. Click the States tab now; you will see the list of all the logical states defined in the current workflow, as shown in Figure 7-13.

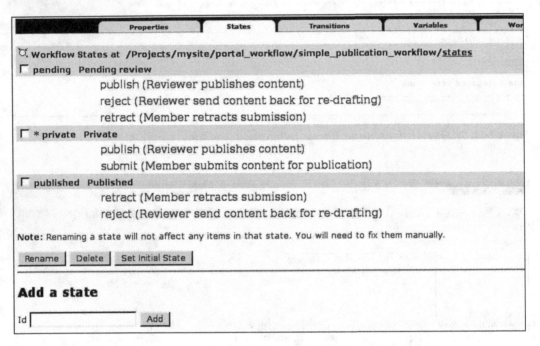

Figure 7-13. *The States tab for the simple_publication_workflow*

Here you'll find the following states for the `simple_publication_workflow`:

- Pending

- Private

- Published

As you have probably noticed, the Private state is marked with an asterisk (*). Only one state can be marked like this because the asterisk indicates the initial state of objects in Plone. That is why when you create a new item on your portal, it is in the Private state. You should also have noticed that for each state some transitions are enabled. For example, from the Private state you can choose a transition that will put items in a different logical state, in this case Publish and Submit. From this tab, you can also create new states, or you can rename and configure an existing state.

Clicking each state allows you to configure it. You can define which transitions you want to enable for that state and configure what users can acquire permission settings (such as viewing, editing, and so on). Let's inspect the Private state and try to find out what you can do through its configuration panel (see Figure 7-14).

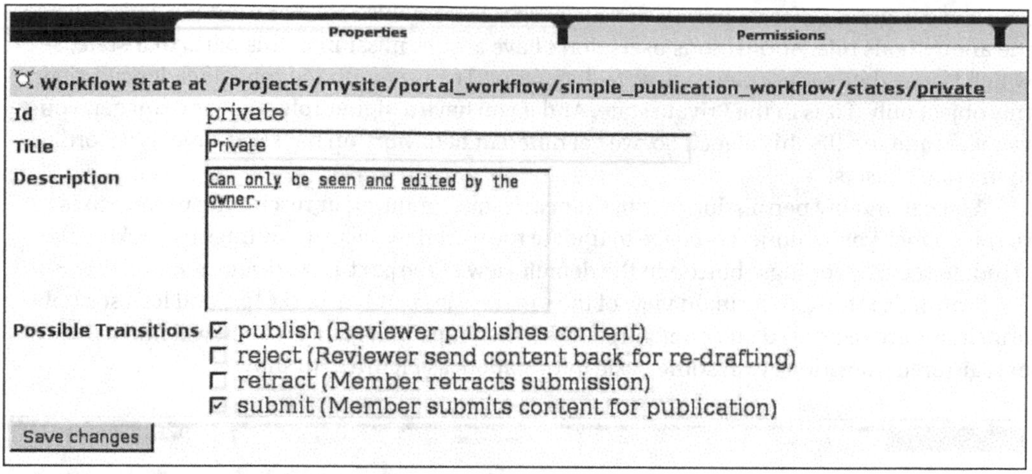

Figure 7-14. *The configuration panel for the Private state*

If you want to manage permission settings for this state, you have to click the Permissions tab, which lets you define a custom permission-roles mapping for that particular state. Figure 7-15 shows the permission settings for the Private state.

Caution Be aware that this is not the same Permissions tab we have already discussed! Previously, we talked about the Permissions tab for each type of workflow registered in the `portal_workflow` tool. Here we are talking about the tab that refers to permission mappings that is different for each workflow state. The same is true for the Groups and Variables tabs. The Groups tab lets you define a group-roles mapping for that particular state. The Variables tab for a particular state allows you to assign values to workflow variables for when objects move to the relevant state.

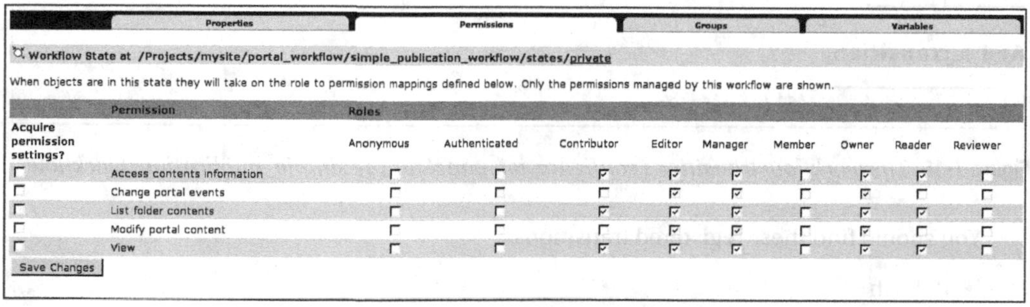

Figure 7-15. *The permission settings for the Private state*

You can grant different permissions to each role from this tool. For example, let's consider the anonymous role. Anonymous users don't have any permission in this particular state, which is why they cannot view a private document. The user with the role of reader can view this object only if it is in the Private state. And if you have a higher role such as manager, you can view and modify this object. So, we get different behaviors on the same objects according to the role of users!

You can modify permission settings for each state, granting or rescinding permissions to roles. Once you're done, you have to update the workflow security settings by clicking the "Update security settings" button in the default view of the `portal_workflow` tool.

Now let's return to the main view of the `simple_publication_workflow`, and let's see how transitions are registered and configured. Click the Transitions tab, and you will find a listing of registered transitions with some basic information, as Figure 7-16 shows.

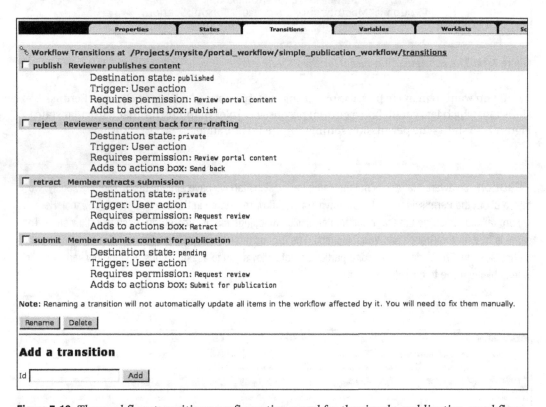

Figure 7-16. *The workflow transitions configuration panel for the simple_publication_workflow*

You should find these registered transitions:

- Publish
- Reject
- Retract
- Submit

For each transition, this listing shows other information. The most important here is the "Destination state" value that lets you define the destination state after the transition, if triggered. For instance, under the reject transition, you can see that if an item undergoes reject, its destination state sets it to Private.

From this panel you can also add new transitions. You can add a new transition from scratch or take a look at how other transitions are configured. Just be sure that you enable your new transition in other states.

To change the settings related to a transition, you need to click the link on that transition to open its configuration panel. To take a closer look at how transitions are configured, click the Publish transition link, and look at the corresponding panel (see Figure 7-17).

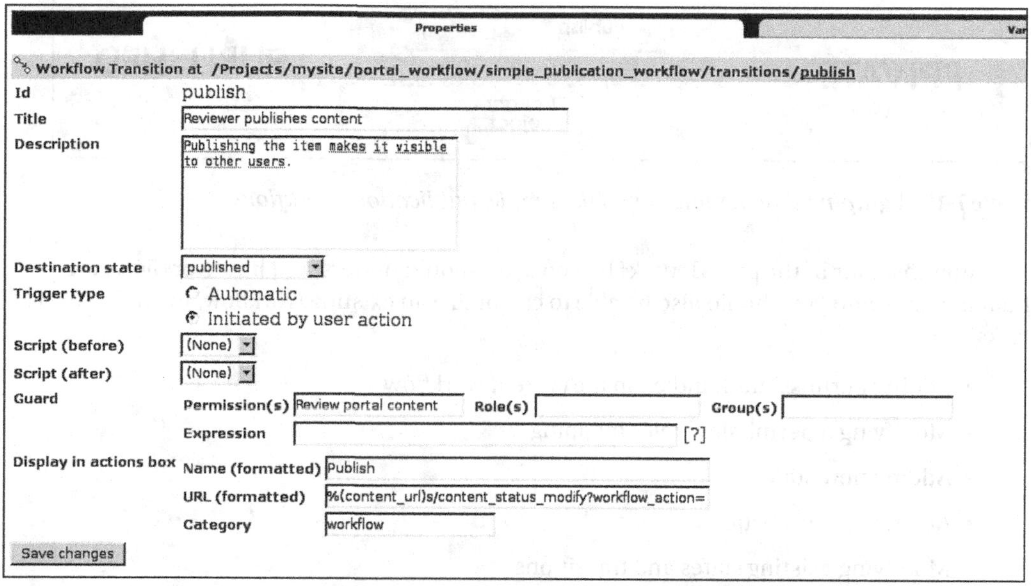

Figure 7-17. *The configuration panel for the Publish transition*

Here you will find a title and some description text, which is useful in order to quickly understand what kind of transition it is. Below that you will find a "Destination state" drop-down menu that lets you set the destination state (in this case Published). You can also select some Python scripts, if there are any, to be launched before or after this transition.

For each transition, you can also configure how it's triggered: by a permission, by a role, by a group, or by an inline generic Python expression. In this case, the Publish transition is protected by the "Review portal content" permission. You can alter this setting with another Zope permission, and this transition will be displayed only to allowed profiles of members. Finally, at the bottom, you'll find the "Display in actions box" area, where you can change the text shown to you in the State menu.

If you can imagine a workflow like a graphical states diagram with transitions that lead you from state to state, on each state you may have a different permissions-roles mapping, and your object behavior will change from role to role! Figure 7-18 shows how the simple_ publication_workflow could graphically appear.

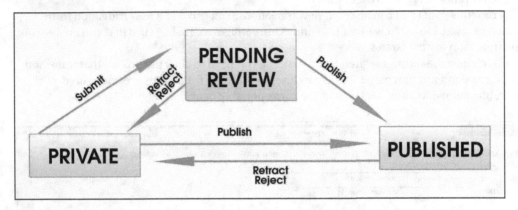

Figure 7-18. *A graphical representation of the simple_publication_workflow*

After this tour of the portal_workflow tool, you should understand how workflows are built in Plone, and you should also be able to customize an existing workflow, including these tasks:

- Adding permissions handled in the current workflow
- Modifying a permission-roles mapping
- Adding new states
- Adding new transitions
- Modifying existing states and transitions
- Using the Types Settings area in the Plone control panel
- Changing the default workflow for different content types
- Setting a workflow for your objects and migrating them to the desired workflow states

After all your changes, you can easily export the workflow settings using the portal_setup tool. In this way, you can create a snapshot/backup configuration; otherwise, if you are a developer, you can include all the configurations you made in the file system product you are developing. With just a few clicks within the portal_setup tool, you can install your product, automatically getting all your workflow settings!

Adding Plone Policy Support

Now we'll introduce the concept of workflow policies. *Workflow policies* are local configurations on site areas and objects so that you can map each content type to existing workflows or custom ones and give different permissions in a specific section of your site. With just a couple of clicks, workflow policies let you create an intranet area within your web site, or a special section with a particular workflow for news items and events, so that the editorial office of a big company can have a custom workflow, for example.

We will not work in the ZMI; we will use the Plone user interface this time, so don't worry! This feature is very easy to manage.

First, enable the Workflow Policy Support product (CMFPlacefulWorkflow) available (but not installed) by default in Plone. To do so, go to the Plone control panel, click Add-on Products, select the Workflow Policy Support item, and confirm the installation. After that, a new item, named Workflow Policies, should appear in the Plone control panel; clicking it will lead to a new configuration form.

Through the Workflow Policies configuration panel you will be able to modify the global portal_type-workflow mapping (you will be able to select the workflow you want for each content type in a certain area of your web site), modify existing local workflow policy settings, and create or duplicate a new workflow policy that you can apply locally on content.

The Workflow Policies configuration panel presents two configuration tabs, as you can see in Figure 7-19. The Global Content Type to Workflow Mapping tab lets you select the workflow you want to apply to each content type.

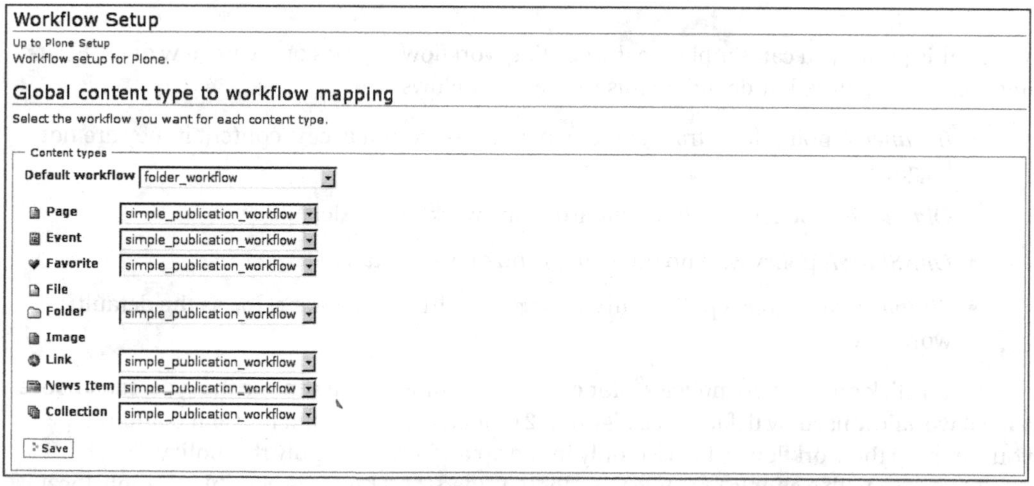

Workflow Setup

Up to Plone Setup
Workflow setup for Plone.

Global content type to workflow mapping

Select the workflow you want for each content type.

Content types	
Default workflow	folder_workflow
📄 Page	simple_publication_workflow
📅 Event	simple_publication_workflow
♥ Favorite	simple_publication_workflow
📄 File	
📁 Folder	simple_publication_workflow
🖼 Image	
🔗 Link	simple_publication_workflow
📰 News Item	simple_publication_workflow
📚 Collection	simple_publication_workflow

[Save]

Figure 7-19. *The Global Content Type to Workflow Mapping tab for workflow policies*

If you change something here, whatever you change will be reflected in the portal_ workflow tool, which we already discussed. In fact, this configuration panel is more than a user-friendly front-end view for the portal_workflow tool—it also introduces some new useful features! We'll discuss them in a moment.

The second tab, Local Content Type to Workflow Mapping (shown in Figure 7-20), leads you through the Workflow Policies configuration panel; it lets you define new custom workflow policies and configure the existing ones, if needed, by changing the default mapping for content types and used workflows.

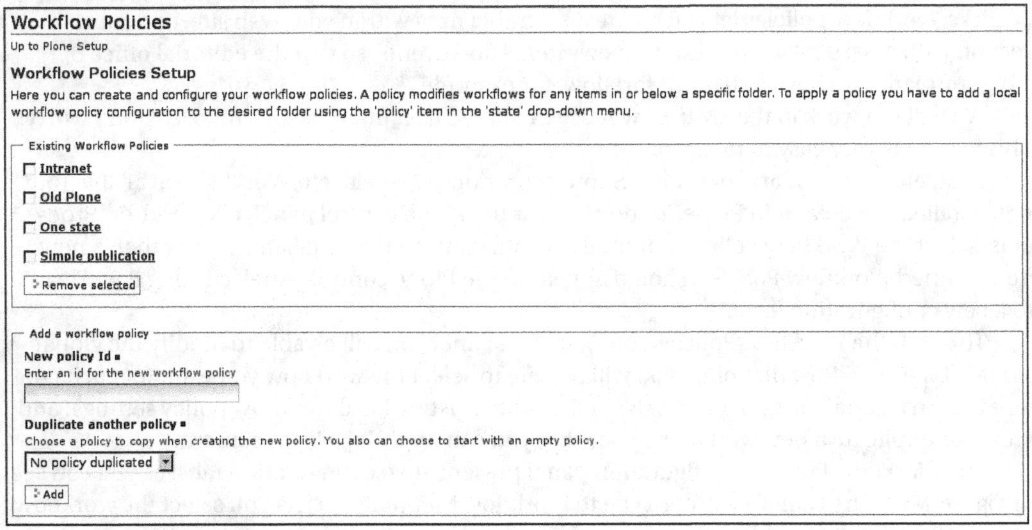

```
Workflow Policies

Up to Plone Setup

Workflow Policies Setup
Here you can create and configure your workflow policies. A policy modifies workflows for any items in or below a specific folder. To apply a policy you have to add a local
workflow policy configuration to the desired folder using the 'policy' item in the 'state' drop-down menu.

┌─ Existing Workflow Policies ──────────────────────────────────────────────────────────────────────────────┐
│  ☐ Intranet                                                                                                 │
│  ☐ Old Plone                                                                                                │
│  ☐ One state                                                                                                │
│  ☐ Simple publication                                                                                       │
│  ⬥ Remove selected                                                                                          │
└────────────────────────────────────────────────────────────────────────────────────────────────────────────┘

┌─ Add a workflow policy ───────────────────────────────────────────────────────────────────────────────────┐
│  New policy Id ■                                                                                            │
│  Enter an id for the new workflow policy                                                                    │
│  [                                        ]                                                                  │
│                                                                                                             │
│  Duplicate another policy ■                                                                                 │
│  Choose a policy to copy when creating the new policy. You also can choose to start with an empty policy.   │
│  [No policy duplicated ▼]                                                                                   │
│  ⬥ Add                                                                                                      │
└────────────────────────────────────────────────────────────────────────────────────────────────────────────┘
```

Figure 7-20. *The Local Content Type to Workflow Mapping tab for workflow policies*

At this point, you can simply use the existing workflow policies or create new ones. Existing policies, registered by default in this tool, are as follows:

- *Intranet*: A policy for intranet areas where users cannot access content if they are not logged in

- *Old Plone*: A policy with the standard Plone workflow as default

- *One State*: A policy with no transitions and only one state

- *Simple publication*: A policy with the `simple_publication_workflow` as the default workflow

If you click one of these policies—for example, Intranet—you can see that you can choose a local workflow used by default (see Figure 7-21 for an example), and for each content type you can map the workflow to be used only in the area where you apply this policy.

Let's start with a simple example in order to understand how it is possible to apply local workflow mappings. Imagine you have to deal with a public web site powered by Plone, but you want also to add a reserved area, reachable only by registered users. In this area, different profiles of users can create, view, and modify content depending on user roles. You can also publish some content externally if you want, letting anonymous users view the content; otherwise, nobody can see inside this area.

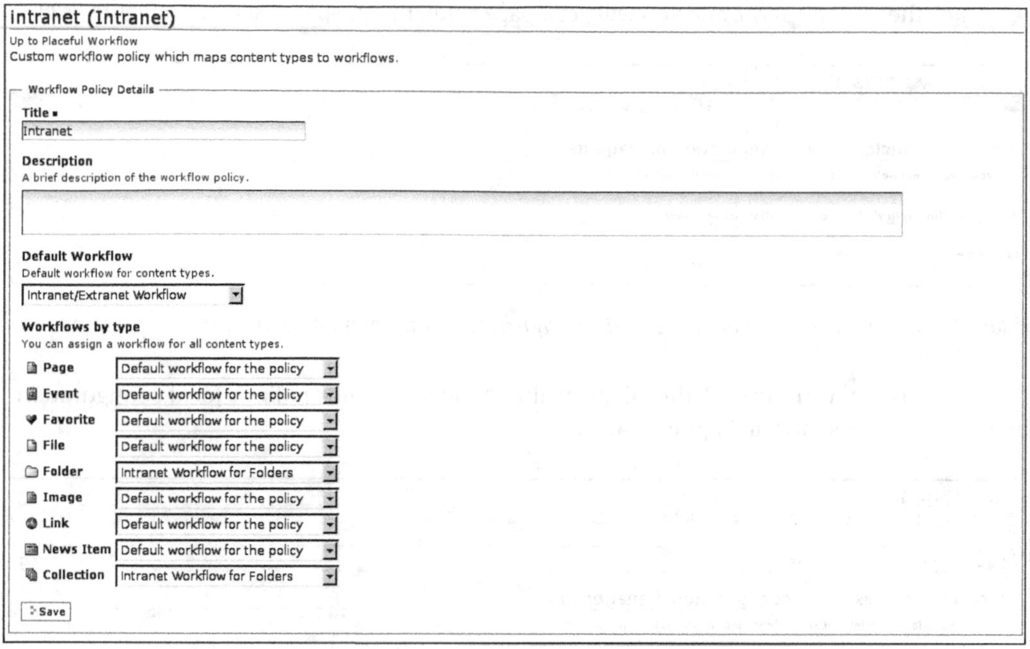

Figure 7-21. *The workflow mapping configuration panel for Intranet*

How can you do this? Go into the root of your web site, and create a new folder named, for example, Intranet. At this point, if you have correctly installed the workflow policy support, look at the State drop-down menu, and you will see a new item, Policy, as shown in Figure 7-22.

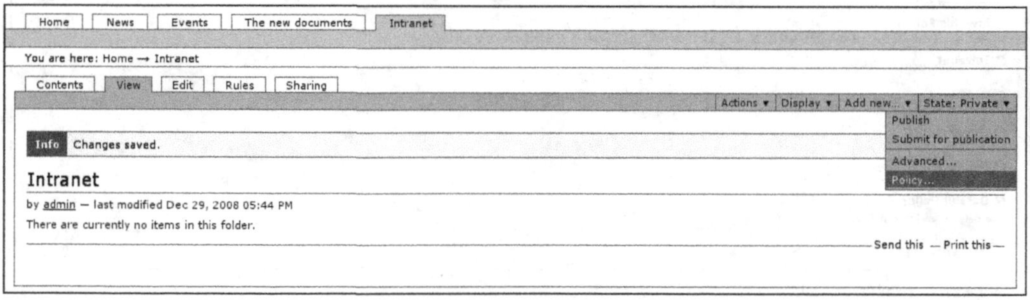

Figure 7-22. *The new option that will appear in the State menu: Policy*

Click the Policy option, and you will get a page similar to the panel shown in Figure 7-23.

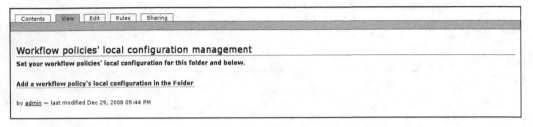

Figure 7-23. *The Workflow Policies' Local Configuration Management panel for new folders*

At this point, you can click the following link: "Add a workflow policy's local configuration in the Folder," as shown in Figure 7-24.

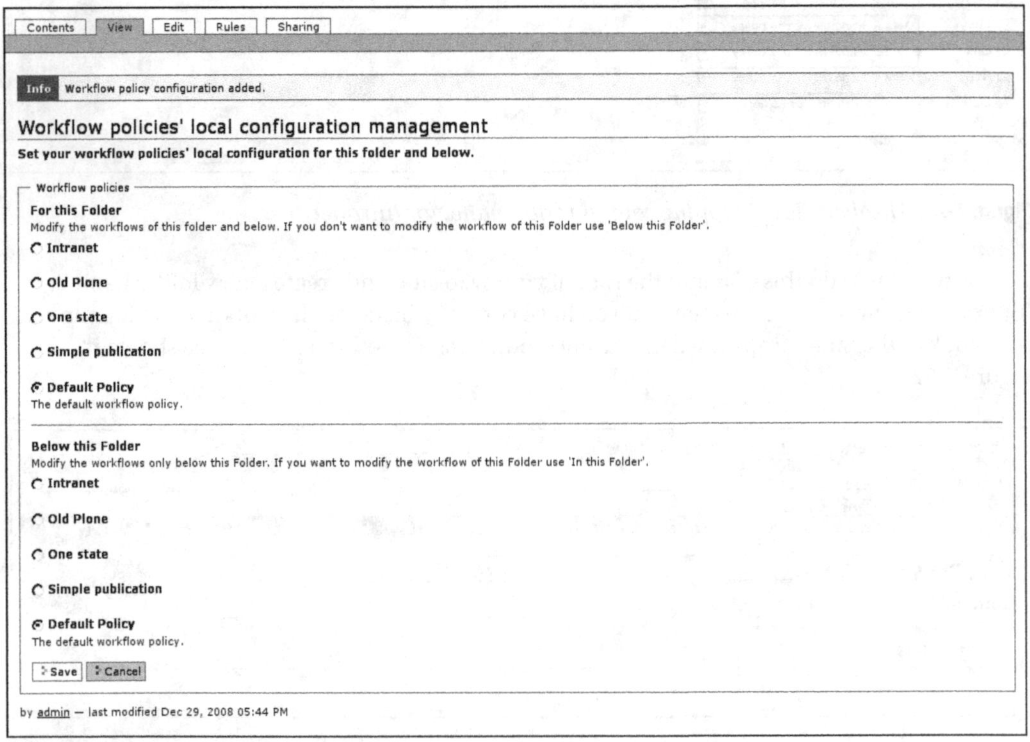

Figure 7-24. *Adding a new workflow policy in a folder*

You can choose a workflow policy for the current folder and also for other content that the folder contains. Toggle the Intranet option for both sections of the configuration panel (you can choose any other option, of course, according to your needs).

With just a couple of clicks of your mouse, you've created an entire intranet area—wow! The entire web site now has a global workflow definition. In the Intranet folder only, you have a custom workflow policy that puts at your disposal an intranet/extranet area. If you take a closer look at the Intranet folder, you will notice that both the Intranet folder and the items it contains have different workflow states, as you can see in Figure 7-25, for example.

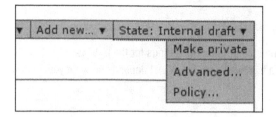

Figure 7-25. *The State menu for the intranet area*

If you want to find out more details of how the intranet workflow works, you can go to the portal_workflow tool in the ZMI. You can see these available states:

- *Internal Draft*: Visible to all intranet users; editable by the owner

- *Pending Review*: Waiting to be reviewed; not editable by the owner

- *Internally Published*: Published and visible to intranet users; not editable by the owner

- *Private*: Cannot be seen by simple registered members

- *Externally Published*: Selected content available to people outside the intranet

You can inspect the permission settings for each state in the same manner you inspected the simple_publication_workflow in this chapter.

In this case, you used a workflow policy already available in Plone. The workflow policy configuration panel will also let you create new policies manually or duplicate existing ones. So, if you want a new local configuration workflow policy, you can create it by hand or, if it is similar to an existing one, duplicate it and change only those mappings that you want to modify. In this way, you can duplicate and customize a policy without modifying the original one. Once created, you can create a new area and apply the new policy, as already done, or apply it to an existing folder.

Creating and Customizing Plone Workflows

You have already seen how workflows are organized. In this section, we will show how to build a couple of simple and practical examples.

Customizing an Existing Workflow

You have seen that the intranet_workflow allows you to publish content externally so that anonymous users can also view it. If you want to disable this feature from the default intranet workflow, you can untoggle the publish_externally transition on those states where it is enabled: Pending and Internally Published. To do so, go to the portal_workflow tool of your Plone site, click the Contents tab, and select intranet_workflow. At this point, click the States tab, click the Internal Published state, and deselect the transition called publish_externally. Repeat this operation also for the Pending state. After that you can remove the external state if you want because there are no transitions to this state.

That is it—you have just customized your first workflow! Now if you are using the intranet_workflow, you should not find any publish_externally option in the State menu. You can also export all your manual configurations using the portal_setup tool.

Note Instead of doing it this way, you can also change the permission settings for the publish_ externally transition and protect this transition with a higher permission. It just depends on what you want to do.

Duplicating and Creating New Workflows

Let's say you want to create your own intranet workflow and keep the original Plone's intranet_workflow untouched. Go to the portal_workflow tool, copy and paste the intranet_ workflow, and rename it to myintranet_workflow.

Do this as an exercise, but first remove from the new myintranet_workflow the publish_ externally transition created in the previous example. At this point, you can disable transitions, change permission settings, and add new states and transitions, all by working through your browser. When you have finished, you can use it as a local workflow policy or assign this workflow to one or more content types.

Let's enrich our example. Let's add a new state called to_be_deleted and of course a new transition called request_delete. This means you will be able to mark some content as removed, and this content should not be visible for anonymous users; reviewers can manually decide whether content marked as to_be_deleted should be removed, or you can choose to automatically eventually delete content from a batch script called once a week. We will not implement the batch script, but we will cover the workflow configuration.

Note You can do something similar with several methods. For example, you can put your objects in the state Hidden and mark them with a to_be_deleted keyword. You will be equally able to apply a script that deletes those objects automatically.

It's also a good idea to create the ability to undo any changes if you make a mistake; to do this, we'll create a new transition called undelete. Let's start from the myintranet_workflow. Go to the States tab of this workflow; fill in the "Add a state" form with the name of the new state, to_be_deleted; and finally click the Add button.

At this point, you can click the new state you just created and configure the permission settings. You can copy the same settings of the Private state.

Now return to the default view of your myintranet_workflow, and click the Transitions tab. Then add a new transition named request_delete through the "Add transition" field. Click the new transition, and configure it: insert a title, choose to_be_deleted as the destination state, and allow this transition to trigger only for those users who have the "Review portal content" permission. Then configure the display box: use request_delete as the title, and finally put this expression into the URL section:

%(content_url)s/content_status_modify?workflow_action=request_delete

You can copy this expression from another transition. Note that the last part of the URL is the transition ID!

Repeating these steps, now create a new transition called undelete that will lead the object into another state (such as the Private one), letting users undelete contents marked as to_be_deleted before the batch script will run. In Figure 7-26 you can see what the transition configuration form should look like.

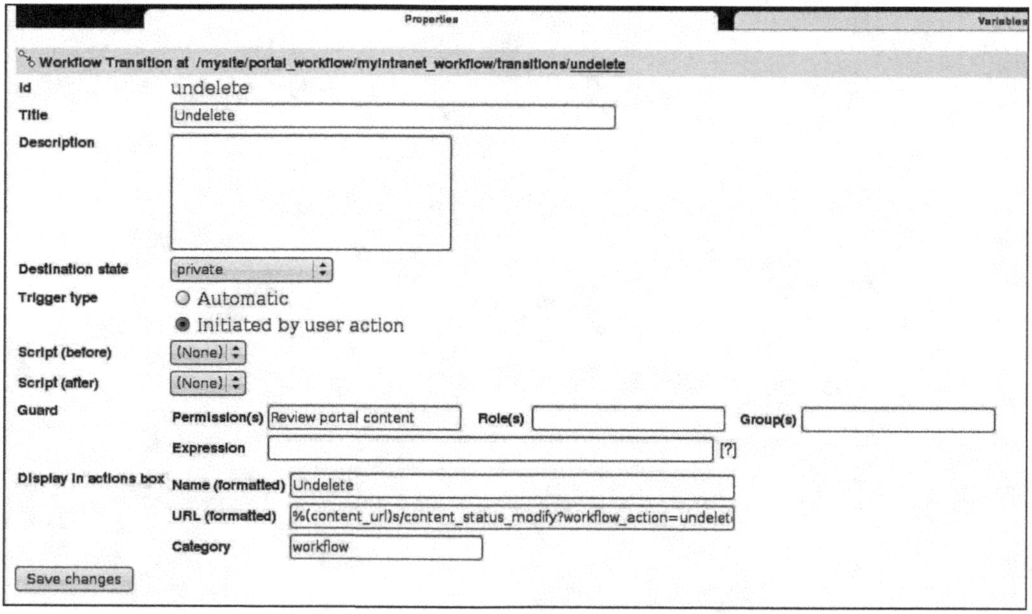

Figure 7-26. *The configuration panel for the workflow transition "undelete" we just created in our example*

Note that we have only created two new transitions; we still have to enable them. So, enable only the first new transition, request_delete, in the Internally Published state (or wherever you need to enable it) by toggling the request_delete transition. Next, do the same for the undelete transition. Go to the to_be_deleted state, toggle undelete, and confirm. You're done! Using only a browser, you have created a custom workflow, and now you can export it using the portal_setup tool.

Summary

In this chapter, you learned how security is handled at the Zope level, and we introduced some basic concepts such as users, permissions, and roles. You also learned how to manage Zope users using the `acl_users` tool, creating and changing roles as necessary.

By now you should know that Zope has a very powerful and granular security architecture and that Plone inherits this solidity. Plone takes advantage of the Zope security architecture; but more important, it adds other concepts such as workflows applied to content.

Finally, you learned how to edit existing workflows provided by default in Plone and how to create new workflows from scratch using just a browser. This way, you can add all the states you need for your objects with different permission settings for each state, where permissions may refer to viewing the whole object, viewing or modifying a particular field, reviewing it, and so on. This lets you build complex state-based workflows that let different users interact, with review steps and other cool things, all from right within your browser.

CHAPTER 8

■ ■ ■

Advanced User Management

Plone is a powerful and flexible system not only for web content management but also for user management. Plone stores all its users inside the Zope Object Database (ZODB) in a separate user list; however, you may need to use another service, such as a relational database that manages your users' information. Thanks to Plone's *pluggable authentication service* (PAS), you can use other services to authenticate your users. The most common alternative system is LDAP, which we will discuss in this chapter. Of course, if you don't have any special requirements, you can just use Plone as it is, with users and groups stored in the ZODB.

Note that you don't need to write any code to integrate your Plone site with another application for user management. As you will see in this chapter, you only have to install the product. Then you will be able to configure your service to authenticate your users directly from Plone without dealing with the ZMI—all with just a couple of clicks! You can also create new plug-ins, if you use different user sources.

In this chapter, first we will introduce some basic concepts about how the authentication service works in Plone. After that, you will see how it is possible to attach Plone to LDAP or relational databases.

Caution In this chapter, you will be playing around with the `acl_users` folders inside a Plone site. Never delete or alter the `acl_users` folder in the root of your Zope instance. If you do that and your user folder breaks for some reason (the server goes down, for example), your entire site will be blocked, and you will no longer be able to get any access, even as an administrator. So, make sure you change only the user folder in the Plone site!

In any case, if you have locked yourself out of your Plone site, don't worry, because you can perform a little rescue mission. The page `http://plone.org/documentation/faq/locked-out` explains how to create a new user without having a manager user account for newer versions, for nonbuildout versions, and for old versions of Zope.

The Pluggable Authentication Service (PAS)

The PAS is Plone's built-in user authentication system. It takes care of user authentication, asks users to log in if needed, allows you to search for users and groups, determines the groups to which a user belongs, and is responsible for extracting credentials from the request and many other things.

It is not built as a monolithic service, but rather it is implemented by several components, called *plug-in*s, that provide the interfaces needed by the PAS. The concepts behind the extreme modularity of the PAS come from the Zope Component Architecture.

In case you are not familiar with this powerful architecture, we'll start with a brief introduction to the concept of *interfaces* in PAS. What kind of functionality does the PAS need? Surely, it needs at least authentication functionality, extraction, properties functionality, and roles and groups membership, as you will see later. For each functionality needed by PAS, there is one or more *plug-in*s, which are small components that provide interfaces related to a specific functionality. The interface describes the PAS functionality; it's like the interface is a contract between two parts (the PAS infrastructure and the plug-in). Essentially, the plug-in promises to provide certain functionalities, and the PAS system knows how to interact with the plug-in thanks to the interface.

Now we'll give you a bit more of a technical definition of *interface*: it is a class with a set of declarations (attributes or methods) that have to be implemented by the object that will declare to provide this interface. So, if you have an object that provides an interface, this object is supposed to work as specified in the interface. That is why interfaces are commonly referred to as contracts; you'll find a similar concept of interfaces in the Java programming language.

What are the advantages? As the Zope Component Architecture teaches, having small and simple components helps in the readability of code, offers maintainability, and allows each component to be better tested. The same considerations apply to PAS and the plug-ins' architecture. There are one or more content components for the storage feature (that is, where users are stored, as in the Zope Object Database, LDAP, relational database, and so on), one or more registered extraction plug-ins for the extraction interface needed by the PAS (how users authenticate), and so on. For each PAS functionality, you can register one or more plug-ins providing that feature needed by PAS.

Why, you may ask, would you want to register one or more plug-ins for the same feature? We'll answer that by providing a simple example. The extraction feature allows PAS to detect how users authenticate, extracting credentials from a request. By default, credentials are taken from HTTP cookies, HTTP login form data, or basic HTTP authentication, but you can also use other methods to authenticate users. For instance, if you want to authenticate users through an IP address, you only have to write a new PAS plug-in providing the extraction interface and plug it in. You're done! Having more than one plug-in for the same functionality also allows you to present users with various authentication methods; the PAS will try the authentication methods in the order you specify, such as HTTP cookie, then HTTP login form, then basic HTTP authentication, and so on. Situations such as these are why Plone allows one or more plug-ins to provide the same feature.

The PAS in Plone

Where is the PAS in Plone? Newer versions of Plone provide a PAS-based user folder by default. If you have an old version of Plone (2.1.*x* and older; you should have at least version 2.5.*x*), you will have to install the Plone PAS products manually. In all cases, you can find the PAS-based user folder by going into the ZMI and clicking the acl_users tool (as shown in Figure 8-1).

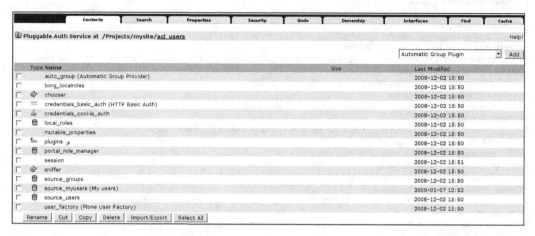

Figure 8-1. *The acl_users tool for your Plone site, where you can add and manage user accounts*

Note In this case, we are talking about the acl_users tool in the Plone site; it is not the http://localhost:8080/acl_users item.

As we discussed in Chapter 7, the acl_users tool has several tabs; one of them is the Search tab that lets you search for users by user ID or login name. But let's go to the default view of acl_users now and click the Contents tab.

You should see a lot of PAS items in this panel. The most important item is Plugins, which is a registry of plug-ins. For each PAS functionality, it registers which plug-ins that feature provides and in which order the plug-ins should be called. The other items you'll see in the acl_users tool, such as source_groups, source_users, and so on, are all PAS plug-ins. Each of them provides some PAS functionality, specified in a particular interface.

The Plug-in Types

There are many other plug-in types, and each of them provides a PAS feature such as adding users, user enumeration, roles and local role issues, and so on, as mentioned earlier. On each of these plug-in items, you will find a different view and several configuration tabs. Click the plugins item in the acl_users tool of your Plone site again; Figure 8-2 shows you what you will find.

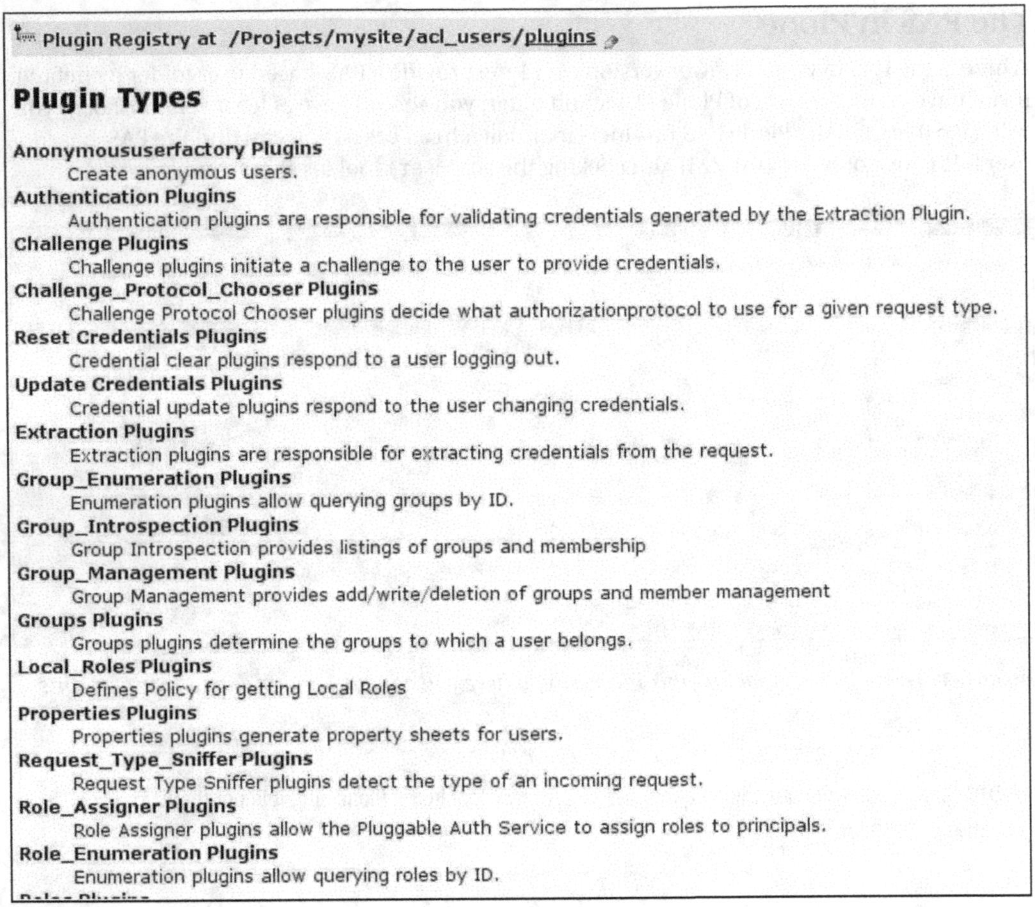

Figure 8-2. *The Plugin Types panel (the figure has been cropped to make the image more readable), where you can click the different plug-ins and configure them*

These are the most important interfaces that you may want to configure:

- *Extraction Plugins*: Extraction plug-ins are responsible for extracting credentials from the request.

- *Authentication Plugins*: Authentication plug-ins are responsible for validating credentials generated by the extraction plug-in.

- *Groups Plugins*: These determine the groups to which a user belongs.

- *Group_Enumeration Plugins*: These allow you to query groups by ID and implement search logic for groups.

- *Properties Plugins*: These generate property sheets for users.

Let's return to the Plugin Types item and inspect one PAS functionality as an example to see which registered plug-ins this feature provides and how they are configured. Let's consider the Extraction Plugins (the interface provided by Extraction Plugins is IExtractionPlugin). Click this item, and a panel like the one shown in Figure 8-3 will appear.

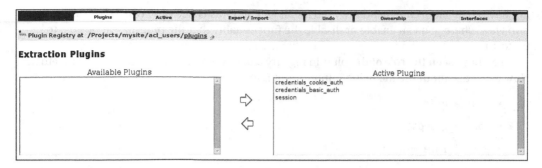

Figure 8-3. *The Extraction Plugins panel, where you can configure the plug-ins that are responsible for extracting credentials from the request*

On the left you should find the available plug-ins, and on the right you'll see the enabled plug-ins providing IExtractionPlugin. Note that the order of registered plug-ins is important because it changes the order in which the plug-ins will be called (the plug-in on top takes precedence). In this case, the select box on the left is empty, and you can see three registered plug-ins on the right for this functionality, in this order:

1. `credentials_cookie_auth`: This is responsible for extracting the credentials of users through HTTP cookies (if used) or from login forms or login portlets in Plone.

2. `credentials_basic_auth`: If you perform basic HTTP authentication from the ZMI before entering Plone, `credentials_basic_auth` manages the extraction.

3. `session`: Finally, the `session` plug-in is configured to use an SHA1-based authentication method to identify login sessions.

This is the chain of extraction plug-ins by default.

Managing Users Through the acl_users Tool

Now let's return to the `acl_users` tool and click one of the plug-ins we just mentioned; for example, click the `credentials_cookie_auth` plug-in (Figure 8-4 shows what you will get).

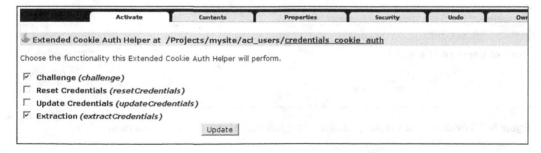

Figure 8-4. *The credentials_cookie_auth panel, where you can choose the functionality this Extended Cookie Auth Helper will perform*

Here you'll see several tabs. The tabs may differ from plug-in to plug-in. For example, with some plug-ins you'll see a Properties tab that lets you configure a plug-in; other plug-ins may not have such a tab. One mandatory tab for all PAS plug-ins is Activate, which is a configuration view where you can enable or disable the functionality that the plug-in will be able to perform.

You have seen the role of the plug-in registry and how components are plugged together. Now we'll talk about the following important plug-ins:

- `source_users`

- `source_groups`

- `portal_role_manager`

These plug-ins are responsible for storing users and groups into the Zope Object Database by default in Plone; for example, you can also change passwords and roles for a particular user by going, respectively, to the `source_users` and `portal_role_manager` plug-ins.

■Note You should always manage users and groups using the Plone interface whenever possible, as you saw in Chapter 4. The next examples are useful only if you are working outside Plone. If you have a particular requirement that compels you to do something different or if you are curious about understanding how Plone users, groups, and roles management work "under the hood," then follow the next examples to discover more about the `acl_users` tool and basic PAS plug-ins.

If you click the `source_groups` plug-in, you will find a listing of groups on your Plone site. In the "Current Groups" section, you can add new groups (or remove existing ones) and assign users to an existing group. If you move on to the `source_users` plug-in, you will find a listing of registered users on the site. This listing will be empty when you're starting with a new site or when users are being handled by another plug-in, but, generally, this is where you can manage your users. You can add and remove users, change login names, and change passwords.

If you want to create a new user, you can click the "Add a user" link, fill in the add form, and confirm your decision by clicking the Add User button, as you already saw in Chapter 7. We've added a user named John, for example, as shown in Figure 8-5.

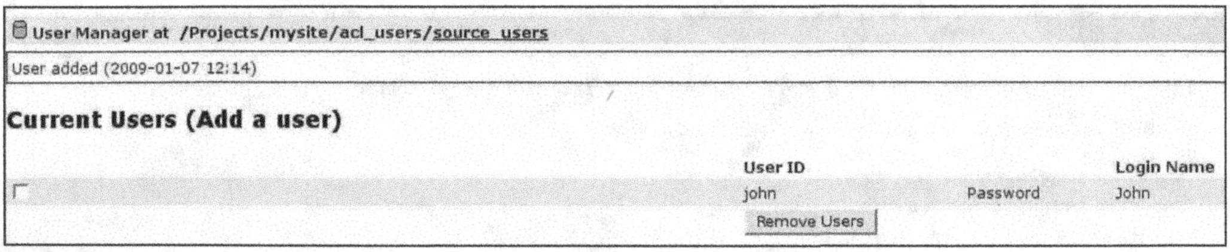

User Manager at /Projects/mysite/acl_users/source_users
User added (2009-01-07 12:14)

Current Users (Add a user)

	User ID		Login Name
☐	john	Password	John

Remove Users

Figure 8-5. *The source_users plug-in, where we just added a new user called John*

Now, if you want, you can remove this new user by selecting its check box and clicking the Remove Users button. You can change the login name by clicking the user ID, and you can change the password for this user by clicking Password.

Suppose you now want to grant user John the manager role. You will have to click the `portal_role_manager` plug-in. When you do, you'll see a tabular listing of existing roles and assignments. In this case, click the manager role (the question mark link in the Assignments column), search for a user named John, and assign that user to the manager role. At this point, John will be considered a manager (for a more complete explanation, review Chapter 7).

Now we'll show a more practical example. You have seen that for each PAS function you can have one or more plug-ins providing the interface. So, now you can manually create a new source for users and play with PAS settings in order to have and manage more than one user manager. This way you will start learning to deal with PAS settings; after that, you should also be able to apply these configurations when you are configuring LDAP or SQL user sources. Go to the acl_users tool of your Plone site, and from the Add drop-down menu select ZODB User Manager. Fill in the form with an ID such as source_myusers, and confirm that decision clicking the Add button. Go to the new source, and click the Activate tab. Here you will find these options, all deselected:

- *Authentication*: Select this option to let users contained in this source authenticate.

- *User_Adder*: Select this option to enable this source to accept user additions.

- *User_Enumeration*: Select this option to allow the enumeration or search for users contained in this source.

By playing with these three options and configuring the order of plug-ins, you will be able to implement some interesting use cases.

Users Will Not Appear in Search Results

Do you want to use this new source (the one we just created called source_myusers) for adding new users that for some reason you don't want to enumerate in search results? (In other words, do you want to make it so that there's no way to search for those new users in the Sharing panel or in the user management area in the Plone control panel?)

If so, select the Authentication and User_Adder options, and click the Update button, keeping the User Enumeration option unselected. Then click the Authentication link, and put your new source on top of the enabled plug-ins. Now, new users will be created automatically in your source of users because your source takes precedence, and they will not appear in user searches. If you go to the Plone control panel and add a new user, it will be created in this source, but it will not appear in user enumerations. This could be useful for managing a forum in which many users will register to add comments and participate in discussions but for which you don't need to enumerate this kind of user in search results; you just need to search and give permissions to the actual site managers.

Users Can Be Searched but Cannot Authenticate

Do you want to set your new source of users so that the users contained in it will be available for searches? In other words, do you want to let them authenticate?

Select only the User_Enumeration option, and confirm by clicking the Update button. The users contained in this source will be available as search results or other listings, but they will not be able to authenticate. It will be impossible to log in for a user contained in this source. This can be useful for sites whose content has been written by an external provider. This way, the authors (who will be registered in the source you are managing) will be available for searches and you will respect their intellectual property, but those users will not be able to authenticate, since there is no reason to let them do so.

No Other Users Will Be Created in This Source

Do you want to plug into Plone a different source for letting users authenticate but you don't want to let anyone create new users on this source? In that case, select the Authentication and User_Enumeration options, and confirm by clicking the Update button. New users will be created in the default source of users. This configuration is very common with external sources that are LDAP or SQL based.

For example, when you plug into Plone an external source of users such as LDAP or a relational database, deselecting the User_Adder option is common. Adding an LDAP user is managed using another tool in order to have a unique management tool. You can mix all these use cases; it just depends on what you need to do.

■**Note** You can easily export and reimport your source with all registered users with the `zexp` import/export tool available in the ZMI.

Authentication with LDAP

In this section you will see how to authenticate users through LDAP. You will have to install the `plone.app.ldap` Python egg only (which was formerly called `simplon.plone.ldap`), and Plone will automatically install all the necessary dependencies. Here are all the dependencies you will need for `plone.app.ldap`:

- `python-ldap`, which provides an object-oriented API to access LDAP directory servers from Python code

- `LDAPUserFolder`, which is a user folder replacement for Zope that authenticates Zope users against LDAP

- `LDAPMultiPlugins`, which provides `PluggableAuthService` plug-ins that interoperate with LDAP

- `Products.PloneLDAP`, which is built upon the `LDAPMultiPlugins` and `LDAPUserFolder` products and contains PAS plug-ins that allow you to use LDAP and Active Directory servers in a Plone site, making it easier to use LDAP connections

Thanks to the `plone.app.ldap` Python egg, it is now easier to create LDAP connections in a Plone web site and manage LDAP and Active Directory servers through a Plone configuration panel with a friendly user interface; in other words, you don't have to deal directly with the `acl_users` tool and the ZMI.

You should know that advanced users may prefer to deal directly with PAS plug-ins instead of working with these wrappers that give a more user-friendly interface but less control. However, if you want to start and install LDAP support quickly, the `plone.app.ldap` product may prove useful for you.

Note This works for Plone 2.5 or newer versions (it is highly recommended you use a Plone 3.x version).

Installing Plone.app.ldap

We'll now show how to install plone.app.ldap and the other dependencies. If you have an existing buildout, you only have to add the plone.app.ldap Python egg to the buildout:eggs section and to the instance:zcml section, as you saw in Chapter 2's "Installing an Add-on Products" section, and shown here:

```
[buildout]
...
eggs =
    ...
    plone.app.ldap

...
zcml =
    ...
    plone.app.ldap
```

At this point, you should run the buildout script and restart your Zope instance:

```
$ ./bin/buildout
$ ./bin/instance restart
```

Note that the python-ldap library is a mandatory dependency. If you have already installed this library in your Python installation, you can prevent the automatic installation from the Python package index. Just look for the [zope2] section of your buildout configuration, and add this line:

```
additional-fake-eggs = python_ldap
```

Otherwise, if you want to make the complete installation automatic, the procedure may be a bit more complicated because of a version mismatch with the python-ldap egg and the Open-LDAP library. You can solve this by compiling the whole OpenLDAP library as a buildout part with the zc.recipe.cmmi recipe; however, we will not cover this installation method because it is outside the scope of this chapter. You can find more information at www.openldap.org.

Configuring Your LDAP Connection

At this point, you can go to the Plone control panel and click the Site Setup link; then click Add-on Products, and install LDAP support. After that, in the Plone control panel a new link in the Add-on Product Configuration area will be available: LDAP Connection. Click this link now, and you will see a screen similar to Figure 8-6.

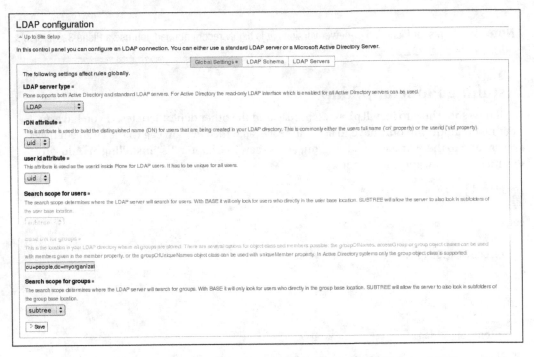

Figure 8-6. *The LDAP configuration panel, where you can easily configure your LDAP connection (part of the panel has been cropped to make the image more readable)*

In this control panel, you can configure an LDAP connection. You can use either a standard LDAP server or a Microsoft Active Directory server. This panel is split into three sections:

- Global Settings, where configuration settings affect rules globally
- LDAP Schema, where you can configure the LDAP schema mapping
- LDAP Servers, where you can add one or more LDAP servers to attach

You will fill in all the global configuration information, specifying the LDAP server type and the other basic properties of your LDAP schema configuration, such as the users/group's base distinguished name (DN) and other specific settings that depend on your LDAP server configuration. Then you'll create the mapping from LDAP user properties and Plone properties. Finally, you'll have to add one or more LDAP servers to attach, assuming they listen on the standard port 389 (the `plone.app.ldap` interface doesn't let you specify the server port, so you have to deal with the basic PAS plug-in in the ZMI). If multiple servers are used, they will be called in top-to-bottom order.

You're done! You have plugged a new LDAP source of users, and now you can search for users defined on your LDAP server.

It is important to remember that you have seen only a front-end configuration panel. All your changes will be reflected in the less-user-friendly `PAS plugin ldap` contained in the `acl_users` tool. If you are curious, you can take a look at the `acl_users` tool—you should find a new item related to your LDAP connection PAS plug-in (type **Plone LDAP plug-in**) named `ldap`. If you enter this plug-in, the Activate tab will let you enable or disable PAS features such as authentication, user enumeration, and so on, as you previously saw with the `source_myuser`

user manager you added in the "Managing Users Through the acl_users Tool" section of this chapter. Note that there is no front end for these settings; you should also know that with the current version of plone.app.ldap (as of press time), if you change something working directly with the ZMI, changes may not reflected in the plone.app.ldap interface because of caching issues.

Configuring Your LDAP Connection Through the ZMI

Dealing directly with the PAS plug-in gives users more control than when using the plone.app.ldap Plone interface. For example, with the current version of plone.app.ldap, you cannot set an LDAP port other than the default one—but with the ldap PAS plug-in, you can. In this case, you will have to configure the connection through the ZMI at http://localhost:8080/mysite/acl_users/ldap/acl_users/manage_servers. You can browse there by going to the acl_users tool, clicking the "ldap" item, clicking the Contents tab, clicking "acl_users (Plone managed LDAP)," and finally clicking the LDAP Servers tab. Once there, fill in a different LDAP port, and confirm by clicking the Add Server button. Note also that changing settings directly on the ldap plug-in through the ZMI will not affect the plone.app.ldap interface.

Another common use case that requires dealing with a PAS plug-in is disabling the User Adder PAS feature on the Activate tab of the new ldap source. You can just deselect the User_Adder option and confirm by clicking the Update button. Now Plone will let you authenticate users through an LDAP source, but it will not create new users on the LDAP source. This is a common setting for closed sites or intranets because sometimes LDAP administrators may prefer to manage users using their well-known custom LDAP tools.

On the Contents tab, you should find a new user manager (type LDAPUserFolder) item with all the configurations you created through the plone.app.ldap configuration panel. Here there are several useful tabs:

- The Configure tab contains the basic properties of LDAPUserFolder (here there are more configurations available than on the plone.app.ldap front end). You can specify all your LDAP settings that depend on your environment such as the base DN for groups or users, the password encryption type, and so on.

- The LDAP Schema tab is where you can map LDAP attributes to Plone user properties.

- The Users tab is where you can search for existing users or add new users specifying the group membership.

- The Groups tab shows all LDAP group records found on the LDAP server and allows deletion and addition. You can also map LDAP groups to Zope roles, thereby conferring a Zope role on members of an LDAP group. Note that with the plone.app.ldap plug-in, the group-roles mapping is not available.

You have seen just how it is possible to set up Plone with LDAP without having to write a single line of code. Once you've installed all the dependencies, you can easily and quickly plug an existing source of users into Plone with little work and plug an existing LDAP source into your Plone. You can use a tool such as plone.app.ldap to perform these configurations with a user-friendly interface that lets you quickly start configuring LDAP with little effort; then, if you are curious, you can take a look at the PAS plug-in directly in the acl_users tool in order to find out how it works. You can have more control or even plug in an LDAP source starting from scratch with PAS plug-ins and getting rid of plone.app.ldap.

Authentication with Relational Databases

In this section, you will learn how to manage user management/authentication from a SQL relational database. First, you will set up the database and the database connection; then, you will see how to install and configure the sqlpasplugin product that lets you easily configure the sql plug-in with just a few clicks.

In real cases, you may have an enterprise relational database with your table of users. This section does not cover the installation of real databases because it isn't part of the aim of this book. But in order to be more practical and to keep things as simple as possible, in the example we'll use throughout this section we use a dummy database type available in Zope by default (the Gadfly database). This way you can quickly create a new database and fill it with a couple of tuples representing users. As a result, you should find many Plone members as items in your database. You will thus be able to test SQL user integration in Plone without having to install any complex databases.

Note In production environments, you should use a professional database. However, the Zope Book covers in detail how to set up access to a relational database; see http://zope.org/Documentation/Books/ZopeBook/2_6Edition/RelationalDatabases.stx.

Let's start! Go to the ZMI, and select the Z Gadfly Database Connection item from the Add list. This will lead you to the add form for a Gadfly database connection. Since it runs inside Zope, you do not need to specify a connection string as other credentials-based database connectors might require. As shown in Figure 8-7, fill in the add form: enter **users_db** as the database ID, select the "demo" item as the data source (you could add other data sources in the var/gadfly subdirectory of your Zope installation), and then confirm your changes by clicking the Add button.

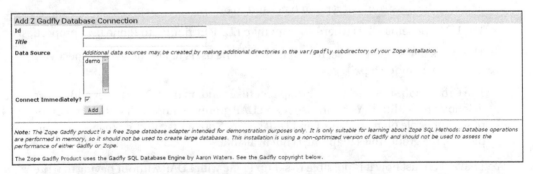

Figure 8-7. *Part of the Add Z Gadfly Database Connection form; you just have to fill in some data and click the Add button. The rest of the panel gives you information about the Gadfly copyright.*

This adds your first database connection. Now click the newly added item. As shown in Figure 8-8, you'll see several tabs; the following are the most important:

- The Status tab shows status and manages database connection.

- The Test tab lets you insert SQL statements (for example, to debug or to create, insert, and so on, tables or items).

- The Browse tab lets you browse the structure of tables of your database.

Figure 8-8. *The available tabs for your database connection*

Your dummy database should be empty. Now you can create a user table and add a new user on the Test tab. Go to the Test tab, fill in this SQL statement, and confirm by clicking the Submit Query button:

```
CREATE TABLE users_table(
username varchar, password varchar, mail varchar, name varchar)
```

We have just inserted the first row as an example; in real cases, your database should be already filled with all registered users. However, if you want to test your SQL integration and quickly add a new user, you can click the Test tab again, insert this simple SQL statement according to the type of table you created, and confirm by clicking the Submit Query button:

```
insert into users_table values ('db_user', '12345',
'john.smith@plonebook.com', 'john')
```

You have filled the dummy database with one user, so you can now query the user table with a select statement, as done for the create and insert statements, with this SQL code:

```
select * from users_table
```

You have created a dummy database with a table containing one user named *db_user*, so now you are ready to start configuring your SQL PAS plug-in and plug new members from a SQL source into Plone. At this point, you are ready to install and configure the sqlpasplugin product. If you have a buildout, you can add this URL to the urls variable of the productdistros section:

```
http://plone.org/products/sqlpasplugin/releases/1.0/SQLPASPlugin-1.0.tar.gz
```

And after that, rerun the buildout script. After restarting Zope, you should find SQLPASPlugin as an installable product in your Plone site. Install SQLPASPlugin via the portal_ quickInstaller tool or the Plone control panel. Otherwise, if you want, you can download the tarball from the Plone.org web site and untar it into the products folder of your instance.

You can find the SQL Authentication Configuration panel in Plone control panel, reachable by clicking the SQL Authentication link in the Add-on Product Configuration area

Figure 8-9 shows what the SQL Authentication configuration panel will look like after your first initialization. The first time you access the SQL Authentication Configuration panel, you will have to choose which database connection you wish to use; in this case, your only choice will be the `users_db` connection we have just created. Select it and confirm.

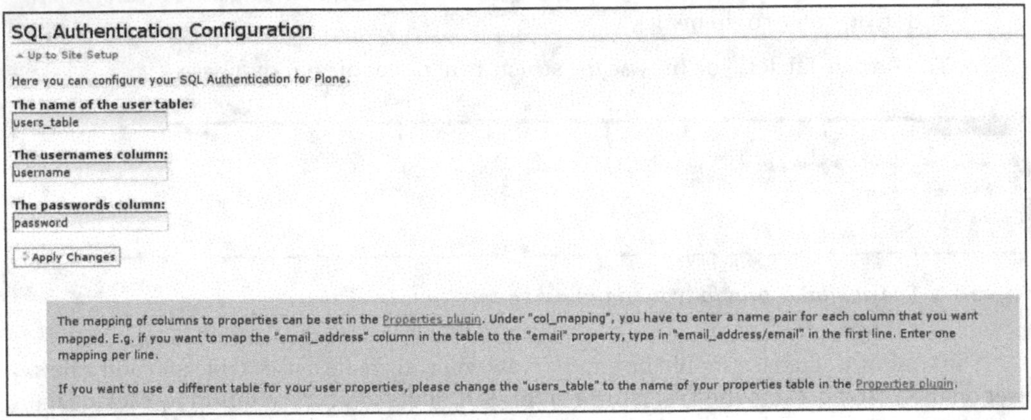

Figure 8-9. *The SQL Authentication Configuration panel*

An important element is the "Properties plugin" link that you can see in the first line of the paragraph shown at the bottom of the panel; by clicking it, you will be able to change the mapping of columns. Clicking this link will lead you to the ZMI configuration tool of the SQL PAS plug-in. Under `col_mapping`, you have to enter a name pair for each column that you want to be mapped, with a forward slash (/) as a separator (this is valid only for the mapping of columns). For example, if you want to map the `mail` column in the table to the `email` property, type in **mail/email** in the first line. Enter one mapping per line, as shown in Figure 8-10.

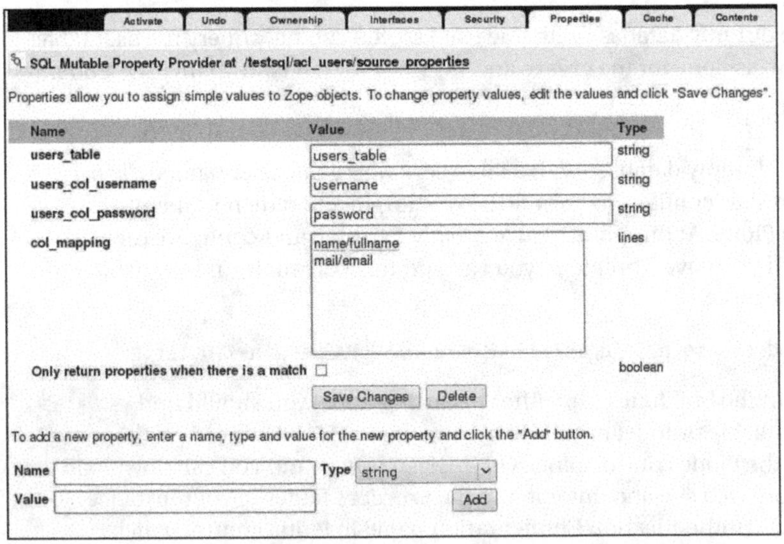

Figure 8-10. *The SQL Mutable Property Provider panel in the ZMI, where you can assign simple values to Zope objects*

You're done! Now you can search for users defined in the SQL source, and users defined on the users_table table are allowed to log in your portal with properties correctly mapped from columns to Plone member properties. Does it work well? Click Users and Groups in the Plone control panel, and search for all users; you should find your user defined in the SQL source, as shown in Figure 8-11.

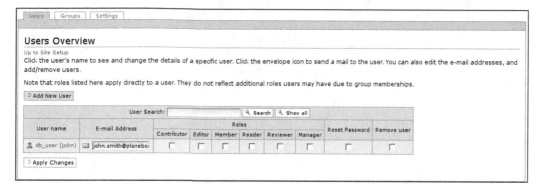

Figure 8-11. *The Users Overview panel shows you the user contained in the database you created.*

A wonderful source of information and practical details about the PAS is the PAS Reference Manual, where you can find instruction for configuring user management in Plone and also for developing PAS plug-ins; visit http://plone.org/documentation/manual/pas-reference-manual.

Summary

In this chapter, we have introduced the concepts that lie behind the PAS and showed you the flexibility you can thus create. You have learned the following:

- How to search for users with the PAS
- How to create a new user with the PAS
- How to change the password for a user with the PAS
- How to change role mapping
- How to create a new source for users and configure the different plug-ins according to your needs

What if your users are on an LDAP server or they are stored in a relational database? No matter. You have seen how to install and configure, with a few clicks, two useful add-on products for plugging in an LDAP connection and a SQL connection. It is easy to integrate a different source of users in your Plone site (OpenID, for example). On the Internet you'll find various useful tutorials to make almost any source of users work with your web site.

## PART 3

Developing Plone

We have arrived at the last part of our journey—the part that's dedicated to web developers. Of course, this part requires some knowledge of the Python language, and more in-depth knowledge of the Plone front- and back-end interfaces, their structure, and their logic.

In this part, you will see how to write an add-on product for Plone, how to integrate Plone with other systems (such as relational databases) and frameworks, and how to access Plone without a browser.

Finally, we will present some of the most common use cases you might encounter as a web developer, considering requirements and possible solutions, in order to give you a further overview of what you can do with Plone.

If you want to deepen your knowledge as a Plone developer, we suggest you also take a look at the following:

- The Zope Book (www.zope.org/Documentation/Books/ZopeBook)

- Zope Developer's Guide (www.zope.org/Documentation/Books/ZDG/current)

- *Professional Plone Development*, by Martin Aspeli (Packt Publishing, 2007)

- *Web Component Development with Zope 3*, by Philipp von Weitershausen (Springer, 2005)

- "A Comprehensive Guide to Zope Component Architecture," by Baiju M (www.muthukadan.net/docs/zca.html)

- Many tutorials available at http://plone.org/documentation

CHAPTER 9

■ ■ ■

Writing an Add-On Product

In the preceding chapters, you have seen what Plone is, what you can do with it, and how to modify its default behavior without writing a single line of code on the file system (e.g., adding content types, manipulating workflow schemas, modifying default page templates, etc.).

So, where do developers come in? They come in whenever you need to change Plone's underlying structure, and a simple reconfiguration of its services isn't enough.

Everything you have to do to configure a Plone instance can be easily distributed among many Zope services using a so-called *product*, which is a Zope synonym for an extension or plug-in. Besides that, working together on the same instance of a Plone site can be a nightmare for a developing team, with everyone risking breaking each other's code without the ability to automatically discover it, as a simple versioning repository could do. Finally, customizing Plone through the web will never let us own the real wheels spinning round at the application server level: you cannot manipulate content, objects, attributes, and schemas as you may with, you cannot create your own viewlets or portlets, you cannot implement any truly distributable extension that adds functionality to Plone itself, and so on.

In the following sections, we'll try to make you understand the anatomy of a typical Plone product, walking through a series of tasks that will take you into the deeper workings of Plone and Zope. In detail, we will create a *Regional News* object for our site that will allow users to create news specific to their locations. This will let us examine the basic structure of a Plone add-on package and how to define custom content types using Archetypes. Also, we will set up a stand-alone CSS file to style the Regional News view, building a Regional News search form, and even creating a configuration panel so that the Plone site manager can configure and maintain the regional news location metadata without needing to read a single line of Python.

Structure of a Plone Product

As we've mentioned, Plone is built on top of the Zope application server, so basically any Plone extension is a Zope extension. Zope is a long-running project, beginning in the 1990s, and it has gone through many different application development approaches. Plone itself is a long-running project in Zope, and besides including different Zope-level development techniques, Plone has introduced and maintains its own techniques.

In the last few years, the Zope 3 framework has been adopted in the Zope 2 environment because of the component architecture. Both the powerful new developing patterns introduced by Zope 3 and the backporting of many Zope 3 technologies have motivated Plone core developers to adopt Zope 3 technologies in Plone development.

Note Zope is the name shared by two different big projects. As described on the Zope.org site, Zope 2 was first released in September 1999, based on Zope 1 libraries that were being developed since 1996 by Zope Corporation, previously known as Digital Creation (see `www.zope.org/Products/Zope/swpackage_ releases`).

Zope 2 is great in what it offers to its users, and Plone is proving that, but some "un-agile" development patterns were quickly discovered, and Jim Fulton himself, the Zope concept's technical father, proposed a way to overcome them, by adopting component development as a paradigm and thus founding Zope 3 as a completely new application server environment.

For various unforgivable reasons, Zope 3 is still missing its own site. Although it continues on the path tracked by Zope 2, it deserves much more emphasis on what is different and how. It has been developed to be easily split into independent, reusable components, and thanks to that farsighted feature, it's been able to be incorporated into Zope 2 application server as a library for years. The Five project (`http://codespeak. net/z3/five/`) has built the binding layer that integrates the Zope 3 framework into Zope 2 quite naturally, and that is why Plone has been leveraging the powerful Zope 3 technologies for years.

The most important innovation in Zope 3 is the *component architecture*, which is outside of our documenting scopes. We strongly suggest taking a look at the free "Comprehensive Guide to Zope Component Architecture" (`www.muthukadan.net/docs/zca.html`), or *Web Component Development with Zope 3*, by Philipp von Weitershausen (Springer, 2005).

The most common way of extending Plone is by implementing a Zope product. A Zope product is a Python package located in a special folder called `Products` on the file system, where Zope looks for extensions to load.

There are no particular rules for building a Plone (and thus necessarily a Zope) product, except it must be a Python package and it must use Zope product registration strategy. Of course, as a Python package, it would be best to use a versioning tool like Subversion to establish a development review process, but that is beyond the scope of this discussion.

Note As stated previously, there are some good online documents about the Zope 2 development paradigm and how to extend it. Have a look at the "Zope Products" chapter of the Zope Developer's Guide (`www.zope.org/Documentation/Books/ZDG/current/Products.stx`).

As mentioned in Chapter 1, Plone is built on top of the CMF (content management framework). The core concepts implemented by Plone are established by the CMF, and so are the content types. Each content type object implements various contracts to reach the final effect we can enjoy using Plone: we want to interact with it through UI view and edit forms, we want its information and metadata to be persistent, we want it to obey to our security configuration, we want it to be indexed and allow fine searches to work, we want it to be workflowed, and a lot more. So let's look at what "extending a CMS" in this manner means for Plone. In order to manage your own content types in Plone, you need to understand the paradigm that Plone uses to implement content types. As mentioned, Plone lets you manage content using content types. Thus, the most important Python objects in the Plone world are those that relate to content types.

Note Zope 2 is a general purpose application server, thus not exceptionally good at solving content management hitches. That's why the CMF (formerly named the Portal Toolkit) was born. The CMF was released around 2001 as a bundle of Zope products that specialized Zope to let it build new portals in a rush with all the bells and whistles. It established a series of new concepts and services that are still used to boost Zope's content management ability. Moreover, it included in the bundle a completely working example, CMFDefault, which implements a client-ready portal, but lacks of usability and appeal to the end user. That is where Plone is coming from: its primary aim was to just skin CMFDefault. The online home of the CMF is on Zope.org, at www.zope.org/Products/CMF.

Some of the functionality of Plone content types comes directly from Zope, such as security and storage concerns, because content types are Zope objects, too.

Note While we won't go deeply into detail, a brief explanation of Zope objects is required. Actually, Zope stands for Z-Object Publishing Environment, which implies that a Zope object is something that Zope can publish; that is, Zope lets a user access code object information and functions in a network application environment, using protocols such as HTTP or FTP. For a deeper look into this, read the "Object Orientation" chapter in the Zope Book, at www.zope.org/Documentation/Books/ZopeBook/2_6Edition/ ObjectOrientation.stx.

CMF-level services add some other functionality, like indexing capability (which is based on the portal_catalog tool) and workflow service (which is based on portal_workflow tool). Adopting the CMF as a basic layer, all we need to build a product containing a new content type object class is a proper usage of the CMF's Python mix-in classes, registration functions for our Python classes, and a few lines of code implementing the methods needed by CMF services.

Clearly, prior to getting productive, you should understand some peculiar Zope and CMF development patterns.

In the following section, we will show you how to create a new content type in Plone, and let it act just like the native Plone content types.

This is easy because Plone minimized all the complexity: you can accomplish the mission just by providing an existing content type class as a base and an attribute schema of the new content type!

Building a Regional News Reader: Requirements and Discussion

For the purposes of this chapter, let's imagine you need something like a Plone news content type but with a new attribute such as location. Let's call it the Regional News content type. For this content type, in the next section we will create a new product containing an Archetypes class, put a new field in it named Location, and base the class on the News class. Then everything you need will be in place. Just restart the service, install your new product, and start adding regional news content everywhere in your Plone portal.

If you're wondering about "Archetypes" in the last paragraph, that is the name of the technology responsible for letting our schemas live as Plone content types. You describe how your content type schema is shaped, and Archetypes takes care of rendering its default view and edit form, persists the corresponding information in the safest way possible, indexes what you ask for, and displays it in your searches.

■**Note** As mentioned previously, Plone's primary objective was to rearrange the CMFDefault skin in order to increase accessibility and usability for the end user. And it succeeded. Plone's secondary objective then became to improve the way you can create and add content types to Plone. To this purpose, after some months of buzz, Archetypes was created by Ben Saller (see http://dev.plone.org/archetypes/browser/Products.Archetypes/trunk/Products/Archetypes/AUTHORS). He was able to build the required infrastructure around the core idea of requiring just content type attribute schemas and hiding all the technical issues from the developer. Have a look at Archetypes Developer Manual (http://plone.org/documentation/manual/archetypes-developer-manual) for more information about what you can do with Archetypes. Despite the fact that Archetypes is showing its age and some newcomer technologies, such as Devilstick (http://devilstick.info) and Dexterity (http://martinaspeli.net/articles/dexterity), are getting close to taking its place, lots of Plone projects still base their code on Archetypes, and we will use it to build our content types.

Our Regional News content type will need to follow a workflow schema different from the default one, because we want to differentiate normal regional published items from the ones we need to publish directly on the home page. Thanks to DC workflow, the workflow engine implemented by the portal_workflow tool we'll cover later in the "Plone Configuration" section of the chapter, that just means that we'll have to create our own workflow schema and associate it with our content type. Plone will immediately show our new transitions and states in the contextual state menu, and we will be able to filter the new regional_published state for regional news lists.

Of course, it is easy to perform all these workflow configurations through the Web, using the DC workflow configuration panel. At the same time, we need to keep them in our product so that the workflow for our content type will be automatically configured in every site where we'll install the product. To do this, we need some configuration import/export utility to extract our workflow policy and distribute it within our product. Fortunately, this is exactly what the portal_setup tool does! We will have a closer look at the portal_setup tool in the "Plone Configuration" section.

So, our first Plone product is almost there, at least conceptually. But something is missing before we can consider it complete: a Regional News search form and a portlet to show the latest news by location. To accomplish this, we could use some page templates and Python scripts in out `portal_skin` tool, but thanks to Zope 3 technologies, we can do better.

In the "Forms" section of the chapter, which follows, you will see in detail how to create a custom search page with a browser view to render both the web form and the results.

You might ask, "Why not just register a couple of page templates and a Python script to produce search results in the `portal_skin` tool?" Well, because in the way that we propose, we will separate much better logic from presentation, and we will also avoid the dirty work of web form implementation.

Note While Archetypes can render very specialized web forms based on their attribute schemas, for a long time Plone has been missing a technology able to render web forms out of attribute schemas without any correlated Zope object. This is one of the benefits that comes from the Zope 3 world, which has at least a couple of pure form-rendering libraries: `zope.formlib` (http://pypi.python.org/pypi/zope.formlib) and `z3c.form` (http://pypi.python.org/pypi/z3c.form). Both of them are based on Zope 3 component concepts, and are able to render powerful and flexible web form machinery out of pure interfaces, which in component terminology are the equivalent of Archetypes attribute schemas.

After we create the Regional News content type, we'll build a Regional News portlet as well, taking advantage of the Plone portlet machinery. But first, we'll give you an introduction to this machinery in the "Viewlets and Portlets" section of the chapter. You should now have a good base of knowledge as to what a typical Plone product should do. But before we start putting our hands on some code, let's just sum up what a typical product package should contain.

First of all, it will be a Python package, placed in the Zope `Products` folder. It will have some registration instructions to let the Zope and Plone layers know that it exists, and some Python modules to describe our Archetypes schemas representing our content classes. Besides this, it will also have some page templates to define our user interface skin, and some modules for our browser views and portlets. Finally, it will probably have a folder containing our configuration policies for workflow schemas and all the rest.

Stay tuned—we will get through all these matters before the end of this chapter.

Building a Plone Product the Easy Way

We promised in the preceding section to start building our own Plone product, so let's do it! As we remarked, our product will live on the file system, so let's open a terminal and prepare our development environment to host our code. All these examples are in Linux, so we will assume some basic familiarity with file system operations in Linux.

As examined in Chapter 2, we use Paster commands to build and configure our system. Paster is a powerful Python library that comes from Ian Bicking's Python Paste project (http://pythonpaste.org). It lets us define templates and then reuse them in order to build our products.

Before getting our hands dirty, we'll need one more piece of knowledge: how to let Zope safely know about our product. Zope 2 establishes that products are placed in the `Products` folder, without checking what packages you put there or which dependencies the packages have. Just start the Zope server after you have put a package in, and see what happens.

Fortunately, Python now has effective machinery to build and distribute Python packages, taking care of versions and dependencies too, thanks to distutils and Peak setuptools. Version, author, dependencies, and everything useful to classify a package are bundled around the package itself in a structure known as a Python egg. setuptools provides a shell script named EasyInstall, which is able to find an egg in egg web repositories and download and install it on your local machine with all the requested dependencies.

■Note Python.org offers the most popular of the online packages repositories, PyPI (Python Package Index). You can browse the index online at http://pypi.python.org/pypi, searching by free text or browsing it at http://pypi.python.org/pypi?action=browse. With PyPI, developers can submit their packages automatically to the repository by running a simple command in the terminal; PyPI will make sure to hide all previous releases and give proper visibility to the new one. Nowadays, more and more Zope and Plone packages are published to PyPI, which is why the Products section of Plone.org was recently bound to PyPI in an automatic way, so that developers may update a single site and have the other site remain up to date.

Zope 2 is not aware of Python eggs. That is why, to take advantage of all this, Zope and Plone use buildout technology to define and build a working Zope instance. As a consequence, we need to provide a Python egg wrapping our product, and Paster help us write the code for the egg by providing some boilerplate code. All the templates we need are provided by Zope-Skel, a collection of skeletons for quickly starting Zope projects.

■Note At this point, we need to state some assumptions about your development environment: all the examples in this chapter have been developed on a UNIX machine, using Python version 2.4.4, the version recommended for Plone 3 (see http://plone.org/documentation/faq/plone-versions). Please use this version of Python for the following exercises.

Furthermore, Plone makes use of the Python Imaging Library (PIL—www.pythonware.com/products/pil) to manage image files. At the time of this writing, PIL is not available as an egg for automatic installation, so you will need to install it on your machine manually, using the same Python version you will use for Plone.

For any specific trouble you may encounter, have a look at the "Installation" section on Plone.org (http://plone.org/documentation/phc_topic_area?topic=Installation).

So, let's start. Download ez_setup.py and launch it:

```
$ wget peak.telecommunity.com/dist/ez_setup.py
$ python ez_setup.py
```

Using `easy_install`, install ZopeSkel and all its dependencies:

```
$ easy_install -U ZopeSkel
```

When finished, you should have a new command available in your shell: `paster`. You can try it out with the following command:

```
$ paster create --list-templates
```

It should answer with a list of all the available templates (e.g., `plone3_portlet`, which you can use for creating a new portlet product, and `archetype`, which creates a generic Plone project).

If you don't already have a working instance to create your product in, just execute the following lines in a terminal:

```
$ cd ~
$ paster create -t plone3_buildout plonebook
```

and answer all the questions the script will ask with their default values. Then enter this:

```
$ cd plonebook
$ python bootstrap.py
```

You will see your new `buildout` instance almost ready to be run. Be sure you have an active Internet connection and execute the following:

```
$ ./bin/buildout -v
```

At the end of this process, you should have a new ready-to-run Zope instance correctly configured with the last Plone bundle.

We will assume you are using a Plone buildout named `plonebook` located in your home directory to run your new package in. Just go to the `src` folder and create a new Archetype project:

```
$ cd ~/plonebook/src
$ paster create -t archetype plonebook.regional_news
```

Answer the questions to create a `regional_news` package in the `plonebook` namespace. Have a look at what your `src` folder contains now—you should find a `plonebook.regional_news` folder. Let's explore what is inside.

The Paster template has prepared a brand new egg for us, with a `README.txt` file to fill in and a `setup.py` file to eventually edit. The actual extension code is placed in the `plonebook/regional_news` folder, which contains the following files and folders:

- **__init__.py**: This file makes the folder a Python package and contains the initialize function, which is launched by Zope at startup to register the product into the framework.

- **browser**: This folder contains Zope 3 browser views defined by the product.

- **config.py**: This file contains common configuration constants for the project.

- **configure.zcml**: This file contains Zope 3 configurations for this product.

- **content**: This folder contains Python modules defining content types.

- **interfaces.py**: This file contains Zope 3 interfaces for this product.
- **portlets**: This folder contains portlets defined in this product.
- **profiles**: This folder contains GenericSetup profiles (see the "Plone Configuration" section of the chapter).
- **README.txt**: This is a text file in which you can add generic information about the product.
- **tests**: This folder contains test modules for the product.
- **tests.py**: This file contains a basic test infrastructure for the product.

As it is, this package does nothing. Additionally, Zope doesn't recognize it yet, because it is not a normal Python package in the Zope `Products` folder, but a generic Python egg in the buildout `src` folder. Let's tell the buildout about it, adding these lines to the `buildout.cfg` file:

```
[buildout]
...
eggs =
    ...
    plonebook.regional_news

develop =
    src/plonebook.regional_news

...
[instance]
...
zcml =
    plonebook.regional_news
```

The last line lets Zope know that we want the package to be loaded at startup, and that we need it unless some other package includes it.

As usual, after this modification, run the `buildout` script:

```
$ cd ~/plonebook
$ ./bin/buildout -v
```

If everything went right, we should start our Zope instance and find `plonebook.regional_news` in the Products section of the Zope control panel. Check it by starting the service:

```
$ ./bin/instance fg
```

and then pointing your web browser to `http://localhost:8080/Control_Panel/Products/manage`.

Obviously, installing the product into a Plone instance at this moment would not produce any extension to Plone itself. We just have a very advanced boilerplate!

Let's have a look at how Paster is still useful to us: thanks to its local commands concept, we will add to the package the boilerplate for creating content types. Just run the following in your terminal:

```
$ cd ~/plonebook/src/plonebook.regional_news
$ paster addcontent -l
```

This will produce a list of further available templates that are useful in this project context. We will use them soon to create our first content type, Regional News, and its Plone news–based schema. Just execute the following in your terminal:

```
$ paster addcontent contenttype
```

Then answer the questions the script will ask you, using RegionalNews as the content type name and the defaults for all the rest. At the end of this process, you should notice some updates in your regional_news package: config.py has a new specific add permission, interfaces.py lists an IRegionalNews interface, and, most interesting, the content folder has a new Python module, regionalnews.py, filled in with all that's required to register our new generic content type into Plone.

Here is the interesting part of regionalnews.py:

```
...
RegionalNewsSchema = schemata.ATContentTypeSchema.copy() + atapi.Schema((

    # -*- Your Archetypes field definitions here ... -*-

))


...
schemata.finalizeATCTSchema(RegionalNewsSchema, moveDiscussion=False)

class RegionalNews(base.ATCTContent):
    """Description of the Example Type"""
    implements(IRegionalNews)

    portal_type = "RegionalNews"
    schema = RegionalNewsSchema


...
atapi.registerType(RegionalNews, PROJECTNAME)
```

Notice that the RegionalNews class inherits from the ATContentTypes ATCTContent class. It declares that it implements the IRegionalNews interface, and its schema is based on ATContentTypeSchema. Finally, the class is registered as an Archetypes content type, as needed by Archetypes framework.

Let's try using our product now. Run the Zope service in a terminal:

```
$ cd ~/plonebook/
$ ./bin/instance fg
```

Now the Zope service will remain attached to the terminal process, and, after a long series of log lines, you should see a nice "Zope Ready to handle requests" message. Don't close that window; open a browser, pointing it to `http://localhost:8080/manage`. After you have signed in, the ZMI should appear. Create a new Plone site, selecting the proper "Plone site" item in the Add select box. Name the site plone, click the confirm button to add it, and wait just a few seconds. At the end of this process, you should find a new object, named `plone`, in the ZMI root list. Point your browser to `http://localhost:8080/plone` and you should see the encouraging Plone welcome page.

As soon as you sign into Plone with your admin user, click the Site Setup link at the top of the page, and then go to the Add-on Products panel. Select the Regional News 1.0 item and click the Install button. Next, click the Plone logo to return to the welcome page, and select your new Regional News content type from the "Add new" menu in the green bar. Our content type is as simple as possible, without any special attributes, but nonetheless it exists in Plone and has all the standard metadata, indexing features, the default workflow schema, and so on (see Figure 9-1).

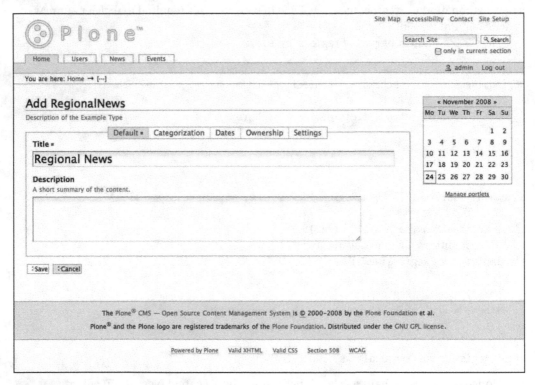

Figure 9-1. *Our simple Regional News object*

Reviewing what we did, we effectively launched a couple of Paster commands—`paster create -t archetype plonebook.regional_news` and `paster addcontent contenttype`—and that was all!

■Note The Archetypes framework was a big step forward in simplifying developing patterns in Plone. But it did not come with Paster templates. Paster is quite a bit younger than Archetypes. The Archetypes developers still had to start up their projects by hand and correctly plug in some mandatory Archetypes registration details before becoming productive.

Philipp Auersperg and Jens Klein were two developers who were not happy with all that early copy'n'pasting. Moreover, they were great UML fans and dreamed of a tool able to translate UML class diagrams into Archetypes projects. They developed a new open source project: a code generator called ArchGenXML (`http://plone.org/products/archgenxml`), which achieved widespread success and is widely used for developing Plone projects. This is due to its flexibility and ease of use, and because it lets the developer maintain a standard way of building products.

While ArchGenXML is a powerful and reliable tool, an in-depth description of it is outside the scope of this book. If you're interested in using it, it has a nice developer's manual at `http://plone.org/documentation/manual/archgenxml2`, and some good tutorials at `http://plone.org/products/archgenxml/documentation`.

In the next section, we will take a deeper look at Archetypes and what you should know about its framework to be able to customize the Regional News content type.

Writing a Custom Content Type

In this section, we will continue to build the custom content type that we started in the last section. At this point, we need to make our Regional News content type more like the Plone news content type, providing the location attribute. We have to build a user interface for our new content type, taking into account the location information, and we have to provide a specialized search form. Finally, we will set up and keep in our package some configuration information useful to our content type, such as the Regional News workflow schema.

First of all, we need it to act as a normal Plone news content item, with all the attributes we need, such as a body and a picture. We'll do this right now.

Thanks to the `ATContentTypes` product, which implements all the default Plone content types as Archetypes classes, fulfilling that as is easy as changing our `RegionalNews` base class to use the Plone news one. Here are the interesting lines in `regionalnews.py` after our adjustments:

```
...
from Products.ATContentTypes.content import newsitem

...
RegionalNewsSchema = newsitem.ATNewsItemSchema.copy() + atapi.Schema((

    # -*- Your Archetypes field definitions here ... -*-

))
```

```
...
class RegionalNews(newsitem.ATNewsItem):
    """Description of the Example Type"""

...
```

To check our modifications, let's restart our Zope service that's been running in the terminal window since last section: first stop the terminal-attached Zope service by pressing Ctrl+C, and then just start it in normal mode:

```
$ ./bin/instance start
```

Now point your web browser back to http://localhost:8080/plone and try to add a new Regional News item in the portal root. You should now find the same attributes that you find on a standard Plone news item. You should also notice another funny detail: when you save your Regional News item, the template in use is not the same as the standard News content one, as you can see in Figure 9-2. We will explain why in the following paragraphs.

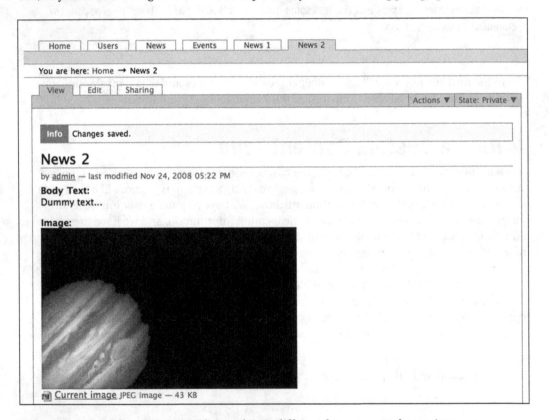

Figure 9-2. *Our Regional News item's template is different from a normal news item.*

We next need to add our first Archetypes schema to Regional News, to store location information. But what is an Archetypes schema?

As you probably expect, a *schema* is a list of fields used by Archetypes to activate our content type. Each field is responsible of storing and retrieving information associated with an Archetypes object.

There is a complete set of provided fields; these include the widely used `StringField` and `TextField`, suited for storing content's title and body, as well as more Plone-specific ones, such as `ReferenceField`, through which we can set relations between Plone contents.

Each field lets the developer set a series of properties to modify its behavior. For instance, we can specify whether a certain field is required or not, and we can specify the `read_permission` the user needs to have to access the field's information. A complete reference on the standard Archetypes fields and their common properties is available at `http://plone.org/documentation/manual/archetypes-developer-manual/fields/fields-reference`.

Obviously, if the standard set of fields don't meet your needs, you can implement and register your own, as is already done by some well-known Plone products. (One such example is `DataGridField`, which offers a table-input component for Plone—see `http://plone.org/products/datagridfield`). We won't create a custom field here—a `StringField` will be enough to start with (we'll get more advanced later in this chapter). Using Archetypes, let's add our new field to the Regional News schema. Remembering that Paster is our friend, go back to the terminal and run the following:

```
$ cd ~/plonebook/src/plonebook.regional_news
$ paster addcontent atschema
```

The Paster script will ask you to provide some parameters: enter **regionalnews** as the module (file) name of your content class, enter **region** as the name of this field, and leave `String` as the default both for the field and widget entries.

Note We use "region" as the field's name because "location" is already in use by the base class as one of the Dublin Core metadata standard fields, and we don't want to override this.

We'll go into details about widgets in a while; for now, just keep on and restart the Zope service:

```
$ cd ~/plonebook
$ ./bin/instance restart
```

Finally, point your web browser back to `http://localhost:8080/plone` and try to add a new Regional News item. Archetypes automatically renders standard view and edit templates for its schema fields, which is why we obtain the same form as for editing a Plone news item, along with a plain text input to enter the region we want to classify the news in.

Let's have a look at the most notable part that Paster added to our `regionalnews.py` module:

```
...
RegionalNewsSchema = newsitem.ATNewsItemSchema.copy() + atapi.Schema((

    # -*- Your Archetypes field definitions here ... -*-
```

```
atapi.StringField(
    name='region',
    storage = atapi.AnnotationStorage(),
    required=False,
    #searchable=1,
    #default='',
    #schemata ='default',
    widget=atapi.StringWidget(
        label=_(u"region"),
        description=_(u"Description of region"),
                ),
            ),
        ))
```

Notice that the code contains a series of common field attributes, some of which are commented. It also contains a widget attribute set to StringWidget, in which Paster has specified label and description properties. This is how Archetypes decides how to render a field: each field is linked to a widget, which knows how to render the information stored by the field itself in view, edit, and search modes.

According to what each field admits, we can choose between many enabling widgets. For instance, in our case, a select box with a list of predefined regions to choose from would be the best choice.

Let's go back to our terminal and ask Paster to create a Selection widget instead of a String one for our region field:

```
$ cd ~/plonebook/src/plonebook.regional_news
$ paster addcontent atschema
```

Open the regionalnews.py module in a text editor, delete the old field part, and add a vocabulary attribute like this to the new one:

```
atapi.StringField(
    name='region',
    storage = atapi.AnnotationStorage(),
    required=False,
    #searchable=1,
    #default='',
    #schemata ='default',
    vocabulary = ('Italy', 'France', 'England'),
    widget=atapi.SelectionWidget(
        label=_(u"region"),
        description=_(u"Description of region"),
    ),
),
```

As usual, restart the service, point your web browser to http://localhost:8080/plone, and add a new Regional News item. You should see a list of radio buttons that lets the user choose the region for the news, as you can see in Figure 9-3. If you're a webmaster, of course, you'll probably prefer to manage the region's vocabulary without having to touch any Python code (or better yet, manage it directly through the Web). This will be covered later in the chapter in the "Tools and Utilities" section.

Figure 9-3. *The user can now choose the region for the Regional News item.*

Of course, Archetypes is a great automator for creating new content types in Plone. It does well at assisting the developer at everything from field storage to widget-rendering problems. For the automatic user interface, it uses our schema order to list the fields, and for the edit form, it offers a grouping feature through the field's schemata attribute. When we need more control over how information is presented to the user, we can modify the Archetypes default user interface as we want. Let's explore how.

Archetypes has a standard set of page templates used to generate standard view and edit user interface for our contents. Every content type looks the same, but changing this is as easy as defining a page template named according to our content type, which contains standard name macros to override the default one.

■Note If you need a deeper understanding of how to modify the user interfaces Archetypes produces for you, see the "Customizing AT View Templates" tutorial on the Plone.org site (http://plone.org/documentation/tutorial/customizing-at-view-templates).

For this example, assume that we want a view template for Regional News that is similar to the standard Plone news template, with some emphasis on the selected region information. To allow for this, we need to implement a browser view named regionalnews_view, containing a ZPT macro named body. Go back to your terminal window and type the following:

```
$ cd ~/plonebook/src/plonebook.regional_news
$ paster addcontent view
```

After asking for a view named regionalnews, Paster will create all that is needed to register a browser view named regionalnews_view in the browser folder of our package: a regionalnewsview.py module and a regionalnewsview.pt page template. We will go deeper into explaining what a browser view is in the "Theming" section of the chapter; just trust what Paster built for us by now.

> **Note** We won't use Plone's `portal_skin` tool for our skinning needs, but it is still possible to register a skin folder in our product and create a `regionalnews_view.pt` file there, in which we could write our `body` macro for the Regional News view template.

We won't need the Python module part of our browser view; we will just use the page template to implement a macro named `body` that contains the string `Hello World!`, just to see what happens. Here is our `regionalnewsview.pt` file as it is before restarting the Zope service:

```
<html xmlns="http://www.w3.org/1999/xhtml" xml:lang="en"
      lang="en"
      i18n:domain="plonebook.regional_news">
<body>
    <div metal:define-macro="body">
        <p>Hello World!</p>
    </div>
</body>
</html>
```

Restart Zope, create a new Regional News item in your Plone site, and see what Archetypes shows you by default: all the fields previously listed below the content title have been replaced with our `Hello World!` string, formatted in the default body text style. We won't go into details about how this technology works here, but you can take a look at Chapter 6 for a refresher.

Archetypes implements the `base_view` template, which is every content type's default view template, through four principal macros: `header`, `body`, `folderlisting`, and `footer`. At rendering time, it looks for a template named after the content type's name (i.e., `regionalnews_view`) and replaces its own macros with the one defined in the most specific template (i.e., `regionalnews_view` in this case). That's why our template removed all Regional News attributes except the title, replacing them with just "Hello World!"—we weren't specific about the `header`, `folderlisting`, and `footer` macros, so Archetypes picked the default ones for these sections.

That easily, just defining a `metal` macro with the ID `body` in a template named `regionalnews_view`, we can render each single field in the place we want within a more complex page template, still keeping in mind that this way we customize our content type's `base_view` template. For instance, let's try this other version of our content's `base_view` template:

```
<html xmlns="http://www.w3.org/1999/xhtml" xml:lang="en"
      lang="en"
      i18n:domain="plonebook.regional_news">
<body>
  <tal:macro metal:define-macro="header">
    <h1 class="documentFirstHeading">
      <tal:field metal:use-macro="python:here.widget('title', mode='view')">
        Title
      </tal:field>
    </h1>
    <h3>Region:
```

```
    <tal:field  metal:use-macro="python:here.widget('region', mode='view')" />
    </h3>
  </tal:macro>

  <tal:main-macro metal:define-macro="body">
    <div class="newsImageContainer"
        tal:condition="here/image_mini|nothing">
      <img src="" alt=""
            tal:replace="structure python:here.tag(scale='mini',
css_class='newsImage')"/>
    </div>
    <tal:field metal:use-macro="python:here.widget('text', mode='view')">
      Body
    </tal:field>
  </tal:main-macro>
</body>
</html>
```

In this template, we override both the header and body macros, leaving the default behavior for the folderlisting and footer macros, and ask the widgets to render their own fields in the proper way. However, since this is a base_view template, it completely forgets about any field not manually listed. So, it would be better not to touch the entire base_view mechanism, and instead prepare a completely new regionalnews_view template based on the original newsitem_view template, and assign it to our content type's default view method. We will leave this as an exercise for you; you can mix what you learned in Chapter 5 about configuration of CMF portal types, and what you will learn in the "Plone Configuration" section of the chapter about how to export those configurations through GenericSetup profiles.

■**Note** As already stated, despite the fact that it is still widely used, Archetypes is slowly getting older. Its monolithic approach to content management issues is quite outdated compared to the Zope 3 techniques we describe throughout this chapter. Martin Aspeli's Dexterity project (http://martinaspeli.net/articles/dexterity) is beginning to be used instead of Archetypes these days because it capitalizes on Zope 3 techniques in a more proper way. Also, Dexterity aims at making it easy to declare new content types, even for nondevelopers.

Through this section, you have seen how easy it is to build new rich content types in Plone using Archetypes. We will discuss the wonders of Archetypes further in the "Forms" section of this chapter, in which we'll focus on customizing our RegionalNews schema attributes. For a more in-depth look at Archetypes, check out the online documentation on Plone.org (http://plone.org/documentation/phc_topic_area?topic=Developing+for+Plone#archetypes).

Theming

In the last section, we stole some visual style magic from the standard Plone news item's template, avoiding having to define our own CSS rules—but let's imagine that we need to do it. For instance, let's create an info box showing the region information at the top-right of the Regional News template. To accomplish this task, we will first register a CSS file of our own as a Zope 3 resource and use the portal_css registry to include it in the standard Plone CSS file. Then we will create a new Zope browser view and register it as the default view method for our content type.

This requires that we discuss *theming*, which relates to everything in Plone connected with presentation. Plone can be skinned quite easily without compromising the application. Thanks to this, it is simple to separate all the files and templates defining our skin into Plone products. Since there are beautiful online tutorials on Plone.org (http://plone.org/documentation/phc_topic_area?topic=Visual+Design#creating-theme-products), we will leave these tutorials as an exercise for you.

For sure, developing a product very often requires some user interface tweaking, and that can be interpreted as theming, because we use the same tools and techniques implemented for core skinning.

The easy part is to modify our regionalnews_view template, separating style rules from content information: we will implement our own CSS file, containing our style rules. Here are the adjustments to the regionalnewsview.pt file:

```
...
<div tal:replace="structure provider:plone.abovecontenttitle" />

<div id="regionalnews_info_box">
    <h3> Region:
        <metal:field use-macro="python:here.widget('region', mode='view')">
        Region
        </metal:field>
    </h3>
</div>

<div class="rnewsImageContainer"
    tal:condition="here/image_mini|nothing">

    ...

</div>
```

Essentially, we moved the region widget into a regionalnews_info_box id div element and changed the newsImageContainer class to rnewsImageContainer to control its style rules.

We now need to publish our static CSS file. We do this by registering it in a Zope 3 browser resource directory. So, let's create a new folder into the browser folder of our regional_news package, name it resources, and create a new file in it, named regionalnews.css. Our simple regionalnews.css content is

```
#regionalnews_info_box {
    float: right;
    width: 202px;
```

```
    border: 1px solid lightgrey;
    background-color: white;
    padding: 0.5em;
}

.rnewsImageContainer {
    float: right;
    width: 202px;
    margin: 0.5em 0 0.5em 1em;
    padding: 0.5em;
    clear: right;
}
```

Then we open the `browser/configure.zcml` file and add to it our new `resources` directory:

```
...
<browser:resourceDirectory
    name="rn-resources"
    directory="resources"
    permission="zope2.Public"
    />

...
```

Note A web user interface is normally implemented using static resources, such as images and CSS files. Zope 3 uses the "browser resource" concept to publish static resources. It is possible to register both single browser resource files and whole browser resource directories. To let us access a browser resource, Zope 3 uses a special namespace named ++resource++. For a deeper understanding of this matter, have a look at the "Customization for Developers" tutorial on Plone.org (http://plone.org/documentation/tutorial/ customization-for-developers).

Let's recap what we've done: we modified our template to implement an info box showing the region attribute of our Regional News content type, we created a Zope 3 resource directory to publish static files, and we added the `regionalnews.css` file to this new resource directory.

What are we missing? Of course, binding the CSS file to our Regional News view template. We could just put an HTML import directive there, but Plone offers something more versatile—a special `portal_css` registry for our CSS import needs, which lets us register a new CSS file to be used by Plone.

So, go back to your terminal and restart the Zope service:

```
$ cd ~/plonebook
$ ./bin/instance restart
```

Then point your web browser to http://localhost:8080/plone and add a new Regional News item. It should work, but notice that the info box on top of it doesn't look like a box. You just need to add your style sheet to `portal_css`: to do so, go to http://localhost:8080/plone/

portal_css/manage_cssForm. On this page, you will be presented with the manage view of the Plone Stylesheets Registry, where you have the current configuration for your Plone site. On top you have a couple of check boxes, among which is the "Debug/development mode" option. (Keep it in mind, since it is very important; we'll switch to this topic in just a moment.) Then you have a long list of registered style sheets, each with a series of properties to manipulate.

Let's go to the bottom of this page and add our style sheet, giving it the ID ++resource++ rn-resources/regionalnews.css and leaving all the rest as suggested. Then point your web browser back to your Regional News item and refresh the page. If nothing changes, just go back to portal_css and set "Debug/development mode" to "true"; it should finally make your box appear, as you can see in Figure 9-4.

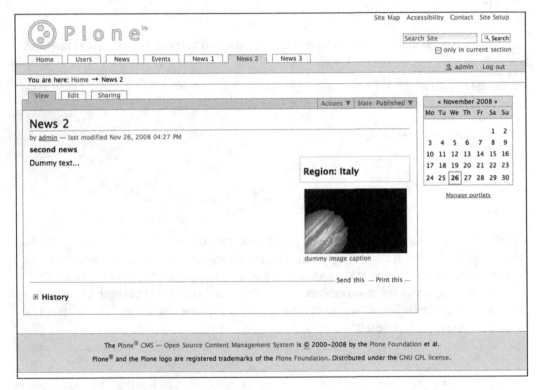

Figure 9-4. *The region for Regional News items is now shown in a box on top of the screen.*

You could complain that, again, we used a web registry while we were supposed to make it a product, but be confident—we will set this up into a distributable package before the end of the chapter. Skip ahead to the "Plone Configuration" section if you'd like to see how to do this.

The Plone Stylesheets Registry is quite powerful and easy to use. There is also a similar tool for JavaScript resources, named portal_javascript, and another for KSS style sheets, portal_kss. We'll use both of these in the "Viewlets and Portlets" section later in the chapter.

■ Note For the sake of completeness, thinking about all the possibilities Paster offers in theming Plone, we must mention the ZopeSkel `plone3_theme` template. If you need to heavily or completely skin a Plone site, consider using this Paster boilerplate to start up your skin product. After launching the command `paster create -t plone3_theme` in a terminal, answer all the questions the script will ask. At the end of the process, you will have a complete theming product, with a series of goodies, such as a new browser view folder with resource directories for images and style sheets, and much more.

Let's now recall how we built our `regionalnews` view, as it is another main aspect of theming from a developer's point of view. In the "Writing a Custom Content Type" section, we asked Paster to create a view named `regionalnews`.

But what does that mean? With the command `paster addcontent view`, Paster creates a Zope 3 browser view, which is one of the standard Zope 3 components for creating user interfaces. A browser view is a convenient way of binding together a page template carrying the presentation layout and a Python class containing the business logic, thus resulting in a clear, easy, reusable development pattern. No more mazy Python expressions and `if...` `then` conditions merged into tricky page templates; just clear, simple page templates and easy-to-manage Python modules and classes.

If you go back and visit your `regional_news` package `browser` folder, you will find `regionalnewsview.pt` containing your page template for `regionalnews_view` and `regionalnewsview.py` with a basic interface class and your main `BrowserView` class, named `regionalnewsView`. But what links the two is in `configure.zcml`, which contains a browser namespace directive like this:

```
<browser:page
  for="*"
  name="regionalnews_view"
  class=".regionalnewsview.regionalnewsView"
  template="regionalnewsview.pt"
  allowed_interface=".regionalnewsview.IregionalnewsView"
  permission="zope.Public"
/>
```

This piece of ZCML is what Zope needs to register a browser view with the name `regionalnews_view`, using `regionalnewsview.pt` as a template and the Python class `regionalnewsView` contained in `regionalnewsview.py` as the business logic code.

So far, we've used the `regionalnewsView` class very little in our template, and we could get rid of it—a browser view can degenerate into a lonely Python class or a lonely page template. But we want to evaluate this browser view pattern, so let's imagine we need to show in the Regional News info box the last two published Regional News items for the specific region, except the one we are visiting.

The template will only need to render a list of dictionaries with the keys title and URL, provided by the view class, to which we will add a new method, get_other_news_items:

```
...
<div id="regionalnews_info_box">
    ...

    <tal:block tal:define="other_news view/get_other_news_items"
            tal:condition="other_news">
    <h3>Other Regional News</h3>
    <ul>
        <li tal:repeat="item other_news">
            <a href="" tal:attributes="href item/url"
                tal:content="item/title">Other News</a>
        </li>
    </ul>
    </tal:block>

</div>

...
```

The view class defined in browser/regionalnewsview.py file will have a new method, get_other_news_items, as well as an interface class:

```
class IregionalnewsView(Interface):
    """

    regionalnews view interface
    """


    def get_other_news_items():
        """ return other last published regional news items
        for the region of the contextual regional news.
        """


class regionalnewsView(BrowserView):
    """

    regionalnews browser view
    """

    implements(IregionalnewsView)

    def __init__(self, context, request):
        self.context = context
        self.request = request

    @property
    def portal_catalog(self):
        return getToolByName(self.context, 'portal_catalog')
```

```
@property
def portal(self):
    return getToolByName(self.context, 'portal_url').getPortalObject()


def get_other_news_items(self):
    context = self.context
    context_path = '/'.join(context.getPhysicalPath())
    query = {'portal_type': 'RegionalNews',
             'review_state': 'published',
             'region': context.getRegion(),
             'sort_on': 'effective',
             'sort_order': 'descending',
             'show_inactive': False}
    brains = self.portal_catalog.searchResults(**query)[:3]

    items = []
    for brain in brains:
        if brain.getPath() <> context_path:
            items.append({'title': brain.Title,
                          'url': brain.getURL()})

    return items[:2]
```

The page template namespace is improved by the "view" term, because it gives access to the view class methods and attributes, according to the allowed_interface specified in the ZCML configuration.

To point at the contextual object, the view class stores in its context attribute the context for which the view has been instantiated—that is, the specific RegionalNews object itself. Notice that you can also access the corresponding request as an attribute on the browser view instance.

Also, we need to state that the class implements the IregionalnewsView interface. In fact, the configure.zcml file requires the .regionalnewsview.IregionalnewsView interface through the allowed_interface attribute.

Finally—the essence of our aim—in the get_other_news_items method, we ask the portal_catalog tool for the Regional News items we want to show, published for the same region as context, ordered according to their effective date, which is the publication date set on the context. At this point, our method will just fail, because portal_catalog doesn't know what the region attribute is supposed to be. So, we need to register this new index before testing our recent efforts. Point your web browser to http://localhost:8080/plone/portal_catalog/manage_catalogIndexes, choose to add a new KeywordIndex, and then enter **region** as the ID and **getRegion** as the Indexed attribute. Don't worry if you don't understand this just now—we will go into further details very soon.

■Note The `portal_catalog` tool is a central service in Plone—not only for the normal search requests from users, but for building every object's listing request. We will take a closer look at it next, in the "Forms" section of the chapter.

To test your new info box details and obtain the result shown in Figure 9-5, you need a few more Regional News items published for the same region. Have a good time with browser views!

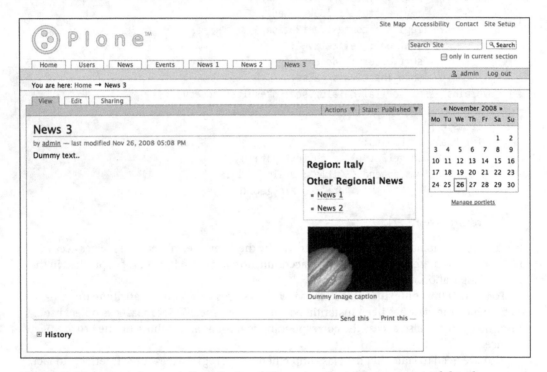

Figure 9-5. *We arranged a specialized Regional News view that shows contextual details.*

So, after having very quickly built a content type of our own, we also put a classification mechanism on it through a content region attribute, and a corresponding index in the catalog. Finally, we arranged a specialized Regional News view, able to show some interesting contextual details.

In the next section, we will build a specialized search form with a "region" parameter—stay tuned!

Forms

Going further with a simple web form useful to our Regional News product, we could imagine implementing a specialized search form, with generic text search using the Plone `SearchableText` index and `region` index as possible criteria. To do this, we will adopt the `z3c.form` library, and use it to build our form browser view, and we will also create a regions vocabulary. Additionally in this section, you will get a good understanding of how to query the portal_catalog tool and present its results. Let's do it!

Until now, we have considered Archetypes our best friend in Plone development. But here is where we miss something: managing web forms without any content object behind them. For instance, sometimes we just use web forms to collect information, not to manage content.

Archetypes web form generation is quite powerful, rich in widgets and validation hooks, and easy to manage, since it's integrated with the fields schema describing our content type.

Unfortunately, we need a fields schema to make it work, which implies instantiating an existing content type object into our database. In fact, every line of code in Archetypes makes the assumption that there is an existing content type object as the context to use.

For some time, this issue could not be solved in any elegant way, but Zope 3 technologies came to help us with a couple of good solutions, both enabling us to manage web forms using Python classes and interfaces: zope.formlib and z3c.form.

The latter seems a bit more flexible and used, so in this section we will look over its development patterns.

Note z3c.form is an advanced HTML form and widget framework for Zope 3—that is, a way to generate and control forms and widgets from Python code. With a pattern similar to Archetypes, it renders a form and its widgets starting from a schema (not a fields schema, but a Zope 3 interface). For a deeper understanding of how z3c.form works, please have a look at http://pypi.python.org/pypi/z3c.form.

Getting and Using z3c.form

First of all, we need to obtain the plone.z3cform package and all of its dependencies for Plone. We can get the eggified package simply by adding plone.z3cform to the eggs option of the buildout section of our buildout.cfg file:

```
[buildout]
parts =
    plone
    productdistros
    instance
    zopepy
    fakezope2eggs

...

eggs =
    elementtree
    plonebook.regional_news
    plone.z3cform

...
[instance]
zcml =
```

```
    plonebook.regional_news
    plone.z3cform

...
[fakezope2eggs]
recipe = affinitic.recipe.fakezope2eggs
zope2-part = instance
zope2-location = ${instance:zope2-location}
additional-fake-eggs =
    zope.testing
    zope.i18n
  zope.component
```

Actually, it is a bit more complicated: plone.z3cform depends on z3c.form, which is an original Zope 3 package. Look at the last section of code: because of the dependencies set on the z3c.form egg, the buildout process would end up getting the wrong dependencies for our Zope 2 environment, which is why we need to use the [fakezope2eggs] section.

After having modified the buildout.cfg file, run the buildout script again:

```
$ cd ~/plonebook
$ ./bin/instance stop
$ ./bin/buildout -v
```

At the end of this process, we should be able to implement our new search view using plone.z3cform. Go to the browser folder of the package and add a new file named regionalnewssearch.py, containing this code:

```
from zope import interface, schema
from z3c.form import form, field, button
from plone.z3cform.layout import import wrap_form

class IRegionalNewsSearch(interface.Interface):

    SearchableText = schema.TextLine(title=u"Text")
    region = schema.TextLine(title=u"Region")


class RegionalNewsSearchForm(form.Form):
    fields = field.Fields(IRegionalNewsSearch)
    ignoreContext = True # don't use context to get widget data
    label = u"Search Regional News"

    @button.buttonAndHandler(u'Search')
    def handleSearch(self, action):
        data, errors = self.extractData()
        self.status = data


RegionalNewsSearchView = wrap_form(RegionalNewsSearchForm)
```

Finally, open `browser/configure.zcml` in your editor and add the registration for the new search view:

```
<browser:page
  for="*"
  name="rn_search"
  class=".regionalnewssearch.RegionalNewsSearchView"
  permission="zope.Public"
/>
```

Note that we did not specify any template for this view. In fact, the `wrap_form` function we got from `plone.z3cform` does the magic, binding the `RegionalNewsSearchForm` class—which is responsible for the web form mechanism—to the `RegionalNewsSearchView` class, the actual browser view class.

So, let's go back to the terminal and start our Zope service:

```
$ cd ~/plonebook
$ ./bin/instance start
```

Then point your browser to `http://localhost:8080/plone/rn_search` and enjoy your first `z3c.form` view (see Figure 9-6). It doesn't do much yet, but it was easy to implement with very little effort, and includes validation on required fields and a working submit button.

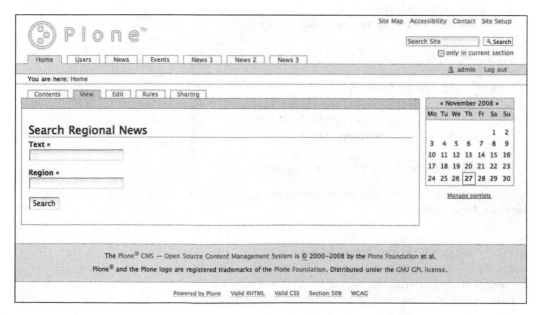

Figure 9-6. *The Regional News search form.*

To accomplish our mission, we still need a couple of important things: implementing the search logic and making it easy to choose the desired region.

Let's start with the latter. When we introduced the region attribute for our content type in the "Writing a Custom Content Type" section, we did not build any web-configurable vocabulary. Remember, we need this so that our portal administrators won't have to mess with any Python code to update the available regions for news items on the site. We won't do it now either, but let's implement a Zope 3 vocabulary to use both for our content type attribute and the search view interface.

Go to the root folder of your package and add a new file named vocabularies.py, containing this code:

```python
from zope.interface import implements
from zope.app.schema.vocabulary import IVocabularyFactory
from zope.schema.vocabulary import SimpleTerm
from zope.schema.vocabulary import SimpleVocabulary


REGIONS = (('Italy', 'Italy'),
           ('France', 'France'),
           ('England', 'England'),
          )


class RegionsVocabulary(object):
    """Vocabulary factory for regional news regions.
    """

    implements(IVocabularyFactory)

    def __call__(self, context):
        items = [SimpleTerm(value, title) for \
                           value, title in REGIONS]
        return SimpleVocabulary(items)


RegionsVocabularyFactory = RegionsVocabulary()
```

Then open configure.zcml in the root folder of the package and register your new vocabulary as a Zope 3 utility:

```xml
...
<!-- -*- extra stuff goes here -*- -->
<utility
  component=".vocabularies.RegionsVocabularyFactory"
  name="plonebook.regional_news.vocabularies.regions"
  />

...
```

We now have a new vocabulary to use. Let's modify the IRegionalNewsSearch interface in browser/regionalnewssearch.py like this:

```
class IRegionalNewsSearch(interface.Interface):

    SearchableText = schema.TextLine(title=u"Text")
    region = schema.Choice(title=u"Region",
            vocabulary="plonebook.regional_news.vocabularies.regions")
```

As you can see, we changed the region attribute to be a Choice attribute, and then used our new vocabulary to fill it.

If you want to know what the results of this are, just restart your Zope service by typing in the following commands:

```
$ cd ~/plonebook
$ ./bin/instance restart
```

Pointing your browser back to http://localhost:8080/plone/rn_search, the region attribute will let you select just the regions you specified in your vocabulary.

You still need to change your content type schema so that it can use your vocabulary, too. Open the content/regionalnews.py module in your package and change the region attribute definition as follows:

```
atapi.StringField(
    name='region',
    storage = atapi.AnnotationStorage(),
    required=False,
    #searchable=1,
    #default='',
    #schemata ='default',
    vocabulary_factory = "plonebook.regional_news.vocabularies.regions",
    widget=atapi.SelectionWidget(
        label=_(u"region"),
        description=_(u"Description of region"),
    ),
),
```

Archetypes is clever enough to use a Zope 3 vocabulary just by passing its name through the vocabulary_factory property.

Now let's try to make our form more interesting by implementing what is missing to let it run the actual search.

Without any further work, we can just redirect what the user is asking for to the standard Plone search view. To do so, edit the regionalnewssearch.py module like this:

```
...
from Products.CMFCore.utils import getToolByName

...
```

```
class RegionalNewsSearchForm(form.Form):
    fields = field.Fields(IRegionalNewsSearch)
    ignoreContext = True # don't use context to get widget data
    label = u"Search Regional News"

    @property
    def portal(self):
        return getToolByName(self.context,
                                'portal_url').getPortalObject()


    @button.buttonAndHandler(u'Search')
    def handleSearch(self, action):
        data, errors = self.extractData()
        if errors:
            return
        base_url = "%s/search" % self.portal.absolute_url()
        qstring = "?portal_type=RegionalNews"
        qstring += "&SearchableText=%s" % data['SearchableText']
        qstring += "&region=%s" % data['region']
        qstring += "&sort_on=effective&sort_order=descending"
        self.request.response.redirect(base_url + qstring)


RegionalNewsSearchView = wrap_form(RegionalNewsSearchForm)
```

Here, we just enabled the handleSearch method of our RegionalNewsSearchForm class to remap the provided criteria into a correct query string and properly redirect to the portal search view. It's that simple, if the standard search view is enough for you.

However, we're going to complicate it a bit: remember from the "Structure of a Plone Product" section at the beginning of the chapter, one of our requirements is that we create our own specialized results view.

Go back to your terminal window and ask Paster to build us a new browser view:

```
$ cd ~/plonebook/src/plonebook.regional_news
$ paster addcontent view
```

Enter **rn_search_results** as the view_name, and then open browser/configure.zcml to change the predefined view name in rn_search_results. We want the template to render the criteria used for the search and the corresponding results: it will render a dictionary containing the chosen criteria and a list of dictionaries corresponding to the actual resulting news, both created by the rn_search_resultsView view class. So let's edit the browser/rn_search_resultsview.pt file like this:

```
<html xmlns="http://www.w3.org/1999/xhtml" xml:lang="en"
      lang="en"
      metal:use-macro="here/main_template/macros/master"
      i18n:domain="plonebook.regional_news">
<body>
    <div metal:fill-slot="main">
        <tal:main-macro metal:define-macro="main">
```

```
        <h1>Regional News Search Results</h1>
        <p tal:define="criteria view/criteria">
            Selected Keys:<br />
            <tal:block tal:repeat="key criteria/keys">
                <strong tal:content="key">key</strong>:
                <span tal:replace="criteria/key">value</span>
                <span tal:condition="not:repeat/key/end">, </span>
            </tal:block>
        </p>
        <ul tal:define="results view/get_results">
            <li tal:repeat="item results">
                [<span tal:replace="item/region">]
                <a href="" tal:attributes="href item/url"
                    tal:content="item/title"> item </a>
            </li>
        </ul>
    </tal:main-macro>
  </div>
</body>
</html>
```

Now for the interesting part—open browser/rn_search_resultsview.py and enter the following code:

```
from zope.interface import implements, Interface

from Products.Five import BrowserView
from Products.CMFCore.utils import getToolByName

from plonebook.regional_news import regional_newsMessageFactory as _


class Irn_search_resultsView(Interface):
    """
    rn_search_results view interface
    """

    def criteria():
        """ return the criteria for our search as a python dict.
        """

    def get_results():
        """ return a list of dicts corresponding to the requested criteria.
        """

class rn_search_resultsView(BrowserView):
    """
    rn_search_results browser view
```

```
    """
    implements(Irn_search_resultsView)

    def __init__(self, context, request):
        self.context = context
        self.request = request

    @property
    def portal_catalog(self):
        return getToolByName(self.context, 'portal_catalog')

    @property
    def portal(self):
        return getToolByName(self.context, 'portal_url').getPortalObject()

    def criteria(self):
        request = self.request
        criteria = {}
        criteria['SearchableText'] = request.get('SearchableText', ' ')
        criteria['region'] = request.get('region', ' ')
        return criteria

    def get_results(self):
        request = self.request
        query = {'portal_type': 'RegionalNews',
                 'SearchableText': request.get('SearchableText'),
                 'region': request.get('region'),
                 'sort_on': 'effective',
                 'sort_order': 'descending'}
        brains = self.portal_catalog.searchResults(**query)

        items = []
        for brain in brains:
            items.append({'title': brain.Title,
                          'url': brain.getURL(),
                          'region': brain.getRegion})

        return items
```

The criteria method is quite simple: we ask the request object for our specific names, and if they're not present, we return an escaped space character.

As for the get_results method, notice that we are using the same pattern we used earlier in the "Theming" section of the chapter. We'll clarify it better in the following section. In Figure 9-7, you can see the rn_search_results view in action.

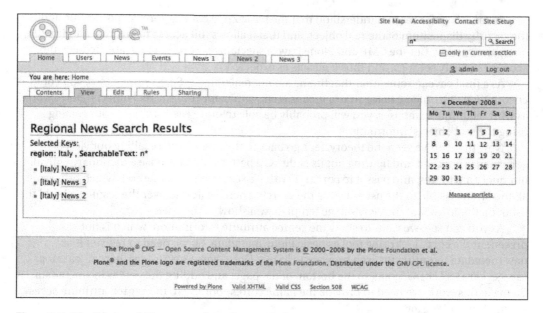

Figure 9-7. *The Regional News search engine works!*

Understanding the Plone Catalog

As you know from the preceding chapters, the portal_catalog tool is one of the most useful services in Plone. It is used for standard searches as well as folder listings.

The ZODB doesn't offer any native indexing service on the objects it stores. That is where Zope catalogs come in. Basically, a catalog indexes an object's information on demand, according to a list of desired indexes, and stores that information for every single object, using a sort of placeholder called a brain, which is by itself an object.

Different kinds of indexes are available, dedicated to specific types of data and queries; for example, we can define a simple field index to store plain string data, a date index to query date fields, a path index to query objects on a position basis, and so on.

Of course, brains store index information in their specific formats to simplify query algorithms. Thus, to show the results of a query in a human-readable format, we would need to look for the real objects corresponding to the resulting brains; but that is quite a heavy operation, especially when we just need to know the real object is there, and are not going to use it.

That's why with indexes, Zope catalogs also store real object metadata into brains: object information annotated into the brain at indexing time, which is useful for building search result pages without awakening the real objects.

Note For a deeper understanding of Zope catalogs, please read the "Searching and Categorizing Content" chapter of the Zope Book (www.zope.org/Documentation/Books/ZopeBook/2_6Edition/ SearchingZCatalog.stx).

So far, it's quite easy to understand that the basic Zope catalog service has no clue about the security disposition of the real object, and that it allows full access to any role admitted to query the catalog. But the CMF and Plone have a specialized Zope catalog, able to take into account security settings, and thus it all acts as expected.

As a final caveat, remember that brains are not real objects. So, in some cases, you could encounter a corrupted catalog that is inconsistent with respect to the real objects. Don't worry: as with relational databases, you will probably be able to quite easily rebuild your catalog using the real objects' information.

Now that you've seen the theory, let's go back to the real world, recalling our view's get_results method and figuring out its code. As a pattern, we compose a dictionary with all our query attributes, and pass it to portal_catalog's searchResults method, which brings out all the brains visible to the user making the search. Then we iterate over the results to build the list of dictionaries that the view's page template will show to the user.

As you can see, we want to show the region attribute information, which is not present in the portal_catalog tool as basic Plone metadata. So we need to register it as new metadata, pointing the web browser to http://localhost:8080/plone/portal_catalog/manage_catalogSchema, going to the bottom of the page, and adding the getRegion metadata. To make this work, we need to provide the name corresponding to the region attribute accessor method: getRegion.

This quick demonstration of z3c.form has left out a lot of powerful features. For a deeper comprehension of z3c.form use in Plone, please read Daniel Nouri's tutorial on Plone.org, at http://plone.org/documentation/how-to/easy-forms-with-plone3.

Viewlets and Portlets

In the last section, we enhanced our Regional News product: we created a nice specific search interface, completing the most common interaction use cases for our content type—making it editable, viewable, and searchable.

We will now concentrate a bit on improving the user interaction. In this section, we'll move our region data from the Regional News info box into a info viewlet, registered to the plone.belowcontenttitle viewlet manager. We will also add a link in order to search all the news from that region through the Regional News search form. Finally, we will implement a portlet to show the latest published news in a specific region.

Thanks to Zope 3 technologies, this is possible without messing with Plone default templates. Since version 3.0, Plone has been widely adopting Zope 3 technologies, and the original template is split up into various viewlet managers, to which any product can register its own viewlets. Point your web browser to http://localhost:8080/plone/@@manage-viewlets and you will see evidence of this.

■**Note** A *viewlet manager* is a Zope 3 component that acts as a placeholder, collecting various viewlets and rendering them where the templates ask for them. To look more deeply into viewlets and the other Zope 3 technologies adopted by Plone to build its user interface, please read the Plone Theme Reference at Plone.org, and in particular look over the section about what a viewlet is, at http://plone.org/documentation/manual/theme-reference/buildingblocks/components/viewletsandportlets.

To accomplish our mission, we will register a simple Regional News info viewlet, which is basically a browser view with a special registration policy.

Create a new file named viewlet.py in the browser folder of your package, and then type in the following lines:

```python
from zope.interface import implements, Interface
from zope.viewlet.interfaces import IViewlet

from Products.Five import BrowserView
from Products.CMFCore.utils import getToolByName
from Products.CMFPlone.utils import safe_unicode

from plonebook.regional_news.interfaces import IRegionalNews
from plonebook.regional_news import regional_newsMessageFactory as _

INFO_SNIPPET = """
    <p><strong>region: %s </strong>(<a href='%s'>search other news</a>)</p>
"""

class InfoViewlet(BrowserView):
    """

    regionalnews info viewlet
    """

    implements(IViewlet)

    def __init__(self, context, request, view, manager):
        super(InfoViewlet, self).__init__(context, request)
        self.__parent__ = view
        self.context = context
        self.request = request
        self.view = view
        self.manager = manager

    def render(self):
        """render the regionalnews info snippet"""
        snippet = ""
        if IRegionalNews.providedBy(self.context):
            region = self.context.getRegion()
            portal_url = getToolByName(self.context, 'portal_url')
            search_url = portal_url() + '/rn_search'
            snippet = safe_unicode(INFO_SNIPPET % (region, search_url))
        return snippet
```

Now edit the browser/configure.zcml file to register your new viewlet, adding these lines:

```
<browser:viewlet
    name="regionalnews.info"
    manager="plone.app.layout.viewlets.interfaces.IBelowContentTitle"
    class=".viewlet.InfoViewlet"
    permission="zope2.View"
    />
```

Notice that the InfoViewlet class just inherits from the standard BrowserView class, and declares that it implements the IViewlet interface, providing a render method. We have no need to use a page template to render our simple viewlet for now—just render the region attribute, if it is available on the viewlet context.

Go back to the terminal window and type in

```
$ cd ~/plonebook
$ ./bin/instance restart
```

Then point your web browser to http://localhost:8080/plone and create a new Regional News item. Save the page, and you should find your new viewlet under the News title.

We obtained what we wanted, but it would be nicer to have the region info just under the title, not behind the "about" line. Remembering the manage-viewlets view, it should be very easy to reorder our viewlets just to match what we are looking for (see Figure 9-8).

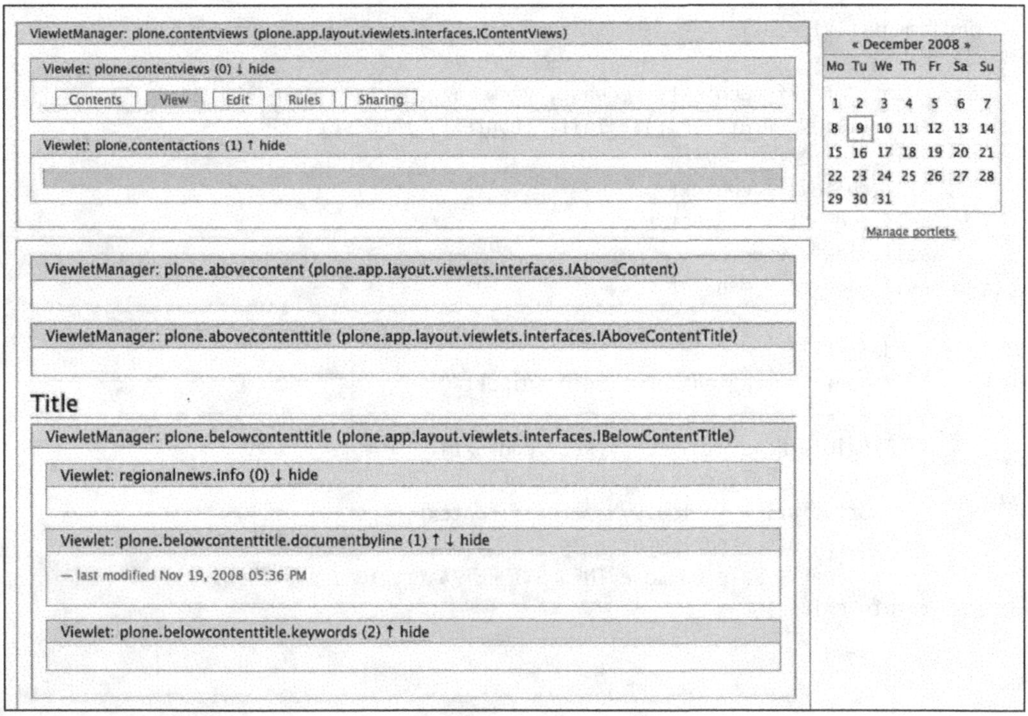

Figure 9-8. *Regional News viewlets*

So visit `http://localhost:8080/plone/@@manage-viewlets` and look for the `regionalnews.info` viewlet; then click its up arrow icon, and you are done.

Again, you may wonder how to register into our product package that the viewlets have to appear in a certain order. We'll describe this shortly: exporting your configuration and storing it in your product using your GenericSetup profile will be quite easy.

As for viewlets, it is quite simple to perform this task—just remember that if you need to manipulate the Plone user interface, you probably won't need to mess with templates: just hide the default viewlet, register your own, and that is it.

To complete our visual refactoring, let's move the other part of the former info box into a portlet of our own. Again, we will need to implement a Zope 3 component and register it, but this time it will be a bit more of a Plone-centric component.

Plone version 3.0 implements its own portlet infrastructure, thanks to the prolific Martin Aspeli. We can register portlets to appear in a specific context according to various rules: in our case, we want our portlet to appear just in the Regional News item context.

So, let's ask for some help from Paster, which provides some boilerplate code for creating a new portlet in our package. Open the terminal window and type in the following:

```
$ cd ~/plonebook
$ ./bin/instance stop
$ cd ~/plonebook/src/plonebook.regional_news
$ paster addcontent portlet
```

Then answer the questions the script will ask you, using `Regional News` portlet as the portlet name and `regional_news` as the portlet type. You can keep the defaults for all the rest. As usual, Paster updates various parts of your package to make the new portlet work: it creates some new files in the portlets folder, as well as a `portlets.xml` file in the `profiles/default` folder, to register the portlet in the GenericSetup profile of the package.

Now we need to edit `regional_news.py` and `regional_news.pt` in the `portlets` folder to make them implement a portlet showing the Other Regional News section of the current info box we have on the `regionalnews_view` template.

Paster produces a rich `regional_news.py` module, providing several class placeholders to fill in. But first, we need to understand what is going on.

Consider how you can manage a portlet in Plone since version 3.0. You can easily add a portlet wherever you want: if you have the needed permissions, you can bind it to a group or a content type through the Plone control panel, or you can place it on any Plone object you like, using the `@@manage-portlets` view.

Besides, according to the kind of portlet you add, you can access a list of portlet attributes to decide how the specific portlet should act (e.g., showing a footer link, searching for a certain kind of content type, etc.).

■**Note** To improve your comprehension of portlet infrastructure, you might want to read the portlet-related chapters in the Plone Theme Reference at Plone.org—in particular the "Portlet Manager" section, at `http://plone.org/documentation/manual/theme-reference/elements/portletmanager`, and the "Anatomy of a Portlet" section, at `http://plone.org/documentation/manual/theme-reference/elements/portlet/anatomy` on portlets.

We will need to implement a couple of forms to add and edit our portlet, and we will need a page template and some business logic to render it.

With this in mind, let's discover what Paster has produced for us. The regional_news.py module uses formlib as its form generation library, which shares a very similar pattern with z3c.form.

The first class we need to fill in is an interface class, inheriting from IPortletDataProvider. If we look over the module, we discover that both the AddForm and EditForm classes will render this interface. So let's change it as follows:

```
class Iregional_news(IPortletDataProvider):
    """A portlet

    It inherits from IPortletDataProvider because for this portlet, the
    data that is being rendered and the portlet assignment itself are the
    same.
    """

    # TODO: Add any zope.schema fields here to capture portlet configuration
    # information. Alternatively, if there are no settings, leave this as an
    # empty interface - see also notes around the add form and edit form
    # below.

    more_url = schema.Bool(title=_(u"All News for this region link"),
                  description=_(u"Tick this box if you want to render "
                                "a link which shows all the Regional News "
                                "for the context region."),
                                required=False)
```

The Paster template's comments invite us to declare the fields we need in order to define our portlet configuration. As an exercise, we will just let the user choose whether he wants to render a region's All News link or not.

We then have an Assignment class, which essentially offers the logic used by the add and edit forms. This class consists of the following code:

```
class Assignment(base.Assignment):

    implements(Iregional_news)

    more_url = False

    def __init__(self, show_search_url=False, more_url=False):
        self.more_url = more_url

    ...
```

Base.Assignment comes directly from the plone.app.portlets.portlets package, which hides the portlet's storing and assigning infrastructure.

The Assignment class teams up with AddForm and EditForm at the end of the module, which derive from the basic plone.app.portlets AddForm and EditForm classes and do not need our intervention.

The most important points here involve the Renderer class. Basically, it acts like a browser view with a few more bindings, and allows us to render the regional_news.pt template properly.

In our case, substantially reusing some code from our regionalnews_view browser view, the following code should suffice:

```
class Renderer(base.Renderer):

    render = ViewPageTemplateFile('regional_news.pt')

    @property
    def is_regional_news(self):
        if IRegionalNews.providedBy(self.context):
            return True
        return False

    @property
    def region(self):
        if self.is_regional_news:
            return self.context.getRegion()
        return ''

    @property
    def all_news_url(self):
        portal_url = getToolByName(self.context, 'portal_url')
        base_url = portal_url() + '/rn_search_results'
        return '%s?SearchableText=&region=%s' % (base_url, self.region)

    @property
    def get_other_news_items(self):

        if not self.is_regional_news:
            return ()

        context = self.context
        context_path = '/'.join(context.getPhysicalPath())
        query = {'portal_type': 'RegionalNews',
                 'review_state': 'published',
                 'region': self.region,
                 'sort_on': 'effective',
                 'sort_order': 'descending',
                 'show_inactive': False}
        portal_catalog = getToolByName(context, 'portal_catalog')
        brains = portal_catalog.searchResults(**query)[:3]
```

```
        items = []
        for brain in brains:
            if brain.getPath() <> context_path:
                items.append({'title': brain.Title,
                              'url': brain.getURL()})


        return items[:2]
```

That is it for the regionalnews.py module.

Have a look now at regionalnews.pt template. Paster offers a good starting point, and we just need to fill in the information from the Renderer class, as follows:

```
<dl class="portlet portletregional_news"
    i18n:domain="plonebook.regional_news.portlets">

    <dt class="portletHeader">
        <span class="portletTopLeft"></span>
        <span>
            <a tal:omit-tag="not:view/data/more_url"
               tal:attributes="href view/data/more_url"
               >More from <span tal:replace="view/region"
                  >region</span></a>
        </span>
        <span class="portletTopRight"></span>
    </dt>

    <dd class="portletItem odd">
        <tal:block tal:define="other_news view/get_other_news_items">
        <p tal:condition="not: other_news"> No other news by now..</p>
        <ul tal:condition="other_news">
            <li tal:repeat="item other_news">
                <a href="" tal:attributes="href item/url"
                   tal:content="item/title">Other News</a>
            </li>
        </ul>
        </tal:block>
        <tal:corners condition="not: view/data/more_url">
            <span class="portletBottomLeft"></span>
            <span class="portletBottomRight"></span>
        </tal:corners>
    </dd>

    <dd class="portletFooter" tal:condition="view/data/more_url">
        <span class="portletBottomLeft"></span>
        <span>
```

```
          <a tal:attributes="href view/all_news_url"
                 >All News from <span tal:content="view/region"
               >region</span></a>
      </span>
      <span class="portletBottomRight"></span>
   </dd>

</dl>
```

Again, thanks to Zope 3 technologies, separation of visual structure and business logic is quite evident, and we gain quite a simple and comprehensible template.

Now that we have all the pieces in place, we should have a look at the portlets/configure. zcml file:

```
<plone:portlet
    name="plonebook.regional_news.portlets.regional_news"
    interface=".regional_news.Iregional_news"
    assignment=".regional_news.Assignment"
    view_permission="zope2.View"
    edit_permission="cmf.ManagePortal"
    renderer=".regional_news.Renderer"
    addview=".regional_news.AddForm"
    editview=".regional_news.EditForm"
    />
```

Just edit the browser/regionalnewsview.pt template to delete the info box part we refactored into our new viewlet and portlet, and finally restart the Zope service to have a look at what we have now:

```
$ cd ~/plonebook
$ ./bin/instance start
```

Then point your web browser to http://localhost:8080/plone and add another news item. Notice that your new viewlet has no more in-context info box, but the portlet does not appear yet.

So, if we want to associate our portlet with every Regional News item, let's go to the Plone control panel, select the Types panel, select our Regional News content type, and then choose the link to access the view for managing portlets assigned to it, at http://localhost:8080/plone/@@manage-content-type-portlets?key=RegionalNews.

Finally, from the "Add portlet" drop-down box, select the Regional News portlet. But, wait ... there is no "Regional News portlet" item in that box!

What's going on here? Well, the answer is linked to the GenericSetup profile portlets.xml file that Paster produced for us.

In the next section, we will take a deeper look at what GenericSetup is. For now, just consider it a service able to import/export Plone configurations using specialized XML files. Unfortunately, GenericSetup must be triggered to import the `portlets.xml` file you prepared, otherwise, the Plone portlet machinery will not register your portlet.

So, in a final effort to register the new Regional News portlet in our Plone portal (whose function we will explain more fully in the next section), go to the `portal_setup` Import tab at `http://localhost:8080/plone/portal_setup/manage_importSteps`, choose Regional News from the Select Profile or Snapshot drop-down box, select the Portlets check box, and finally click the Import Selected Steps button at the bottom of the page.

The service should process our `portlets.xml` file and answer with a confirmation message. Return to `http://localhost:8080/plone/@@manage-content-type-portlets?key=RegionalNews` and try to add our Regional News portlet again. This time you will probably find it there. In Figure 9-9, you can see the new portlet in action.

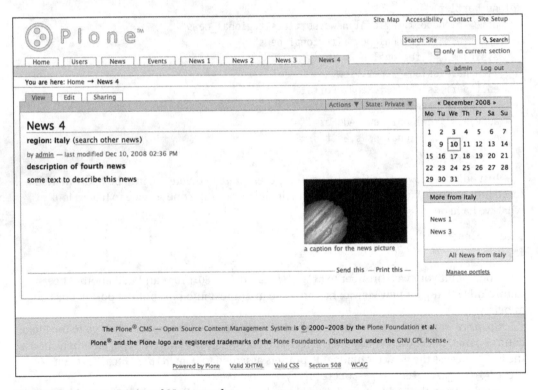

Figure 9-9. *The new Regional News portlet*

Using viewlets and portlets, we provide the webmaster with powerful and yet simple visual components to build the desired user interface in an easier and more flexible way. And with this, we can consider our work for the Regional News package almost done.

In the next section, we will add a specific publication workflow and take a deeper look into the GenericSetup concept.

Plone Configuration

Plone is a very flexible environment to configure, and has become more so since GenericSetup was introduced. Every Plone site has a `portal_setup` tool, accessible through the ZMI, able to manage configuration profiles in various ways. Plone flexibility comes in when you need to adjust properties to match your site's requirements (e.g., creating new content types by cloning the existing one in `portal_types`, adding custom indexes or metadata to your `portal_catalog`, or defining a whole new workflow schema).

Before GenericSetup, it was not possible to easily export to other Plone sites the configurations produced for one particular site. GenericSetup offers a simple way to convert site configurations to XML files and back.

Note For a deeper understanding of the GenericSetup machinery, please read the "Understanding and Using GenericSetup in Plone" tutorial on Plone.org, at `http://plone.org/documentation/tutorial/genericsetup`.

Let's have a look at it by providing a new workflow schema to our Regional News content type, using as a base the default `simple_publication_workflow` schema, and adding the `regional_published` state to it. For example, the new state could be useful to hide regional published news from the top level of our site. We leave it to you to eventually adjust your various views to the new state.

So, point your browser to the `portal_workflow` tool management interface, at `http://localhost:8080/plone/portal_workflow/manage_main`, select the `simple_publication_workflow` item, copy it, and then paste it in place.

You should see a new item named `copy_of_simple_publication_workflow`: select it and rename it to `regional_publication_workflow`.

Finally, visit `http://localhost:8080/plone/portal_workflow/regional_publication_workflow/manage`, and you will have quite an efficient web workflow configuration client. Use it to add the `regional_published` state, entering **Regional Published** as the title, and defining on it the `role-permissions` mapping you want through the permissions tab at `http://localhost:8080/plone/portal_workflow/regional_publication_workflow/states/regional_published/manage_permissions`. Then add the new `regional_publish` transition, entering **Regional Publish** as the title, and associate it with the various states for which you want it to be available.

All this can be done through the Web—content type association included—using the form at http://localhost:8080/plone/portal_workflow/manage_selectWorkflows. Just look for the RegionalNews text box and type in **regional_publication_workflow**. Your new configuration should look like in Figure 9-10.

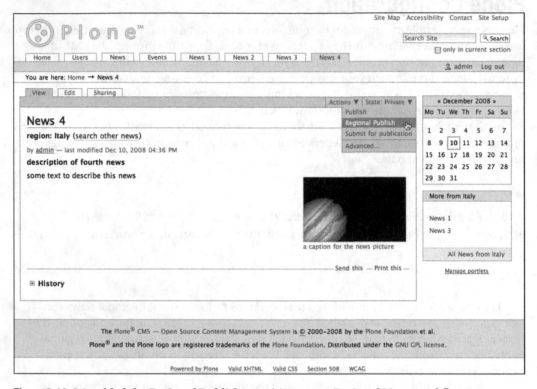

Figure 9-10. *We added the Regional Publish transition to our Regional News workflow.*

You should now be ready to use your new workflow in this site. But what about all the other Plone sites using your product?

You already know the answer is portal_setup, so point your browser to http://localhost:8080/plone/portal_setup/manage, and click the Export tab.

The portal_setup tool shows you a list of available export steps, each corresponding to a specific script able to extract its specific configuration information and turn it into a corresponding XML file or set of files.

We could simply select the check box corresponding to the workflow tool step and obtain its current configuration by clicking "Export selected steps" at the bottom of the page, but we would still be missing a few other configurations we changed during this chapter. So, instead, click the "Export all steps" button to obtain the whole set of the site's configuration information in a single compressed archive.

Unarchive the downloaded file and have a look at its content: each GenericSetup export step produces an easy-to-recognize XML file and, eventually, a folder in which to store other XML files, as in the case of the workflow step. Each export step is autonomous in deciding how to export its own configuration information, as far as the corresponding import step can use it. GenericSetup exports the site's configuration state at the precise moment we ask for it: in this case, we have to filter a whole slew of configurations we won't need in our product. To mitigate this, it is possible to create snapshots of the configuration state and compare them to obtain just the differences as a patch—but in this section we won't go deeper into this matter.

So, from our downloaded `portal_setup` file, let's take just the information we need for our product and store it into our package's `profiles/default` folder, starting with the workflow information.

Create the file `profiles/default/workflows.xml`, and put the following into it:

```
<?xml version="1.0"?>
<object name="portal_workflow" meta_type="Plone Workflow Tool">
 <object name="regional_publication_workflow" meta_type="Workflow"/>
 <bindings>
  <type type_id="RegionalNews">
   <bound-workflow workflow_id="regional_publication_workflow"/>
  </type>
 </bindings>
</object>
```

Then create the folder `profiles/default/workflows`, and copy in it the regional_publication_ workflow folder you find in the configuration's downloaded archive.

Afterward, create the file `profiles/default/catalog.xml`, and type in the following lines:

```
<?xml version="1.0"?>
<object name="portal_catalog" meta_type="Plone Catalog Tool">
 <index name="region" meta_type="KeywordIndex">
  <indexed_attr value="getRegion"/>
 </index>
 <column value="getRegion"/>
</object>
```

These lines are responsible for the creation of the `region` index and the `getRegion` metadata in `portal_catalog`.

Then register our regionalnews_view browser view to be the default one for our content type, changing the `profiles/default/types/RegionalNews.xml` file as follows:

```
<?xml version="1.0"?>
<object name="RegionalNews"
    meta_type="Factory-based Type Information with dynamic views"
    i18n:domain="plonebook.regional_news"
    xmlns:i18n="http://xml.zope.org/namespaces/i18n">

    ...
```

```
  <property name="default_view">regionalnews_view</property>
  <property name="view_methods">
   <element value="regionalnews_view"/>
  </property>
    ...

</object>
```

Continue by adding the following content to the file `profiles/default/cssregistry.xml` to register our CSS resource:

```
<?xml version="1.0"?>
<object name="portal_css" meta_type="Stylesheets Registry" autogroup="False">
 <stylesheet title="" cacheable="True" compression="safe" cookable="True"
    enabled="on" expression="" id="++resource++rn-resources/regionalnews.css"
    media="" rel="stylesheet" rendering="import"/>
</object>
```

After that, create the file `profiles/default/viewlets.xml`, and put in the following lines to order your viewlet as you want:

```
<?xml version="1.0"?>
<object>
 <order manager="plone.belowcontenttitle" skinname="Plone Default">
  <viewlet name="regionalnews.info"/>
  <viewlet name="plone.belowcontenttitle.documentbyline"/>
  <viewlet name="plone.belowcontenttitle.keywords"/>
 </order>
</object>
```

Finally, register the portlet to be displayed in the Regional News context, editing `profiles/default/portlets.xml` as follows:

```
<?xml version="1.0"?>
<portlets>
   <portlet
     addview="plonebook.regional_news.portlets.regional_news"
     title="Regional News portlet"
     description=""
   />
   <assignment name="regional-news" category="content_type" key="RegionalNews"
     manager="plone.rightcolumn"
     type="plonebook.regional_news.portlets.regional_news">
    <property name="more_url">True</property>
   </assignment>
</portlets>
```

We should now be ready to restart our Zope service and create a new Plone site, to verify we don't need to mess with web configuration any more. Let's go to the terminal window and type:

```
$ cd ~/plonebook
$ ./bin/instance restart
```

Point your web browser to `http://localhost:8080/manage`, create a new Plone site named plone2, and install your Regional News product, just as you did in the "Building a Plone Product the Easy Way" section of this chapter.

Then open the `http://localhost:8080/plone2` site's main page in your browser and try to create your first Regional News item for this portal. As in Figure 9-11, you should see a nicely formatted Regional News item with our viewlet and portlet in place, and a working "search other news" link pointing toward a working specialized search form for Regional News.

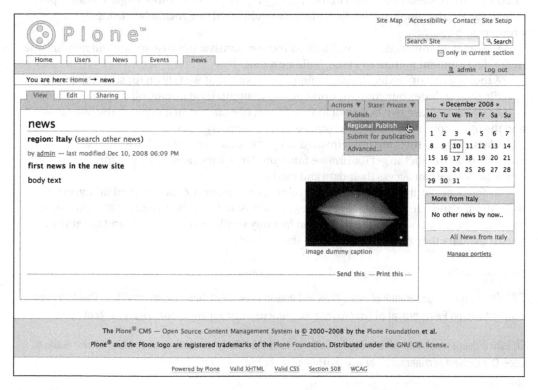

Figure 9-11. *We were able to export our Regional News item to a new Plone site.*

We have finally been able to fulfill all the promises we set forth, except one, which is letting a webmaster easily manage our region's vocabulary through the Web. We will discuss a couple of different ways to accomplish this last mission in the next section.

Tools and Utilities

Throughout this chapter, we have focused on extending Plone content types with our Regional News type. You have seen how to build this Plone extension using a file system product, but without having to understand too much to get up and running, thanks to Paster's aid. We followed quite a good development pattern using Zope 3 technologies, building web forms automatically from schemas, keeping templates and business logic as isolated as possible, and adopting portlets and viewlets to split user interface elements up. Finally, we used Generic-Setup profiles to extract our web configurations and gather them into our product package.

Next, we need to solve a little point we left in the preceding sections: allowing a Plone webmaster to manage the `regions` vocabulary for our Regional News content type through the Web, without asking the developer to change the current items.

Solving this could be done following various approaches: for instance, we could easily build a property sheet of our own in the `portal_properties` tool, with a single `lines` property, able to store our regions one per line. Then we could build our vocabulary using that `lines` property as a source.

However, in this section we will be a bit more expansive, because we are still missing one major development pattern in Plone: building a tool.

A tool is a sort of service, usually unique in the site, that we rely on for something quite specific (e.g., to index our content, workflow our content, send e-mail, etc.).

As usual, we have two flavors of tools in Plone: one classic, belonging to the Zope 2 world, and the other coming from Zope 3 technologies, known as a *utility*.

Classic Zope 2 tools are implemented in Python classes registered in a specific way, and are acquired through the `getToolByName` function. Thus, they need to be instantiated in the portal before we can access their data and methods.

As for Zope 3 utilities, our `regions` vocabulary is already a Zope 3 named utility, but it lacks storage and a user interface to manage its items; in fact it is pure code. We could also adopt local utilities, which are instantiated in a way similar to classic tools and are able to persist the data they need while the Zope service is off.

Note   To have a better look at Plone tools and how to implement them, please read the "Create a Custom Tool" tutorial on Plone.org, at `http://plone.org/documentation/how-to/create-a-tool`.

To take a deeper look into what a Zope 3 utility is, read the "Utility" section of "A Comprehensive Guide to Zope Component Architecture," at `www.muthukadan.net/docs/zca.html#utility`.

So, taking the newer development pattern, we will build a control panel configlet based on a `formlib` class that will store and retrieve configuration data using a local named utility. Of course, we will set up what is needed by working with our GenericSetup profile.

Note A *configlet* is a special component useful for building a configuration user interface in the Plone control panel.

At the end, we will update our regions vocabulary implementation to use this new local utility.

Let's start! First, define the configuration interface in the package's interfaces.py file, as follows:

```
class IRegionalNewsConfig(Interface):
    """Description of Regional News Configuration Panel"""

    regions = schema.List(
                 title = u"Available Regions",
                 default = [u'Italy', u'France', u'England'],
                 value_type = schema.TextLine(),
                 unique = True,
                 required = False,
                 )
```

We declare a regions field, which in fact is a list of TextLine fields, providing a convenient default value.

Then, we have to define our configlet component. To do this, let's create the browser/configlet.py file, and enter the following lines:

```
from zope.formlib import form
from zope.i18nmessageid import MessageFactory
from plone.app.controlpanel.form import ControlPanelForm

from plonebook.regional_news.interfaces import IRegionalNewsConfig
from plonebook.regional_news import regional_newsMessageFactory as _

class RegionalNewsConfigForm(ControlPanelForm):

    form_fields = form.Fields(IRegionalNewsConfig)

    label = _(u"Regional News Configuration Panel")
    description = _(u"define settings for Regional News content type")
    form_name = _(u"Regional News Config Panel")
```

The RegionalNewsConfigForm class inherits from plone.app.controlpanel.form.
ControlPanelForm, so it is easily plugged into the Plone control panel user interface.
It just needs to specify a few mandatory attributes, and also specify that it renders the
IRegionalNewsConfig interface.

Of course, we need to register our new component, so add the following to browser/
configure.zcml:

```
...
<browser:page
    for="Products.CMFPlone.Portal.PloneSite"
    name="regionalnews-config"
    class=".configlet.RegionalNewsConfigForm"
    permission="cmf.ManagePortal"
    />

...
```

Next, we need to provide the local utility in which to store our configuration; so, open the
config.py file in the root of our package, and add the following code to the bottom:

```
from zope.interface import implements
from zope.schema.fieldproperty import FieldProperty
from zope.component import getUtility
from OFS.SimpleItem import SimpleItem

from plonebook.regional_news.interfaces import IRegionalNewsConfig

class RegionalNewsConfig(SimpleItem):
    implements(IRegionalNewsConfig)

    regions = FieldProperty(IRegionalNewsConfig['regions'])
```

As you can see, we just store our configurations in a Zope SimpleItem class, using zope.
schema FieldProperty. This is a convenient way to easily annotate our instance with data coming from our interface.

Presently, you will see how to create our local utility at the product's installation time
using GenericSetup, naming it regionalnews_config and instantiating it at the site root level.

Of course, we need to bind our configlet formlib class with this local utility; so, we register
a function as an adapter, returning our local utility and providing IRegionalNewsConfig. So, at
the bottom of the config.py file, add the following lines:

```
def rn_config_adapter(context):
    return getUtility(IRegionalNewsConfig,
                      name='regionalnews_config',
                      context=context)
```

Clearly, we'll have to register it in the package `configure.zcml` file as follows:

```
...
<adapter
  for="Products.CMFPlone.Portal.PloneSite"
  provides=".interfaces.IRegionalNewsConfig"
  factory=".config.rn_config_adapter" />

...
```

Everything we need is there! Let's add some XML configuration files to instruct Generic-Setup to install the configuration utility and our shiny new configlet for the Plone control panel.

So, to add the local utility to the site root at install time, create the `profiles/default/componentregistry.xml` file, and put the following code into it:

```
<?xml version="1.0"?>
<componentregistry>
 <utilities>
  <utility name="regionalnews_config"
     factory="plonebook.regional_news.config.RegionalNewsConfig"
     interface="plonebook.regional_news.interfaces.IRegionalNewsConfig"/>
 </utilities>
</componentregistry>
```

Then create the `profiles/default/controlpanel.xml` file, and fill it with the following lines:

```
<?xml version="1.0"?>
<object name="portal_controlpanel" meta_type="Plone Control Panel Tool">
 <configlet title="Regional News" action_id="RegionalNewsConfig"
     appId="RegionalNewsConfig" category="Products" condition_expr=""
     url_expr="string:${portal_url}/regionalnews-config"
     visible="True">
  <permission>Manage portal</permission>
 </configlet>
</object>
```

This will add our configlet to the Plone control panel.

Finally, let's restart the Zope service, going back to the terminal window and typing

```
$ cd ~/plonebook
$ ./bin/instance restart
```

Now, open the URL `http://localhost:8080/manage` in your web browser, create a new Plone site named plone3, and install the Regional News product.

If everything went fine, you should find a new Regional News item in the Add-on Products configuration section of the Plone control panel. Click the link, and enjoy your new web-managed list of regions (see Figure 9-12).

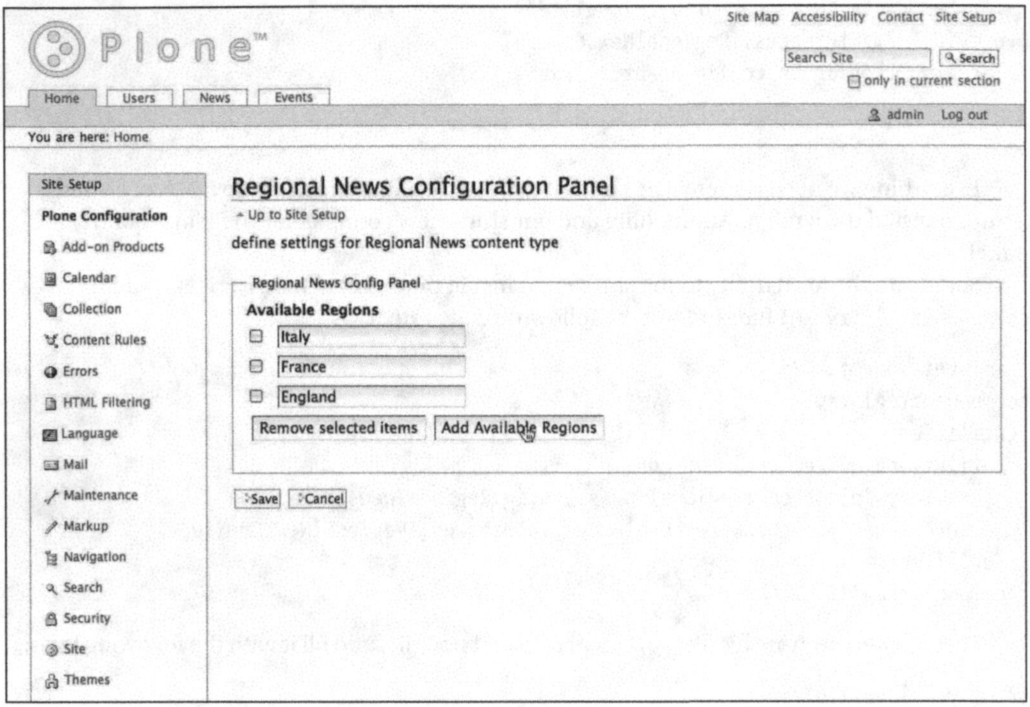

Figure 9-12. *We now have a web-managed list of regions.*

We'll leave it as an exercise for you to add a nice icon for the new Regional News configlet. Just remember GenericSetup is your friend!

So, now we have the configlet, but we haven't bound our regions vocabulary to the local utility data. Don't worry—nothing could be easier! Let's open the vocabularies.py file in the package root and change it to obtain what follows:

```
from zope.interface import implements
from zope.app.schema.vocabulary import IVocabularyFactory
from zope.schema.vocabulary import SimpleTerm
from zope.schema.vocabulary import SimpleVocabulary
from config import rn_config_adapter


class RegionsVocabulary(object):
    """Vocabulary factory for regional news regions.
    """

    implements(IVocabularyFactory)
```

```
def __call__(self, context):
    rn_config_utility = rn_config_adapter(context)
    items = rn_config_utility.regions
    if not items:
        items = (u"n.d.",)
    items = [SimpleTerm(el, el) for el in items]
    return SimpleVocabulary(items)
```

```
RegionsVocabularyFactory = RegionsVocabulary()
```

As you can see, we just get rid of the REGIONS constant to pick up the regions stored in our local utility. Also, our rn_config_utility function turned out to be useful to easily get the local utility in this module, too.

Just restart the Zope service, and add a new Regional News item in the site root. You will get the regions you specified through the configlet.

Summary

Well, we've finally reached our goal, which is clearly a simple goal as far as the Plone framework's possibilities go, but this should inspire you with many ideas for following up.

Along the way, we touched on some of the most common development patterns in Plone. We covered how you can build your own content type, the primary brick in Plone's structure. We investigated how to customize the default views on content types, as well as how to search manually for and automatically collect your content.

Plone is an evolving technology, based on actively developed frameworks. That is why we underlined the fact that, at present, Zope 3 techniques are on the way to completely replace the old-school patterns. Zope 3 is introducing amazing new technologies, such as browser views and z3c.form, as discussed in this chapter. Zope 2 is based on the concept of object orientation, which Zope 3 strengthens with the component architecture machinery, to allow developers to customize their applications and reuse code in easier and more effective and ways.

In the next chapter, we'll have a look at how to integrate Plone with other systems. In particular, if you're a developer, you may find the "Relational Databases" section interesting. Keep on reading!

CHAPTER 10

■ ■ ■

Integrating Plone
with Other Systems

Plone's nature is well-connected with the goal of managing web content through the Web and using proprietary (albeit open source) tools, such as the Python coding language and the ZODB object database. But Plone is more than this as well. If you investigate a bit, you'll discover that Python is an easy-to-learn, powerful tool with a complete set of extensions, enriching you with loads of extra possibilities. And Plone *is* Python. As well, Plone *is* Zope. And this opens to many other possibilities.

For instances, ZODB provides a nice storage layer for your content because it's so transparent and robust in its operation behind the curtain of Zope. And thanks to its roots in Python and Zope, Plone can go far beyond what you would expect from an application aiming at such an "easy" task as managing web content through the Web. In this chapter, we will delve into how to access Plone using methods different from the standard web user interface, as well as how to integrate Plone with other systems. First, we'll discuss how to link Plone with a file system, both through Plone's web interface and as a network share. Then we will make a foray into integrating a relational database in Plone, adopting classical Zope 2 techniques and using the SQLAlchemy library as a bridge. Next, we will figure out how to access Plone content without a web browser, using the WebDAV or FTP protocols; and, finally, we will take a look at Plone as a web service, glancing over the RSS, XML-RPC, and WSGI technologies.

Publishing the File System

Publishing folder content on the server file system requires a few steps, and this is because of security concerns. Of course, you could bypass the security issues by enabling Apache or an equivalent proxy web server to serve such folders directly, but every time a user wants to publish new folder content, a systems administrator will be needed to help.

The problem we want to solve here is, "How can a Plone user register a folder local to the server to be accessed as a normal Plone folder, but using its original files as objects, and all without asking a sys admin to lend a hand?" You might run into this use case in many circumstances, such as when you have a whole slew of documentation files and you would like them to be rapidly accessible through your intranet/extranet, giving access to them as you do for standard Plone folders.

You can provide this functionality within your Plone instance by extending it with some special products, like the one we suggest here: Reflecto. At the time of writing, Reflecto 2.0 is one of the most adopted solutions given by the Plone community to this special issue; it comes, in fact, after some other long-adopted products, such as LocalFS. You can find it on the Plone.org site, at http://plone.org/products/reflecto.

As stated by its official description, "Reflecto is a tool to incorporate part of the file system into a Plone site" as Plone content. Reflecto acts as a window for browsing the local file system and accessing the files in it as if they were Plone file objects. Using Reflecto, files in the mapped parts of the file system are indexed and searchable in Plone's catalog, can be copied and pasted, and can be renamed. They can be added from the file system or through Plone.

Let's now examine Reflecto more deeply. First, install Reflecto by unarchiving the downloaded package in your Products folder, or running your buildout script after having added Products.Reflecto to eggs in the buildout section, and to zcml in the instance section of your buildout.cfg file. You have seen these operations in detail in Chapter 9.

Start your local Zope service and create a new Plone site. Go to the Plone Control Panel and choose Add/Remove Products, and then select Reflecto from the list and click Install (if you have any doubt about this step, see the "Adding/Removing Products in Your Site" section of Chapter 4). At the end of this process, you should have a new content type named Reflector available in the Add New menu of your Plone folders.

A Reflector is a standard Plone object you can create in any Plone folder to open a window on the local file system. Just specify a title and a local file system folder path in the edit form of your Reflector object, and you will be able to navigate the contents of the folder corresponding to the path you give, subfolders included. You will also be able to rename, delete, and create new files using the Plone Contents tab, just as you would expect. As a note and invitation to read the Reflecto documentation, notice that files with file names that would clash with Plone's naming conventions will be ignored by Reflecto; for instance, Reflecto will not display files whose file name starts with @@, or contains a +.

Note Of course, the local file system has its own security machinery. For this reason, to access the local file system through Plone as expected, you need to give read/write permissions to the system user running the Zope service.

Reflecto is an easy and effective tool, but those files you can see in Plone using a Reflector object are not standard Plone objects in the ZODB database! If you choose the "Show live data" option in the Reflector object edit form, you can create a new file on the file system folder, and it will appear in Plone, without any further manual operation on your Reflector object. Nonetheless, if you want to change the Plone state on that file, you will find that it is not possible, and if you try to search for that file through the Plone search form, it will not show up. Let's try to understand the reasons of this in the next paragraph.

Almost every standard Plone behavior bases its operations on information stored in the objects it makes use of. For instance, for security and workflow services to work, they need to annotate the objects on which they are applied with specific information, and this is not easy to do with a file outside the ZODB storage. Furthermore, some services maintain a separate registry and need complete control over the content they manage. As an example, the portal_ catalog tool maintains its own registry for indexing purposes, and standard implementation of the indexing mechanism in Plone is based on synchronous calls. Each content object calls methods on the portal_catalog service, such as reindexObject, every time it is known that something new needs to be registered.

In the case of Reflecto, if some third-party application or manual intervention changes the files directly on the file system, the Plone registries will not be up to date. That is why Reflecto 2.0 proposes a trade-off between showing live data, or indexing file system contents, and advising that the live data mode could slow down Reflecto quite a lot. That is also why you cannot provide any working standard workflow or security function on these kinds of content. Plone security and workflow services are very advanced features, so it should be fairly obvious why you cannot quickly apply them to a file system folder and its content.

Relational Databases

For many years, relational databases have been the de facto standard for storing data in business applications, web CMS applications included. However, Zope doesn't need a relational database to store its data. Let's try to understand the reasons of this.

ZODB vs. Relational Databases

Relational databases are founded on mathematic theory and some efficient and well-known design techniques, not to mention various powerful database management systems (DBMSs) such as PostgreSQL. Relational databases need some conditions to efficiently apply their principles to our data, and these conditions are often mismatched by generic web applications. The most important reason for this is that a typical web application has a tree-like data structure, but relational databases are most suited to flat data structures: this is usually pointed out as an "object-relational impedance mismatch." Zope applications are developed as object hierarchies, so it would be quite difficult to store each object instance we need in generic relational structures while building an application. This is why Zope developers developed the ZODB, which is now a very robust and scalable object database, with transactional support and much more. Certainly it is one of Zope's secret weapons, especially if we consider all the attention paid to ORM technologies nowadays.

Many Zope applications are completely at ease without the need to even define a relational database structure. And developers use the ZODB transparently almost everywhere. Nonetheless, there are some Zope applications that need some integration with or functionality of a relational database management system (RDBMS). Next, we'll show you how Zope has no problems solving those situations.

Adopting a Relational Database in Zope

Without providing excessively complex use cases that would be out of the scope of this book, we will glance over some of the various ways to adopt a relational database in a Plone application.

Note The Zope Book provides a complete chapter on relational databases connectivity, available at www.zope.org/Documentation/Books/ZopeBook/2_6Edition/RelationalDatabases.stx. This documentation gives the official way to integrate a relational database in a standard Zope application, but remember that we can adopt anything that Python supports to solve this problem.

First of all, we should solve the simplest problem, in which we have a relational database table storing data we need to publish in our Plone site. This can be solved easily using particular Zope 2 tools. Specifically, we can add a Database Adapter object to open a connection to the relational database we want to query, create a ZSQL Method object to set our SQL query and run it, and finally use the result produced by the ZSQL Method execution, publishing it through a Zope page template.

For the following to work, you will need access to a PostgreSQL database service. We will also assume you installed in your Zope server instance the ZPsycopgDA product, which you can get from http://pypi.python.org/pypi/psycopg2. ZPsycopgDA is part of the psycopg2 package because it depends on it, so please read its install documentation carefully to understand how to make it work on your system.

Note You can use a different database than PostgreSQL as long as you have a working Zope Database Adapter object for it.

We will also need a table to query, so let's execute this script on our PostgreSQL database service to create our database:

```
CREATE DATABASE plonebook
  WITH OWNER = postgres
      ENCODING = 'UTF8';
```

Then create the "contacts" table:

```
CREATE TABLE contacts
(
  id serial NOT NULL,
  name text,
  surname text,
  telephone text,
  mail text,
  CONSTRAINT id PRIMARY KEY (id)
)
WITH (OIDS=FALSE);
ALTER TABLE contacts OWNER TO postgres;
```

Finally, insert some records into the table so that our test will provide some data. We are now ready to start with the Zope side.

If you correctly install ZPsycopgDA and restart your Zope service, a new item, named Z Psycopg 2 Database Connection, will appear in the ZMI Add select box in the top-right corner. Assuming we are customizing our site at `http://localhost:8080/plone`, let's visit the custom skin directory at `http://localhost:8080/plone/portal_skins/custom/manage`. In this directory, select the Z Psycopg 2 Database Connection item from the Add box. Enter **postgresDA** as the ID, and then enter the correct connection string to your PostgreSQL database (in our case, `host=localhost dbname=plonebook user=pg_zope password=pg_zope`). Leave all the other fields as is, and click Add.

You should have a new connection to your database open, and you can test it simply by visiting `http://localhost:8080/plone/portal_skins/custom/postgresDA/manage_testForm`, and selecting everything in the `contacts` table by typing in the following line:

```
select * from contacts
```

Then click Submit Query. If the connection is on, you should see the contacts you inserted in the table. Next, you need to create a proper way to use the database adapter. You'll do this using a new ZSQL Method that you'll add to the custom skin directory. As before, select the ZSQL Method item from the ZMI Add select box. Then enter **getContacts** for the ID and the title, and specify **postgresDA** for the connection ID. Now, in the Query Template box, type the following:

```
select * from contacts
```

Click the Add and Test button, and finally click Submit Query. Again, Zope should publish your contact records now, and also any time you call this ZSQL Method object (which you're going to do next).

Now, all you're missing is a nice page template to publish this data using Plone as a publishing box. So, add a new page template object named `contacts_board` to your custom skin directory and insert code to execute the `getContacts` method, acquiring it from the context. Then cycle over the resulting records. It should look like the following lines:

```
<html xmlns="http://www.w3.org/1999/xhtml" xml:lang="en"
      xmlns:tal="http://xml.zope.org/namespaces/tal"
      xmlns:metal="http://xml.zope.org/namespaces/metal"
      xmlns:i18n="http://xml.zope.org/namespaces/i18n"
      lang="en"
      metal:use-macro="here/main_template/macros/master"
      i18n:domain="plone">
<head>
    <metal:block fill-slot="top_slot"
                 tal:define="dummy python:request.set('disable_border',1)" />
</head>
<body>
<div metal:fill-slot="main">

    <h1 class="documentFirstHeading">
       Contacts
    </h1>
```

```
<ul tal:define="contacts here/getContacts">
<tal:block repeat="contact contacts">
    <li tal:define="name string:${contact/name} ${contact/surname};
                    details string:${contact/telephone}, ${contact/mail};">
        <strong tal:content="name">contact's name</strong><br/>
        <span tal:content="details">contact's details</span>
        </li>
    </tal:block>
    </ul>

</div>
</body>
</html>
```

If you open the URL http://localhost:8080/plone/contacts_board in your browser, you should see a nice formatted template with the records from your contacts table, as Figure 10-1 shows.

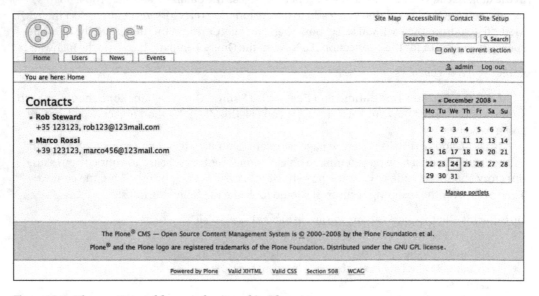

Figure 10-1. *The contacts table records viewed in Plone*

Obviously, this is a convenient way of accessing your relational database from Plone, especially considering that the ZSQL Method object is far more flexible than the simple case just shown. But this approach has some problems if you want to obtain more reusable code; besides, it adopts a specific Zope pattern that can become unmanageable if development issues arise.

We will skip all the various hybrid approaches you can adopt mixing up specific Zope and Python ways of accessing a relational database. For instance, Archetypes (covered in Chapter 9) proposed a SQL storage concept, which did not prove itself as a viable integration pattern. If you would like to examine this possibility, you might have a look at the article "Archetypes

Using MySQL and PostgreSQL" on Plone.org (http://plone.org/documentation/how-to/archetypes-using-mysql).

SQLAlchemy and Plone

In this section, we will create a simple product package, implementing something similar to what we did in the previous section, but in a more Pythonic way, and without writing any SQL query to accomplish our mission, thanks to SQLAlchemy ORM technology.

■Note ORM (object-relational mapping) is a programming technique to convert data from relational database structures to object-oriented coding structures. SQLAlchemy (www.sqlalchemy.org) is a popular Python SQL toolkit and object-relational mapper. It's easy to use in Python to abstract the relational database logic layer. As you will see throughout this section, SQLAlchemy let us access a relational database as we would do with a normal classes hierarchy, leaving out SQL commands as much as possible.

SQLAlchemy is not a Zope-aware package, so we will adopt Martin Aspeli's collective.lead package (http://pypi.python.org/pypi/collective.lead) to integrate the SQLAlchemy machinery with Zope. It works simply by linking SQL transactions to Zope transactions and making databases available as named utilities.

Let's start! Recalling what we did in Chapter 9, we'll create a new product package using Paster in our buildout environment. Type the following commands in a terminal window:

```
$ cd ~/plonebook/src
$ paster create -t plone plonebook.contacts
```

Answer the questions the script will ask you to create a contacts package in the plonebook namespace. In this case, we need a much less structured package than the one we implemented in Chapter 9, which is why we use the ZopeSkel plone template (using the -t plone switch). If you examine the plonebook.contacts/plonebook/contacts folder, you will find just a few files as boilerplate; that is sufficient for our basic task.

First, you'll update the configuration a bit. As stated before, you will need the collective.lead package to link SQL transactions to Zope transactions, so let's specify collective.lead as a dependency for our egg. Open the setup.py module in the root of your plonebook.contacts package, and add collective.lead in the install_requires parameter list, as follows:

```
...
zip_safe=False,
install_requires=[
    'setuptools',
    # -*- Extra requirements: -*-
    'collective.lead',
],
entry_points="""
...
```

Next, open the buildout.cfg file in your buildout root directory, and add the plonebook. contacts entries where needed under eggs, develop, and zcml parameters, as follows:

```
...

eggs =
    ...
    plonebook.contacts

develop =
    ...
    src/plonebook.contacts

...

[instance]
...
zcml =
    ...
    plonebook.contacts

...
```

Then type the following in your terminal window:

```
$ cd ~/plonebook
$ ./bin/buildout -v
```

This should download and configure everything you need to connect to your relational database through collective.lead and SQLAlchemy.

As specified in the collective.lead package documentation, to connect to the relational database, you have to configure a named utility based on the Database class provided by the package. So, let's create a new file named database.py in src/plonebook.contacts/plonebook/ contacts. We'll use the empty Contacts class to bootstrap the database connection, asking SQLAlchemy to autoload the contacts table associated Python class. Type in the following:

```python
from collective.lead import Database
import sqlalchemy as sa
from sqlalchemy import orm

class Contacts(object):
    pass

class PlonebookDB(Database):

    @property
    def _url(self):
        return sa.engine.url.URL(drivername='postgres',
                                 host='localhost', port='5432',
                                 database='plonebook',
```

```
                                    username='pg_zope', password='pg_zope',
                                    )

    def _setup_tables(self, metadata, tables):
        tables['Contacts'] = sa.Table('contacts', metadata, autoload=True)

    def _setup_mappers(self, tables, mappers):
        mappers['Contacts'] = orm.mapper(Contacts, tables['Contacts'])
```

The PlonebookDB class is your database connection named utility implementation.
You specify your connection parameters through a special method named _url, used by
the collective.lead Database class to open a connection to your PostgreSQL database. Then
you define the table you want to map in the _setup_tables method, and finally you extract its
shape from the database using the SQLAlchemy mapper class in the _setup_mappers method.
The mapper defines the correlation of class attributes to database table columns. In your
case, you have asked SQLAlchemy to automatically determine such correlations by setting
the autoload parameter to True in the _setup_tables method.

Now, to define the final named utility, we just need to open the configure.zcml file of our
package and register the plonebook.db utility within it:

```
<configure
    xmlns="http://namespaces.zope.org/zope"
    xmlns:five="http://namespaces.zope.org/five"
    i18n_domain="plonebook.contacts">

    <include package="collective.lead" />

    <utility
        provides="collective.lead.interfaces.IDatabase"
        factory=".database.PlonebookDB"
        name="plonebook.db"
        />

</configure>
```

As you can see, you also need to explicitly include the collective.lead package, because
its configure.zcml file defines a specific factory adapter you need to let your PlonebookDB class
work as expected. At this point, you should have everything in place to connect to your relational database. Easy enough!

Let's go on now with providing a browser view that's able to produce the same results we
had with our Zope-specific connection method. Create a subfolder in your package, named
browser, and create an __init__.py file to make it a Python package. In the terminal window,
run the following commands:

```
$ cd ~/plonebook/src/plonebook.contacts/plonebook/contacts
$ mkdir browser
$ cd browser
$ touch __init__.py
```

Next, create a file named `contacts.py` in the `browser` folder, containing the following code:

```
from Products.Five import BrowserView
from zope.component import getUtility
from collective.lead.interfaces import IDatabase

from plonebook.contacts.database import Contacts

class ContactsView(BrowserView):

    def getContacts(self):
        db = getUtility(IDatabase, name='plonebook.db')
        contacts = db.session.query(Contacts).list()
        return contacts
```

Also create a `contacts.pt` file to ask the view class to provide the contact data, and then copy into it the `contacts_board` template we used in the previous section. Then make the following single-line modification:

```
...
<ul tal:define="contacts view/getContacts">
    ...
</ul>
...
```

Next, to register the browser view, create a `configure.zcml` named file in the `browser` directory, containing the following lines:

```
<configure
 xmlns:zope="http://namespaces.zope.org/zope"
 xmlns="http://namespaces.zope.org/browser"
 >

  <page
      name="contacts"
      for="*"
      class=".contacts.ContactsView"
      template="contacts.pt"
      permission="zope2.Public"
      />

</configure>
```

Finally, update the `configure.zcml` file in the package root to include the `browser` package, adding the following line:

```
...
<include package=".browser" />
...
```

Now start your Zope service, running the following commands in the terminal window:

```
$ cd ~/plonebook
$ ./bin/instance fg
```

Point your web browser to http://localhost:8080/plone/contacts; you should see the same list of contacts as before, but this time no SQL queries will be involved. Likewise, there will be no specific DBMS dependencies—you just specified postgres as the drivername parameter in the _url method of your utility. Not bad at all!

Just to push it a bit further, we will now introduce a simple form to query our contacts table by name. Modify your contacts.pt template, adding the following lines:

```
...
<h1 class="documentFirstHeading">
   Contacts
</h1>

<form tal:attributes="action view/name" method="get">
   <label for="contact_name">Name</label>
   <input type="text" name="contact_name" id="contact_name" />
   <input type="submit" value="Search" />
</form>

<ul tal:define="contacts view/getContacts">
...
```

Here, we've submitted the form to the same browser view, passing contact_name as a parameter to filter by. Now update the ContactsView class as follows:

```
...
class ContactsView(BrowserView):

    @property
    def name(self):
        return self.__name__

    def getContacts(self):
        db = getUtility(IDatabase, name='plonebook.db')
        query = db.session.query(Contacts)
        name = self.request.get('contact_name')
        if name:
            contacts = query.filter(Contacts.surname.like("%"+name+"%")).list()

        else:
            contacts = query.list()

        return contacts
```

To build the form action URL, we have provided the browser view name with a specific name method. We have also modified the getContacts method to get the contact_name parameter from the request object, and, if given, to use it to filter the SQLAlchemy query, adopting a "like" syntax. Again, we didn't need to provide any specific SQL queries.

So far, you should understand that, although relational databases are not Plone's first choice, there are no problems using them with Plone. Moreover, there are many different ways to do it—some more Zope-specific, others more Pythonic.

Note We should mention a nice Plone-related project that involves a relational database: ore. contentmirror (see http://plone.org/products/contentmirror for more details). Kapil Thangavelu released this great package in 2008, and presented it at the annual Plone Conference as a transparent layer able to mirror the content of a Plone site into a structured external data store. As stated in the package documentation, it primarily focuses on and supports out-of-the-box content deployment to a relational database, but it can be useful in a variety of cases as a way to integrate Plone with other systems without too much effort.

Accessing Plone Without a Web Browser

While Plone is an empowering application for managing content using the Web, the Web is not the only way to access Plone's management capabilities. Zope is a solid application server, providing the infrastructure for its applications to be accessed in a variety of different ways, among which are WebDAV and FTP.

Accessing Plone over FTP

It is quite easy to modify the Zope configuration file, zope.conf, to automatically start the internal FTP server or enable access to the dedicated WebDAV server. Just add the following lines to the zope.conf file:

```
<ftp-server>
    # valid key is "address"
    address 8021
</ftp-server>

<webdav-source-server>
    # valid keys are "address" and "force-connection-close"
    address localhost:1980
    force-connection-close off
</webdav-source-server>
```

You can also do the same using buildout—just add the following parameter to your buildout.cfg file in the zope2instance recipe section:

```
...
zope-conf-additional =
```

```
<ftp-server>
        # valid key is "address"
        address 8021
    </ftp-server>
    <webdav-source-server>
        # valid keys are "address" and "force-connection-close"
        address localhost:1980
        force-connection-close off
</webdav-source-server>
...
```

Remember to run the `buildout` script after you modify the `buildout.cfg` file!

Next time you start your Zope service, it will activate the specified protocols' servers on the indicated ports.

Note FTP (File Transfer Protocol) has been widely used as the standard way of transferring files on the Internet. Zope 2 lets us access its objects using this protocol. For a more comprehensive reading about accessing Zope objects via FTP, have a look at the "Managing Zope Objects Using External Tools" section of the Zope Book, at `http://docs.zope.org/zope2/zope2book/source/ExternalTools.html`.

WebDAV (Web-Based Distributed Authoring and Versioning) is an extension to the HTTP protocol, advocated by the W3C, specifically aimed at enabling users to collaboratively edit and manage files on web servers. Unfortunately, it is quite a new standard, and therefore not supported by as many applications as FTP, nor always fully implemented. So, be prepared to look for the right tool to manage it on your operating system, as suggested by the "Using WebDAV" tutorial on Plone.org (`http://plone.org/documentation/how-to/webdav`).

But what does all this mean for the end user? Not that much—it's just FTP access we enabled, which isn't that amazing or useful to add to Plone, because Plone already does all those file transactions in an elegant, polished web user interface. The Plone web user interface is usually an easy choice both for readers and content managers: you can get full access to all of the core functionalities wherever you can log on to the site with a web browser, no matter if you are on your PC or a complete stranger's machine.

Nonetheless, some special use cases would preferably dictate simpler and more effective user interaction than the one offered by the Plone web user interface—for instance, when you need to move a large number of images or files, or when you need to upload a massive amount of original content to a new portal from the file system. In all these cases, something like an FTP client would be very useful.

Using Plone Through the WebDAV Protocol

In some other cases, it could be great to have network share–like access to your site directly in the file manager, especially if you use Plone as an intranet system, storing projects, documents, and the like in it.

This is where WebDAV comes in. However, standard WebDAV clients cannot achieve full-featured access to Plone content. For instance, Plone workflow and security are quite difficult to manage without Plone's web user interface, and, in any case, it's not possible with a standard FTP or WebDAV client.

Nevertheless, the closer we stay to the file management pattern, the better we could be satisfied with Plone FTP and WebDAV standard access. Instead, if you want to access the whole set of metadata of your Plone objects, such as their workflow state or publication dates, then you will need the Plone standard web user interface. If you are inclined to give a try to FTP or WebDAV access to Plone, it will be helpful to keep in mind the existence of the content_ type_registry tool, which we introduce in the next paragraphs.

Plone inherits some of its services from the CMF layer, and one of them is especially useful to our purpose: content_type_registry. For example, when you add an image through the Plone web interface, you explicitly ask Plone to create an image content type. But what will happen if you add a new image file using an FTP or WebDAV client? You may be surprised to discover that Plone will create the right content type for you!

Plone does this via the content_type_registry tool, which has a list of default rules that define which CMF content type will be created based on specific conditions of the uploaded file. These rules may use the file extension, as well as its MIME type or some specific name-based regular expression. You can define your own rules and create your own content types as appropriate.

Note Plone reveals another advanced behavior: the ability to let you manage web pages without the need to learn HTML, and without allowing you to break the site with incorrectly entered page body text. To accomplish this, Plone's WYSIWYG HTML editor, Kupu, supplies a powerful filtering and transforming layer, which alters the page. Among other things, it doesn't allow you to insert dangerous HTML tags (as discussed in Chapter 4).

Of course, this implies that if you import HTML files through FTP or WebDAV, the files may end up showing quite a different look due to Plone's filtering feature. Additionally, if you try to modify your pages with a standard HTML editor through FTP or WebDAV, then Plone will transform your modifications to meet its filter rules.

As a final note to this section, if you need finer-grained control over Plone folders mounted via WebDAV as network shares on a Windows-operated PC, you could try Enfold Desktop. Enfold is a Plone company that has been offering both open and closed source extensions to Plone for years. One of these extensions, recently passed to the open source side, is Enfold Desktop, which offers advanced access to Plone content through the Windows file manager, such as extending its contextual menu to add workflow support at the file manager level.

Note Plone.org offers a good read about issues you may encounter while importing content in Plone: "Importing existing HTML content into Plone," at http://plone.org/documentation/faq/ importing-existing-html-content-into-plone.

Integrating Plone with Other Frameworks

Plone as a CMS is quite independent with regard to integration with different systems, able to solve any need it meets autonomously. Nonetheless, Plone is a web-based CMS, and thus genuinely part of the inherently integrated ecosystem that is the Web in general.

Plone portals are coherent and self-reliant, and it is also quite easy to build a constellation of different Plone sites connected to each other in various forms.

In this section, we will outline some techniques that let Plone play with other systems: RSS files exchange, XML-RPC access to Plone, and WSGI integration.

RSS Integration into Plone

Let's start with the basics: integration techniques involving sharing content with other sites and services over the Web. For example, it's often useful to share certain types of content, such as news, with other sites automatically. The standard mode for doing this is called RSS (Really Simple Syndication). Fortunately, Plone offers RSS functionality out of the box.

■Note The ability to share information among sites, or to stay tuned with our preferred news source using an automated process is a notorious problem with as big and prolific an information source as the Web. Many years ago, Netscape launched the first version of RSS. Since then, various versions of RSS and alternative formats have spread out, among which are Atom and OPML.

First of all, any `Collection` object exposes its content's RSS version. So, if you need to share some kind of content corresponding to some specific criteria, just create a collection stating those criteria (refer to the "Gathering Disparate Elements into Coherent Collections" section of Chapter 3 to see how to do so), and you will get a content listing in RSS form. (This is, in fact, exactly what happens if you go to a new Plone site and click the "RSS feed" link at the bottom of its News section; it actually contains a `Collection` object providing the link.)

Second, Plone lets you build your own RSS feeds through the Advanced Search form. Any time you go to search in Plone, on the results page you will find a link offering you search results for the same criteria in RSS format. With a good RSS reader or just Mozilla Firefox, you can easily create a personal notification system to alert you any time you want to be informed about something (e.g., the creation of new pages in a section or updated content from a specific author) using an automated Advanced Search query. Try it!

Plone 3.0 supports only RSS version 1.0, although there are products extending it to various other formats, like RSS version 2.0 and Atom, the most promising of which is Vice (http://plone.org/products/vice). We can easily implement our own RSS template, extending the default one, as well as completely rewriting it to support other standards or cover different requirements. The Zope Page Templates (ZPT) language is not HTML-specific and can be a good XML-templating language, which makes such tasks even easier.

In the case we want to publish external RSS feeds in our site, we can use the Plone RSS portlet, which we can add to any section of Plone: when you add an RSS portlet through the Plone portlet management interface, just indicate in the edit form of the portlet the number of items to show, the URL of the RSS feed, and the reload timeout to refresh the feed from the source service, and Plone will do the rest. You have seen how to configure an RSS portlet in the "Managing and Adding Portlets" section of Chapter 4. For achieving more advanced functionality, consult the "Products" section at Plone.org (http://plone.org/products) and search for "RSS."

XML-RPC and Plone

If you need a more specific automatic interaction with other services, especially online services, there are various possibilities to consider, but the simplest and most productive one is probably the XML-RPC protocol: a Remote Procedure Call protocol that uses HTTP as the transport layer and adopts XML to encode communications. We won't go into details, but a typical use case involving the adoption of XML-RPC access to Plone would be the creation of objects from external services. One specific example of an XML-RPC solution is the LeMill FSE, part of the LeMill project (http://lemill.net and http://lemill.org). LeMill FSE is a Federated Search Engine layer, which enables running a standard Plone search over multiple federated Plone sites, and it is just a matter of a few lines of Python code in which communications between different Plone sites are implemented via XML-RPC, as you can see at http://lemill.org/trac/browser/trunk/LeMillSearchTool.py.

Note XML-RPC is a forefather of SOAP (Simple Object Access Protocol). Basically, it defines a handful of data types and commands in XML used by client and server services to communicate through HTTP. A good tutorial about Zope and XML-RPC can be found on the Zope web site at www.zope.org/Members/Amos/XML-RPC.

Zope offers a very strong platform for supporting XML-RPC based applications. In fact, Zope and Plone are accessible via XML-RPC, requiring you to pass the same security checks of the standard web access.

And Now for Something Completely Different: Plone on WSGI

If you immediately got the heading title, then you are a real Pythonist! (If not, you have some Monty Python that you need to watch.) If we consider integration between different applications, the Python world offers something that shouldn't be missed: WSGI.

The Python Web Server Gateway Interface (WSGI) was proposed in 2003 by Phillip Eby, who wished to create an easy way to integrate different application server frameworks and to obtain unique final applications (www.python.org/dev/peps/pep-0333). At that time, the Python world of web application frameworks was quite crowded, and his proposal quickly reached some acknowledged implementations. Nowadays, the Python world of web application frameworks is still very crowded, but almost all of the frameworks already support WSGI or are likely to do it.

The WSGI layer is placed between the web server and the application server, so that the choice of framework is separated from the choice of web server. As declared by Eby, the goal of WSGI is "to facilitate easy interconnection of existing servers and applications or frameworks, not to create a new web framework."

The proposal suggested that WSGI would also allow for the "possibility of an entirely new kind of Python web application framework: one consisting of loosely coupled WSGI middle-ware components." And that is exactly what is coming true, as you will see in a while; in fact, a middleware component could act as a server to some application(s), and as an application to some server(s), all at once. Adopting such an architecture, a middleware component could, for instance, route a request to different application objects based on the target URL, after rewrit-ing the environ parameters accordingly, or allow multiple applications or frameworks to run side by side in the same process.

The Zope 2 world was a bit behind, until Agendaless and its Zope superstars decided to recover, founding the Repoze project. Chris McDonough and Tres Seaver are the parents of a reliable collection of technologies that bridge WSGI and Zope. Agendaless reimplemented some core Zope features as WSGI middleware and applications. In this way, it's easy for Python developers to plunge Zope pieces into a WSGI environment.

As part of the Repoze project, the `repoze.plone` WSGI application provides a completely working Plone application served by a WSGI environment.

If you want to install it on your machine, you just need to download a working buildout and run it locally. Open a terminal window and type the following to check out the basic build-out provided with `repoze.plone`:

```
$ cd ~
$ svn co http://svn.repoze.org/buildouts/repoze.plone/trunk repoze.plone
```

Next, just launch the buildout in this way:

```
$ cd ~/repoze.plone
$ python bootstrap.py
$ ./bin/buildout -v
```

If everything goes right, read the instructions to continue: launch the `supervisord` daemon to start all the configured services, and then run the `addzope2user` script to create the admin user:

```
$ bin/supervisord
$ bin/addzope2user <username> <passwd>
```

Finally, just visit your running service at `http://localhost:8080/manage` using your web browser, log in, and create your new Plone site. It will be the same, but served in a completely different way!

At this point, you should be curious enough to ask for more information about how to fit different pieces of WSGI together with Plone—for instance, to obtain a really decoupled single-sign-on layer—but that is a matter for another book.

Summary

If you need your Plone site to integrate with other systems and applications, then this chapter should have been extremely useful for you. In this chapter, we have covered how to directly publish a file system folder through a Plone site, how to access a relational database and publish its information using Plone as a front end, how to access Plone via FTP and WebDAV, and how to syndicate your Plone content to other sites via RSS. We also introduced the XML-RPC protocol and WSGI. You could look deeper into many aspects of this chapter, and you could look into many related topics as well.

In the next chapter, you'll discover how to tackle various system architecture and deployment configuration cases.

System Architectures and Deployment Configurations

You know how to install Plone and set up small to medium sites. Plone is a great tool for managing large and complex sites as well, but to use it for that, you'll need to speed up and tune your system. That is the aim of this chapter: learning how to build and manage a system architecture that will allow you to get the best performance for your web site, even in mission-critical cases. This chapter is also intended to be a technical reference with configuration examples for common use cases.

We should remind you that since Plone works very well as a stand-alone service anyway, you won't need to build any particular system architecture if you don't have any special needs; thanks to its built-in web server, Zope, which can directly serve requests.

What are the main problems or common requirements you could have managing a big site or an intranet? Let's list a few:

- Slow page display

- Many visitors and high load

- Large Data.fs file

- Concurrent writing on the Data.fs file

- Managing a site with a lot of large images or attachments

- Managing a site with a lot of large documents to be indexed

- Securing Zope behind a web server

We will introduce new system architectures in the context of considering these requirements and problems you may have to face. For each of those requirements, we will discuss one or more solutions we can adopt.

Tip All the system architectures we will describe can be mixed up together in different combinations, in order to meet any requirement that you might find in a complex environment like a big intranet or portal. All the examples we will provide are in a Linux environment.

Optimizing Storage Configurations

Objects published by the Zope application server are stored by default into the ZODB. The ZODB provides an object database and stores *pickles* of objects and transactions in a file named Data.fs (remember that you can have more than one ZODB).

Note When we talk about "pickles," we are talking about a concept that concerns Python. *Pickling* is the process whereby a Python object hierarchy is converted into a byte stream; briefly, the pickle module implements a fundamental and powerful algorithm for serializing and deserializing a Python object structure.

The Data.fs file can grow too quickly and become too big if, for example, big attachments and transactions are stored in the ZODB. This is one thing you never want to occur, because it makes the site hard to manage and it slows down the entire site-maintenance process. In order to prevent ending up with too big a Data.fs, we can do the following:

- Store images and attachments outside the Data.fs file—for example, on the file system using Binary Large Object (BLOB) storage, thanks to the plone.app.blob package. In this manner, uploaded attachments or images will not affect the Data.fs file.

- Schedule the automatic packing of the Data.fs file once a week or daily, removing previous versions of objects. (Note that when you remove old versions of objects, you will not be able to restore them!) If you pack the ZODB, there may be a little performance improvement, it will be easier to manage, and you can avoid high disk space consumption. We will face this case in the "Automatic ZODB Packing" section.

If the solutions don't solve your particular problem well enough, you might use another storage implementation strategy on relational databases for the ZODB, like RelStorage, or consider the solutions in the "Relational Databases" section of Chapter 10.

Configuring BLOB Storage

BLOB support can be integrated into Plone thanks to the plone.app.blob package. Using BLOB storage, you will keep your Data.fs file lighter and in general get better performance. BLOB storage allows large binary data to be managed directly by the ZODB but separately from your Data.fs, so that images and attachments aren't stored in the Data.fs file—they're saved on the file system instead.

If you want to install BLOB support, you have to configure where to store it, and then add plone.app.blob to the eggs variable in the [buildout] section of your buildout configuration. The same line should be added in the zcml variable of the [instance] section, as follows:

```
[buildout]
...
eggs =
    ...
    plone.app.blob
....
```

```
[instance]
....
blob-storage = var/blobstorage
....
zcml =
    ....
    plone.app.blob
```

Note here that the blob-storage option lets you choose a folder into which attachments will be saved; in this case, we have set it to var/blobstorage; you may wish to set a different directory. After you've saved your changes, stop the Zope instance, run the buildout script, and restart the service as follows:

```
$ ./bin/buildout
$ ./bin/instance start
```

After that, you have only to install the plone.app.blob package in the portal_quickinstaller tool or in the Site Setup area of Plone. That's it! Now, your attachments are no longer stored in the Data.fs file, but in the var/blobstorage directory; so you will avoid having a huge Data.fs file on your system. You can get more information at http://plone.org/products/plone.app.blob.

■**Note** BLOB support is a tool with a lot of potential, but it is still a work in progress. So, keep in mind that for now it works only with Plone 3 and later versions. Older versions are not supported, and there is no official release out yet. However, the experimental release of the BLOB support tool is already used in production sites, and a stable release will soon be available.

Configuring RelStorage

RelStorage is a storage implementation for ZODB that stores pickles in a relational database. It supports many popular relational databases, including MySQL, PostgreSQL, and Oracle. The way RelStorage is installed depends on whether you have a traditional Zope instance or a buildout.

Actually installing RelStorage requires applying a patch to the ZODB, customizing the zope.conf file if you have a traditional instance, or modifying buildout.cfg and putting the access credentials of your relational database into the rel-storage option.

Note that installing RelStorage is an advanced task that only experienced webmasters and developers should perform. Also, RelStorage doesn't have a stable release at the time of this writing, and developers are still working on this project. So, some of the details we describe in this book may change in the future. For updates about the latest developments of the project, stay tuned on http://pypi.python.org/pypi/RelStorage.

RelStorage requires a version of ZODB with the invalidation-polling patch applied. You will be asked to manually apply a patch or to use a buildout configuration that uses a patched version of the ZOBD. You can find the patch already applied here: http://packages.willowrise. org. The patches are also included in the source distribution of RelStorage.

If you want to actually try RelStorage, you can install a database (e.g., PostgreSQL) and use a buildout configuration similar to the following one:

```
[buildout]
...

find-links =
http://packages.willowrise.org
...


versions = versions

eggs =
...
psycopg2
RelStorage

[versions]
ZODB3 = 3.8.1-polling-serial

[instance]
...

 rel-storage =
type postgresql
dbname relstorage_zodb
user pgzope
host localhost
password postgres
```

To install a PostgreSQL database on a Debian-like distribution (or on Ubuntu), you will have to type the following commands:

```
# apt-get install postgresql
# apt-get install postgresql-server-dev-8.3
```

After you've installed PostgreSQL, you will have to start it, create a new user named pgzope, and enter the password postgres when required. You'll also have to create a database for support, which we will call relstorage_zodb. To do so, type the following commands:

```
# sudo su - postgres
$ createuser -P pgzope
$ createdb relstorage_zodb
```

Once you have initialized the instance, the system will save everything in the new database, instead of in FileStorage. Figure 11-1 shows what has changed in the ZMI, in the Database Management panel for the new database connection we have just set up.

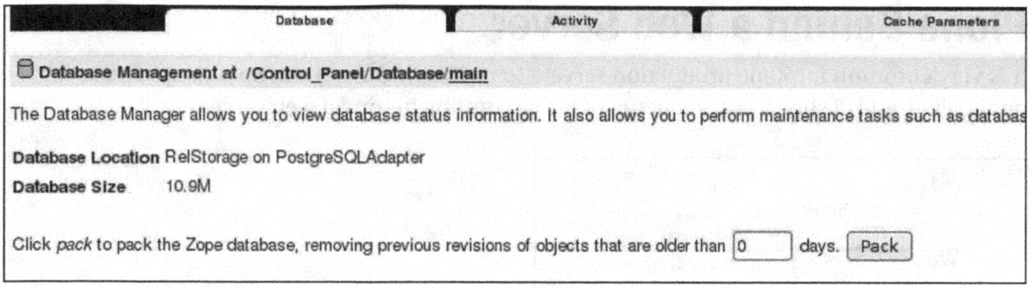

Figure 11-1. *The Database Management panel, where you can see that the database location is now RelStorage on PostgreSQL*

You can find more information on RelStorage at `http://wiki.zope.org/ZODB/RelStorage`.

Asynchronous Indexing

If your site contains many large documents (such as DOC or PDF files), and you often perform searches, normal searching-and-indexing configurations can be inappropriate. Synchronous and repeated indexing operations of big attachments can seriously slow down your Plone site.

The solution is performing indexing asynchronously with searching with a more efficient queuing system. For this purpose, you can install the `collective.indexing` package, which lets you optimize indexing operations in Plone, thanks to an approach that provides an abstract framework for asynchronous queuing. This package allows you to take advantage of a more efficient indexing queue that gets rid of redundant indexing operations.

If you want to enable asynchronous indexing in Plone, you just have to install the `collective.indexing` package. Stop your instance and modify the buildout contained in `buildout.cfg` as follows:

```
[buildout]
...
eggs =
    ...
    collective.indexing
....
[instance]
....
zcml =
    ....
    collective.indexing
```

Then run the `buildout` script and restart your instance:

```
$ ./bin/buildout
$ ./bin/instance start
```

Finally, go to your Plone site and install the `collective.indexing` package from the `portal_quickinstaller` tool in the ZMI or in the Plone Site Setup area. Visit this link to find out more information about `collective.indexing`: `http://pypi.python.org/pypi/collective.indexing`.

Plone Behind a Web Server

It is very common for Zope production servers to run behind a web server like Apache or ngnix. Figure 11-2 shows you a schema of Plone running behind a web server.

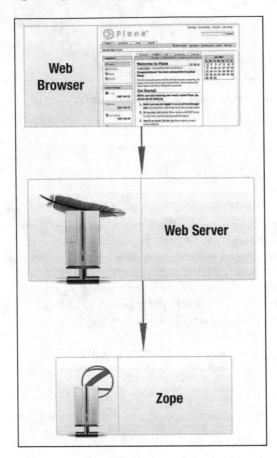

Figure 11-2. *A schema of a Zope installation behind a web server*

Although Zope has its own embedded web server, you may have to deal with certain scenarios that require a more complex structure. For example, you may want to take advantage of the well-tested and full-featured Apache SSL layer provided by Apache. This way you will be able to use rewrite rules in order to have one or more domains served by the same server, or disallow direct access to your Zope instance (in order to prevent invalid HTTP requests or denial-of-service attacks). How can we configure Zope behind a web server in order to handle one or more virtual hosts on the same server?

As an example use case, let's configure virtual hosting for several sites in one Zope instance (remember, of course, that different mixed options are possible). Start by creating a new Plone site in the root of Zope with the ID myexampledomain. We will assume that we are working with the Apache web server, and we'll configure a virtual host. We want to end up with several domains served by the same web server. For example, myexampledomain.com should correspond to our first Plone site at http://localhost:8080/myexampledomain.

First check that the Apache web server is correctly installed. Then add the following lines to the /etc/hosts file:

```
127.0.0.1    myexampledomain.com
```

This way, we can easily simulate a domain configuration and make our new domain point to localhost. If you ping, for example, myexampledomain, your local machine should respond.

Now that our basic Plone site is set up, let's configure Apache to serve it. Create a file named myexampledomain.com in the directory /etc/apache2/sites-available, with the following configuration:

```
<VirtualHost *>
 ServerAlias    myexampledomain.com
 ServerAdmin    youremail@myexampledomain.com
 ServerSignature On
 LogLevel warn
  <IfModule mod_rewrite.c>
   RewriteEngine On
   RewriteRule ^/(.*) \
     http://localhost:8080/VirtualHostBase/http/%{SERVER_NAME}:80/
myexampledomain/VirtualHostRoot/$1 [L,P]
 </IfModule>
</VirtualHost>
```

Now you just have to enable this site and reload the Apache configuration by typing the following into your shell:

```
# a2ensite myexampledomain.com
# /etc/init.d/apache2 reload
```

Finally, if you enter the URL http://myexampledomain.com in your browser, you should get our Plone site. You can add one or more domains—you just need to repeat the preceding steps. See the following links for more details:

- http://plone.org/documentation/tutorial/plone-apache
- http://plone.org/documentation/how-to/apache-ssl

Caching, Clustering, and Load Balancing

So, is the rendering of your pages too slow? Let's *cache*! You can make your portal up to 40 times faster or more (depending on what configuration you choose) by integrating Plone with a caching proxy, using a combination of memory, proxies, and browser caching. There are many system architectures available. Plone with caching proxies not only gives you the flexibility of a powerful CMS environment with user facilities, but also serves dynamic pages immediately—as fast or faster than for static HTML!

Another common issue we should mention concerns *clustering*. What happens if your portal gets so many visits that it slows down? In this case, you can balance the higher load using a *cluster* of Zope instances: ZEO allows you to use one database to share the workload among different servers. And when there is the need, you can always add another Zope instance to help in scaling and balancing the load.

In this section, you will see how to scale and balance the load of your system and speed up your site by configuring a ZEO environment integrated with a caching proxy.

Zope Clustering with ZEO

Let's start confronting the concept of Zope clustering by looking at ZEO. If your use case matches the classic web pattern of many reads and few writes, you may want to take advantage of ZEO. Briefly, ZEO works like this:

- Concurrent requests are served by two or more Zope clients at the same time, thanks to a load balancer.

- The ZEO servers manage a common ZODB shared between ZEO clients.

Using ZEO, you can provide a distributed object architecture to Zope instances. ZEO allows multiple processes, machines, and locations to work together as one transactional object system. All this will be a big advantage in many practical use cases, compared with a simpler architecture where you have a transactional object system like a stand-alone Zope server with an in-memory cache of objects. This is ZEO!

With ZEO, you can create many Zope instances that are connected to a Zope Storage Server (ZSS or, commonly, ZEO server). When one Zope instance (or, as it is commonly referred to in this context, ZEO client) changes an object, the changes are sent to the ZEO server, which sends a message to the other ZEO clients. The other ZEO clients then remove the object from their local cache. When a ZEO client already has an object in its local cache, then there is no need to fetch it another time from the ZEO server, as long as it hasn't been modified.

The great thing is that ZEO clients can be added whenever you need to scale the workload, and they can also be set up on different machines. On very complex systems, ZEO clients can even mount one or more shared ZODBs from one or more ZEO servers.

As the load balancer for our concurrent requests, we use Pound. Pound was originally developed to enable distributing workload among several web servers, so we can use it as load balancer for our ZEO clients. With Pound, you can manage complex persistent session policies. Figure 11-3 shows you a possible configuration.

Note This is only one possible configuration. You can, for example, reserve a ZEO client for heavy batch jobs, among other configurations. See in Chapter 12 for a more complex use case.

Note that outside the classic web pattern just mentioned (many reads and few writes), the ZEO system architecture pays a penalty. For example, when the number of writes starts to get close to the number of reads, you should use an alternative storage like RelStorage that better handles loads of concurrent writes. For more information about ZEO, see the "Scalability and ZEO" chapter of the Zope Book, at www.zope.org/Documentation/Books/ZopeBook/2_6Edition/ZEO.stx.

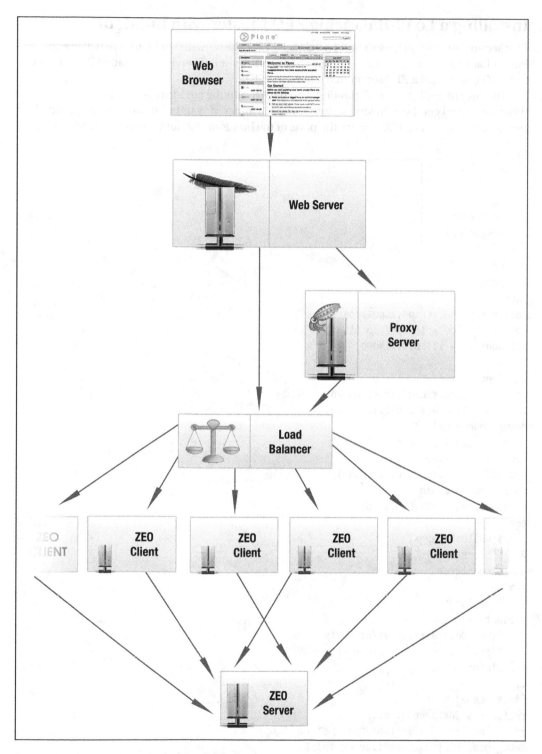

Figure 11-3. *Distributing the load among web servers thanks to Pound: a possible configuration of the ZEO server and ZEO clients*

Installing a Load-Balancing ZEO Cluster with buildout

This section shows you how to build a balanced ZEO cluster with buildout. We will use the Pound load balancer (note that you may choose other similar services instead of Pound), and two ZEO clients and a ZEO server that share the ZODB.

In order to apply this configuration, you have to run the buildout script. When you do this, you should get the following scripts in the bin folder of your buildout: zeo, instance01, instance02, and poundctl. Here are the parts of the buildout that let you set this configuration:

```
[buildout]
parts =
    ...
    zeo
    instance01
    instance02
    ...
    pound-build
    pound
[zeo]
recipe = plone.recipe.zope2zeoserver
zope2-location = ${zope2:location}
zeo-address = 127.0.0.1:8000
...
[instance01]
recipe = plone.recipe.zope2instance >=2.0
zope2-location = ${zope2:location}
debug-mode = off
verbose-security = off
zeo-client = True
zeo-address = ${zeo:zeo-address}
user = admin:admin
http-address = 127.0.0.1:8010
eggs =
    ${buildout:eggs}
    ${plone:eggs}
    elementtree
zcml =
    ${buildout:zcml}
products =
    ${buildout:directory}/products
    ${productdistros:location}
    ${plone:products}
...
[instance02]
recipe = ${instance01:recipe}
zope2-location = ${instance01:zope2-location}
debug-mode = ${instance01:debug-mode}
verbose-security = ${instance01:verbose-security}
```

```
zeo-client = ${instance01:zeo-client}
zeo-address = ${instance01:zeo-address}
user = admin:admin
http-address = 127.0.0.1:8011
eggs = ${instance01:eggs}
zcml = ${instance01:zcml}
products = ${instance01:products}
[instance03]
...
[pound-build]
recipe = plone.recipe.pound:build
url = http://www.apsis.ch/pound/Pound-2.3.2.tgz
...
[pound]
recipe = plone.recipe.pound:config
daemon = 0
timeout = 90
balancers =
        myplone 127.0.0.1:8002 127.0.0.1:8010 127.0.0.1:8011
```

Here, we get a ZEO server running on port 8000 (see the [zeo] section) and two ZEO clients, instance01 and instance02, running respectively on ports 8010 and 8011. Both ZEO clients are balanced, thanks to Pound running on port 8002. You can of course add one or more ZEO clients.

Take a look at the [instance02] section; note how it is different from [instance01]. What this shows is that you can have ZEO clients with different configuration settings.

After running the buildout script, you can start your ZEO cluster. Do this by calling the executables in the bin directory (poundctl, zeo, instance01, and instance02) in the following order:

```
$ ./bin/poundctl start
$ ./bin/zeo start
$ ./bin/instance01 start
$ ./bin/instance02 start
```

These commands will start your load balancer, the ZEO server, and the two Zope instances. All requests received on port 8002 (served by Pound) will be balanced on the two ZEO clients listening on ports 8010 and 8011.

You can also use the supervisord utility to monitor and control the processes of your buildout. For more information, take a look at http://supervisord.org and http://pypi.python.org/pypi/collective.recipe.supervisor.

If you want to know more about the configuration of these recipes, take a look at the following links:

- See http://pypi.python.org/pypi/plone.recipe.pound for a recipe for installing and configuring Pound.

- See http://pypi.python.org/pypi/plone.recipe.zope2zeoserver for a buildout recipe for installing a Zope 2 ZEO server.

Caching Proxies and Your Plone Site

You have seen that a caching server can help performance a good deal. You can increase performance using a caching proxy in front of your Plone site. A *caching proxy* keeps local copies of frequently requested resources, so that they will be served directly from the proxy server without having to ask to the Zope server. This can dramatically speed up the display time of your pages!

A good product for speeding up your site is CacheFu. *CacheFu*, as mentioned on `http://plone.org/products/cachefu`, "is a collection of products that aggregate and simplify various caching settings, speeding up Plone sites using a combination of memory, proxy, and browser caching. CacheFu can be used by itself or with Squid, Varnish, and/or Apache. Configuration files can be generated for Squid, Varnish, Squid-behind-Apache, Varnish-behind-Apache, and Apache cache proxy (if you are using a noncaching Apache by itself or just Zope-only, no extra configuration files are needed)."

To install CacheFu, you have to include `Products.CacheSetup` (a package that installs all CacheFu dependencies) in your buildout configuration, just as for Plone products released as Python eggs (see the "Installing an Add-on Product" section of Chapter 2 for more information). You can find details on installing CacheFu on this page: `http://pypi.python.org/pypi/Products.CacheSetup`.

After you update the buildout configuration, you have to restart your instance and install CacheFu on the site you want to speed up. Once installed (as usual, click Add-on Products in the Plone control panel, and install the product in your Plone site), CacheFu can be configured through the Cache Configuration tool, available in the Plone control panel. This tool lets you select which kind of proxy cache purge configuration you want to enable (Zope-only, Zope behind Apache, Squid/Varnish in front, etc.), provides you with a list of domains for your site (along with HTTPS versions of your domains if you use them), and gives you a list of domains for any purgeable proxy caches if needed (e.g., if you are using Squid with Apache, there will commonly be a single Squid instance at `http://localhost:3128`).

Changing other default settings of this tool requires a deep knowledge of the HTTP protocol. Fortunately, the default values are commonly valid for the main use cases, so you generally won't need to change them. For these purposes, you just need to know that the Cache Configuration tool lets you add or edit existing cache policies and rules to apply to certain content types. For example, standard content types refer to a particular rule for views of Plone content types. As the description of the rule says, anonymous users are served content object views from memory, not the proxy cache; authenticated users are not cached in memory or proxy (because caching personalized pages is inefficient), but an ETag is added to enable proper HTTP `not modified` responses. The member ID (a parameter that is for identifying a site member) is used in the ETag because content is personalized. The time of the last catalog change is included so that the navigation tree stays up to date.

■**Note** If you are using a noncaching Apache server by itself or just a stand-alone Zope instance, no extra configuration files are needed to run CacheFu.

CacheFu allows Plone to explicitly invalidate old caches when operations such as editing content are performed, so that your content is always fresh, even if you have an aggressive caching policy. Figure 11-4 shows you a logical configuration of a common system architecture with proxies.

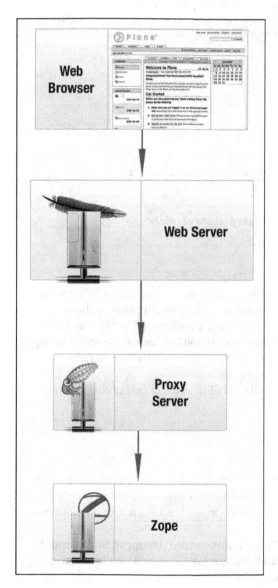

Figure 11-4. *A logical configuration with a caching proxy*

Be aware that the scheme described depends on your environment. If you want to support advanced session-persistence policies, support or not support HTTPS, and so on, there are many other possible configurations.

Installing a Proxy Cache Server with buildout

You can install a proxy cache server manually or using a specific buildout recipe that lets you build and configure the desired proxy server (e.g., Squid or Varnish) automatically. The main buildout recipes to do that are plone.recipe.squid and plone.recipe.varnish.

Let's take Varnish as an example. There are many settings, depending on your environment. The basic buildout configuration to build and configure Varnish is as follows:

```
[buildout]
parts =
    ...
    varnish-build
    varnish
[varnish-build]
recipe = zc.recipe.cmmi
url = http://downloads.sourceforge.net/varnish/varnish-2.0.2.tar.gz
[varnish-instance]
recipe = plone.recipe.varnish
daemon = ${buildout:directory}/parts/varnish-build/sbin/varnishd
bind = 127.0.0.1:8000
backends = 127.0.0.1:8002
cache-size = 1G
```

After having changed the buildout configuration, don't forget to run the buildout script to build Varnish. In this case, the [varnish-build] section will build our proxy cache server and the [varnish-instance] will be used for configuring our Varnish service. Varnish will be listening on port 8000 and will use a service running on port 8002 as back-end service (a Zope instance, a load balancer, or a web server, depending on your environment). For reference, take a look at http://pypi.python.org/pypi/plone.recipe.varnish.

After setting up the cache proxy, you can install CacheFu, as described in the previous section.

Multiple ZODBs

A ZODB has its own caching mechanism. For each mounted ZODB, you can choose the cache size in number of objects, tuning it as needed for your environment. The general idea is to keep as many objects in cache as possible, but this value depends on the amount of RAM you have available.

We should mention what we mean by "objects" in this context. We mean both standard heavy objects like Plone content, and smaller catalog information objects (in Plone slang, these are known as "brains") that Plone uses instead of dealing with real objects (for performance reasons).

While you have the same cache for all fetched objects, you will want to have as many brains as possible in cache as well. Brains should always be ready to be used, because they are frequently used by Plone for things like object listings, searches, and so on.

Depending on your environment, your site may slow down if you have thousands of objects stored. The solution is to create a separate ZODB, with a larger cache size for your objects, to serve only the portal_catalog tool of your portal. This will give you two separate ZODBs, each with dedicated caches: one for the main site and another dedicated to the portal_catalog tool. This way, you will keep all the brains in the ZODB cache, and your site will perform better. You can increment the cache dedicated to the ZODB serving the portal_catalog tool and keep all the brains in memory, ready to be used for searches or listings with comparatively little memory consumption (because brains are small objects).

Depending on what you have to implement, you may want to split the main ZODB into smaller ones, each served by one or more ZEO servers if needed. In this section, you will see how to mount sections (e.g., the portal_catalog tool) served by multiple ZODBs with both stand-alone installations and ZEO clusters. We will assume that you already have a buildout. However, it is also simple to adapt these configurations to a traditional Zope installation as well.

Speeding Up Plone by Putting portal_catalog on a Different ZODB with a Stand-Alone Zope Instance

In this section, you'll see how to serve the portal_catalog tool on a different ZODB with a stand-alone Zope instance. To do so, we will assume we are working on a Plone site named myplone, and we will for simplicity start by duplicating our Data.fs file, which is used by default in Plone as the file store. We will call our copy of the Data.fs file CatalogData.fs. To perform the duplication, run the following command after you have stopped your Zope instance:

```
$ cp var/filestorage/Data.fs var/filestorage/CatalogData.fs
```

Why did we duplicate the Data.fs file? So that we can have a duplicate of the portion of the file storage (i.e., the portal_catalog tool) that we want to be served by a different ZODB. Note that you can also use this technique for other portions of your system—even an entire Plone site. Copying the Data.fs file, you will have an exact copy of the data, and it will be served by a different ZODB.

So, we created a new file store called CatalogData.fs; now we have to make our Zope instance know that this new file store exists and has to be mounted. To do so, we have to modify the zope-conf file. In a traditional instance, you can modify it directly; if you use buildout, you will have to modify buildout-cfg as follows, adding a zope-conf-additional option to the [instance] section of your buildout, as shown here:

```
zope-conf-additional =
  <zodb_db catalog>
    # Catalog database
    <filestorage>
      path ${buildout:directory}/var/filestorage/CatalogData.fs
    </filestorage>
    mount-point /myplone/portal_catalog:/myplone/portal_catalog
    container-class Products.CMFPlone.CatalogTool.CatalogTool
    cache-size 10000
  </zodb_db>
```

In the configuration we have just made, we specified the name of the Catalog database that will use the CatalogData.fs file as the file store, and we configured the parameters we need for the mounting.

You can also tune the cache-size value, depending on how many objects you want to have in cache. The final aim is to have all the brains in cache memory, although this depends on software settings and hardware architecture. As mentioned, the idea is to have as many objects as possible in cache for your environment.

Next, run the buildout script as shown:

```
$ ./bin/buildout
```

Then restart your instance, go to your myplone site, and from the ZMI, delete the portal_catalog tool. You're doing this because the portal_catalog tool will be served by another file store (in this example called CatalogData.fs). Don't worry, this won't break your site forever!

After that, we have to mount our portal_catalog tool served by the CatalogData.fs file. To do so, we have to add a ZODB mount point from the Add drop-down menu in the ZMI, which we will call "catalog." Use the form that will appear to finalize the mount point configured in zope.conf. On this form, select your mount point without modifying the other options, and confirm by clicking the "Create selected mount points" button. Finally, in some cases you will have to recatalog the portal_catalog tool (e.g., mounting a folder with content from one database into another one). In this case, it might not be necessary, but it won't do any damage to perform it anyhow.

Now, in the database management area (http://localhost:8080/Control_Panel/Database/manage_main), you should see our new mount point, called catalog, that uses as its file store the CatalogData.fs file. If you click the catalog mount point, you should see the cache settings.

Speeding Up Plone by Putting portal_catalog on a Different ZODB with a ZEO Cluster

In the case of a ZEO cluster, the ZEO server will serve both the main Data.fs file and the ZODB containing the portal_catalog tool. All databases will be shared among ZEO clients. In the ZEO server configuration, we have to register a new file store; each ZEO client will mount and share this new database. Basically, you should stop your cluster and copy the main Data.fs to a new file (CatalogData.fs):

```
$ cp ./var/filestorage/Data.fs ./var/filestorage/CatalogData.fs
```

The CatalogData.fs file will provide the portal_catalog once mounted. Now modify your existing buildout.cfg configuration, adding to the ZEO recipe a zeo-conf-additional option, registering the new file store, and adding a zope-conf-additional option for each ZEO client, as shown here (the added options are in bold):

```
[zeo]
recipe = plone.recipe.zope2zeoserver
...
zeo-conf-additional =
  <filestorage 2>
    path ${buildout:directory}/var/filestorage/CatalogData.fs
  </filestorage>
[instance01]
recipe = plone.recipe.zope2instance
...
zope-conf-additional =
  <zodb_db catalog>
    mount-point /myplone/portal_catalog
    container-class Products.CMFPlone.CatalogTool.CatalogTool
    cache-size 10000
    <zeoclient>
      server ${zeo:zeo-address}
      storage 2
      name catalogstorage
      var ${buildout:parts-directory}/instance01/var
      cache-size 400MB
    </zeoclient>
  </zodb_db>
  <environment>
    DISABLE_PTS 1
    TEMP ${buildout:directory}/tmp
  </environment>
```

Save and rerun the buildout as shown:

```
$ ./bin/buildout
```

After you have restarted the cluster, delete the `portal_catalog` tool of your myplone Plone site in the ZMI, select ZODB Mount Point from the Add drop-down menu, select your ZODB to be mounted, and leave the other default settings untouched, as in the previous paragraph.

That's it! In this example we have cloned a ZODB `CatalogData.fs` file from the `Data.fs` file. Note that it is also possible to keep only the mounted area of `CatalogData.fs` and remove the other sections (so your ZODB will be lighter).

■Caution Once you have mounted a new ZODB, you should usually begin a tuning phase wherein you can change ZEO client or ZODB settings. However, since that depends on your server and what kind of application you are developing, we won't delve into those issues here.

Automatic ZODB Packing

Why does the ZODB grow to a size that makes us need to pack it? The ZODB provides all of the *ACID* properties—properties that are well known and used often in computer science and relational databases theory. *ACID* stands for *atomicity, consistency, isolation, and durability* in database transactions; these properties exist in order to guarantee that transactions are processed reliably. If you want to find out more information about ACID properties and relational databases, take a look at http://en.wikipedia.org/wiki/ACID. In order to support the rollback of transactions, changes written to a ZODB database are appended to the Data.fs file.

Let's better define the concept of *packing*: the ZODB keeps a record of transactions, which can be used, for example, by an application to allow undo functionality. But with the passing of time, the database file can grow in size, storing a longer and longer list of changes to each object. Packing the ZODB is the operation of shrinking it back to a more efficient size. This operation can also be scheduled so that it will be performed automatically—we'll show you how presently.

It is a good idea to schedule the automatic packing of the ZODB if you use FileStorage, the default storage system in Zope (of course, if you have configured RelStorage, the mechanisms will be different), so that you are sure that periodically you will get performance and disk space benefits.

If you want to pack the ZODB of a stand-alone Zope instance, you can put the following command in a cron job:

```
wget http://localhost:8080/Control_Panel/Database/main/manage_pack?days:float=7
  --http-user=admin --http-passwd=admin -q --delete-after
```

As an alternative, you may want to try the PortalMaintenance Plone product, which lets you add a pack task without having to use the admin password of your instance (see http:// plone.org/products/plonemaintenance).

If you want to pack a ZODB that's served by a ZEO server, you can put the following command in a cron job, assuming again that you're working in a UNIX-like environment:

```
./PATH_TO_BUILDOUT/bin/zeopack -p 8000 -h 127.0.0.1 -S 1 -d 7
```

The parameters used are as follows:

- -p stands for the ZEO server listening port.
- -h stands for the ZEO server listening address.
- -S stands for the storage name (the default is 1).
- -d removes transactions that are older than the number of days the value indicates.

Running this command, you should now find a packed ZODB in the var/filestorage directory of your buildout, and the addition of a .old extension to the original ZODB file name.

For more information, see the tutorial at http://plone.org/documentation/tutorial/introduction-to-the-zodb/tutorial-all-pages.

Summary

At this stage you should know that, thanks to Plone and Zope flexibility, you can use a stand-alone installation when you are developing your system and for normal use cases, but when the going gets tough, you can set up auxiliary services such as caching and load balancing to make the Plone application more scalable. In place of having a stand-alone Zope installation, you can mix together the techniques described in this chapter to achieve a more performant system for the specific needs you are facing (e.g., managing large Internet sites or intranets).

In the next and final chapter, we'll cover some of the most common cases that you may encounter in your experience as Plone webmaster or developer. You will learn how to solve some common problems and how to set up a web application able to solve many of your needs. We will cover the management of enterprise workflows, the automatic handling of documents and images, the management of multimedia files and big objects, the integration of external applications and single-sign-on, and the creation of custom member profiles. You will see how you can realize with Plone an efficient e-commerce site, a social network, a community site, and a company intranet, among others. Let's get to work!

CHAPTER 12

■ ■ ■

Case Studies

We've almost gotten to the end of our journey, a journey that has let us learn about a very powerful CMS, as well as a flexible development environment. Throughout the previous chapters, you built an understanding, brick by brick, of all the basic concepts and features of Plone, and you started to build your personal experience as a user, integrator, and developer.

We will conclude the book with a dive into real life. In this chapter, we'll cover some of the most common cases that you may encounter in your experience as Plone webmaster or developer. We will cover many of the requirements that a business might have, and how Plone can meet them. This will also give you a further overview of what you can really do with Plone.

Some of the use cases we will face in this chapter deal with simple Plone configurations—just changing some settings in the Site Setup area provided by the default Plone user interface. You will see, for example, that to create an intranet for your company, if you don't have any special requirements to accomplish, you can simply go with a standard Plone installation, add some configurations about workflow and groups of users, and you're done!

Other use cases, however, will instead require solid Plone development experience. We will talk about writing ad hoc products and integrating other systems in our Plone site. The point will be always the same: Plone is not only a good CMS out of the box, but also a very flexible development framework and a powerful application environment. With it you will be able to meet almost all of your needs.

Finally, this final chapter has another aim: showing you where you can push your Plone experience to, so that you can continue learning and expanding your knowledge involving Plone. For this reason, this final chapter could be also be a good first chapter to read—it will keep clear in your mind why you are going to learn Plone.

Management of Enterprise Workflow

Let's try to start deepening your understanding of Plone versatility and examine a possible use case related to a realistic enterprise workflow. You'll find that in adopting Plone, you can easily solve various document-management needs of your department, and it will probably do its best just as it is, right out of the box.

Before going into specific cases, let's note some general features of Plone that make it applicable to several use cases. In Plone, you can easily create specific content types, or just use specific folders to separate different kinds of documents, as well as define various groups of users to delegate specific activities at your ease. Besides this, you can outline your own document workflow in minutes, with specific states and transitions, thus creating dynamic behavior for your content, the same way that the publication workflow that comes with Plone acts as a publication engine for its content. You can have all these with a basic Plone installation, and much more, as far as you can master the whole set of its features and capabilities. And of course you can! We covered all the features you need to build your information architecture in Chapter 3, and how to administer the site in Chapter 4. Furthermore, if you need to do some more complex configuration, you can refer to content types and indexing services in Chapter 5, customizing Plone's look and feel in Chapter 6, and advanced user management in Chapter 8.

Let's try now to push forward our use case a bit. Imagine we wish to support a specific enterprise workflow like the following: we have our operational data accessible and manageable through enterprise resource planning (ERP) software. Its standard workflow starts by focusing on an "order" document; when it is time to send it out, after some adjustments to its data through the ERP, we produce the order document, send it to our supplier, and store it in a specific shared folder.

Of course, in the middle, someone has to manage the order, receiving a request and looking for the right supplier and price; and then someone else will have to approve it; and finally some low-responsibility personnel will send it to the supplier by mail and fax, and properly store the document in the right place.

Here is where Plone can help in both organizing the workflow and suitably supporting a rational and efficient scheme for storage and retrieval of the yielded digital documents, and content in general.

If we have at our disposal a legacy ERP, such as any Oracle-based operational software or SAP, we can easily start generating the final document out of "raw" database information. Just create a relational view on your ERP database, where order data can be read by Plone, and then show this data to the user and let him select which order should be transformed (into, for example, a PDF document). To do so, you will have to pick some document-generating solution, like Reportlab (`www.reportlab.org`), or OpenOffice Python binding, to effectively produce the content file. This document could also be produced by the ERP itself directly: we could just save it into a shared folder and let Plone process any files it finds there (e.g., an OpenOffice document or a plain CSV text file).

At this point, we have a PDF or OpenOffice document in Plone, and we can easily attach to it some ERP metadata, like "Order Date" and "Order Number," to make subsequent classification and retrieval easy. We could set on it a specific order workflow diagram, including three states: to_approve, approved, and notified. Of course, we should let only a certain group of users approve the documents; besides, we should set the notification accordingly, so that the corresponding users have a simple-to-manage to-do list—for example implementing a dedicated portlet that shows all the documents that have to be approved or notified. To improve the support, we can set a mail notification system for orders, and that could be done directly through the Plone user interface, using the powerful content rule tool we discussed in Chapter 4, in the "Managing Automatic Rules" section.

We can easily imagine a more elaborate approval phase, where the user digitally signs the order document using a personal smart card and specific client software. In this situation, we could provide a special download link to make the digital signature software open automatically, and receive the signed files back into the system if the user saves them in some special shared folder. We could then recognize each file just by reading a special key in the uploaded file name, and link it to the original document to approve.

Of course, this workflow could be as complicated as you like. However, it should be clear enough by now that you don't have to think of Plone's out-of-the-box features as a cage, but rather as a proposed way to tackle content management issues "the Plone way" (and we know the Plone way allows us to meet nearly any need!).

Plone is very apt for these kinds of enterprise workflows. The more unstructured they are, the more easily Plone will succeed, as it gives you a strategic support environment through which you can rapidly improve the enterprise knowledge base (e.g., a Plone-based application can help you easily switch from share folders and personal mailboxes to a central and reliable documents repository).

E-Commerce with Plone: Your Business Online

You have learned how to build amazing web sites and provide good services to your users. Now it is time to get paid. Plone has a long history in business-oriented features, but the efforts have not been focused toward the creation of the typical monolithic e-commerce platform. Instead, the Plone way is to provide reusable and flexible modules that can be used in any site.

Integrating E-Commerce Functionality into a Plone Portal

This means that in your site you can take the classic approach of providing product catalogs and a cart for the buyer, managing payments, and so on. What you will have to do is integrate into your Plone site new functionalities through add-on products. You will also have to manage some complex cases. For example, say that what we are selling isn't a product with a simple material value. For instance, imagine a web portal that sells training; the primary purpose of the site is to manage courses and training materials, so it can't be designed for typical e-commerce. Instead of building a second site to sell these kinds of products, we can instead quite easily assign a price and number of available seats to our courses, so that users can put courses in their cart together with training materials, and this material can include both online documents and real books. After the payment, they obtain the access to the courses and receive the books. You can also set up a particular workflow for the online documentation, so that students can even fill in exercises and submit them, or propose changes (see Chapter 7 for more details on workflow).

Plone extends well to many other complex e-commerce use cases. For instance, if we deal with goods that have an expiration date for the user (suppose we also sell, for example, the right to view content for a certain amount of time), and we allow recurring payments (a sort of subscription), we can simply set the good so that when it expires, it will no longer be available to the user; you can simply use the expiration date feature Plone provides by default (see the "Setting Page Metadata" section of Chapter 3), or build an ad hoc module for more complex features.

This type of Plone setup is wonderful for the managers of the portal, because they can edit and manage all the course information in the same place and won't have to keep two different platforms aligned (one for the anonymous visitors, and one for subscribers). When a new course is ready and published, it will be also buyable. As you probably already know, you can build all this by creating a "courses" workflow, with new states and transitions.

Atypical E-Commerce Use Cases with Plone

In other cases, you may not need an e-commerce infrastructure at all, but you simply want to allow your users to give you money—for example, for a donation or to sponsor a project or an event. You do not need a cart and you do not need to record the details of your users. To achieve this with Plone, all you need are some pages that describe what you will do with the users' money and some fields to let users choose their type of donation, and then you can send everything to your payment gateway. You should be able to manage all this in a pluggable way. You can just start with PayPal, which has an efficient e-commerce service you can integrate into your site (visit the official site to see how to create a personal business account that accept payments on the Internet: `https://www.paypal.com/us/cgi-bin/webscr?cmd=_registration-run`), and then move to a bank so that your money transfers will be directly processed.

Another common use case that you can easily satisfy with Plone is the creation of a personal request for payment. It's simple: you can create invoice objects and share them only with the recipient, who can be a registered user. We have covered how to reserve content in depth in previous chapters (above all in the "Sharing Your Content" section of Chapter 3). For more complex needs, you can use a particular workflow policy (see the "Adding Plone Policy Support" section of Chapter 7).

You can even avoid the traditional login procedure, recognizing the user with a *token* (a long code that allows access to a nonregistered user) generated and sent by the system. In both cases, only the selected user will be allowed to see his invoice and pay it.

When all is said and done, using Plone for business does not require a different approach for your web applications. Its modular structure allows you to inject payment features into a live site.

It is even possible to use the same commerce tools and modules for other aims. For example, one interesting cross-application would be to have your users use the cart to select the most interesting content in your web sites, and then send you feedback or subscribe for changes.

Automatic Handling of Documents and Images

Throughout the previous chapters, we have emphasized a basic concept: Plone is not simply a CMS—it is a complex framework, a dynamic development environment that allows you to extend and customize features. In this section, in particular, we will cover the possibility of handling and publishing images and documents. You can easily perform these tasks with many CMSs, but with Plone you can also solve various complex use cases involving your document and image data. For example, you can add watermarks to images and allow for dynamic document generation from your web content.

We will briefly discuss these use cases and figure out a good way to meet our needs. But remember, there is always more than one solution that can meet a demand.

Watermarks on Images

Our first use case is the following: suppose we publish a rich photo gallery on our Plone site. The image content type is automatically published so that any anonymous visitor can view the images, and this is what we expect to happen. But what if we don't want people to be able to download them and use them in any manner they wish (e.g., publishing them on their own site without citing the source)?

To solve this drawback, you can integrate into your Plone site a product for watermarking, so that identifying information is embedded into the image's data. You can, for example, mark the images of your photo gallery with a copyright notice and/or a logo.

The watermarking can be automatically applied when you or a member of your site creates or edits an image, or just if the user decides to enable that feature. In addition, the watermarking can be performed with different styles—for example, transparency of watermarks, tiled watermarks, random or localized watermarks, staggered marks, and so on.

Implementing these features in your Plone site is not complicated, but of course you need to be familiar with the Python language and the structure of Plone: working with the Python Imaging Library (PIL, which is already installed with your Plone installation), you will be able to create an ad hoc product that will meet your needs.

Dynamic Document Generation from Your Web Content

This time, let's assume we have an e-commerce site; suppose we sell cameras, and we therefore have a Products section in our Plone site that contains a lot of objects—one for every product we sell—divided into categories. For each product, we provide the visitor with a data sheet with all the technical specifications.

Wouldn't it be great to give visitors the chance to download a PDF file that summarizes all the characteristics of the product, using a nice template with your logo and contacts, that you can customize, for example, on the occasion of periodic promotions? Even better, you could enable the possibility of downloading the entire product catalog!

With Plone you can realize this desire, and you can do it in different ways. There are various add-on products that let you export various types of Plone content to a PDF, DOC, RTF, or simple TXT document. The best thing you can do is write a product that lets you and your collaborators easily operate on the template to apply to the files that will be generated and exported. The user will just have to click a button you will add to the view of each product on your site, or to the view of the container that contains the entire catalog, to download, for example, a PDF file that they can easily consult offline or print.

Plone and Multimedia

As a CMS, Plone enables its users to upload and share any sort of binary file—this of course includes audio and video files. However, if you want to get more complex and use Plone as a specialized multimedia portal, you will need to handle some specific issues and requirements. We'll discuss some of the most common ones.

In a site that deals with multimedia content, we'll probably have to deal with some types of metadata that are not part of the Dublin Core set of metadata normally managed by Plone, such as metadata that involves resolution or codecs. Besides this, we'll also need some specialized preview mechanism, or, better yet, some streaming functionality—which introduces one of the biggest problems of multimedia: how to handle big files and long-running requests. On top of all that, we'll want to offer specialized features, such as podcasting or user tagging of multimedia content.

So, is Plone the right tool to achieve all this and more? Of course it is! But we will need to rely on some extension products if we don't want to write too much code on our own. And we will also need to choose a good deployment configuration for our service to enable the system to handle big files and long-running requests.

The first and most important set of products for multimedia handling in Plone comes from the Plone4Artists project (see `www.plone4artists.org` and `http://plone.org/products/plone4artistssite`), supported by Jazkarta, which aims to strengthen Plone to become the perfect artist community web site. Plone4Artists provides us with some new content types to handle audio and video files in the ways that we expect.

For every type of file we will upload, the system will recognize it and will make it act in the proper way. So, for example, if we add a video file to our Plone site, Plone will extract its proper metadata automatically, and will show the player on the default view page. If we add a link object with a URL pointing to a video file on YouTube, Vimeo, or other common video-hosting portal, Plone4Artists will enable Plone to extract the metadata from those portals, and also to embed the appropriate video player. Plone4Artists also offers standard specialized views for the folders hosting our video objects, and adds Plone video-feed capabilities, as well as capabilities for user ratings, comments, and tagging on videos.

If you want to see all this in action in a real case, just visit `http://plone.tv`, a Plone4Artists-based Plone portal where you can enjoy both a multimedia-specialized portal and some good videos and audio from the Plone community. Of course, Plone4Artists provides for audio files the same functionality it provides for videos, as well as specific functionalities for content managers, such as a massive file uploader.

A major alternative to Plone4Artists (though built on Plone4Artists roots) is the Plumi project (`http://plumi.org`). Plumi is supported by the EngageMedia Collective to power the EngageMedia site (`http://engagemedia.org`), a video-sharing site that focuses on social justice and environmental issues. We won't go into details on the differences between Plone4Artists and Plumi here, but note that Plone4Artists is a bit closer to "pure technology," with all its stand-alone and reusable modules, while Plumi is a bit more use case–specific, since its development is driven by the needs of the EngageMedia portal.

You've received a good introduction to multimedia management with Plone, but you still need to face the issues of handling big files and long-running requests. Clearly, you will have many big files to manage in your multimedia portal, as well as requests that could take more time to process than typical Zope/Plone requests.

To get a deeper understanding of how to correctly deploy a production Plone instance in general, we invite you to look over Chapter 11 again, and also pay particular attention to the following section in this chapter, "Handling Many Large Objects with Plone."

As for the issue of long-running requests, in our multimedia scenario we could get long-running requests both during management activities, such as massive file uploads, and in normal usage, as when serving some really big file. To solve these problems, you need to understand your specific use case and go for some kind of clustering techniques mixed with application-side care and deployment configuration tricks.

For instance, if just a few users are enabled to upload content, it could be smart to offer a dedicated virtual host exclusively for them, and to keep them on an exclusive ZEO client (see Chapter 11 for a deeper look into this topic). On the other hand, if we need to build a reliable streaming portal, it could be essential to implement this feature in such a way that Plone doesn't do the streaming directly. For example, we could implement a more specialized and "static" streaming service using the Tramline technology (`www.infrae.com/products/tramline`), which bypasses files upload and download issues, delegating them to a specific Apache module in a very clever way.

Clearly, those are not the only technical problems to be aware of when dealing with multimedia portals. For instance, we could mention server-side file-processing requirements to obtain conversions and the like, but that is well outside of the scope of this book.

Handling Many Large Objects with Plone

Handling many large objects is a low-level problem, but Plone has been working out a solution at the application level for years. Zope empowers Plone in many ways, but, until recently, was missing an important feature: BLOB (Binary Large Object) management. In the most common cases, as for the standard Plone 3 file content type, the actual binary file is stored as an attribute on the file object, and is thus duplicated every time the object is touched, even if the binary file is not involved. This behavior stresses the default ZODB FileStorage, which tends to increase its `Data.fs` file size rapidly; as well, it raises the amount of resources needed to run a Plone instance. In fact, the ZODB loads entire objects in RAM when it thinks they are needed, binary files included, even if they're not going to be used.

That is why, especially for binary file–centric Plone portals (such as multimedia or documental services), it is important to adopt a specific BLOB strategy to store all the binary files we will manage directly on the file system. As it is a very common case, (despite not being a Zope priority until recently), many alternatives have been proposed to overcome this problem. Some of them are provided by specific content types, like the famous PloneExFile, which acts at the application level to separate the file object from the actual binary file. However, this approach is a bit obsolete nowadays. Thanks to Archetypes' storage concept, we can specify which type of storage we prefer per-field, independently from the ZODB, which normally continues to store the object itself. In the "Writing a Custom Content Type" section in Chapter 9, you have seen in detail that Archetypes transforms a field's schema into a Plone portal type. You can specify what kind of storage Archetypes will use for each field, and that is what we are heading toward.

When it comes to binary file fields, we can choose FileSystemStorage (`http://plone.org/products/filesystemstorage`), supported by Ingeniweb, as a well-known solution to the problem.

FileSystemStorage (FSS), and its eggified version, `iw.fss` (`http://pypi.python.org/pypi/iw.fss`), are quite simple to use and configure. They're useful for creating a per-site file system repository where binary files are stored according to one of four provided strategies. In addition, FSS comes with full RDF metadata support and a series of goodies, including a script to rebuild a pure file system version of the repository if needed.

FSS is a good solution, but it comes with a few important caveats: You have to keep in mind that FSS stores files on the file system assuming that you will not access them using the file system directly. In fact, if you do this, you could mess up FSS quite easily—for example, what if FSS needs to delete a file while you have it opened in your editor? You should expect some kind of failure. Furthermore, it solves our problem only for Archetypes-based content, which is not a general solution. Finally, it solves a low-level problem at the application level, which is not the most elegant and versatile solution.

But why are we stressing FSS's weakness instead of its good features? Well, because a proper low-level solution is available, and it is known as BLOB support for ZODB. Of course, if we adopt BLOB support for ZODB, the application-level flexibility we gain with FSS is lost; in fact, its files repository is a much more cryptic beast than the one implemented by FSS—quite obscure from a Plone point of view. Nonetheless, using BLOB support for ZODB, we gain a clearer and more efficient solution: the ZODB is Zope's standard storage method, and it precludes us from needing to solve our problem at the application level (unless we want to duplicate our efforts to guarantee reliability and robustness). Of course, we won't have direct access to our files, but that is typical of any relational DBMS, and should not be so hard to accept, unless you prefer the FSS solution.

BLOB support has been at the core of ZODB since version 3.8.0, and the `plone.app.blob` package, which fits ZODB BLOBs into Plone, is almost in a stable release. `plone.app.blob` provides a replacement for `ATFile`, changing the standard `ATFile`'s file field with a BLOB support–enabled one. As well, `plone.app.imaging` provides a replacement for the standard `ATImage`'s image field, covering the basic standard content types with binary fields in Plone. Plone's next releases will probably propose a standard way of tackling the problem of adopting ZODB BLOB support. As for your projects, have your choice, and go down that road as needed.

Now, let's approach our second issue for this section: what to do when your Plone site hosts many objects. First of all, if you need to host thousands of files in a single folder in Plone 3 or earlier, remember to use a Large Plone Folder and not a standard one, at least until the current Plone developers' effort to implement a unique kind of folder with the ability to manage many objects by itself is finished. You can enable the creation of Large Plone Folders just by visiting the Types configlet page in the Plone control panel, choosing Large Plone Folder, and selecting the "implicitly addable" check box. Large Plone Folders are important when you just need to access real objects; in the cases of listing and searching objects, you can use a catalog query instead. So, now let's focus on the `portal_catalog` tool and its features.

A primary notion you need to understand is that the catalogs store their indexes and information in the ZODB using a special kind of object called a *brain* (we introduced this concept in Chapter 11). However, the standard Zope configuration is based on a single ZODB database, and it is not possible to tune the ZODB cache to keep all the brains you need separate from all the other kinds of objects in the ZODB cache.

The trick here is to configure a second ZODB database, where we store only the `portal_catalog` tool, for which we will safely set an extremely high number of objects in cache. This works great for brains, since brains are tiny objects compared to standard Plone content types. Setting up a separate ZODB database for the `portal_catalog` tool makes it so that after the first few requests, all the brains we need are calculated and cached in RAM, making Plone's catalog queries much quicker and more efficient. (This technique was examined in detail in Chapter 11.)

The last tool we would like to introduce is ContentMirror, which lets us approach the many-files performance issue from a different point of view, and could be useful in some specific cases. Imagine you need to continue to use Plone for your content management, but you also need to publish the same content to a much larger audience and with way less flexibility. In this case, you would just need to let the readers access published and updated content, perhaps with simple access control, like a token on the request. This is quite typical in many cases where Plone is used to manage news sites, or big database sites with many anonymous visitors asking for information but never contributing to the content.

In this and similar cases, you could think about building a simple and efficient publishing application, able to consume the Plone content database. Not that easy, you think? Well, not that hard, either, if you adopt ContentMirror, which we mentioned at the end of Chapter 10. Content-Mirror synchronously pushes Plone content and its metadata into a relational database, so that any other specialized content publication application can safely publish it as needed, and always keep it up to date.

Of course, a lot of other possible strategies could be chosen, depending on the specific use case, but that is part of the art of building powerful Plone sites. As always, you will need to balance Plone and application-centric methods with proper service configuration as well as possible.

Integration of External Applications and Single-Sign-On

All IT managers know that the curse of IT infrastructure consists of an uncontrolled proliferation of applications: different interfaces, different search engines, different ways of managing data, and different types of authentication. If you are lucky enough to have your company mission, requirements, and means let you do so, you can move all your applications into Plone and solve all your problems.

This is wonderful because it does not matter if the sentence you read the last month was in a commercial offer, in a PDF document you received in an e-mail, in the documentation of a project, in the description of a book in your company library, in a post on the company forum, or in the blog of the CIO. If it's in Plone, you will find it. You must remember that Plone does content management, which extends beyond web pages, and all the contexts we listed in the previous example are content-oriented. Having the same interface for creating, editing, and managing content is a great advantage. This will save time when you have to learn how to use new features and avoid mistakes due to lack of knowledge of the less-used ones.

One of the most appreciated strong points of a fully integrated enterprise system is unified authentication and authorization. For example, you no longer have to deal with dozens of passwords that you risk forgetting or have to write down. Instead, you're provided with a unique tool that lets you decide if a user or a group can access a specific resource.

However, integrating different applications in a single platform is not always possible. Sometimes applications are complex, not open source, bound to a specific operating system, not web-oriented, and so on. In these cases, you do not have to give up—Plone can still be a collector of resources. You have already seen in Chapter 10 how you can index a file system with Reflecto; in the same way, you can index remote file servers. This makes all your company documents searchable by Plone. You can even carry over the same privileges from Reflecto so that site members can search only what they have permissions to see.

However, in most companies, information isn't stored only in files, but also in a database. Fortunately, it does not matter what the front-end application is—Plone can access any common database (at least any database supported by the Python language).

Plone can access databases directly with traditional SQL queries. We can show information as Plone content, or simply make the databases searchable by the Plone search engine (see Figure 12-1 for an example of this kind of structure).

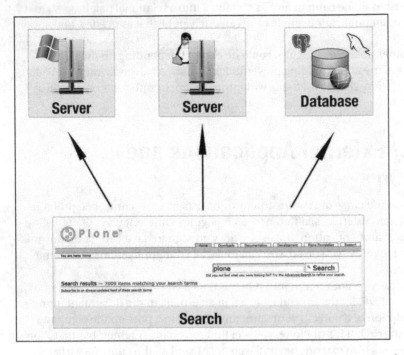

Figure 12-1. *The flexibility of the Plone search engine allows you to search not only through the site content, but also through external data sources, like databases and servers.*

To go further with the integration of our external applications, we will describe how to share authentication among them; to do so, we will divide our task into two stages. The former is to use the same authentication parameters for all the applications. This is easy for Plone because it can easily use various back ends for authentication (see Chapter 8).

The latter stage in integrating authentication is to provide a single-sign-on (SSO) among your applications. This can be achieved using an external SSO server and a corresponding PAS plug-in; on Plone.org you can find many of them. But you can also use Plone directly as an SSO server. This can be very effective when you do not have many applications and you can modify their source code. Using XML-RPC, applications can ask Plone if a user is valid, and they can let Plone manage the whole login process and even share users' data (see Figure 12-2 for an example of this kind of integration system). This can be an important step toward full Plone integration.

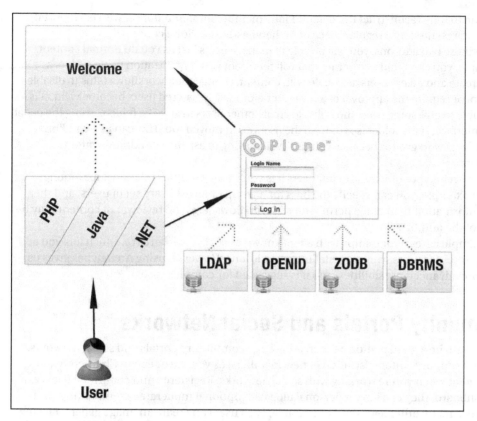

Figure 12-2. *Plone can take care of user authentication even for queries that come from other platforms, regardless of the user's source.*

Custom Member Profiles

Sometimes the users of a web site consist of more than a username and a password. Plone includes some extra fields for users, the most famous of which are the full name and e-mail fields. But if these are not enough, you are free to add more fields according to your requirements.

As usual, the Plone philosophy is to follow modularity, so we do not have to reinvent the wheel. We can rely on the Archetypes framework, which lets us create content with all the fields we need, and on the pluggable authentication service (PAS), which lets us choose where to get login data (for more details, see Chapter 8).

To exploit these features, you have to use the Plone add-on products Membrane and Remember. Membrane (http://plone.org/products/membrane) is a set of PAS plug-ins that allow for user-related behavior and data (authentication, properties, roles, groups, etc.) to be obtained from content within a Plone site. In other words, it allows you to support members as content types in Plone. Remember (http://plone.org/products/remember), as the project description says, "provides a set of plug-ins that let developers use content objects to provide information about user properties, groups, and roles. Remember builds on this, using

Membrane to fully reconstruct the default Plone member implementation with each portal member represented by a regular piece of Archetypes-based Plone content."

With these two add-ons, you will be able to manage users just as you do normal content. For example, you can build a structure that will represent your organization using folders as groups, create and delete users as you do with content, change their workflow status to disable their login, or require the approval of a reviewer before self-registered users become valid. It is also possible to give some users the rights to create other users in specific folders, using the usual sharing interface. If the folder is removed, the users are removed too. This can be incredibly useful for local workgroups because you can avoid having to ask the site administrator to create users.

Using Archetypes objects for your users lets you create complex relationships among users. For example, you can specify the boss for a group or an arbitrary set of users, and then use this information to manage permissions in workflows (e.g., the reviewer of content may be the boss of the author).

For simple cases, Plone ships with a tool known as `portal_memberdata`, which lets you add new properties for users without installing any add-ons. However, using Archetypes gives us many more advanced possibilities, and it is suggested for complex cases.

Community Portals and Social Networks

Plone can also be a good platform for creating large community portals and social networks. Plone itself supports autoregistration of new members, as you have seen in Chapters 3 and 4, which is great when you're working with social networks. Registered and confirmed users can use a dashboard, they can have a personal blog with optional moderated commenting, and they can use many other features. For example, each user can create an image gallery, tagging photos in certain areas with names and notes; identify community members; create an internal inbox message service from users; implement internal chat; and so on.

What about community portals? A great example of their use can be seen with Plone.org itself. With a simple out-of-the-box Plone site, you can quickly create a community portal that provides community members and your visitors with

- Updated news and important announcements about the main projects of the community

- Events and appointments related to the main projects of the community

- Training courses

- The latest software releases

- Documentation

- Support

You can of course take advantage of the powerful internal search engine (e.g., restricting search to a certain area, or performing an advanced search).

It is the big community of users itself that can create and update the content on your community site—all you have to do with your Plone site is enable the self-registration of users, as described in the "Managing Security Settings" section of Chapter 4. Of course, the entire system will have to be regulated by an appropriate workflow: for example, visitors can register and, when the team that manages the site approves the request, users will have their own account. All the content they will add, such as a news, a training course, a new project, and so on, will be submitted for revision, and the review team will have the power to publish it. Only then will anonymous users see this content. To review how to manage and customize workflows, review Chapter 7 and 8. You'll be able to create new and custom workflow states or transitions in order to meet your specific needs.

If you want to periodically update your users about new products, events, documentation, and so on, you can use the RSS feeds. As we discussed in Chapter 3, in the "Gathering Disparate Elements into Coherent Collections" and "Finding Content in Your Site" sections, Plone by default lets visitors subscribe to a search or a collection, so that they will receive alerts every time new content that matches certain criteria is added, without their having to check on the site. (For even more information on this, see the "RSS Integration into Plone" section of Chapter 10.)

As you have just seen, you can create your own community portal just by configuring a standard Plone site! You already know all the steps you need to perform. Additionally, it's easy to find useful extensions to integrate (e.g., internal chat, forums, or blog support). A good product for integrating online chat in your Plone site is PloneChat (http://plone.org/products/plonechat). To create a discussion board in your Plone site, a good product is Ploneboard (http://plone.org/products/ploneboard). Finally, a survey section can also be a big help for sharing feedback and new ideas; a good product for this purpose is Plone Survey (http://plone.org/products/plone-survey).

Intranets and Document Management Systems

With Plone, we can build well-constructed and flexible intranets with wide user bases. By *intranet*, we mean a private area to securely share any part of an organization's information. Of course, in practice, intranets can be way more than this. Nowadays, almost all companies use intranets as a collaboration tool—and for them to be as efficient as possible, they have to be based on the enterprise's specific needs.

Thanks to Plone's features and extensions, you cannot only improve content management and internal communication within your intranet by adding various tools and specific workflows, but you can also implement subsidiary services that will be useful to intranet users.

The Plone CMS, as described in the "Setting Up Your Dashboard" section of Chapter 3 and the "Managing Security Settings" section of Chapter 4, provides a personal area—the dashboard—that any user can manage autonomously, setting different portlets that will show updated information any time the user logs in. With the dashboard, the user can configure RSS feeds, choose to view recently modified content, set up shortcuts with links, and so on. Just like with an intranet, you can also enable a personal folder for any user, with particular security settings so that only that member (and administrators) will be able to add and edit content in that folder.

It is easy to create entire areas that can be accessed only by certain groups of users, apply different workflows and workflow policies, and integrate user management with LDAP or relational databases. You can index and search information—even PDF and DOC files—intelligently, and keep track of structured metadata about the content. And many of these features and capabilities are of course integrated into Plone by default.

With regard to internal enterprise communication, you can also create news, events, and alerts easily in Plone. Never forget the importance of social networks: you can create a blog, a forum to enable the sharing of knowledge, a survey section, an internal chat mechanism (see the previous "Community Portals and Social Networks" section). You can even integrate tools for project management, such as a ticketing system.

Note The references we mention for add-on products to integrate into your Plone site are only a few solutions among many that you may want to use. To see even more of the possibilities you have at your disposal, go to the Downloads section of Plone.org and perform an advanced search.

A very common use case in enterprise communication is the use of a portion of the file system shared through the enterprise network. With the Reflecto product, it is possible to incorporate part of the shared file system into a Plone site, so that each file is treated as Plone content, and the files in the mapped parts of the file system are indexed, searchable, and manageable directly in Plone. Reflecto lets you manage and access files contained in a defined area of the local file system as Plone content, taking advantage of the collaboration tools you enabled, and all the usual content management policies you are used to working with in Plone. Content can be added through the Plone interface or from the file system.

Enterprise intranets can benefit a lot from Plone. Plone allows you to, of course, access databases in read mode, even if they've been written by other applications. But you can also integrate them into your intranet so that you can implement search features and make queries on data that comes from other systems, or integrate and manage data that comes from ERP systems within Plone.

Plone also allows for the capability of sending content as faxes and integrating messaging features to send alerts via SMS messages to certain groups of users.

We could go on with many other examples and specific use cases, but the point is that Plone is not just a CMS! It offers the chance to meet almost any enterprise need regarding internal communication and project management, thanks to its default features and extensions.

Plone: Faster Than Light

It is a common belief that CMSs are slow. This might be true for other CMSs, but not Plone. Thanks to its architecture, Zope/Plone can have very good performance in both speed and load. With the right tuning and tools, it is possible to build systems that satisfy every need. The first step is to understand what you are looking for. In this section, our goal is not to analyze any particular solution, but rather to let you understand what you can tweak to improve the performance of your applications. So, we will use a general-purpose enterprise architecture.

In this general example, we'll assume an Apache (or nginx) web server as a front end to our web application (see the "Plone Behind a Web Server" section in Chapter 11), which allows us to do virtual hosting and HTTP and HTTPS request management, if required. The web server will act as a reverse proxy, sending users' requests to two different back ends. If the request is coming from an anonymous user, it is sent toward a Squid proxy server, which is followed by a load balancer. Logged-in requests are instead sent directly to the load balancer.

The presence of Squid permits us to provide dynamically generated pages at the same speed as static ones. This is primarily very useful for images and files (e.g., CSS and JavaScript). However, normal Plone content can benefit from caching as well, particularly with the use of the CacheFu add-on product, through which you'll be able to manage the persistence and validity of pages and avoid providing expired content.

When installed in Plone, CacheFu provides a configuration area in the Plone control panel (we discussed CacheFu at length in Chapter 11—chiefly in the "Caching Proxies and Your Plone Site" section). Through this area, it is possible to configure many parameters to have the right caching for each need; the more expert you are about the HTTP protocol, the more advantage you will get with the right tuning. But even if you do not know anything about it, you can improve your site performance simply by installing this product with its default options.

Note that a proxy cache is most effective for anonymous users, because content besides CSS and JavaScript that can be cached in the browser is usually user-specific. Proxy caches are usually avoided for logged-in users.

The next step involves the load balancer: its job is to spread requests among ZEO clients. An open source solution for load balancing is Pound, as mentioned in Chapter 11. Pound acts as a reverse proxy, forwarding requests according to the performance of the recipients, which are the core of the system: ZEO clients. They do the hard job. All the computation is done by them, so they are very important for the performance of our applications. But the good news is that you can have all the ZEO clients you want, spreading the load among different machines (at least as many as you can afford!). You can easily clone a ZEO client, add a new one in the balancer pool, and improve the capacity of your system.

Behind ZEO clients, there are one or more ZEO servers that keep application data. Both servers and clients can be spread out geographically (e.g., you could have a ZEO server in one city and the ZEO clients in others). Depending on your application's requirements, the various ZEO servers can store different parts of the application's data for structural and also performance reasons. Obviously, all this makes sense only in particular cases; in most cases, Plone will satisfy your needs out of the box.

At this point, you have seen how to organize your system to increase the speed and load it can bear, but you can also work on the application side. By default, Zope provides two ways to enhance the application's speed: caching the results of computations on the server, and modifying the HTTP response headers in order to manage persistence of web pages in the browser or in the proxy.

Summary

We have come to the end of our journey. You should now be able to use Plone, configure it, integrate it with other systems, and develop web applications. Throughout this last chapter, we've given you some real reasons why you should choose to learn the functions of this powerful CMS.

We went through many common use cases, such as building an e-commerce site, a community portal, a social network, and an enterprise intranet. We covered how to manage big files, how to integrate automatic handling of documents and images, multimedia management, custom member profiles, and SSO.

Of course, we could have chosen other examples; but it is time to take your bag of skills and start to build the most important thing that will allow you to use Plone: a wealth of experience. We are sure you will find out that Plone is exactly what you were looking for!

■ ■ ■

Creative Commons Legal Code

Attribution-NonCommercial-ShareAlike 3.0 Unported

Reprinted from http://creativecommons.org/licenses/by-nc-sa/3.0/legalcode

License

THE WORK (AS DEFINED BELOW) IS PROVIDED UNDER THE TERMS OF THIS CREATIVE COMMONS PUBLIC LICENSE ("CCPL" OR "LICENSE"). THE WORK IS PROTECTED BY COPYRIGHT AND/OR OTHER APPLICABLE LAW. ANY USE OF THE WORK OTHER THAN AS AUTHORIZED UNDER THIS LICENSE OR COPYRIGHT LAW IS PROHIBITED.

BY EXERCISING ANY RIGHTS TO THE WORK PROVIDED HERE, YOU ACCEPT AND AGREE TO BE BOUND BY THE TERMS OF THIS LICENSE. TO THE EXTENT THIS LICENSE MAY BE CONSIDERED TO BE A CONTRACT, THE LICENSOR GRANTS YOU THE RIGHTS CONTAINED HERE IN CONSIDERATION OF YOUR ACCEPTANCE OF SUCH TERMS AND CONDITIONS.

1. **Definitions**

    a. **"Adaptation"** means a work based upon the Work, or upon the Work and other pre-existing works, such as a translation, adaptation, derivative work, arrangement of music or other alterations of a literary or artistic work, or phonogram or perfor-mance and includes cinematographic adaptations or any other form in which the Work may be recast, transformed, or adapted including in any form recognizably derived from the original, except that a work that constitutes a Collection will not be considered an Adaptation for the purpose of this License. For the avoidance of doubt, where the Work is a musical work, performance or phonogram, the synchronization of the Work in timed-relation with a moving image ("synching") will be considered an Adaptation for the purpose of this License.

b. **"Collection"** means a collection of literary or artistic works, such as encyclopedias and anthologies, or performances, phonograms or broadcasts, or other works or subject matter other than works listed in Section 1(g) below, which, by reason of the selection and arrangement of their contents, constitute intellectual creations, in which the Work is included in its entirety in unmodified form along with one or more other contributions, each constituting separate and independent works in themselves, which together are assembled into a collective whole. A work that constitutes a Collection will not be considered an Adaptation (as defined above) for the purposes of this License.

c. **"Distribute"** means to make available to the public the original and copies of the Work or Adaptation, as appropriate, through sale or other transfer of ownership.

d. **"License Elements"** means the following high-level license attributes as selected by Licensor and indicated in the title of this License: Attribution, Noncommercial, ShareAlike.

e. **"Licensor"** means the individual, individuals, entity or entities that offer(s) the Work under the terms of this License.

f. **"Original Author"** means, in the case of a literary or artistic work, the individual, individuals, entity or entities who created the Work or if no individual or entity can be identified, the publisher; and in addition (i) in the case of a performance the actors, singers, musicians, dancers, and other persons who act, sing, deliver, declaim, play in, interpret or otherwise perform literary or artistic works or expressions of folklore; (ii) in the case of a phonogram the producer being the person or legal entity who first fixes the sounds of a performance or other sounds; and, (iii) in the case of broadcasts, the organization that transmits the broadcast.

g. **"Work"** means the literary and/or artistic work offered under the terms of this License including without limitation any production in the literary, scientific and artistic domain, whatever may be the mode or form of its expression including digital form, such as a book, pamphlet and other writing; a lecture, address, sermon or other work of the same nature; a dramatic or dramatico-musical work; a choreographic work or entertainment in dumb show; a musical composition with or without words; a cinematographic work to which are assimilated works expressed by a process analogous to cinematography; a work of drawing, painting, architecture, sculpture, engraving or lithography; a photographic work to which are assimilated works expressed by a process analogous to photography; a work of applied art; an illustration, map, plan, sketch or three-dimensional work relative to geography, topography, architecture or science; a performance; a broadcast; a phonogram; a compilation of data to the extent it is protected as a copyrightable work; or a work performed by a variety or circus performer to the extent it is not otherwise considered a literary or artistic work.

h. **"You"** means an individual or entity exercising rights under this License who has not previously violated the terms of this License with respect to the Work, or who has received express permission from the Licensor to exercise rights under this License despite a previous violation.

i. **"Publicly Perform"** means to perform public recitations of the Work and to communicate to the public those public recitations, by any means or process, including by wire or wireless means or public digital performances; to make available to the public Works in such a way that members of the public may access these Works from a place and at a place individually chosen by them; to perform the Work to the public by any means or process and the communication to the public of the performances of the Work, including by public digital performance; to broadcast and rebroadcast the Work by any means including signs, sounds or images.

j. **"Reproduce"** means to make copies of the Work by any means including without limitation by sound or visual recordings and the right of fixation and reproducing fixations of the Work, including storage of a protected performance or phonogram in digital form or other electronic medium.

2. **Fair Dealing Rights.** Nothing in this License is intended to reduce, limit, or restrict any uses free from copyright or rights arising from limitations or exceptions that are provided for in connection with the copyright protection under copyright law or other applicable laws.

3. **License Grant.** Subject to the terms and conditions of this License, Licensor hereby grants You a worldwide, royalty-free, non-exclusive, perpetual (for the duration of the applicable copyright) license to exercise the rights in the Work as stated below:

a. to Reproduce the Work, to incorporate the Work into one or more Collections, and to Reproduce the Work as incorporated in the Collections;

b. to create and Reproduce Adaptations provided that any such Adaptation, including any translation in any medium, takes reasonable steps to clearly label, demarcate or otherwise identify that changes were made to the original Work. For example, a translation could be marked "The original work was translated from English to Spanish," or a modification could indicate "The original work has been modified.";

c. to Distribute and Publicly Perform the Work including as incorporated in Collections; and,

d. to Distribute and Publicly Perform Adaptations.

The above rights may be exercised in all media and formats whether now known or hereafter devised. The above rights include the right to make such modifications as are technically necessary to exercise the rights in other media and formats. Subject to Section 8(f), all rights not expressly granted by Licensor are hereby reserved, including but not limited to the rights described in Section 4(e).

4. **Restrictions.** The license granted in Section 3 above is expressly made subject to and limited by the following restrictions:

a. You may Distribute or Publicly Perform the Work only under the terms of this License. You must include a copy of, or the Uniform Resource Identifier (URI) for, this License with every copy of the Work You Distribute or Publicly Perform. You may not offer or impose any terms on the Work that restrict the terms of this License or the ability of the recipient of the Work to exercise the rights granted to that recipient under the terms of the License. You may not sublicense the Work. You must keep intact all notices that refer to this License and to the disclaimer of warranties with every copy of the Work You Distribute or Publicly Perform. When You Distribute or Publicly Perform the Work, You may not impose any effective technological measures on the Work that restrict the ability of a recipient of the Work from You to exercise the rights granted to that recipient under the terms of the License. This Section 4(a) applies to the Work as incorporated in a Collection, but this does not require the Collection apart from the Work itself to be made subject to the terms of this License. If You create a Collection, upon notice from any Licensor You must, to the extent practicable, remove from the Collection any credit as required by Section 4(d), as requested. If You create an Adaptation, upon notice from any Licensor You must, to the extent practicable, remove from the Adaptation any credit as required by Section 4(d), as requested.

b. You may Distribute or Publicly Perform an Adaptation only under: (i) the terms of this License; (ii) a later version of this License with the same License Elements as this License; (iii) a Creative Commons jurisdiction license (either this or a later license version) that contains the same License Elements as this License (e.g., Attribution-NonCommercial-ShareAlike 3.0 US) ("Applicable License"). You must include a copy of, or the URI, for Applicable License with every copy of each Adaptation You Distribute or Publicly Perform. You may not offer or impose any terms on the Adaptation that restrict the terms of the Applicable License or the ability of the recipient of the Adaptation to exercise the rights granted to that recipient under the terms of the Applicable License. You must keep intact all notices that refer to the Applicable License and to the disclaimer of warranties with every copy of the Work as included in the Adaptation You Distribute or Publicly Perform. When You Distribute or Publicly Perform the Adaptation, You may not impose any effective technological measures on the Adaptation that restrict the ability of a recipient of the Adaptation from You to exercise the rights granted to that recipient under the terms of the Applicable License. This Section 4(b) applies to the Adaptation as incorporated in a Collection, but this does not require the Collection apart from the Adaptation itself to be made subject to the terms of the Applicable License.

c. You may not exercise any of the rights granted to You in Section 3 above in any manner that is primarily intended for or directed toward commercial advantage or private monetary compensation. The exchange of the Work for other copyrighted works by means of digital file-sharing or otherwise shall not be considered to be intended for or directed toward commercial advantage or private monetary compensation, provided there is no payment of any monetary compensation in connection with the exchange of copyrighted works.

d. If You Distribute, or Publicly Perform the Work or any Adaptations or Collections, You must, unless a request has been made pursuant to Section 4(a), keep intact all copyright notices for the Work and provide, reasonable to the medium or means You are utilizing: (i) the name of the Original Author (or pseudonym, if applicable) if supplied, and/or if the Original Author and/or Licensor designate another party or parties (e.g., a sponsor institute, publishing entity, journal) for attribution ("Attribution Parties") in Licensor's copyright notice, terms of service or by other reasonable means, the name of such party or parties; (ii) the title of the Work if supplied; (iii) to the extent reasonably practicable, the URI, if any, that Licensor specifies to be associated with the Work, unless such URI does not refer to the copyright notice or licensing information for the Work; and, (iv) consistent with Section 3(b), in the case of an Adaptation, a credit identifying the use of the Work in the Adaptation (e.g., "French translation of the Work by Original Author," or "Screenplay based on original Work by Original Author"). The credit required by this Section 4(d) may be implemented in any reasonable manner; provided, however, that in the case of a Adaptation or Collection, at a minimum such credit will appear, if a credit for all contributing authors of the Adaptation or Collection appears, then as part of these credits and in a manner at least as prominent as the credits for the other contributing authors. For the avoidance of doubt, You may only use the credit required by this Section for the purpose of attribution in the manner set out above and, by exercising Your rights under this License, You may not implicitly or explicitly assert or imply any connection with, sponsorship or endorsement by the Original Author, Licensor and/or Attribution Parties, as appropriate, of You or Your use of the Work, without the separate, express prior written permission of the Original Author, Licensor and/or Attribution Parties.

e. For the avoidance of doubt:

    i. Non-waivable Compulsory License Schemes. In those jurisdictions in which the right to collect royalties through any statutory or compulsory licensing scheme cannot be waived, the Licensor reserves the exclusive right to collect such royalties for any exercise by You of the rights granted under this License;

    ii. Waivable Compulsory License Schemes. In those jurisdictions in which the right to collect royalties through any statutory or compulsory licensing scheme can be waived, the Licensor reserves the exclusive right to collect such royalties for any exercise by You of the rights granted under this License if Your exercise of such rights is for a purpose or use which is otherwise than noncommercial as permitted under Section 4(c) and otherwise waives the right to collect royalties through any statutory or compulsory licensing scheme; and,

    iii. Voluntary License Schemes. The Licensor reserves the right to collect royalties, whether individually or, in the event that the Licensor is a member of a collecting society that administers voluntary licensing schemes, via that society, from any exercise by You of the rights granted under this License that is for a purpose or use which is otherwise than noncommercial as permitted under Section 4(c).

f. Except as otherwise agreed in writing by the Licensor or as may be otherwise permitted by applicable law, if You Reproduce, Distribute or Publicly Perform the Work either by itself or as part of any Adaptations or Collections, You must not distort, mutilate, modify or take other derogatory action in relation to the Work which would be prejudicial to the Original Author's honor or reputation. Licensor agrees that in those jurisdictions (e.g. Japan), in which any exercise of the right granted in Section 3(b) of this License (the right to make Adaptations) would be deemed to be a distortion, mutilation, modification or other derogatory action prejudicial to the Original Author's honor and reputation, the Licensor will waive or not assert, as appropriate, this Section, to the fullest extent permitted by the applicable national law, to enable You to reasonably exercise Your right under Section 3(b) of this License (right to make Adaptations) but not otherwise.

5. Representations, Warranties and Disclaimer

UNLESS OTHERWISE MUTUALLY AGREED TO BY THE PARTIES IN WRITING AND TO THE FULLEST EXTENT PERMITTED BY APPLICABLE LAW, LICENSOR OFFERS THE WORK AS-IS AND MAKES NO REPRESENTATIONS OR WARRANTIES OF ANY KIND CONCERNING THE WORK, EXPRESS, IMPLIED, STATUTORY OR OTHERWISE, INCLUDING, WITHOUT LIMITATION, WARRANTIES OF TITLE, MERCHANTABILITY, FITNESS FOR A PARTICULAR PURPOSE, NONINFRINGEMENT, OR THE ABSENCE OF LATENT OR OTHER DEFECTS, ACCURACY, OR THE PRESENCE OF ABSENCE OF ERRORS, WHETHER OR NOT DISCOVERABLE. SOME JURISDICTIONS DO NOT ALLOW THE EXCLUSION OF IMPLIED WARRANTIES, SO THIS EXCLUSION MAY NOT APPLY TO YOU.

6. Limitation on Liability.

EXCEPT TO THE EXTENT REQUIRED BY APPLICABLE LAW, IN NO EVENT WILL LICENSOR BE LIABLE TO YOU ON ANY LEGAL THEORY FOR ANY SPECIAL, INCIDENTAL, CONSEQUENTIAL, PUNITIVE OR EXEMPLARY DAMAGES ARISING OUT OF THIS LICENSE OR THE USE OF THE WORK, EVEN IF LICENSOR HAS BEEN ADVISED OF THE POSSIBILITY OF SUCH DAMAGES.

7. Termination

a. This License and the rights granted hereunder will terminate automatically upon any breach by You of the terms of this License. Individuals or entities who have received Adaptations or Collections from You under this License, however, will not have their licenses terminated provided such individuals or entities remain in full compliance with those licenses. Sections 1, 2, 5, 6, 7, and 8 will survive any termination of this License.

b. Subject to the above terms and conditions, the license granted here is perpetual (for the duration of the applicable copyright in the Work). Notwithstanding the above, Licensor reserves the right to release the Work under different license terms or to stop distributing the Work at any time; provided, however that any such election will not serve to withdraw this License (or any other license that has been, or is required to be, granted under the terms of this License), and this License will continue in full force and effect unless terminated as stated above.

8. Miscellaneous

a. Each time You Distribute or Publicly Perform the Work or a Collection, the Licensor offers to the recipient a license to the Work on the same terms and conditions as the license granted to You under this License.

b. Each time You Distribute or Publicly Perform an Adaptation, Licensor offers to the recipient a license to the original Work on the same terms and conditions as the license granted to You under this License.

c. If any provision of this License is invalid or unenforceable under applicable law, it shall not affect the validity or enforceability of the remainder of the terms of this License, and without further action by the parties to this agreement, such provision shall be reformed to the minimum extent necessary to make such provision valid and enforceable.

d. No term or provision of this License shall be deemed waived and no breach consented to unless such waiver or consent shall be in writing and signed by the party to be charged with such waiver or consent.

e. This License constitutes the entire agreement between the parties with respect to the Work licensed here. There are no understandings, agreements or representations with respect to the Work not specified here. Licensor shall not be bound by any additional provisions that may appear in any communication from You. This License may not be modified without the mutual written agreement of the Licensor and You.

f. The rights granted under, and the subject matter referenced, in this License were drafted utilizing the terminology of the Berne Convention for the Protection of Literary and Artistic Works (as amended on September 28, 1979), the Rome Convention of 1961, the WIPO Copyright Treaty of 1996, the WIPO Performances and Phonograms Treaty of 1996 and the Universal Copyright Convention (as revised on July 24, 1971). These rights and subject matter take effect in the relevant jurisdiction in which the License terms are sought to be enforced according to the corresponding provisions of the implementation of those treaty provisions in the applicable national law. If the standard suite of rights granted under applicable copyright law includes additional rights not granted under this License, such additional rights are deemed to be included in the License; this License is not intended to restrict the license of any rights under applicable law.

Creative Commons Notice

Creative Commons is not a party to this License, and makes no warranty whatsoever in connection with the Work. Creative Commons will not be liable to You or any party on any legal theory for any damages whatsoever, including without limitation any general, special, incidental or consequential damages arising in connection to this license. Notwithstanding the foregoing two (2) sentences, if Creative Commons has expressly identified itself as the Licensor hereunder, it shall have all rights and obligations of Licensor.

Except for the limited purpose of indicating to the public that the Work is licensed under the CCPL, Creative Commons does not authorize the use by either party of the trademark "Creative Commons" or any related trademark or logo of Creative Commons without the prior written consent of Creative Commons. Any permitted use will be in compliance with Creative Commons' then-current trademark usage guidelines, as may be published on its website or otherwise made available upon request from time to time. For the avoidance of doubt, this trademark restriction does not form part of this License.

Creative Commons may be contacted at http://creativecommons.org/.

Index

- (not phrase), 78, 153
? (single wildcards), 78, 153
" " (phrases), 78, 153

A

access control list (ACL), 184
Accessibility link, 39
ACID (atomicity, consistency, isolation,
    and durability), 312
ACL (access control list), 184
acl_users folder, 205
acl_users tool, 184, 207, 209–212, 214
acquisition, 133, 136
actions, 142–143
Actions menu, 40, 64
"Add collection" option, 76
Add Collection panel, 72
Add Comment button, 80
Add File panel, 54
"Add new" drop-down menu
    events, 55
    files, 54
    icons, 141, 146
    images, 52
    links, 56
    news items, 57–58
    restricting content types in folders, 63–64
Add New Search Criteria section, 74, 76
Add New User button, 102
Add Page panel, 48–49
Add Role button, 183
Add RSS Portlet option, 43
Add Rule panel, 123–127
AddForm class, 260–261
Add-on Product Configuration section, 82
add-on products
    building, 227–233
    configuration, 265–269
    custom content type, 233–239
    forms, 246–247, 254–256
    installing, 33–34
    overview, 6–7, 223
    portlets, 256–265
    structure of, 223–227
    theming, 240–246
    tools and utilities, 270–275
    viewlets, 256–265

Add-On Products section, 161
Add/Remove Products panel, 95, 278
addzope2user script, 293
administrators (admin), 17, 105
adminPassword.txt file, 24
advanced user management. *See* user
    management, advanced
Ajax, 79, 175–179
"Allow comments" option, 79
Allow discussion value, 139
Allowed content types value, 139
allowed_interface attribute, 245
Always show option, 120
and keyword, 78, 153
Anonymous role, 101
anonymous users, 101
Apache, 306, 328
Applications folder, 20
/Applications/Plone/zinstance/bin/buildout
    file, 20
/Applications/Plone/zinstance/buildout.cfg
    file, 20
Apply Changes button, 103
archetype attribute, 229
Archetypes, 7, 223, 226–227, 233, 237, 321
ArchGenXML code generator, 233
Assignable roles, 101
Assignment class, 260
asynchronous indexing, 299
ATContentTypes product, 231, 233
ATContentTypeSchema class, 231
ATCTContent class, 231
ATFile file, 322
atomicity, consistency, isolation, and
    durability (ACID), 312
ATTopic class, 158
AttributeError class, 92, 153
Attributes tab, 115
Authenticated role, 101
authenticated users, 105
authentication
    with LDAP, 212–215
    pluggable authentication service, 206–212
    with relational databases, 216–219
Authentication Plugins, 208
autoload parameter, 285
Automatic option, 99

automatic rules
   assigning, 127–128
   creating, 123–127
   overview, 122–123
automatic ZODB packing, 312
Automatically generate tabs option, 93
Available view methods value, 139

■ B

banner.jpg file, 137
base_properties object, 168, 173–174
base_view template, 238–239
Base.Assignment class, 260
bin folder, 27, 304
$ ./bin/instance fg directory, 27
BLOB (Binary Large Object), 296–297, 321
blob-storage option, 297
Block option, 120
Block/unblock portlets section, 119–121
Blogspot, 40
body macro, 238
</body> tag, 166
bootstrap.py file, 27
brains, 149, 153, 322
breadcrumbs, 39
Browse button, 52
Browse tab, 217
browser caching, 301
browser directory, 286
browser folder, 229, 237, 243, 248, 286
browser/configlet.py file, 271
browser/configure.zcml file, 241, 249, 252,
   258, 272
browser/regionalnewssearch.py file, 251
browser/regionalnewsview.pt template, 263
browser/regionalnewsview.py file, 244
browser/rn_search_resultsview.pt file, 252
browser/rn_search_resultsview.py file, 253
BrowserView class, 243, 258
buildout directory tree, 27–30
buildout newest option, 30
buildout script
   installing load-balancing ZEO clusters
      with, 304–305
   installing proxy cache servers with, 308
[buildout] section, 296
buildout.cfg file, 24, 28–31

■ C

CacheFu applications, 306, 328
cache-size value, 310
caching
   installing proxy cache servers with
      buildout script, 308
   overview, 301–302
   proxies, 306–307
Caching allowed option, 172

Calendar Settings panel, 96
Can add permission, 71
Can edit permission, 71
Can review permission, 71
Can view permission, 71
Cascading Style Sheets. See CSS
case studies
   automatic document and image handling,
      318–319
   community portals, 326–327
   document management systems, 327–328
   e-commerce, 317–318
   enterprise workflow management,
      315–317
   external application integration, 323–324
   intranets, 327–328
   large object handling, 321–323
   member profiles, custom, 325–326
   multimedia, 319–321
   single-sign-on, 323–324
   social networks, 326–327
   speed, 329
CatalogData.fs file, 309–311
CentOs, 21–22
Central Intelligence Agency (CIA), 6
"Change note" field, 49, 69
"Change state" button, 53
check links button, 112
Chicago History Museum, 6
Choice attribute, 251
CIA (Central Intelligence Agency), 6
Classic portlet option, 121–122
clustering
   installing load-balancing ZEO clusters
      with buildout script, 304–305
   overview, 301–302
   Zope clustering with ZEO, 302
CMF (content management framework), 8–9,
   224
CMFCatalogAware class, 149
CMFDefault class, 225–226
CMFPlone/skins/plone_kss/plone.kss folder,
   176
CMFPlone/skins/plone_styles/mobile.css.
   dtml file, 167
CMSs (content management systems), 1, 3–5
col_mapping tool, 218
collection content types, 43, 46
Collection Indexes panel, 97–98
Collection Metadata panel, 97–98
Collection object, 291
Collection Settings panel, 97–98
collective.indexing package, 299
collective.lead Database class, 285
collective.lead package, 283, 284, 285
Comment column, 69
Comments field, 63

community portals, 326–327
component architecture, 224
Comprehensive Guide to Zope Component
    Architecture, A, 221
Compression type option, 173
Condition option, 172
configlets, 271
config.py file, 229, 272
configure.zcml file, 34, 229, 245, 250, 273,
    285–286
Contact link, 39
contact_name parameter, 288
Contacts class, 284
contacts package, 283
contacts table, 281–282, 284
contacts_board template, 281, 286
contacts.pt template, 287
contacts.py file, 286
ContactsView class, 287
content
    customizing, 7
    defined, 4
"Content editor" field, 45
content folder, 229, 231
content management framework (CMF), 8–9,
    224
content management systems (CMSs), 1, 3–5
Content Rules panel
    Add Rule panel, 123–127
    assigning rules, 127–128
    overview, 122–123
content statement, 169
Content type condition, 125
"Content type portlets" menu, 120–121
content types
    changing icons for, 140–141
    configuring, 137–140
    creating from existing types, 145–146
    overview, 224
content_type_registry tool, 290
ContentMirror tool, 322
content/regionalnews.py module, 251
Contents tab, 40, 42, 53, 215
contextual permissions, 182
control panel, 81–82, 89–90, 120, 278
Controller, 17–18
Copy button, 41
Copy to folder condition, 126
Create a Group panel, 106
create statement, 217
credentials_basic_auth plug-in, 209
credentials_cookie_auth plug-in, 209
criteria method, 254
Criteria tab, 74
"Criteria type" field, 74
cron job, 312

CSS (Cascading Style Sheets)
    DTML, 167–169
    editing, 172–173
    examples, 173–175
    managing viewlets, 169–172
    overview, 161
    ZPT, 167–169
CSS Media option, 172
custom folder, 121, 168
custom layer, 165–166, 175
custom tags, 114
customizing sites
    automatic rules, managing, 122–128
    CSS
        DTML, 167–169
        editing, 172–173
        examples, 173–175
        managing viewlets, 169–172
        overview, 161
        ZPT, 167–169
    HTML filtering, 113–115
    JavaScript, 175
    KSS, 175–179
    Kupu visual editor, 108–113
    portlets, managing, 116–122
    quickly, 161–163
    setting up
        Add/Remove Products panel, 95–96
        Calendar Settings panel, 96
        Collection Settings panel, 97–98
        error log, 89–92
        Language Settings panel, 85–86
        Mail Settings panel, 88–89
        Maintenance panel, 89
        Markup Settings panel, 98–99
        Navigation Settings panel, 93–94
        overview, 81–83
        Search Settings panel, 94
        Security Settings panel, 86–87
        Site Settings panel, 83–85
        Theme Settings panel, 87–88
        Type Settings panel, 99–100
    skins, 163–166
    users, managing, 100–108
Cut button, 41

D

-d parameter, 312
Database class, 284
Database Management panel, 298
database management systems (DBMSs), 279
database manager, 184
Data.fs file, 295–296, 309–310, 321
DataGridField class, 235
date index, searching, 151
DateIndex method, 148
DateIndexRange method, 148

DBMSs (database management systems), 279
Debian-Like distributions, 21
Debug Mode, 19
default page templates, 223
Default view method value, 139
Delete object condition, 127
description attribute, 40
Description field, 32
description property, 236
Description value, 138
/develop-eggs directory, 28
Devilstick technology, 226
Dexterity technology, 226, 239
Digital Creation, 224
Display as Table check box, 73
Display menu, 40
distinguished name (DN), 214
distutils attribute, 228
document handling, automatic, 318–319
document management systems, 327–328
Document Template Markup Language
        (DTML), 167–169
document workflow, 315
documentation, 7
Documentation tab, 112
/downloads directory, 28
drivername parameter, 287
DTML (Document Template Markup
        Language), 167–169
<dtml-var fontFamily> tag, 167
Dublin Core, 319
dynamic development environment, 318
dynamic document generation, 318–319

E

easy_install tool, 229
e-commerce, 317–318
Edit panel, 79
edit properties page, 40
Edit tab, 43, 49, 59, 71, 74
EditForm class, 260–261
egg-based product, installing, 34
/eggs directory, 28
eggs option, 247
eggs variable, 296
email property, 218
"Enable external editing" field, 45
enable_inline_editing property, 179
Enfold Desktop, 290
EngageMedia Collective, 320
enterprise resource planning (ERP) software,
        316
enterprise workflow management, 315–317
Error Log panel, 89–92
Event content type, 46
event log, 92
Excel spreadsheets, 54

exceptions, 92
Execute button, 53
exporting configurations, 144–145
extensibility, 7
Extension Profiles field, 32
extensions, 223. *See also* add-on products
external application integration, 323–324
Externally Published state, 201
Extraction Plugins, 208
ez_setup.py tool, 228

F

[fakezope2eggs] section, 248
Fall back to default view value, 139
Fedora, 21–22
Feed reloaded timeout, 118
"Feedback for author" box, 46
field index, searching, 150–151
"Field name" drop-down menu, 74
FieldIndex index, 150–151
File content type, 46
File extension condition, 125
File System Directory View (FSDV), 165
file system, publishing, 277–279
File Transfer Protocol (FTP), 18, 47, 277,
        288–289
FileSystemStorage (FSS), 321
Filter content types value, 139
Filtered classes section, 115
filtering, 113, 154
Folder content type, 46
folder_workflow tool, 189
foldercontents ZPT code, 176
foldercontents_update_table action, 176
FolderContentsKSSView class, 177
folderlisting macro, 238
fontColor property, 168
fontFamily variable, 167
footer macro, 238
Forgot your password? link, 37
formlib class, 260, 270, 272
forms
        overview, 246–247
        z3c.form, 247–254
        Zope catalogs, 255–256
Framework Team, 10
frameworks, integrating, 291–293
FSDV (File System Directory View), 165
FSS (FileSystemStorage), 321
FTP (File Transfer Protocol), 18, 47, 277, 288–289
FTP Access field, 18

G

General Public License (GPL), 3, 15
Generate tabs for items other than folders
        option, 93
GenericSetup profile, 259, 264–265, 270

get_other_news_items method, 244–245
get_results method, 254, 256
getCatalogResults script, 155
getContacts method, 281, 288
getObject method, 153
getPath method, 153
getRegion method, 256, 267
getRID method, 153
getToolByName function, 270
getURL method, 153
GIMP (GNU Image Manipulation Program), 53
Global Settings section, 214
globbing, 78, 153
Gnu, 20–24
GNU Image Manipulation Program (GIMP), 53
GPL (General Public License), 3, 15
graphical user interface (GUI), 18
Group Membership tab, 105–107
Group portlets menu, 120
Group Portlets tab, 108
Group Properties tab, 106
Group_Enumeration Plugins, 208
groups
    adding new, 106
    changing details of, 106–108
    overview, 101–105
Groups Overview panel, 105–106
Groups Plugins, 208
Groups tab, 191, 193, 215
growth, 8
GUI (graphical user interface), 18

H

-h parameter, 312
handleSearch method, 252
header macro, 238
Hello World! string, 238
here/title_or_id statement, 169
History button, 63
History tab, 68
/home_view string, 168
HTML (Hypertext Markup Language), 4–7,
    168, 290
HTML Filter Settings panel, 113–115
HTTP (Hypertext Transfer Protocol), 14, 206,
    328
HTTPS request management, 328
http-server section, 22
Hypertext Markup Language (HTML), 4–7,
    168, 290
Hypertext Transfer Protocol (HTTP), 14, 206,
    328

I

i18n Domain value, 138
Icon value, 138
icons, 88, 140–141

Id field, 32
if statements, 137
IIS (Internet Information Services), 14
Image content type, 46
image handling, automatic, 318–319
Implicitly addable value, 139
Indexed attribute, 245
indexing content, 148–149, 225
InfoViewlet class, 258
__init__.py file, 229, 285
Initial view name value, 139
insert statement, 217
Install button, 161
Install Log link, 95
install_requires parameter, 283
installing Plone
    adding sites, 31–33
    add-on products, 33–34
    on Gnu/Linux, 20–24
    load-balancing ZEO clusters, 304–305
    on Mac OS X, 19–20
    overview, 13–14
    proxy cache servers, 308
    on Windows, 14–19
    with zc.buildout, 24–30
[instance] section, 296
[instance02] section, 305
instance:zcml section, 213
integrating Plone with other systems
    accessing without browsers, 288–290
    frameworks, 291–293
    overview, 277
    publishing file system, 277–279
    relational databases, 279–288
interface class, 244
interfaces, searching by, 157–158
interfaces.py file, 230–231, 271
Internal Draft state, 201
Internally Published state, 201
International Planetary Data Alliance, 6
International Training Center of the Interna-
    tional Labour Organization (ITC ILO), 6
internationalization, 6
Internet Information Services (IIS), 14
Intranet folder, 201
intranet_folder_workflow tool, 189
intranet_workflow tool, 189, 201–202
intranets, 327–328
IPortletDataProvider class, 260
IRegionalNews interface, 231
IRegionalNewsConfig class, 272
IRegionalNewsSearch interface, 251
IregionalnewsView interface, 245
IResult interface, 157
ITC ILO (International Training Center of the
    International Labour Organization), 6
IViewlet interface, 258

J

JavaScript, 161, 175
Jazkarta, 320

K

KeywordIndex class, 148, 151–152, 245
KSS (Kinetic Style Sheets), 175–179
Kupu Configuration panel
    Documentation tab, 112
    Kupu Libraries panel, 109–110
    Kupu Resource Types panel, 111–112
    Links tab, 112–113
    overview, 108–109
    Toolbar tab, 113
Kupu HTML filter, 113
Kupu Libraries panel, 109–110
Kupu Resource Types panel, 111–112
Kupu visual editor
    documentation, 112
    library configuration, 109–110
    links, 112–113
    overview, 108–109
    resource types, 111–112
    toolbar configuration, 113

L

label property, 236
Language Settings panel, 85–86
languages, 6
large object handling, 321–323
Large Plone Folders, 322
layers, 161, 163–165
LDAP (Lightweight Directory Access
        Protocol), 212–215
ldap plug-in, 215
LDAP Schema section, 214
LDAP Schema tab, 215
LDAP Servers section, 214
LDAPMultiPluginsc class, 212
LDAPUserFolder class, 212
Lightweight Directory Access Protocol
        (LDAP), 212–215
Limit Search Results option, 73
lines property, 270
Link content type, 46
Links tab, 112–113
Linux, 14, 20–24
List of values option, 76
LiveSearch feature, 94
load balancing, 301–302, 304–305
Local Content Type to Workflow Mapping,
        198
LocalFS product, 278
Location field, 50
Log In button, 38
Logger condition, 126

login_form object, 136
logo.jpg item, 174

M

Mac OS X, 19–20
Mail Settings panel, 88–89
mailing lists, 10
main_template tool, 163, 165–166, 170
Maintenance panel, 89
/manage file, 134
Manage Portlets panel
    Block/unblock portlets section, 119–121
    Classic portlet option, 121–122
    overview, 116–119
Manager role, 101
manage-viewlets view, 258
Managing Security Settings section, 326
Markup Settings panel, 98–99
max range, 151
member profiles, custom, 325–326
Member role, 101
Membrane plug-ins, 325
Merging option, 172
metal macro, 238
Metatype value, 138
Microsoft Excel spreadsheets, 54
min range, 151
minmax range, 151
Move to folder condition, 126
multimedia, 319–321
multimedia portal, 319
myintranet_workflow tool, 202
myproject directory, 26
/mysite file, 136
/mysite/login_form path, 136
MySpace, 40

N

nasty tags, 114
navigation portlet, 40
Navigation Settings panel, 93–94
"New categories" field, 50
News class, 226
News Item content type, 47
News portlet, 57
newsImageContainer class, 240
newsitem_view template, 146, 239
Nonassignable roles, 101
not keyword, 78, 153
not modified responses, 306
not phrase (-), 78, 153
NotFound error type, 92
Notify user condition, 126
Novell, 6
Number of Items field, 73
NuPlone theme, 161

O

object publishing and acquisition, 135–137
object_provides index, 157–158
object-oriented web development, 133–134
object-relational mapping (ORM), 283
.old extension, 312
one_state_workflow tool, 189
OpenOffice, 316
/opt/Plone3.x/zinstance/ file, 24
or keyword, 78, 153
ore.contentmirror relational database, 288
ORM (object-relational mapping), 283
Owner role, 101

P

-p parameter, 312
packaging, 6
packing, 312
Page content type, 47
page metadata, 49–52
pagenumber argument, 176
Parent portlets drop-down menu, 120
/parts directory, 28
PAS (pluggable authentication service)
    acl_users tool, 209–212
    folder object, 184
    overview, 206
    in Plone, 207
    plug-in types, 207–209
passwords, 86
paster addcontent contenttype command,
        232
paster addcontent view command, 243
Paster commands, 227
paster create -t archetype plonebook.
        regional_news command, 232
paster create -t plone3_theme command, 243
Paster utility, 25, 227–229, 231–233
PathIndex, searching, 152
payment gateway, 318
PayPal, 318
PDF (Portable Document Format), 4–5
Pending Review state, 61, 201
Permissions tab, 190, 193
Permitted styles section, 115
Personal Preferences panel, 46, 105
Personal Web Server (PWS), 19
personalization, 7
phrases (" "), 78, 153
pickling, 296
PIL (Python Imaging Library), 228, 319
Plone
    adding and editing content
        events, 55–56
        files, 54
        images, 52–53

links, 56
        news items, 57
        overview, 46–47
        pages, 47–52
    automatic item locking and unlocking,
            59–60
    CMSs, 4–5
    collections, 72–76
    commenting content, 79–80
    community, 9–11
    features of, 5–8
    finding content, 77–79
    inline editing, 59
    installing
        adding sites, 31–33
        add-on products, 33–34
        on Gnu/Linux, 20–24
        load-balancing ZEO clusters, 304–305
        on Mac OS X, 19–20
        overview, 13–14
        proxy cache servers, 308
        on Windows, 14–19
        with zc.buildout, 24–30
    integrating with other systems
        accessing without browsers, 288–290
        frameworks, 291–293
        overview, 277
        publishing file system, 277–279
        relational databases, 279–288
    interface, 38–40
    managing and sharing content, 60–72
    new user log in, 35–38
    organizing site, 40–46
    origins of, 8–9
    overview, 3, 35
    pluggable authentication service (PAS),
            207
Plone Conference, 8
Plone Configuration section, 82
Plone Contents tab, 278
Plone Controller, 17–18
Plone Default skin, 171
Plone folder, 20
Plone Foundation, 8, 10
Plone HTTP field, 18
Plone installer, 19
#plone IRC channel, 24
plone object, 232
Plone Survey, 327
Plone Version Overview section, 82
plone_images layer, 174
plone_lexicon tool, 152
plone_setup tool, 170
plone_templates layer, 166
plone_workflow tool, 189
plone3_theme template, 243
Plone4Artists project, 320

plone.app.blob package, 296–297, 322
plone/app/content/browser/configure.zcml
    folder, 176
plone/app/content/browser/foldercontents.
    py folder, 177
plone/app/content/browser.pt folder, 176
plone/app/content/browser.py folder, 177
plone.app.controlpanel.form.ControlPanel-
    Form class, 272
plone.app.imaging package, 322
plone.app.ldap interface, 213, 215
plone.app.portlets.portlets package, 260
plone.belowcontenttitle viewlet manager,
    256
Ploneboard, 327
plonebook attribute, 229
plonebook namespace, 229, 283
plonebook.contacts package, 283–284
plonebook.contacts/plonebook/contacts
    folder, 283
PlonebookDB class, 285
plonebook.db utility, 285
plonebook/regional_news folder, 229, 230
PloneChat, 327
plone.css file, 168
ploneCustom.css file, 173
/Plone/Members/danae folder, 152
Plone.net, 11
Plone.org, 11
plone.portaltop viewlet manager, 170
plone/portlet/collection/collection.py folder,
    158
plone.recipe.squid configuration, 308
plone.recipe.varnish configuration, 308
/Plone/testing/danae folder, 152
plone.z3cform package, 247
pluggable authentication service. See PAS
plug-ins. See add-on products
Plumi, 320
Portable Document Format (PDF), 4–5
portal catalog
    indexing content, 148–149
    making search form, 154–157
    overview, 147
    searching catalog, 150–153
    using search results, 153–154
    ZCA, 157–158
Portal Toolkit, 225
portal_action tool, 143
portal_catalog tool, 147–150, 225, 246–247,
    255–256, 309–311
portal_css tool, 172–173, 240–241
portal_javascript tool, 242
portal_javascripts tool, 175
portal_kss tool, 176, 242
portal_memberdata tool, 326
portal_membership tool, 143

portal_properties tool, 270
portal_properties/site_properties configura-
    tion tool, 179
portal_quickinstaller tool, 217, 297, 299
portal_setup tool, 144, 196, 202–203, 226,
    265–266
portal_skin tool, 227, 238
portal_skins tool, 121, 140, 163–165
portal_type tool, 190
portal_types tool, 137, 140, 145, 265
portal_type-workflow mapping, 197
portal_workflow tool, 146, 186–188, 201–202,
    225–226, 265
PortalContent class, 149
PortalMaintenance Plone product, 312
portlet infrastructure, 259
portlets
    Block/unblock portlets section, 119–121
    Classic portlet option, 121–122
    defined, 43
    moving items to, 259–265
    overview, 116–119
portlets folder, 230, 259
portlets/configure.zcml file, 263
portlets.xml file, 259, 263–264
ports, changing, 18–19
Ports page, 18
postgres parameter, 287
postgresDA ID, 281
PostgreSQL database service, 280, 298
Pound application, 329
Press Release content type, 146
pressrelease_view tool, 146
Private Draft state, 61
Private state, 60, 192, 201
Product Description link, 95
Product factory method value, 139
Product name value, 138
/products directory, 28
Products folder, 224, 227, 278
Products namespace, 34
Products.CacheSetup package, 306
Products.Reflecto file, 278
Professional Plone Development, 221
Profile link, 44
profiles, defined, 144
profiles folder, 230
profiles/default folder, 259, 267
profiles/default/catalog.xml file, 267
profiles/default/componentregistry.xml file,
    273
profiles/default/controlpanel.xml file, 273
profiles/default/cssregistry.xml file, 268
profiles/default/types/RegionalNews.xml
    file, 267
profiles/default/viewlets.xml file, 268
profiles/default/workflows folder, 267

profiles/default/workflows.xml file, 267
Properties Plugins, 208
Properties tab, 209
proxy cache servers, 308
psycopg2 package, 280
Public Draft state, 61
publication control system, 60
publication state history, 63
publication workflow, 316
publish_externally tool, 201–202
Published state, 61
publishing
    documents, 60–63
    file system, 277–279
publishing engine, 133
Publishing Process panel, 63
PWS (Personal Web Server), 19
PyPI (Python Package Index), 30, 228
Python, 3, 9, 134, 228, 316
Python Imaging Library (PIL), 228, 319
Python package, 135, 224
Python Package Index (PyPI), 30, 228
Python Paste project, 227
python-ldap egg, 212–213
python-ldap library, 213

Q

query list, 151
Query Template box, 281

R

ranges, 151
RDBMS (relational database management
    system), 279
read_permission tool, 235
README.html file, 20
README.txt file, 23–24, 229–230
Really Simple Syndication (RSS), 72, 291–292
Recent Changes portlet, 120
Red Hat, 21–22
Redirect error type, 92
ReferenceField field, 235
Reflecto, 278, 323, 328
Reflector object, 278
region attribute, 241, 250–251, 256, 258
region field, 236
region index, 246, 267
region widget, 240
Regional News object, 223, 274
Regional News portlet module, 259
Regional News reader, 226
regional_news package, 229, 231, 240, 243
regional_news tool, 259
regional_news.pt template, 259, 261
regional_news.py module, 259–260
regional_publication_workflow folder, 267
regional_publish tool, 265

regional_published state, 226, 265
regional_published tool, 265
RegionalNews class, 231, 233, 245
RegionalNews schema, 239
regionalnews view, 237, 243
regionalnews_config tool, 272
regionalnews_info_box id div element, 240
regionalnews_view browser view, 261
regionalnews_view tool, 237–240, 243
regionalnews_view.pt file, 238
RegionalNewsConfigForm class, 272
regionalnews.css file, 240–241
regionalnews.info viewlet, 259
regionalnews.pt template, 262
regionalnews.py file, 231, 233, 235–236, 262
RegionalNewsSearchForm class, 249, 252
regionalnewssearch.py file, 248, 251
RegionalNewsSearchView class, 249
regionalnewsView class, 243
.regionalnewsview.IregionalnewsView
      interface, 245
regionalnewsview.pt file, 237, 238, 240, 243
regionalnewsview.py tool, 237, 243
REGIONS constant, 275
regions field, 271
regions vocabulary, 271, 274
Register link, 37
registration, 7
reindexObject method, 149, 279
reindexObjectSecurity object, 149
rel option, 173
Related Items field, 50
relational database management system
    (RDBMS), 279
relational databases
    adopting in Zope, 280–283
    authentication with, 216–219
    overview, 279
    SQLAlchemy, 283–288
    versus ZODB, 279
relative path, 112
reliability, 8
RelStorage, 297–299
rel-storage option, 297
Remember application, 325
Remove button, 80
Remove Group column, 106
render method, 258
Render type option, 173
Renderer class, 261–262
replace statement, 169
Reply button, 80
Reportlab, 316
repoze.plone WSGI application, 293
repurposing, 145
request object, 288
request_delete tool, 202–203

Reset Password column, 104
++resource++rn-resources/regionalnews.css
    file, 242
resources directory, 241
Result object, 157
Reverse option, 76
"Revert to this revision" link, 71
Reviewer role, 101
reviewers, 105
Revisions panel, 69
rn_config_utility function, 275
rn_search_results tool, 252
rn_search_resultsView view class, 252
rnewsImageContainer class, 240
roles, 101–102, 181–184
root user, 22
RSS (Really Simple Syndication), 72, 291–292
RSS Feed portlet, 118
Rules tab, 128

S

-S parameter, 312
Scalable Vector Graphics (SVG), 5
schema, 235
schemata attribute, 237
Scripts tab, 191
Search button, 71
search engine optimization (SEO), 6, 32
Search Settings panel, 94
SearchableText index, 246
searchResults method, 150, 156, 256
Secondary types check boxes, 64
security, 7, 181–186, 197–201
Security Settings panel, 86–87
Security tab, 182
Select a content item as default view option,
    68
select statement, 217
Select values from list option, 74
Send mail condition, 127
SEO (search engine optimization), 6, 32
session plug-in, 209
Settings panel, 52
Settings tab, 79
_setup_mappers method, 285
_setup_tables method, 285
setup.py file, 229
setuptools module, 25, 228
Sharing tab, 71–72
short names, 48
"Show code differences" link, 70
Simple Object Access Protocol (SOAP), 292
simple_publication_workflow tool, 186,
    188–189, 265
SimpleItem class, 272
single wildcards (?), 78, 153

single-sign-on (SSO), 323–324
Site Map link, 39
Site Settings panel, 83–85
Site Setup area, 161, 315
Site Setup link, 39, 134, 213, 232
sitemap.xml.gz file, 85
skins, 161, 163–166
SOAP (Simple Object Access Protocol), 292
social networks, 326–327
sort_limit keyword parameter, 150
sort_on keyword parameter, 150
sort_order keyword parameter, 150
source_myusers tool, 211
SQL Authentication configuration panel, 218
SQLAlchemy class, 284
SQLAlchemy library, 277
SQLAlchemy ORM technology, 283–288
SQLPASPlugin class, 217
sqlpasplugin product, 216–217
Squid, 306, 328
/src directory, 28
src folder, 230
src/plonebook.contacts/plonebook/contacts
    file, 284
SSO (single-sign-on), 323–324
Standard view option, 65
State drop-down menu, 186
State menu, 40, 53, 61
States tab, 192
Status tab, 217
storage configurations, 296–299
String class, 235
StringField field, 235
StringWidget class, 236
Stripped attributes section, 115
Stripped combinations section, 115
stripped tags, 114
Styles tab, 115
Submit Query button, 217, 281
"Subscribe to an always-updated feed of
    these search terms" link, 78
sudo command, 20, 23
Summary view option, 66
supervisord utility, 293, 305
SVG (Scalable Vector Graphics), 5
system architectures
    asynchronous indexing, 299
    automatic ZODB packing, 312
    caching, 301–302, 306–308
    clustering, 301–302
    load balancing, 301–302, 304–305
    multiple ZODBs, 308–311
    overview, 295
    Plone behind web servers, 300–301
    storage configurations, optimizing,
        296–299

T

Table Columns field, 73
TableKSSView class, 177
Tabular view option, 67
Tag Attribute Language (TAL), 175
Tags tab, 114–115
TAL (Tag Attribute Language), 175
TAL (Template Attribute Language), 133, 155
tal:repeat syntax, 155
tar.gz file, 144
Template Attribute Language (TAL), 133, 155
templates. *See* CSS
Test tab, 217
tests folder, 230
tests.py file, 230
Text option, 75
TextField field, 235
TextLine fields, 271
Theme Setting panel, 87–88
theming, 7, 240–246
through-Web development, 134–135
Thumbnail view option, 67
title attribute, 40
Title field, 32
Title option, 172
Title value, 138
to_be_deleted tool, 202–203
tokens, 318
Toolbar tab, 113
tracking history, 68–71
Tramline technology, 320
Transform tab, 53
Transition workflow state condition, 127
traversal, 136
Type Settings panel, 99–100

U

Ubuntu, 21
uids option, 113
UML (Unified Modeling Language) tools, 7
Unauthorized error type, 92
undelete transition, 203
Unified Installer, 22–24
Unified Modeling Language (UML) tools, 7
Uniform Resource Locators (URLs), 136
Uninstall button, 95
uniqueValuesFor method, 156
UNIX, 14
Unlock button, 60
unlocking, automatic item, 59–60
Update button, 212
update_table method, 177
URLs (Uniform Resource Locators), 136
usability, 6
Use parent settings option, 120

User Enumeration option, 211
User Folders, 87
user management, advanced
    authentication
        with LDAP, 212–215
        pluggable service, 206–212
        with relational databases, 216–219
    overview, 205
User Name field, 38
User Properties panel, 104
user registration, 7
User Search box, 103
User_Adder option, 211–212
User_Enumeration option, 211
User/Groups Settings panel, 108
users, managing
    adding, 102–103
    changing details of, 103–105
    groups, 101–108
    overview, 100–102
    roles, 101–102
    User/Groups Settings panel, 108
User's group condition, 125
User's role condition, 125
Users tab, 215
users_table table, 219
utilities, 270–275

V

ValueError error type, 92
/var directory, 28
var/blobstorage directory, 297
var/filestorage directory, 312
var/gadfly subdirectory, 216
Variables tab, 191, 193
/var/lib/zope/etc/zope.conf file, 22
Varnish application, 306
[varnish-build] section, 308
VERSION installer, 23
versioning feature, 70
View panel, 63
View Plone button, 17
View tab, 44, 49, 76
View your Plone site link, 35
view_name tool, 252
viewlet manager, 169, 256
viewlet.py file, 257
viewlets, 169–172, 256, 259, 264–265
viewlets.xml file, 171
Vimeo, 320
Visual Transforms tab, 178
vocabularies.py file, 250, 274
vocabulary attribute, 236
vocabulary_factory property, 251

W

watermarks, 318–319
web CMSs, 4
Web Component Development with Zope 3, 221
Web Server Gateway Interface (WSGI), 292–293
web servers, Plone behind, 300–301
WebDAV (Web-Based Distributed Authoring and Versioning) protocol, 18, 47, 277, 289–290
WebDAV Source field, 19
wget utility, 25
widget attribute, 236
Windows
    configuring server on, 18–19
    installing Plone on, 14–17
workflow
    case study, 315–317
    creating and customizing, 201–203
    managing existing, 188–196
    overview, 7
    portal_workflow tool, 186–188
Workflow policies, 197
Workflow Policy Support product, 197
workflow service, 225
Workflow state condition, 125
Workflow transition condition, 125
Worklists tab, 191
wrap_form function, 249
WSGI (Web Server Gateway Interface), 292–293
WYSIWYG editor, 168

X

XML-RPC, 292

Y

YouTube, 320

Z

Z Gadfly Database Connection, 216
Z Psycopg 2 Database Connection item, 281
z3c.form, 246–254
ZCA (Zope Component Architecture), 157–158, 206
ZCatalog, 77
zc.buildout tool, 13, 22, 24–30
zcml parameters package, 284
zcml variable, 296
zc.recipe.cmmi recipe, 213
ZCText Index, 152–153

ZCTextIndex method, 148, 152
ZEO (Zope Enterprise Objects), 22–23, 302, 304–305, 311
zeo-conf-additional option, 310
zinstance folder, 20
ZMI (Zope Management Interface)
    actions, 142–143
    configuring LDAP connection through, 215
    content types
        changing icons for, 140–141
        configuring, 137–140
        creating from existing types, 145–146
    control panel, 82
    exporting configurations, 144
    overview, 137
    through-Web development, 134–135
ZMI Add select box, 281
ZMI root list, 232
Z-Object Publishing Environment, 225
ZODB (Zope Object Database)
    automatic packing, 312
    multiple, 308–311
    versus relational databases, 279
Zope
    overview, 8–9
    relational databases, 280, 283
    security in, 181–186
Zope Book, 221
Zope catalogs, 255–256
Zope clustering, 302
Zope Component Architecture (ZCA), 157–158, 206
Zope Database Packing section, 89
Zope Developer's Guide, 221
Zope Enterprise Objects (ZEO), 22–23, 302, 304–305, 311
Zope Management HTTP field, 18
Zope Management Interface. *See* ZMI
Zope Management Interface button, 17
Zope Object Database. *See* ZODB
Zope Page Templates (ZPT), 7, 155, 167, 291
Zope Storage Server (ZSS), 302
zope.conf file, 22, 288, 297
zope-conf file, 309
zope-conf-additional option, 309–310
zope.formlib interface, 247
zope.schema FieldProperty class, 272
ZopeSkel, 25, 228–229
ZPsycopgDA product, 280
ZPT (Zope Page Templates), 7, 155, 167, 291
ZSQL Method object, 280, 282
ZSS (Zope Storage Server), 302

You Need the Companion eBook

Your purchase of this book entitles you to buy the companion PDF-version eBook for only $10. Take the weightless companion with you anywhere.

We believe this Apress title will prove so indispensable that you'll want to carry it with you everywhere, which is why we are offering the companion eBook (in PDF format) for $10 to customers who purchase this book now. Convenient and fully searchable, the PDF version of any content-rich, page-heavy Apress book makes a valuable addition to your programming library. You can easily find and copy code—or perform examples by quickly toggling between instructions and the application. Even simultaneously tackling a donut, diet soda, and complex code becomes simplified with hands-free eBooks!

Once you purchase your book, getting the $10 companion eBook is simple:

❶ Visit **www.apress.com/promo/tendollars/**.

❷ Complete a basic registration form to receive a randomly generated question about this title.

❸ Answer the question correctly in 60 seconds, and you will receive a promotional code to redeem for the $10.00 eBook.

THE EXPERT'S VOICE™

2855 TELEGRAPH AVENUE | SUITE 600 | BERKELEY, CA 94705

Offer valid through 10/27/09.